The Rural and Peripheral in Regional Development

The countryside has often been marginalised in discussions of economic and societal development, in favour of the urban. This book aims to stimulate a debate and a re-evaluation of how the concepts of the rural, peripheral and marginal are treated in academia and policy.

Approaching this theme from geographic, demographic and economic perspectives, Peter de Souza makes a compelling case for giving the periphery a prominent role as an integral part of a holistic and balanced society. The book carefully deconstructs the concept of the urban, and critiques the idea of urban-rural or centre-periphery comparisons, and presents an alternative approach to spark future discussions.

The Rural and Peripheral in Regional Development will be of interest to those studying and researching in the areas of rural economics, sustainability and development, as well as those involved in rural policymaking.

Peter de Souza is a Doctor of Economics and Associate Professor at the Inland Norway University of Applied Sciences. He has also worked at the universities of Göteborg, Uppsala and Örebro in Sweden, and has worked extensively as a consultant on regional and local development issues. A former member of the International Board of Regional Studies Association and Chairman of its Nordic Section, he is author of *Territorial Production Complexes in the Soviet Union* (1989) and co-editor of *Towards New Nordic Regions* (2008) and *Regional Development in Northern Europe* (2012).

Regional Studies Association
THE GLOBAL FORUM FOR CITY AND REGIONAL RESEARCH, DEVELOPMENT AND POLICY

Routledge
Taylor & Francis Group

Regions and Cities

Series Editor in Chief
Joan Fitzgerald, *Northeastern University, USA*

Editors
Ron Martin, *University of Cambridge, UK*
Maryann Feldman, *University of North Carolina, USA*
Gernot Grabher, *HafenCity University Hamburg, Germany*
Kieran P. Donaghy, *Cornell University, USA*

In today's globalised, knowledge-driven and networked world, regions and cities have assumed heightened significance as the interconnected nodes of economic, social and cultural production, and as sites of new modes of economic and territorial governance and policy experimentation. This book series brings together incisive and critically engaged international and interdisciplinary research on this resurgence of regions and cities, and should be of interest to geographers, economists, sociologists, political scientists and cultural scholars, as well as to policy-makers involved in regional and urban development.

For more information on the Regional Studies Association visit www.regionalstudies.org

There is a **30% discount** available to RSA members on books in the ***Regions and Cities*** series, and other subject related Taylor and Francis books and e-books including Routledge titles. To order just e-mail Joanna Swieczkowska, Joanna.Swieczkowska@tandf.co.uk, or phone on +44 (0)20 3377 3369 and declare your RSA membership. You can also visit the series page at www.routledge.com/Regions-and-Cities/book-series/RSA and use the discount code: **RSA0901**

126. Smart Transitions in City Regionalism
Territory, Politics and the Quest for Competitiveness and Sustainability
Tassilo Herrschel and Yonn Dierwechter

125. Geopolitics of the Knowledge-Based Economy
Sami Moisio

124. The Rural and Peripheral in Regional Development
An Alternative Perspective
Peter de Souza

123. In The Post-Urban World
Emergent Transformation of Cities and Regions in the Innovative Global Economy
Edited by Tigran Haas and Hans Westlund

The Rural and Peripheral in Regional Development

An Alternative Perspective

Peter de Souza

Routledge
Taylor & Francis Group
LONDON AND NEW YORK

First published 2018
by Routledge
2 Park Square, Milton Park, Abingdon, Oxon OX14 4RN

and by Routledge
711 Third Avenue, New York, NY 10017

Routledge is an imprint of the Taylor & Francis Group, an informa business

British Library Cataloguing-in-Publication Data
A catalogue record for this book is available from the British Library

Library of Congress Cataloging-in-Publication Data
A catalog record for this title has been requested

ISBN: 978-0-415-79323-0 (hbk)
ISBN: 978-1-315-21118-3 (ebk)

Typeset in Bembo
by Apex CoVantage, LLC

To Lisa

Contents

Preface

Looking back through the years, contemplating how the idea for a book actually materialised, it is fascinating to see the combinations, the causalities, connections and coincidences becoming partly systematic and logical, ultimately systemic. I started out with a planner's education, turning to a generalised interest in the real functioning of economies. I spent a couple of decades trying to understand the anomalies of the so-called planned society of the Soviet Union/Russia, watching its disintegration, while at the same time investigating the continuous tug-of-wars between different constellations of forces trying to win the upper hand of power, ownership and control. I became fascinated as an academician, consultant, activist in matters concerning core-periphery, urban-rural, centrality, etc.

Returning to similar issues and, often enough, systemic generalities in a European, mostly Northern setting, I discovered the fascinating issues of contextual preconditions in regional and local development processes with a looming central state authority working its mysterious ways.

This travel through time has also been a fascinating social experience, with a framework of friends, colleagues, authors and creators continuously providing food for thought, challenges, penetrating discussions and debates. Often enough in scientific fields, also from other competence areas, this brings a necessary extension to the present author's limited capacities. It is impossible to register all the persons contributing to this process, but there are a few that could be 'blamed' more than others, although not for the way their impact has been used. Mike Danson, Svante Karlsson, Anne Lorentzen, Henrik Halkier, Håvard Teigen among the multitude. Complementing these are the attendants of the organised activities of the PEMABO network, helpfully financed by the Regional Studies Association.

This has ended up a book, not following classical academic rules, but hopefully initiating important discussions and further systematic academic research and development.

There are also institutions to be mentioned. My early academic career at the Department of Human Geography, University of Göteborg. My East European orientation at the Department of Soviet and East European Studies, University of Uppsala; my years at the University of Örebro; and finally, at present, the supportive, collegial, atmosphere at Inland Norway University of Applied Sciences, Campus Rena.

A crucial important framework contribution has been the role of the Regional Studies Association, where important instruments like network facilitation as well as the progression of high-quality conferences, where ideas have been tested and discussed, have been provided. The special contributive role of the VRI (Virkemidler for regional FoU og innovasjon) programme in the Norwegian Research Council should be noted as well.

And last but not least, especially in the final phase of the manuscript, these wonderful librarians, always with a suggestion, a solution and extensive flows of information. A special thanks to Anette Danielsen, Magni Melvær and their colleagues.

The result, this book, of this extended and rollercoaster ride is possible due to all this. Any mistakes, misconceptions, etc., still remain with me.

Peter de Souza
Försteamanuensis
Institute of Economics
Inland Norway University of
Applied Sciences (Campus Rena)

1 What is this all about?

Introductory positioning

Background and a general problem description

This book concerns the treatment of the periphery, the rural, in scientific and popular contexts. Primarily, it is about stereotyped areas (structures and processes) that have been, are or seem to have clear negative tendencies or profiles. It will be argued that a combined lack of substantiated knowledge and taken-for-granted profiles are hiding potentials and alternatives, beneficial for a future societal development, beyond what is outlined today.

Part of the problem, as will be noted, is the fact that the issues approached are under-researched and, which will be argued, when empirical and theoretical work actually is taking place, seemingly biased. An important ingredient of the picture/image/reality is the way the subject has been and is approached and treated in the academic community. Descriptions in literature and policy documents in universal terms, tend to be neither examined nor explored with regard to the periphery,[1] with the same kind of approach as urban structures and processes. Emanating results cannot, with conviction, discuss the situation in the periphery, compared to the dominating tradition. It will be argued that in many contexts (e.g. primarily within the economic, economic-geographic or political science disciplines), research on the periphery is marginal to the careers of the academic community, its individuals, and treated as of lesser worth in publications, promotions and similar areas. These biases have had and still have far-reaching effects in the political and policy fields. An explanation could be based on inadequate knowledge among policymakers, as already Chambers (1983) suggested, or on more penetrating ideological concerns, defined in dimensions of centre, top-down and macro perspectives. The state of art show that there has been much research and attention paid to the regions in the core of Europe in general, focused especially on cities, city-regions, old industrial areas, border regions and to some of their more important underlying characteristics, but the peripheral/rural is left wanting. The present monograph is not standing at the forefront of this opinion; neither is the argument discovered here. It has already been raised and will continue to be so in the future. Already in the 1970s, Michael Lipton published a book on world development issues: *Why Poor People Stay Poor: A Study of Urban Bias in World Development* (1977).

There is a special focus today on agglomerations generally and clusters and regional innovation systems in particular. Earlier approaches to agglomeration theory and its more up-to-date appearances includes specific statements, defining it as the good and probably only alternative. This is, however, as will be shown, technically doubtful and often methodologically meaningless. Specific features of geographical and functional peripheral and marginal regions have, in the light of this, been neglected. Peripheral or non-central regions are, by definition not included, or considered superficially or in specified limited roles as, for instance, resource providers (Petrov, 2012).

Focusing on this general state-of-the-art description, it is natural to face the issue whether this book is important. Complementing the basic question whether the development we are looking forward to, in the long run, is sustainable, when fundamental imbalances in society are maintained, primarily in the centre-peripheral dimension. Focusing on these in future development considerations makes that position clear.

When discussing the periphery, the core,[2] is presented as an absolute role model in a dichotomy carrying categorical flavours of good and bad. The 'core' being generalised in such discourses hides the reality of being many things and not all of them beneficial for either growth or mankind.

Focusing at the moment on the agricultural sector, it remains outside of mainline concern for general development processes, as the focus, still, remains on manufacturing, nowadays extended to the service and knowledge sectors.

> In other words, the agricultural sector/the periphery/remote regions are being somewhat left behind, and tend to fall outside the scope of the analysis.
>
> (Gruber and Soci, 2010, p. 44)

Further emphasising the point made above, related to the type and quality of information and knowledge flows, raises pertinent questions about aspects of power and interests. A questioning of the flows of resources reflecting negatively on the need for a subsidised countryside while the cities and especially the larger cities are not really under any scrutiny, is not opening all avenues for consideration. The large city coffers foster interest-based corruption and nepotism, not necessarily explicit, but included as ingredients of an urban culture of dominance. National politics and holding on to power is interpreted as keeping the urbanites satisfied/contented

> since these communities are invariably better educated, more articulate, organized in trade unions and other groupings, and therefore likely to be a much greater potential threat to economic and political stability than the less educated and less well-organised rural poor.
>
> (Potter, Binns and Smith, 2008, p. 445)

Substantive differences existing between the compositions of labour force and economic status in the core and peripheral industries, is not explained by the labour force composition in itself, but in significant sectoral variations, making comparative ambitions questionable (Beck, Horan and Tolbert II, 1978).

There is also another and enforcing proposition, in regard to the periphery, that indicates us not really knowing what we actually are talking about "a mythic heartland . . . a zone of otherness . . . geographies of other people and places become marked as Other – exotic, transgressive, extraordinary, and by no means representative" (Shields, 1991, p. 4).

Whether it comes down to this or 'just' a way of presentation is still to be explored. This introductory chapter is, among other things, presenting how this exploration will be organised.

Development perspectives

The proposition of an urban/core preference or bias, in the development process, is valid and needs – even more, demands – much more of qualifications and analytically penetrative ambitions. Perspectives and ideologies where cities, and especially larger ones, are acting as primary brokers for knowledge, societal processes and development, should be scrutinised and questioned. "But this assumption is needed precisely because local institutions do not work properly and cannot reasonably be reformed, due to the entrenched and longstanding self-interests of major urban-political elites" (OECD, 2011a, p. 208). The argument includes a number of taken-for-granted propositions, for instance, the centre-periphery dichotomy. This model or metaphor is continuously criticised as being too simplistic as an explanation for the complexity of differentiated development, whether in Europe or elsewhere. Regions with designations as economically lagging, deprived or peripheral exist in core areas and, simultaneously, economically dynamic, innovative regions are found in geographically peripheral areas (Eskelinen and Fritsch, 2006). An emerging consensus is found where the supposed dichotomy is actually described in terms of a multiplicity of relationships outlined within a scope of different theoretical endeavours, the urban-rural complexity a part of a remaining necessity of interdependence and complementarity. The awareness of global-local, interconnectivity enhanced in policy importance. Accomplished and often spontaneous changes based on a global scale relate, to a large degree, on issues of land-use and, through this directly to the rural. Turning to the examples of improved ecological practices, "rural areas and their contribution to sustainable development have set new issues for both policy making and research" (Dax, 2014, p. 59).

Different results are not competing but complementing, in terms of differentiating the object of study – the term multichotomies – used and the heterogeneity of cores and peripheries highlighted. An unknown number of logics seem to be acting, or taking place, simultaneously. Scale sensitivities with imbalances define different cultures of core/periphery positions "each operating at particular spatial level, but with all levels interconnected" (Petrov, 2012, p. 61).

Furthermore arguments for centralisation and large-scale production, carry illogical rationalities in terms of efficiency, cost reductions, etc., for the provision of welfare, in general terms. The argued relevance for this – in terms of schools, hospitals, universities, the population level of municipalities, the organisation of policy and types of settlement patterns – continuously highlights in positive terms propositions that are not always qualified. Simplified models approach social problems with standardisation severely questioned already by Myrdal (1982, p. 94), comparing them with the then much-criticised Weather Forecast Service.

The periphery is not peripheral only in physical terms, it is also a periphery in conceptual aspects as is 'the' rural, remaining in an intellectual periphery. The potential for change is there, and this book wishes to provide some input into this change. The substantiated status of the periphery is, as should be known, far from rigid/static. The transformation and extension of the EU has placed regions, positioned in the periphery of the Soviet empire, in a transitory role, a core position, in the redirection of political, economic and cultural interests of former Central and Eastern Europe (Cooke, 2012).

The picture/image/reality could carry potential scenarios that stand in stark contrast to the present ones. There are many questions mentioned or, partly or hesitantly, answered in this monograph, approached in a more systematic manner than has been the case before. For instance, is the periphery a burden, or a contribution to a larger society? Is the periphery a container for specific groups/kinds of people – the inhabitants of the periphery? Is the periphery the outcome of the centre's development? Is the periphery the spoils of a special kind of historical and economic/political development? Should the definition of the periphery be, by what it was, what it is or what it is becoming? Could one identify different roles for the periphery in different stages of societal development – what is generalisable within the always unique trajectory? Depending upon the functional pattern and/or place in the geographical space, could something be said about the past, present and future – within the same kind of analytical framework? "What is of interest within these questions and among those questions not put forward? Do we care and for what do we care?" (Danson and de Souza, 2012, p. 4).

Looking back to development processes in historical times is not only a nostalgic trip. The idea of the rural creating a foundation for the centre/urban should be inspiring. The historical background where the agricultural surplus created markets and potentials for urban agglomerations is not only a historical fact. Industrialisation did not appear out of the blue. Agricultural innovation and rural productivity – where a fundamental precondition of early development, released capital and surplus labour necessary for the establishment of industrial activities and the urbanities – is a historical absolute:

> [A]n economy from "one that is dominantly rural and agricultural to one that is dominantly urban, industrial and service-oriented in composition."
>
> (Potter, Binns and Smith, 2008, p. 444)

Driven by the rural, development was capitalised when the farmer bought the technology. In the Swedish case:

> [T]he milk machines and separators came from Alfa Laval, stoves from AGA, housewares from Kockums, sewing machines from HUSQVARNA and electrical engines from ASEA. Electric motors that drove harvesters were from Thermaenius that later came to be acquired by Bolinder-Munktell, that accompanied Volvo. Almost all of the successful Swedish export companies have their roots deeply buried in the Swedish agricultural soil and the forest topsoil.
>
> (Sylwan, 2011, p. 13, my translation)

The present progress remains dependent, in absolute terms, for foodstuffs, raw materials of diverse kinds and energy. The outline inspires thoughts that have to do with the properties of development in more general terms, where explanations as to changes range through the whole ideological field, from Marxism to Liberalism, although, naturally in different appearances. A latter day, surprisingly late, contribution to this we find with Paul Krugman, introducing spatial dimensions into traditional macroeconomic theoretical modelling. He identifies emergent properties, in terms of self-organisation, as spontaneous summations of micro-behavioural activities and interactions.

> [T]he spatio-temporal manifestation of powerful self-organising tendencies [are] driven by emergent properties and mechanisms. . . . The geographical forms that make up that landscape – cities, industrial districts, clusters, centre-periphery patterns of development, and the like – are not usually imminent in the motives of economic agents (firms, workers and consumers).
>
> (Martin and Sunley, 2012, p. 339)

The scope will widen further, looking from the general process as such in a chapter of its own, at its creation of the 'urban', in some of its differentiated substances, including the fragmented and kaleidoscopic nature of the counter-urbanisation tendencies, always there as an undercurrent, changing in nature and outcome. The latter tendencies have had a surprisingly low analytical attraction, in spite of being clearly identified manifestations. New developments in ICT, for instance, create locational independence appropriate for rural frameworks. Spontaneous survival and quality of life (QOL) issues specific to the countryside, the dynamics of private initiative and special dimensions of the public sector are of basic interest as well. Which of these trends are counter-tendencies and by what properties?

Another approach, another generalised logic, is a substantial share of EU territory is rural. What does it mean, what does it really mean!? What implications should be considered in the supposed responsibility for the delivery of foodstuffs, etc., in the coming decades and the substantial contribution to the solution of upholding biodiversity, positively influencing climate change and keeping the urbanites alive and thriving in future terms? Evolutionary, even revolutionary changes in society should place the rural, peripheral areas geographically and functionally at the nexus of our attention.

> The very idea of development implies a dynamic of change over time. But when development dynamics are not conceptualized in terms of the systemic logics of the capitalist growth machine . . . we are able to imagine many other dynamics that operate and could be purposefully stimulated.
>
> (Gibson-Graham, 2011, p. 229)

Climate change and long-term sustainability, relating primarily to land-use dynamics and extended rural development processes, needs not only attention, it also needs systemic approaches for research geared to a much higher level and changing directions, founding consecutive policy changes and implementation with clear quality concerns, including "ecological practices, the economic viability of rural areas and their contribution to sustainable development" (Dax, 2014, p. 59). Attention should be shifted from the traditional concern for agriculture and forestry and their futures to a much larger scope concerning these economic functions in the biosphere in a multitude of its complexities. A dimension of the modern rural, in the special variants of entrepreneurial and innovative activities, the special conditions and therefore processes for economic life and survival in economic terms, is seldom interpreted in terms of peripheral and marginal structures. It is taken for granted that there is another way about life out there, a sparsely populated one, etc., one that, in general is unique, but when studied more in depth, returns to the analysis with more generalised findings. The special nature of processes taking place cover, in general terms, diversification and specialisation, and at the same time segregation and conservation (Forsberg, Grimsrud, Jakobsen, Jansdotter and Stubberud, 2006).

The book ends up with the summarised questioning of a dominant and paradigmatic structure, and at the same raising the awareness of a possible other societal logic, much more than economic, but social, balanced and, above all, holistic.

> Rural development seems, in many important respects, to have a life of its own. Despite concerted efforts by both state agencies and private-sector firms to discover a secret recipe for economic success in the countryside, . . . it is not surprising that the supposed ingredients of success in rural development are hard to discern and that they should vary over time.
>
> (Murdoch, 2000, pp. 407–408)

Some contextual considerations

The necessity of the present effort is promoted and provoked by some fundamental changes in the societal logic. It is founded on the combined philosophical and ideological structural changes, with deep-going impacts in several directions, primarily and at present, in terms of neo-liberal interpretations of globalisation. It defines an ideology with global implications and results, in terms of state-market relations, promoting the idea of the prominence of the market and within this the individual and differentiated collectives. These ideas, ideologies, political processes, do not appear from nowhere. The question stands, whether the economic-socio-political fabric in its continuous transformation stands in confrontation with this response to fundamental and continuous challenges, from a number of structural and provoking patterns and phenomena.

> Globalisation facilitated the expansion and restructuring of international trade which was accompanied by rising living standards, but also by rising interpersonal inequalities . . . as well as intra-national – although, curiously not international – disparities.
>
> (Tomaney, Pike and Rodríguez-Pose, 2010, p. 618)

While globalisation described as a general contextual framework may be too abstract, different aspects of it are not. Another contemporary process, with increasing impacts on global issues in their local interpretations, is climate change. In the upcoming pages, references made to other pattern-forming pre-conditions defining change in different temporal patterns, are approached in this regard. Terroristic acts and movements, refugee and other migratory patterns movements are also relevant cases/processes at present. Important dimensions of balancing welfare policies and their financing are important in the framework analysis as well. The impact of the Web on cultural changes, movements and life-to-death progression in generational and intergenerational relations in no way finalise the included ambition.

Another contextual development is that, in spite of the ongoing urbanisation, much of the global population, even in the industrialised world, remains and continues to live in the countryside. The peripheral parts of each nation are complemented by a noted trend, especially in the affluent part of the world for Quality of Life (QOL) considerations, built-on established basic tiers of satisfactory material standards.

Within the framework of all, and even more, of these general processes, are issues regarding the place and role of the locality, increasingly brought to attention, both in general terms and as a focus for specific interests and interest groups. Sometimes, they appear as worthwhile of defending, sometimes a continuously budding alternative for ideologies and policies. Social and cultural processes are becoming manifest in local, place-related patterns, interacting to facets of the global. Creating and partaking in the global is at the same time clearly distinct (Follo and Villa, 2010).

The necessity of the present effort has to do with the general increase of interest in the field of regional development, within this contextual framework, promoted by an increase in importance of alternative perspectives of development, especially in economic growth and its political *foci*[3]– decentralising in former centralised states and deepening the decentralising level in others.

Bringing the basic argument into the book format

Summing up the general approach, it seems valid to make the following hypothetical proposal, based on the existence of a persistent and dominant paradigm, including theoretical constructs, methods, ways to measure, choices of problems/cases – noting and not accepting that this captures the complexity that characterises the periphery/rural in its present and future progression. The identified construct plays an important role in hiding the functioning and alternate logic and potential of the periphery/rural, in turn, having negative implications on societies' 'positive' development choices, especially in the medium and long-term.

> In such a country [Finland] an urban-based logic appears like a cripple, to say the least. The field of spatial development policies needs other forms of logic too – what could be the walking aids, the stick that complements the set of policies?
>
> (Schmidt-Thomé and Vihinen, 2006, p. 46)

As proposed earlier, one of the fundamental issues raised is that the core, centre, capital, urban dimensions set the agenda in analytical and therefore in policy terms. This appears in the form of a collection of general system-defining characteristics. Some of these have a bearing on choices of theory, methods and analytical variables, and through this, tendentious implications for the analytical outcome, and eventually on policies and implementation.

One of the returning themes is the way we describe and define the kind of development we are seeking. This is pertinent, especially when it comes to aspects of environmental and resource dimensions. The basic idea of the Brundtland Commission, i.e. not to send forward the consequences of an economy that exploits and reduces the potentials for future generations, does have implications in this reading. Taking a sharper look at the rural/peripheral potential, we find a large number of issues with direct consequences for biological resources. In future energy solutions the biocycles have, for instance, to be considered compared with urban materialistic and exploitative lifestyles and choices.

> Perhaps it would be useful for all who strive with rural development to consider it as a testing ground for ideas of a society that can offer a real hope that the generated objective is for real.
>
> (Westholm, 2014, p. 2, my translation)

The paradigmatic ideas, elaborated in holistic approaches, taking place in functions, sectors and orientations of society, carrying an analytical dimension in different kinds of social categories, occupations, roles and positions. For example, in the continuing process of unequal exchange. Where the urban 'classes' – the urbanites – in the prerogative of the urban, therefore maintaining the urban bias (Potter et al., 2008). Sometimes versed in even stronger phrasing:

> The centre has been able to grow and raise its standard of living by stealing increasingly the resources of the periphery, particularly its natural resources in the form of food, energy and minerals.
>
> (Schön, 2012, my translation)

From these 'simple', nearly boastful, statements, the intention is to dive into the field of more penetrative exploration with an excursion into a conceptual-analytic organisation of terms and concepts involved. The first step is, whether there are some problematic dimensions of the concepts in themselves, which brings analytical complexity in terms of distortions. Secondly, whether there exist some consensual agreement, making these into stereotypes carrying preconceived values.

After that, the analytical process forwards some basic questions relating to whether one can be satisfied with the way that traditional theory is used in relation to the periphery/rural and identifying whether the theoretical foundations have any in-built tendencies and where these are to be found within the existing theoretical arsenal. Whether the theories used concerns the periphery in the first place? If they have an explanatory value with regard to the periphery and if they are sufficient? When and if they are used in a proper manner? Returning to asking whether the starting point for discussions of modern theoretical representations – in terms of clusters, innovation systems, triple helixes, learning regions – is satisfactory. Whether they are actually theoretical constructs by themselves, parts of a larger theoretical system or, primarily policy development/offensive, presented in an aura of academic polish, with efforts to becoming established theory. In other words, is the acceptance and promotion of the latest version of theory or policy based on the established core, taken as a natural expansion or outside the centre, and if relationships, linkages, values and norms are recognised, is their significance evaluated appropriately?

From concepts and theories, we approach general and more specific methods. Questions put forward here are whether good standards for inductive and deductive reasoning are maintained. Are the methods of analysis adequate? How are measurements taking place? What happens to the 'unmeasurable'? Granqvist (2012, pp. 242–243) provides an intellectual fragment proposing that channels of funding are mainly preserved for quantitative approaches and the periphery finds itself being under the radar, caused by 'littleness'. "It is hard for a small community to be noticed in a larger political context and in survey studies they tend to disappear among the results from the cities." Restrictions in data gathering make conclusions impossible, but on the positive side, stimulate alternative scientific avenues, with an orientation towards interdisciplinary approaches (Mendas, 2016, p. 29).

Taking a counterpoint and progressing into a more in-depth analysis of old economic and societal structures and processes, a general presumption of positive elements in the periphery, usually described as exceptions, are anomalies and unique. If that is a correct statement, is it then possible to see other patterns in structures and processes, tendencies and trends?

> [F]or example, [they] have to overcome their peripheral location by capitalising on strengths in relation to ICT, research, educational and environmental opportunities.
>
> (ESPON, 2013, p. 8)

Furthermore, is it possible to see the newly arising or discovered phenomena in the rural/peripheral economies, in the same manner, as a generalised, positive alternative?

Leaving the safety of primarily socio-economic analysis, the position where the periphery is a place, one focuses on post-modern values and consumption, possibly also making it into a territory more occupied with existential rather than material matters. This route identified by Akgün, Baycan-Levent, Nijkamp and Poot (2011) is driven by considerations for QOL encompassing aspects of health and medicine, social, demographic, economic, environmental, etc., concerns – i.e. focusing on status and attitudes, an orientation still lacking qualitative research (Ulver, 2012) and ignored by the quantitative. Following this line of thought, complicating the analytical progress, we are not discussing absolutes, neither absolute dichotomies, nor absolute categories, but a large amount of varieties of the unique, and an emphasis of accepting uniqueness in a drive for generalities. Uniqueness reigns all the way in the range of the periphery to the urban. We can accept the diversity of the local/regional

> due to e.g. geographic location, demographic structure, economic strength, human capital, labour force, machinery and age of plant, trading links, (with other regions and internationally), consumption patterns and productivity.
>
> (Littke, Foss, & Rauhut, 2012, p. 1)

Identify this as strength:

> they are differentially capacitated to facilitate life in populations of different sizes, with different rates of social and geographic mobility, and different degrees of labor specialization and hierarchic integration.
>
> (Wood, Fels and Krygier, 2010, p. 27)

Through process analysis, the OECD (2009b) noted that social changes are sometimes of such a nature and magnitude that they alter a region's competitive position within the framework of the national/global system. Relative periphery is not only defined by physical distance or affected by technology changes and in aspects of time and cost. Structural causes like customs and other trade barriers are changed by a multitude of material and immaterial factors. Or approaching through a counter-image where small is beautiful (Svensson, 2012), and where the local situation, imaginative and creative solutions see the light of the day, an ideology of never giving up predominates. Within a constantly experienced confrontation to what Big Brother produces forwards a further deconstruction of peripheral societies. Administrative reform often strikes blunt and uneven, depending upon the regional and local resonance, resource packages and preparedness for change. The central message is that there is a solution that fits, will benefit all and a search for administrative shortcuts is hardly a socially optimal strategy.

The following chapter continues the effort of defining the concepts around rural and peripheral, changing focus to a discussion of their 'opposites'. The major elements of substance, defining the concepts of rural and peripheral, are their distinctions as reflections and/or antonyms of other concepts and terms like urban, central, core, etc. The outline of urban deconstruction is meant to question the nature of the concept of the generalised urban, in its capacity to be directly identified by development (in positive terms), constituting agglomerations forming the basis for advanced processes of innovation. One could favour the idea that a deconstruction discloses those parts, functions, relations that actively contribute, and which do not. How to find them?

The continuation of the presentation then focuses on a collection or construction of a case or maybe a skeleton of a case (with missing parts), where a combination of empirical fragments and deductive reasoning is under a heavy impact of continuous change. Fragments, structures, sentiments are found in the periphery but invisible from the paradigmatic standards of the present (Schmidt-Thomé and Vihinen, 2006).

There is hardly any need to legitimate the present effort in policy terms, but what is considered is also the impact on policy, policy development, appearing in many disguises. Existing generalised policy creates the argument, complemented by identified structurally induced patterns of behaviour. This will turn to an analytical starting point, where the peripheral development – suggested to have another logic, or life of its own, where present prescriptions seem to turn the healthy into patients making it on their own – sometimes seems better.

> [R]ural areas continue to follow their own stubborn logics of change and stasis. Seemingly hopeless rural economics either remain hopeless, despite the best efforts of developmental actors, or suddenly show quite unexpected signs of health and vitality.
>
> (Murdoch, 2000, pp. 407–408)

Of importance is to take on perspectives of major societal processes, where an alternative logic and preserved settlement structure could, and maybe should, regain importance and become an absolute in long-term future perspectives. Rurality, not only as a way of life, but as an absolute in development, existence, i.e. for survival.

> Rurality is thus an essential element and must be protected and allowed to develop. It is here that inequalities are often the most pronounced. It is also the people living there who are best capable of looking after the natural heritage.
>
> (Delors, 2012, p. 7)

Changing towards new policies needs new research questions and analytical *foci*, where economy and society have to become locally oriented. Small-scale and local adaptations will increase in importance in overall policy orientation and daily efforts:

> Contemporary insane roaming between different locations around the globe for a few hours of superficial experience, may be replaced by local environment rich variety and the inner journey opportunities.
>
> (Schön, 2012, my translation)

Peripheral/rural as in 'negative'

> The yearn for the urban has left the image of the countryside to its fate, to be portrayed either as a stigmatised, dying relic that nobody wants to touch, or as a romantic idyll so that no one dares to believe in its existence. Looking only at these representations, creating a kind of "internal orientalism" . . . the Swedish countryside is approaching a pitch-dark future.
>
> (Ulver, 2012, p. 3, my translation)

Interpreting this into a flowery and taken-for-granted dichotomy:

> problems of relative poverty, social anomie and decay [lie] in contrast with the mainstream vital and creative, renewed, rich and high-tech, global post-industrial urban centres.
>
> (Lindegaard, 2012, p. 78)

This is not the place to explore the concepts of 'negative' or 'negativism', but instead to make a shortcut to something bad, the opposite of good and positive. This could be an attitude, a way of describing a situation, a status or a process. It could also be direct and unequivocal, or defining an absence of positive attributes or indirect by nuances in interpretations and transmitted in varying forms – verbal, printed, through body language or absence.[4] The negative could also be in the form of self-identification. A formidable basis for important decisions for life and future, possibly even taken into the socio-economics of enterprises and locational behaviour.

The negative approaches, based and focused on structural preconditions and patterns, also present in some parts of theoretical endeavours of development economics, appearing in explanations to the causes behind peripherality. The closeness of these traditions to ideology is noted. In the radical tradition, references are made to structural patterns – socio-cultural, political-administrative and environmental – to dominance and dependency, to cumulative causation, in short by exploitation (Lorentzen, 2012b). The liberal, classical, often economic tradition is related to the presumed functioning of the market economy, witnessed or analysed. The monetised dimensions of development versus growth are to be discussed and questioned.

The negative, geographic and functional 'peripherality', and the main or alternate words appear in themselves in a range from pejorative to affirmative/positive. Peripherality has, in its popular/general appearance mainly derogatory values as attributes. For example, 'peripheral' and 'peripherality' are described together with poor local accessibility, and/or sparse population as a 'basic handicap' (Gløersen, Dubois, Copus and Schürmann, 2006, p. 17). The connotation automatically refers to undefined settlements, considered with additional 'handicaps', presented in economically 'rational' terms (Schmidt-Thomé and Vihinen, 2006). Alternate related concepts like 'marginal' carry the meaning 'at the edge', 'on the boundary', etc., and also have negative connotations. 'Peripheral' linked with 'marginal' define a tendency towards a further emphasised 'negative' mutual reinforcement.

Part of the framework, found within legislation, norms and standards, either in formulation, interpretation and/or implementation, shows a negative, often unintended, bias. A well-known example could be the principles of full competition within the EU *acquis*, with priorities extended on to the entire Union to the disadvantage of the local level and smaller and closer market participants. This kind of general framework is culturally encompassing and penetrating:

> administrative boundaries, existing fiscal schemes for transfers to local governments, and legal instruments often do not correspond to the functional boundaries that may contain the necessary elements to attain a sufficient level of resources to support self-sustaining growth.
>
> (OECD, 2009b, p. 130)

It is possible to find complementary descriptions, in generalised complex/multifunctional categorisations like 'lagging', 'backward', 'vulnerable', 'less favoured', 'disadvantaged', 'derelict', 'pure countryside'. "In other words, the conventional view has been that of 'laggards' which need to be encouraged to 'catch up' with core areas" (Herrschel, 2012, p. 35). Similar descriptions are enforced or enhanced in terms of climate and weather conditions and preconditions: 'harsh climatic conditions', 'short growing seasons', 'reduced agricultural potential', 'dismal transport system'.

Remaining on a balanced approach, references are appearing in versions of ideological populism where the opposite (rural, countryside, etc.) is presented as 'better' than the city (Follo and Villa, 2010, p. 122), compared to an urbanity loaded with a factual negative counterpoints to the rural, or rusticity, as used for discussion by Creed and Ching (1997). They emphasise ghettos, corrupt corporate headquarters, random violence as realities, with a credo of political, economic and cultural power defining a generalised proposal: "In fact, the presence of this power is one reason for high urban crime rates; there are simply more resources to contest, legally or illegally, than in the country" (p. 17). The balance turning out where and when:

> cities may include drug dealers and 'city slickers' among their inhabitants, it is linguistically difficult to denigrate urbanites as a group, whereas the

> opportunities for criticizing the rustic are vast: crackers, rubes, hayseeds, hicks, hillbillies, bumpkins, peasants, rednecks, yokels and white trash.
>
> (p. 17)

By this, returning to the 'negative', often appears as a counterpoint, in a distinction of 'lack of'. Historically and semantically, the periphery always seems to need a comparison to the core/urban and often, in this light, is viewed as a place of underdevelopment. In the normative aspects of this urban-rural dichotomy, the 'negative' is quite distinct but, appears in shades and nuances, where intentions are neither clear-cut nor consciously sought for: "Strong anti-aesthetic that characterises the stories of rural areas" (Ulver, 2012, p. 11, my translation).

Being a farmer carries the burden of the dominating urban perspective, brought forward by an urban cultural language. "What speaks against rural areas in this contemporary culture has much to do with these structures of status, . . . the social identity of the people in the middle class of today" (Ulver, 2012, p. 10, my translation). 'Farmer' is used as invective; it carries automatically a low status, implicating the continuous stigmatisation of a supposedly subsidised population category, using large shares of government's capacity and tax incomes – being well fed, and protected by monopolies and custom tariffs.

Perspectives act as generalisations, where villages, hamlets or rural areas are described in terms of fringe areas, peripheral regions or, as in Denmark 'the rotten banana', as problem areas filled with hopelessness (Møller, 2009). This happens in all countries, generalising the bleakness. Part of Sweden (Norrland), is ascribed these kind of features. It does contain remote areas, but the image of periphery could not really be applicable to the whole (Hedlund, 2016). Still different actors with different interests are ending up with similar standardised pictures.

A further alternative – ignoring, avoiding mentioning, avoiding describing, not knowing – takes the argument even further, defining a role and position. Lack of knowledge is a special case in point. "[K]ey national decision makers and development institutions more widely had inadequate knowledge about rural dwellers and their needs due to a number of 'biases' in research practice" (Potter et al., 2008, p. 445).[5] Thematic maps of Europe do sometimes not include territories above Helsinki, Oslo or Stockholm, indirectly presenting an assumption of 'emptiness', of nothing and "fail to adequately represent whole sections of Europe's economic development perspectives" (Gløersen, 2009, p. 11). This is a crucial example of lacking, found in the concept of the development discourse defining the prerequisites for knowledge-driven economic and social processes:

> These interaction and information-related disadvantages of peripherality are likely to be increasingly important in today's knowledge-driven economy and deserve greater attention in future research.
>
> (Crone, 2012, p. 52)

The periphery is identified as distant from the core and in this complex aspect, therefore, without any capability of interfacing for innovative development (Virkkala, 2007, p. 513). Profiles of low average educational levels and limited access to public research and knowledge are mentioned.[6] Also a subsidised culture is nurtured, indicating low rates of entrepreneurship and innovation. This is complemented by the lack of relevant research, specified to the needs of the periphery. References identifying a lack of agglomerative advantages are common.

Municipalities in the peripheries, most often described by their narrow economic profiles, by the presence of a past, 'factory'-dominating culture. Patriarchal relations in industrial and company townships implicate: "a lower diversity in product and commodity markets" (Margarian, 2013, p. 16), indicating potential limits in the resource base and enforcing a position of vulnerability.

Picture, image, experience and analysis

> We thus propose looking in the places that are culturally the most remote: in the sticks, in the middle of nowhere, in the backwaters of this country and many others, in a word, in the countryside.
>
> (Creed and Ching, 1997, p. 1)

Information, pictures and images play a key role. Centralising processes within the media industry makes the unbalance successively more problematic. In Sweden there has been a reduction of journalists of 25 percent in the countryside, between 2004 and 2014. Of local newspaper offices, a third, about 100 local news points, have disappeared and the profile of journalism has changed from general coverage to blue light (Mittnytt 9.10.2014).[7] Another kind of deficit or ignorance is the focus on non-positive aspects of rural development, more or less ignoring advantages or achievements, and if disclosed, presented with an aura of surprise. Recognising the important marks of status-defined categories, Creed and Ching write: "Ironically, the rural-identified may experience their marginalization as both invisibility and as a spectacularly exaggerated denigration" (1997, p. 4).

A special version on how the periphery (and other categories) is treated or maltreated in 'popular' and some versions of 'scientific' descriptions with analytical ambitions is through different representations where the Latin word *imago* is translated into 'picture'. The translation does not catch the full value of the concept(s). 'Image' carries an extra weight of experience, with individual and collective interpretations, while 'picture' represents more of a scope of primary 'real' and fake. The concept of 'image' does also open a vista of the 'myth'. Fosso (2004) refers to a number of idealised narratives linked to the value-rich words like 'freedom' and 'room for diversity of the city', where 'conformity' pertains the place of birth (rural). Where tranquillity, peace and control of the rural stands in contrast to the exciting, adventurous traits of the city.

The simple method used here is by exploring a list of negatives or negative attributes, in more detail. The nature of the conceptual substance has an impact, both on the general picture and in its details although the systematic treatment of conceptual analysis and registration of nuances are left to the full book. The term 'position' refers to two alternate aspects: either as location and place, in geography, or as a function or role, as in system or organisation. This approach opens for a discussion of relative positions both in geographical and functional and, in this case, normative terms, leading towards a systematisation of disadvantages. Lorentzen (2012b, p. 17) writes, "absence of agglomeration advantages, low rates of entrepreneurship and innovation . . . population will be sparse . . . depend on primary industry, poorly developed infrastructure." Within the inherited administrative structures and boundaries, issues and instruments, communities are less able to take care of themselves, being too small, too sparsely populated, with "a lack of influence in the wider governance arena" (Copus, 2001, p. 540) making 'powerlessness' a central feature of periphery, "which predisposes the community to inaction".

There is a time dimension, when the periphery, indicated with evaluations attached, provides other time-defined values and attributes. A dynamic argument refers to the projection of development as in a negative or positive progression, or analytically, when past performance influences the evaluation of today. Structural phenomena by a historically defined division of labour favours core over hinterland, wealth over poverty, political power over non-influence, big business over local entrepreneurs. At present, the identification of problems pertains to the countryside appearing as "a simple reflection of the emergence of a new geography of flows, wherein rurality is (once again) reconfigured by forces emanating from urban centres" (Murdoch, 2000, p. 408). But this work also provides interpretations of these flows. A central, structural issue of the rural image automatically includes support, subsidies etc., in spite of the fact that the periphery/rural/countryside provides a fundamental share of the necessary provisions for keeping the urban going.

This, more or less, consistent picture/image has the added consequence of what we can call self reinforcement – a kind of negative logic. Much of the stigma is created when compared with a given 'positive', often in terms of the centre/core, especially the urban.[8] The rationale for this exemplified:

> The crisis of the urban and the inability to cope with urban problems is one possible point of departure for reawakened interest in the rural. Finding areas that can be defined as 'behind' or 'backward' may be a way to present the urban in a favourable way and to strengthen the picture of the urban selves in metropolitan areas.
>
> (Stenbacka, 2011, p. 243)

A special image, within the 'periphery' are areas far from large cities being primarily 'sparsely populated', not carrying any specific positive, compensating, idyllic characteristics. "The term is mostly associated with the problem of areas being too sparsely populated" (Eriksson, 2010, p. 96). Sparsity appears in demographic processes, settlement patterns and economic activity. Demographic processes lead to a reduced population, being the sum total of different tendencies, dwindling populations a 'negative' in themselves. The 'negative' is also found in more ultimate consequences. The author continues with the linkage between sparsely populated areas to a territory named Norrland referred to earlier.

> Thus, in the popular geographical imagination, Norrland is a sparsely populated area and has become a negatively charged category referring to people as reactionary, stagnant and backward. In this sense, it is also an abstract rural space that is constructed as wild, empty and underdeveloped.
>
> (Eriksson, 2010, p. 96)

Demographic processes, defining, or complementing a status/stage – sparsity – are conduits to other negatives and vice versa. Sparsity is, however, a much more multifaceted phenomenon, sometimes a constraint but not an absolute, sometimes an advantage, a point that will be returned to.

Focused on specific structural preconditions and patterns like sparsity, 'thinness' and incompleteness, ideological-theoretical preconditions are noted, with evaluations – based on liberal, classical economic traditional norms – of the approach defining the workings of the economy and transference to a kind of 'grand theory status'. Their power to explain or rather legitimise patterns of today make them also part of the denigrating rhetoric. Hörnlund explains that the attribute of sparsity usually carries negative taken-for-granted implications in spite of real economic realities: "Is not then the sparse rural communities a certain burden? No, quite the opposite, by far. It is the large-area municipalities that deliver in lots of hydropower billions" (2009, my translation).

Another image-building category is linked to the concepts 'remote' and 'remoteness' – a simple matter of 'distance' counted in kilometres, miles, time and cost, and often used as a generic term indicating a wide range of handicaps. It is a status defined by large urban centres, with the negative of the remote defined by distance to the implicit good of the urban (Gløersen et al., 2006, p. 81). Also a geographical and functional distinction related to centres in general. 'Remote' implicates less favourable conditions, including interacting infrastructure (part of the substance of being 'remote'). As to infrastructure there is a noted "relative absence of physical infrastructure (road, rail, telecommunications), qualified labour and research and technological development (RTD) activity, etc." (Morgan, 2007, p. 109). Distance complemented with location makes climatic, pertinent constraints, leading to erratic seasonal variations, especially for communication. The image, from the outside, is one of hardship.

Living in a 'remote' neighbourhood, the heralded IT backup makes for improvement, but never on a scale and quality good enough for restrictions in the periphery to be taken for granted. Limited IT skills are an individual restriction; improvements of technical levels do not close that gap. Mastering potential is deemed more or less impossible. For business in terms of market potential, this remoteness/isolation is deemed an explicit structural obstacle if the firm has expansionary ambitions (Tödtling and Trippl, 2005). There exist fewer opportunities for business community interaction and local networking capabilities, also implying an absence of local competition, in turn, indicating less encouragement for innovation, compared to areas where competition is fierce. Consequences appear in the form of vulnerability, where the international and national financial markets and state budget changes have a profound and sometimes devastating impact.[9] Remoteness does not isolate from global implications.

In descriptions of the labour market, the extent of entrepreneurship and enterprises is, primarily, a question of accessibility to jobs and labour. The level of accessibility[10] goes in both directions. Rural labour markets are described as 'thin' in terms of size, density and there is 'slack' in the number of jobs relative to the size of the potential workforce. Even noting that reliability and low turnover possibly cause disincentives for productivity efforts, reductions of labour are avoided through introducing new technology. The isolated local labour market, in relative terms and small labour markets, indicates high unemployment rates and lower median or average incomes (Morgan, 1997). A 'wrong' composition is usually described as less specialised with general low education and skill levels. Limited access to higher education is the historic explanation, including a culture where intellectual efforts were, and remain, frowned upon. Causalities are not really researched. Furthermore, the negative identification of low (relative and nominal) incomes, indicates a smaller scale in terms of local consumption and market for production. All this adds up to an economy described as fragmented, with, on average, small entities, reduced contact with information, knowledge and therefore also inspiration and market stimuli.

> Where networks both intraregional and extra-regional – are weak, innovations are unlikely to originate or to be adapted in meaningful ways. These regions thus struggle to catch up.
>
> (Virkkala, 2007, p. 513)

Lacking institutional capacity, 'organisational thinness' in terms of lack of critical mass, of entrepreneurial resources and a general mismatch between the science base and the knowledge users also contributes to the picture. Descriptions of institutional capacity, described in degrees of complexity blend together with fragmentation, plausibly related to lack of oversight and range of remedies (Green and Orton, 2010). These authors make references to the uncertainty within the governance types of development, promoting efficient policy, possibly hindered by a too-adaptive institutional response. A possible positive interpretation of that could be a potential for flexibility on local levels.

Within the framework of institutional capacity, a picture and experienced low supply of public welfare services in terms of total volume, per capita and quality, are part of a generalised negative reputation. At the same time the image of a public sector can be perceived as 'unhealthily' large, due to the reliance on public spending emanating from the centre (James, Midmore and Thomas, 2012,

p. 448). Relative and increasing costs for providing these services, infrastructure and competence promotion have an impact on tax incomes, tax levels and therefore also on individual expenditures.

Turning to another commonly identified negative, the branch structure, where production and growth are dominated by agriculture, forestry, fishing and hunting, defined by substantial technological development with a direct negative impact on the local and regional labour markets, but deemed good for productivity. The combination of a decline in the manufacturing industry and economic activity reinforcing this is part of the profile. Part of the picture at the same time, as noted, includes a lack of technological development.[11] Descriptions of the profiles in terms of 'sunset branches', argue that these combined with a 'too-good' welfare system, makes the labour market less dynamic. Being on the 'dole' maintains an acceptable standard of living for the individual, described as 'conventional thinking' enforcing the main argument (Aarsaether and Nyseth, 2007). Terms such as 'conservative', 'old', even 'archaic' are used.

A knowledge-driven economy needs the results of mainline research and knowledge, but also specialised and relevant research, profiled to specific needs. But the image is instead one of:

> low education and traditional occupations that fit. High education and modern vocations belong to key locations and city. Such marginalises also the identities of places of upbringing; they are suitable only for young people without any particular ambitions in life.
>
> (Fosso, 2004, p. 133, my translation)

The negative image of the intellectual capacity of the periphery is also downgraded by the notion of a brain drain within general migratory patterns, a picture of a failing or faltering local mobilisation of potential, weakening the social fabric. The compensation of a voluntary sector and social economy lacks volume and intensity. Another way of saying that there is a difference in the appearance and potential of network activity: "less favoured regions (LFRs) seem to have little or no social capital on which they can draw" (Morgan, 2007, p. 109).[12] This brings us from a position of geography (peripheral) deeper into cultural representation.

There are aspects where even the 'positive' turns around and becomes negative. A mentioned possibility of a growing local population still carries negative connotations. "[I]t does not follow that this necessarily enhances local living conditions" (ESPON, 2013, p. 41). Increasing housing prices, stimulated by external demand, has a negative impact for local couples looking for their first dwelling. Commuting to locations with better access to financial and other service facilities reduces the demand for providing these services locally, in turn, resulting in higher-on-average costs for service provisions. Individuals in the higher income brackets using their own car reduce the fundament for public transport. These kinds of impacts exclude groups with a different standard in material and life status and thereby impact quality of life for these even further.

The concept of resources seems, in general terms, to be a positive quality. This identification is, however, quite different inside looking out or outside looking in. Natural resources, climate, landscape and the development of tourism could be objects for exploitation, aspects of oppression or aspects of quality of life.

Research on young people in the countryside point at a number of qualitative issues in and for this group: a general climate and structure of not having; isolation, limited social networks and a local society putting up obstacles (the word used is 'claustrophobic'); limited possibilities for organised leisure activities; rudimentary service and public transport facilities; small and limited labour markets; small range of local education facilities. They look at their outmigrating peers with envy and feel even less successful (Möller, 2012). A migrant population of the 'successful', looking for the Holy Grail of a career and a 'better' lifestyle, integrate a possible fear of failure in being forced to return. A cloak of education and competence-building leaves the 'losers' behind, included in a white trash discourse, linked to a reality of low-average health, psychological problems, lack of education, self-destruction, indifference and poverty (Ulver, 2012).

Ulver (2012) further elaborates on the image-, picture-building, referring to a flow of cinematic projects where the peripheral countryside is presented in Hollywood, action style, where violent criminals hide, where blue-light journalism is the collection of hardship and violence, serial killers, racists, motorcycle gangs. This stands in stark contrast to the middle-class ideals of the rural, being more secure etc., and instead, anonymity in the town is replaced by a rural inhabitant being the outcast, where life exists in the urban culture and the farmer slowly, culturally starving, forgotten.

The image building is relevant also in other dimensions. In a discussion on the rural and urban masculinities, Stenbacka (2011, p. 235) registers within the context of family farming that men are "backward, lonely, vulnerable and marginalised. . . . [I]t is possible to identify a competition between urban and rural symbolic space, where the urban ends up as dominant." This discussion also encompasses a more penetrative dimension in gender, especially masculinities:

> do not describe rural masculinities as hegemonic, but rather the rural as deviant, unequal and in need of assistance compared to urban counterparts, which are not mentioned but taken for granted and seen as superior.

Noting that this is not a conspiracy it is "unconsciously created and women as well as men help to perpetuate them" (Stenbacka, 2011, p. 236). The image and/or reality are much more complex than that:

> Rural men and their identity expressed through rural masculinity are portrayed as being closely connected to primary industries, gender inequality and a low level of 'civilisation' – collectively contributing to presenting the rural man as 'the other'.
>
> (Stenbacka, 2011, p. 242)

The role of media emphasises the gap, giving an advantage to the urban side.

> Popular culture returns to the retrograde a kind of unsuccessful man all the time. In the news, the themes are more subtle, but the coverage is partly based on some of the stereotypes about uneducated and outdated people. The inhabitants of the countryside are singled out as 'the other'.
>
> (Nordström, 2015, my translation)

What is described/listed here is a somewhat unsystematic collection of attributes for functions, lifestyles, milieu and social images, found in everyday practices overflowing into the scientific agenda, referring to the creation of place/territorial identities and transferred narratives of the negative and positive. In the weak and strong regions, localities, the weak could explicitly and/or implicitly, identify characteristics in this regard. Representations of these regions also include images of the people living there and their presumed identity and/or role models. The experienced rural is usually expressed in the pejorative version of periphery/margin. Life at the rustic margin "in which rustic people (wherever they reside) are marginalized and their culture devalued vis à vis urban(e) culture" (Creed and Ching, 1997, p. 5). These stereotypes are generally promoted, reinforcing the image of the region/locality. "As a result, the problems within these areas are implicitly blamed on the people living there" (Eriksson, 2008, p. 369).

Personal philosophy and methodological considerations

As should be evident by now, this book is not a conventional scientific endeavour. It is clearly and admittedly apologetic in its approach. As such, it's controversial, but not forbidden . . . ? Its legitimacy is found in a conviction of the existence of a field of research, so far underexploited, definitely underfunded and confronting/opposing a major paradigmatic structure that, as is logical, does not seem to be aware of the need to question its own preconditions or presuppositions. There is ideology, but not standardised versions, and the formulated viewpoints and/or opposition is a conglomerate of kaleidoscopic character.

The nature of the approach has implications as to ramifications in theoretical and methodological excuses, needing further and future references to the validity and reliability of at least some of the results. The approach is, however, not grandstanding, in the way of ignoring the empty argument or the unsubstantiated proposition in order to make the case. The unconventional approach and method is endorsed "because of the problematic nature of enterprise" (Anderson, 2000, p. 98).

Holism is a major ingredient of the approach. As exemplified but not automatically or convincingly reachable:

> By addressing current challenges and acknowledging the interrelations between land use, regional economy, ecological changes, societal drivers and governance issues it provides a comprehensive framework for rural

> development research that aims to take account of the increasing complexity of development in rural areas.
>
> (Dax, 2014, p. 59)

Being holistic, within the limited framework of one monograph and the limited capabilities of one author, says something about the overambitious personality, but even more about the relation between generalisations and analytical substance. Part of it being apologetic contains an ambition to start out on an intellectual adventure, inviting to sharing, disputing all that is contained in the upcoming pages. This does not always raise results, but maybe will launch questions in need for answering in the coming years. I not only replace results with further questions, but also accept levels and systematisations of empirical information that by methodological approach could be questioned. The ambitions are also raised for one substantial presupposition. There is development, development presupposes changes, and the context of *now* is a forming and deforming exercise. Take for instance this 'small' outline:

> In pre-industrial times, the city was associated with freedom and with professional groups, crafts and guilds. . . . This raises a second debate whether 'urbanisation' actually describes a deeper societal change and not just the concentration of population.
>
> (Bosworth, 2009, p. 5)

There is also an important analytical entrance, concerning methodological consequences in the relation between the unique and the generalised or generalisable. Here, the degree of empirical penetration will not always be in terms of an acceptable level of analytical impact, and I am wilfully opening the door for future confirmation or not, by way of more directed and methodological elaborations. What will also be, partly, considered is that within this outline of periphery, margin, rural, etc., there are tremendous varieties of societal profiles connected with natural-given prerequisites. This recognises, in general terms, the existence of qualitative differences within what could be called, artificially homogeneous entities, different forms with different patterns of action, reaction and ideology. So what is to be generalised, cannot be disclosed, weakening possibly the case, although, also possibly, qualifying a multifaceted argument with several, even a large number of variations.

The effort to opening doors, as many doors as possible, makes shortcuts in the way of handling references. Sometimes ignoring distinctions of first- and second-hand sources, by transferring sources and with them possibly mistakes, false logic – although hopefully, not outright lies – without a full-fledged control of quality, and referring to quite a high number of direct quotes. The relation between the author, the source and the reader is such that the references used and exploited are in terms of their merit in contributing to the ongoing discussion, not as a final scientific point (Østrem, 2015, p. 36). Accepting that, in order to cover a fundamental societal problem, no apparent alternative seems available.

Notes

1 The word 'periphery', in its different connotations, will be used for 'rural', 'countryside'. 'margin', etc., to simplify the reading. This is qualified with references to different nuances when necessary and conceptual, further developed in Chapter 2.
2 The concept of 'core' treated in a similar fashion as 'periphery' covering 'centre', 'urban', etc.
3 The intellectual, theoretical and practical conflict found in the relations between the concepts of 'economic growth' and 'development' is a basic ingredient in the full discussion.
4 'Absence' meaning 'ignoring', 'lack of attention', 'missing qualities'.
5 Use of the past tense is not necessary.
6 Aspects of action research – preconditions and consequences as potentials – are not discussed here.
7 The source was a television programme.
8 A dichotomy that will be returned to in a much more explorative and thorough manner in Chapter 5.
9 See the comment on public-sector spending on the preceding page.
10 Accessibility is about availability and the degree this is so. It is a quality of a system or entity.
11 This could possibly be a result in the period discussed.
12 A suggestion questioned in other sections of this monograph.

2 The periphery,[1] the marginal and the rural

Conceptual discussion

Introduction

Before going any further, there is a need to relate to the primary terms/concepts[2] and some of their consequential links and roles. This is central for the whole idea/ideology of the upcoming presentation. One thing should be explicit – maintaining obscurity pertaining to the terms will continue to stand as a crucial issue to the future of policymaking and policy implementation. Agreeing with Rokkan (1987, p. 234), these words/concepts are still useful as introductory keys for further theoretical work. The present contribution emphasises a conceptual/analytical approach with reference to some earlier conceptual and taxonomic discussions (Danson and de Souza, 2012), while at the same time further elaborating on some possible preconditions and intellectual highways for theoretical and empirical exploration.

Giving a full chapter to this exercise seems also essential, as the terms/concepts are frequently used or abused by others, in metaphorical extensions, active propagandistic activities and misinterpreted nuances. It seems necessary to bring further substance, both to the concepts involved, and to what is described and analysed, and hopefully also provoke the reader to reflect for a future constructive debate. In spite of the fact that the terms are continuously used, and as noted abused, the broadness and depths of them have impressive dimensions and could beneficially be employed for discussions of the local, of the region, of development, of the future. One of many caveats, however, in their collective meaning encompasses being non-urban, non-central, etc., at least in the eyes of dominating perspectives.

Their interconnectivity is an analytical dimension in itself, as similarities and non-similarities disclose and define the limits of some of their common nuclei, which will have a forward-reaching importance. Similarities, although not total congruence, with dimensions of the rural and the countryside are not surprising. We will also find out about counter-definitions, like in 'non-urban', where socio-economic patterns stand out in historical processes, carrying the brunt of industrialisation and technical achievements, but focusing on the direct link to the exploitation of different aspects of natural resources. Distance matters for the ongoing processes, creating structures and sub-processes that do not manifest themselves in the same way on a micro level, due to contextual prerequisites.

The periphery/rural is integrated in the general societal change of globalisation, neo-liberalistic policies, as well as in other ideological, political and similar features. The periphery/rural also represents a mixture of characteristics, not different from the urban in its elements, but differently categorised in its mixtures. Appearing from this we will also see how individuals and groups defined by themselves and others through belonging, in turn reinforcing forces that create definitions and meanings. For the sake of the analysis, it is also necessary to include the role of sub-centres, as well as the analytical impact of in-between zones and activities. The latter highlight special aspects of place and locality, neighbourhood and social community seen from an individual and collective perspective. Finally, there are some necessary comments on issues relating to the outer, geographical and functional edges or borders of, and in, rurality.

At times one could identify how different 'academic tribes' or disciplines apply the terms differently. Considering the importance of spatiality in geography, this prism provides a complementary analytical dimension of value. Spatiality acts as a common denominator categorising social, economic and other variables in one presentable dimension. The other way around, economics and social sciences link through geography within its sub-disciplines to natural sciences. The basis for periphery and marginality within other social sciences is primarily on functional categories, and could, but not always, become more explicit when appearing on a map.

Turning to a quite basic background question, at least for a geographer, is whether space is a dominant explanatory variable. This has to be qualified by contextualising the kind of space that is analysed. When it comes to periphery and margin there could sometimes (often enough) be dominant spatial aspects. A general survey of the literature indicates that this tendency is more evident when it comes to the concepts of periphery/peripheral than margin/marginal. Construction of the functional rural, in turn, takes place at different geographical scales and changes substance and focus depending on the specific levels in relevance for attitudes, behaviours, practices and decisions, often carrying a spatial interpretation, although a complementary one. Important aspects lead into the functional and experiential by way of the spatial or letting functionality or experience choose its own alternative and also returning path.

An argument pointing to a general lack of systematised empirical analysis in these still undefined areas, functions and experiences is necessary. Meaning that aspects of regional and/or rural policies, usually developed with perspectives, are given special treatment to areas with a regional/central orientation or location, or areas defined by some kind of threshold indicators for population, densities of activities, etc. It should be noted that peripheral, marginal and rural enter a stage of qualifying identifications, including the concept of 'sparsity',[3] occurring in a combination of low population densities, dispersed settlements, further implying specific challenges and considerations (Gløersen et al., 2006). This defines the number of persons and/or the functional population base in a significant way (economic, etc.). Distance to work, services and dispersed settlements and houses is also important. Sometimes, the industrial profile – agriculture, forestry and fishing – are significant as markers. The relationship between the statistical/empirical base and its role in defining the bounded entity or place, and further on, in specific spatial categories, are cases in point. Different definitions of the boundary, minimum scale, geography, community, etc., from core and peripheral perspectives tend to disadvantage attempts to undertake research in and of more peripheral, sparsely populated or isolated territories – bringing in the potential explanatory powers of social constructs, finding characteristics qualifying the substance and explaining the construction of it. Physical features historically form obstacles for communication and interaction. Other obstacles appear in the form of borders and boundaries: neighbouring populations, marginal political positions. "[T]hrough their definition of insider/outsider status in relation to territorial organization. . . . Supranational and regional and local boundaries can also have powerful marginalization impacts" (Syrett, 2012, p. 67).

At the same time, this tries to identify the historical situation as different in such a way that is not directly relevant for up-to-date interpretations. In one example, Moe (2010, p. 15) notes the importance of specific families or persona among the nobility and/or city states where centrality (defined in terms of power and market) created a hierarchical structure, while the periphery remained segmented rather than stratified. Other cultural-forming structures/processes like religion or war are also relevant. These kinds of arguments are conditional for a more penetrating analysis of a contextual approach; the widening framework will, however, question the extent of the present author's (economic geographer) ability as:

> Social spaces or rurality are no longer seen necessarily to overlap with geographical spaces of rurality, as cultural constructs of the rural pervade various aspects.
>
> (Johnston, 2000, p. 720)

Concepts and terms will simultaneously discuss an elaboration of definitions through identifying methodological considerations, practical implications and policy regulations. The analysis has no ambition of being the final answer or a systematically encompassing approach, but draws together a representative number of examples.

As a slight diversion in legitimising the still remaining, complex ambition, a fundamental and interesting question is the fact that the definition of problems of living in the periphery appears at the same time as the definition itself develops, encompassing the status of being peripheral. This raises a question of relations between experienced and exogenously determined definitions. The natural inclination or situation of a need or demand is for 'hard' statements and facts and 'rules' standing in contrast to the denigrating substance of the terms. Having noted the dimension of living, there is also a crucial dimension of 'acting'. This is a peripheral response towards the centre, in terms of 'we and them', mobilising the 'we'. A similar process takes place in the centre, resulting in a power-game in controlling resources and impacting policies of:

> openness versus isolation in relations with foreign standards, intellectual or ideological innovation. Fighting in the periphery is about maintaining individuality, autonomy with respect to the territorial center, the fight in the center stands on border marker towards other systems.
>
> (Rokkan, 1987, p. 225)

Peripheries and margins – peripheral and marginal

The idea that places, regions and territories are social constructs is, naturally, transferable to peripheral or marginal areas or locations, in the way that these designations are prisms through which the status of peripheral is substantiated.

The term 'periphery' is derived from Greek – i.e. to move around a circumference with an emphasis of being, primarily, a spatial concept. In abstract terms, a periphery is a boundary or outer part of any space or body. The perimeter of a circle, another closed curve or also, the perimeter of a polygon is a line that determines the limit of an area, the outermost part or region within a precise boundary, a zone constituting an imprecise boundary in itself. Other descriptions where the term is used is, for instance, 'peripheral vision', that part of the visual perception that occurs in the periphery, i.e. near the edges of the field of view. The periphery indicates the outer ring of the hinterland defined by a centre, or a kind of intermediary zone, distinct from the outer periphery. Periphery, used in a distinction of peripheral countries, includes nations/states not described in terms of core, capitalist or industrialised, all within the definitions of the World System Theory. Periphery also refers to the boundary of a town or city, also known as outskirts or suburbs, what is not mainstream or central.

When extending to adjectives or verbs, peripheral/peripheralisation is highlighting the dynamic properties of causality leading up to the stages/status of peripheral and peripheries, being in the periphery, being peripheral, being less core, etc., notable at a given time. Peripheralisation becomes peripheral through (changes in): the operation of markets, sectors or market forces, (national or international) borders, etc. The same kind of approach could be used, when referring to margin/marginalisation. Approaching the substance has quite a reach:

> The world is broken into centers and peripheries that index degrees of significance, create and reflect distribution of power, and articulate standards and deviations. To explore peripheries, therefore, is to raise questions not only about geography but also about hierarchy, power, and social norms.
>
> (Platt, 2011, p. 1)

Exemplifying into the phenomenology of relative geography: "Another weakness of the Stockholm metropolitan area is its peripheral location with regard to the Pentagon area" (Smetkowski et al., 2011, p. 210). The concept of peripherality encompass maybe too much of variation and qualitative differences, so the term needs further qualifications. What seems evident from day-to-day utilisation, is that it tends to be applied to quite a wide range of issues, sometimes losing contact with its own essential nucleus. Similarly, all its potential derivations are usually exploited loosely: 'peripheral', 'peripheralisation', 'peri-urban' (though terminological versions with a more technical tendency seem to be applied more carefully).[4] The reflection does also pertain to other concepts in the same general category, like rural, lagging, deindustrialised, etc.

The use of peripheral and marginal space defines peripherality. The use being activities connected with experiences, differentiated actors, geographical and functional positions and locations:

> at the edge of a communication system, where they are away from the core or controlling centre of the economy.
>
> (Anderson, 2000, p. 93)

The substance and picture/image of peripherality and/or marginality, is a conceptualisation of the relations (social and economic constructs) between the core and the periphery, used as a metaphor for the totality of the different operational facets of this prism. Copus (2001) identifies three groups: causal, contingent and associated. Causality is defined by combined time and cost factors where relative distance and sparsity combine to create higher per capita or unit costs, further enhanced by poorly developed – i.e. quality in general terms – infrastructure, summarised into an effect of weak development potential and position. This exemplifies further dimensions and/or layers, with aspects of political accessibility although the notion of periphery and accessibility are here described "as notoriously vague and variable concepts" (Copus, 2001, p. 540). This introduces the notion of the centre as the defining category. At the same time, it increases the complexity of the theoretical endeavour, eliminating the possibility of a single conceptual or theoretical interpretation.

An exemplifying projection of what a periphery is describes lacking in economic activity or rather, aspects of economic activities. "In relation to a more economically diversified centre, the periphery is a distant (*utmark*) area with a relatively limited number of export products in exchange for a relatively diversified import" (Westlund, 1998, p. 11, my translation). This notion is often used when discussing the spatial and functional positions of islands. It also represents the specific notion of northern Nordic and other similar peripheralities (Johansen, Bjørnsen, Hagen and Juvkam, 2006, p. 29). The same source refers to municipalities lacking settlements and centres and therefore not conducive to commute to in any meaningful numbers. Processes in local communities progress according to internal causalities that may influence structural and social change. "Both cores and peripheries are thus continuously being produced by different coexisting mechanisms" (Lorentzen, 2012b, p. 17). Exemplifying the complex interactions from which the particular unfolds:

> Hence 'peripherality' can be seen to be culturally specific, a social construct, best explained within the interplay of culture and economics.
>
> (Anderson, 2000, p. 93)

The picture also orientates the other way, giving the dweller, an inhabitant, an identity, some kind of collectivity, carrying not only a name but also, among other things, a normative complex of characteristics – peripheral or marginal, positive or negative.

As part of an opposite, an antonym to peripheralisation we find centralisation. In a functional sense, it contains processes where an individual's locational behaviour, together with other structural conditions (industrial processes and structures, the structures and processes of the labour market, etc.), work together and define directional flows, to and from an identified centre. Peripherality as a condition defining and defined, at the edge of the system, far away from the main control, found in the centre, the core. It lies at the outer reaches of the state's spokes. The manifestation appears in a number of differently defined and described processes like decentralisation, separation and processes of conscious, regulated regional formation. It is sometimes integrated, sometimes differentiated. Its meaning is well represented in:

> [t]he European Union's decades-old regional policy. . . . There, peripherality, or marginality, have usually been geographically defined as edges of a territory, based on distance from a centrifugal core, and this has been projected as a negative condition that needs to be tackled by reaching out to the margins and reducing distance through improved communication lines (infrastructure projects).
>
> (Herrschel, 2012, p. 30)

Approaching , on the one hand, simultaneous aspects of geographical, functional and relative distances and structures and, on the other, different interpretations of advantages and disadvantages, constituted by dimensions of these distances, closeness and place-related issues. The former also includes relations between centre and periphery like dependence, difference and discourse. To exemplify, transborder zones, described or identified as 'weak', in terms of participation in the economic landscape are simultaneously conducive for separatist tendencies and new formations of cross-border character. The latter activities neutralise state borders and impose on issues of sovereignty.

There is always a story/history about periphery/ies, margins. Part of the present is based on the past with preconditions shaping or hindering different development paths, where human settlements were defined by the presence or non-presence of cultivable land, exploitable opportunities and state power. Places found on the periphery are marginalised in cultural systems. Spaces ranked in power-hierarchical structures are relative to each other. It is nearly impossible to change the position of a functionally marginalised/peripheralised area/place. Being part of an earlier historical legacy or modern functionalities that were not of major importance as status definitions becomes prominent (Jönsson, Tägil and Törnqvist, 2007). In analysing the causes of peripheralisation, the complexity of historical legacies, social structures and governance issues necessarily coincide. Changes in relative positions in the centre/periphery dichotomy are noted. Changes in the political and transport infrastructural landscape made Györ (HUN) move from a national periphery to a central European location. Cultural "openness, language skills, or experience in regional cooperation – often driven by INTERREG (EU interregional) projects – nowadays work as a competitive advantage" (Cooke, 2012, p. 91).

The reason for the inclusion of accessibility as a conceptual distinction is that it represents, in a major way, an impact that could be generalised, not in its negative but in its constructive substance. Introduced here are aspects of the concept, used both geographically and functionally. For example, distance and costs are measured in terms of competence and settlements. Perspectives like this form a basis for the study of extended functionality, a

> difference in terms of skills, entrepreneurialism, policymaking capabilities, general human resources, or local ways of doing things.
>
> (Herrschel, 2012, p. 34)

The image emanating from the stereotype of backwardness implicates a lack of potential innovativeness (Pasquinelli and Teräs, 2011). This dimension has an impact on people, on actors, on self-identification. To many it is a dimension of experiencing: "the edge of a communication system, where they are away from the core or controlling centre of the economy (Goodall, 1987)" (Fuduric, 2012, p. 167). Periphery is concerned with identifying the relation with something, distinguished with elements of the centre, core. Its essence infused by power relations is "founded upon territory-based practices . . . especially for those living in less privileged areas" (Lagendijk and Lorentzen, 2007, p. 462). Issues around power, control and ownership are emphasised by development economists in classical representations like Myrdal (1957) and Hirschman (1958) and by representatives of the dependency school like Cardoso and Faletto (1979) and Frank (1966). Westlund (1998) refers to some of these, highlighting the importance these relations have had for development processes in different directions.

> The structure of the periphery has been shown to be dynamic rather than fixed. The paradoxical aspect of this peripheral change is the values attributed to the 'otherness' of the periphery, those very characteristics that helped to make it peripheral.
>
> (Anderson, 2000, p. 105)

Attributes also vary, geography could be complemented by social,[5] political, economic characteristics and defined on different spatial levels. "Reflection on these studies reveals a fourth important facet of peripherality, namely its multiscalar nature" (Crone, 2012, p. 51). Identifying peripheries on a global level includes categories like 'underdeveloped', 'third world', etc. On a national level, categories can be 'North', 'distant', etc. The other end of the scale distinguishes "spatial peripherality of places as the backdrop to actor engagement, shaping their ambitions, interests, priorities and expertise" (Herrschel and Tallberg, 2011, p. 91). Actor and interest are defined and appear in normative dimensions like in "the degree to which localities or regions are perceived as 'peripheral' by those outside (that is in the core areas) and thus little 'advantageous' to engage with" (Herrschel and Tallberg, 2011, p. 91). 'Peripheral' and 'peripherality' must be understood here primarily as geographical terms, although I disagree with the view that "attempts to broaden their scope beyond the geographical (e.g. 'aspatial peripherality' after Copus, 2001) risk contributing to the fuzziness of the concept" (Crone, 2012, p. 50).

It is also possible to catch the concepts, as noted, within a hierarchical approach. Being thematically constructed, the hierarchies chosen usually have something to do with centralisation and concentration, examples being urban, power and wealth-defined. This kind of approach discloses some of the processual dynamics – power emanating from inequality, periphery subordinated to the core.

Another approach avoids the concept of periphery but introduces 'non-core' as the designation – Lorentzen's (2012b, pp. 24–25) referring to Arzeni, Esposti and Sotte (2002). This designation is defined by activity, meaning that it has an impact in defining degrees of peripherality. A further dimension to introduce is a reality perspective. When given a name attributed with a quality of uniqueness:

> In their influential analysis of European peripheries Stein Rokkan and Derek Urwin characterised peripheral regions as being, in relation to the capital areas of the respective countries, geographically distant, culturally different and economically dependent (Rokkan and Urwin, 1983, p. 13).
>
> (Baldersheim and Fimreite, 2005, pp. 764–765)

. . . and more specific. Within aspects of the experience industry peripheral connotations can refer to resources for some and lack of for others, leading to progressively more permanent marginalisation and abandonment or a potential positive development. In a concluding comment on the construction and definition of the periphery, the reader is left with what could be called an academic cliff-hanger:

> Consequently in place of the stable objectification of periphery as distant and remote, interpretations of the periphery have become more subjectified and must now be recognized as more fluid.
>
> (Anderson, 2000, p. 92)

In relation to added dimensions of margin and marginal, a number of interesting entrances or nuances are found. As in a zone with a certain width, a beach, there is room to act or react in the essence of a safety margin. In a spatial/functional sense, we have room (elbow room) in allowing/leaving a margin. In a functional sense, we are finding or defining room to manoeuvre. Similar to periphery we find circumference, border, boundary but also symbolic/immaterial aspects like living on the margins of society. To estimate a margin is to include a possibility, a dimension, sometimes of error. In a similar functional sense, we have the idea of being marginal in relation to sources of and for power, identifying the implications of asymmetric power relations (Syrett, 2012).

Although there are various understandings of marginality, basic aspects refer to a dimension of disadvantages due to situation/context whether cultural, social, political and economic, and locational factors, or all together. It is an experienced distance to a non-specified centre or core, representing power and other societal *foci* (Petrov, 2012). The notion of margin and marginal is also in the category of fuzzy concepts. "In the introduction to this book Rob Shields (1991) characterizes marginal places as left behind, and that those places on the margin form a 'mythic heartland . . . a zone of otherness' (Shields, 1991, p. 4)" (Nyseth, 2009, p. 1).

This is conceptually a complication as the two terms/concepts, quite substantially, enter into each other's explanatory sphere and similarly reflected in each other's interpretations. Is the question one of nuances or more, one of direction? One interpretation is in degrees of peripherality "the term 'margin' is used to designate ultimate peripheries, which are distinct in the level of isolation, disintegration, and marginal from less isolated and disintegrated peripheries" (Petrov, 2012, p. 61). A rough distinction between things being peripheral and people being marginal and people in the periphery being marginalised. Being on the margin includes the possibility of appearing in a functional or geographical peripheral or location:

> contexts ranging from geographically peripheral positions rural areas through to the marginalized spaces located in the most economically prosperous city-regions.
>
> (Syrett, 2012, p. 65)

As noted, the interpretation of being marginalised does indicate primarily a functional (not a geographical) definition, but does not exclude the possibility. For example in the argument of the marginal appearing, as a defined substance of the peripheral. Herrschel (2012, p. 31) quotes "effective marginalization *as a quality of* in-between peripherality". Actors, whether conscious or not, partake in creating peripherality. Individuals or groups, due to ongoing activities, changes, timetables leading to marginalisation, often participate in defining and are defined in geography.

Returning to the main dichotomy, the investigation often treats the concepts in their static manifestation/interpretations, while changes are continuous. Therefore, the spatial and historical context in its specificities has to be interpreted. Is there a specially profiled kind of margin active in a special type of region or geography? (Syrett, 2012). For the description of these processual and changing conditions, identified as trigger factors, impacts contribute to define the direction, nature and progress of 'the general process' in itself. What are the major variables/structures and the essence of their change? What are the timescales: some background processes are so long-term, that they could be experienced and described as static. Similarly, continuous or discontinuous variables are described as dependent or just pure coincidence. What is the significance of the interdependent processes of peripheralisation and marginalisation becoming (more or less) peripheral or (more or less) marginal? What forces are involved? Are the identified forces (always) derived from the core, and are there major elements in the scientific problem? As methodological considerations, structures and processes are naturally necessary in order to understand the manifestation of the concepts in real-world dimensions, being determinants of each other. The nature of the process is mostly defined by the situation at a given time with all its contextual properties.

However, turning some of the arguments around, the basic nature of the processes are fundamental reflections of the general and dominating process of centralisation. A basic characteristic here is an aspect of economic processes appearing in spatial connotations. This is exemplified, for instance, by Selstad (2004) in the centralising city-region and also in discussions on a conceptual understanding of the metropolis.

It is possible, before venturing into the field of even more complex attributes and characteristics, that the two words/concepts, in most cases, appear as attributes/criteria in themselves, describing the nature of an area, function or position. Sometimes, they are accompanied by enhancing negative attributes in loaded wording and can

> signal the relative absence of physical infrastructure (road, rail, telecommunications), qualified labour and research and technological development (RTD) activity, etc.
>
> (Morgan, 2007, p. 109)

'Symptoms' refer to sickness, 'poor' to lacking, while 'weakness' is situational and 'disposition' is dependence, reliance. A multitude of other sources, attributes/criteria, with different degrees of complexity/multifunctionality are found, exemplified previously in representations as lagging, backward, vulnerable, disadvantaged and derelict, which can be summarised as 'basic handicaps'.

Historically, the rationale for a creation/establishment of a settlement, was guided by the suitability of natural conditions (soil, climate, protection and other natural advantages). Accumulated experience combined with different kind of 'pressures' and 'necessities' defining, and being basic determinants for production forms, survival and the eventual possibility to earn a living. Peripheral and marginal have been indirectly substantiated by factors like harsh climatic conditions, short growing seasons, i.e. low agricultural potential; marginality is further emphasised by erratic seasonal variations and long-term climate changes and other combined impacts, making accessibility, margins and peripheries in a geographic sense even harder. Peripheral regions and locations differ in many aspects of conditions for development, as in terms of resources, accessibility and market potential. On the road to:

> marginalization and abandonment of certain areas and a growing demand for 'nature' and 'rural heritage' in others.
>
> (Lorentzen, 2012b, p. 25)

Before going further, there is an interesting diversion: the idea of using politically defined districts, i.e. subsidiary definitions (Johansen et al., 2006). Peripherality is identified by borders distinguishing areas with focusing (primarily subsidiary) policies. Calculated delimitations are based on specific criteria, (returning to the starting point), and through weighing the importance of these in relation to each other or based on political expediency or a combination of both. This recognises a dynamic approach and a changing result of what at every time is the 'type' of peripheral/marginal area.

Synonyms, antonyms and categorisations

Synonyms appear primarily in three configurations in this conceptual substantiation. First, as alternate wordings for the same phenomena, second, as reflections with possible different interpretations, and third, carrying a structure of alternate language cultures. Another major element of substance is distinctions as counter-reflections of antonyms, defining their own substantive definitions by their opposite/counterpart. The nature of the relation and relativity are carried by each of their own categorisations. Categorisations appear as instruments creating substance through the concepts in the manner of their utilisation. Policy works with this all the time and if using policy (for example geographical coverage), it means accepting ladders or scales of centrality, peripherality and marginality in different appearances. Teigen (1999, p. 18) ranks seven levels where number seven is the ultimate opposite of centrality. The main variable used is distance to centres of different sizes. This accepting the concepts as variants of continuous, not only discrete phenomena. Other peripheries or categories of peripheral functions, on a scale could redefine a periphery seen from a core as semi-periphery, or seen from the outside or outer periphery as semi-core, or whatever denomination that is useful.

Complicating the issue somewhat is when the functional periphery simultaneously is defined as spatial. The concept of dependency is an example of ways and means to operationalise. Relating to the capital or major urbanities the periphery (or locality) becomes relatively dependent in general dimensions of economy, knowledge, culture and politics, while also creating an existence on the localised provision of services (Fimreite and Selle, 2006).

To exemplify the complexity, the question is whether and how the concept of core defines and determines the periphery? The logic of dichotomies is the interdependency. "Conventionally, peripherality has been understood in a spatial context, usually in the context of core-periphery models and here variable (uneven) economic development" (Herrschel, 2011, p. 93).

The periphery tends to be the opposite of the main focus of attention – so the economic/social system defines, analyses, establishes policies for the centre or core, and the periphery is 'the other',[6] the rest, the remainder. Being peripheral and marginal relate to something being core/central, according to the specification of these designations, which indicates that a comparison, through substantiating aspects of their common opposite is a meaningful process. A mentionable example being 'core cities' or 'core regions', where the antonym – 'peripheral cities, hinterland, region' is mainly undetermined.

The practical application of the concepts tends to be driven by actors/groups (read interests, roles, etc.) differently, with hidden or disclosed agendas, and subtleties and nuances in interpretation. For instance, within core or city-regions, the periphery of this entity is, more or less, irrelevant, especially when local government or administrative areas are focused as a basis for analysis. In understanding and interpreting, the relationship creates efforts to defuse some of their potential consequences. Political power in Norway is functionally centralised, but legitimised through peripheral elements of the representative system having had a presence in the political centre.[7] This devolves some of the political power, while maintaining a central control function (Fimreite and Selle, 2006).

Another approach that relates to what has been mentioned above, is a definition of periphery and marginality based on what is not there, what they are deprived of. They are defined by not having characteristics or features of a core, i.e. the absence of these, rather than the positive presence of having their own definable and defining factors. For example, periphery = lack of agglomeration = lower level of resources. Dispersed or peripheral organisations lack the advantages of knowledge spillovers, due to distance factors. An utilisation of the term robust regions, defined by large population potentials and strong centres, localisation of international production activities and facilities and connected with strong growth and development contexts, highlights this kind of approach. The opposite to the characteristics of peripherality and robust will therefore be an extended antonym.

Another dichotomy of interest is local/global. Conceptually, local is at the bottom of a hierarchy of geographical entities, slightly above or on the same level as place and subordinated the region. Being an antonym to global has placed the term/concept prominently in development theory and practice of today. The term encompass a meaning where the local is describing a geographical point with varying spatial extent, describing aspects of actors, things, processes taking place somewhere, being localised. A locality defined in relative terms. It's a dichotomy where urban may stand at the other end, also indicating its potential in aspects of rural, peripheral. Local should not only be interpreted in a geographical sense, but also as functional, as it encompasses a number of social, economic and political practices, manifesting something quite specific, only describable with reference to the unique locality or in a generalised 'locale'. The local understood as those places where we live, as individuals or groups, giving a specific meaning, a meaning returned to and on us. Being part of the formation of a community, in a continuous interaction with a surrounding society. The concept of place could be either a subcategory in this or a limited synonym. Places carry names. A similar distinction found between space and area. Local and place defined relative to other localities and places, in categories of sparsity, urbanities, megapolis, etc. Local development (in its dominating aspect) also in this perspective seen as a process of progress and/or adaptation, constructing the local. It contains a specific world of nature, social relations and meanings. A local place has much more than cultural significance.[8]

Preconditional variables, like natural resources, are unevenly distributed and with varying climatological preconditions; the built and organised infrastructure are others, just to take the most frequently used contexts. In more detail, preconditions for agricultural activities of different kinds have created historically defined patterns and processes (Hegrenes, 2004, p. 45). On the other hand as noted by Onsager and Selstad (2004, p. 298), the fact that high-tech firms are found in the periphery does prove that the impact of contextual determination in the analysis has to be qualified in much, further, operational detail. It could be of interest to define some kind of hierarchical structure of such descriptions.

Context has also dynamic properties. The nature of peripherality could and does change over time and places and areas in the periphery, but does not necessarily remain there and through specific policies (long and short term) and other exogenously given processes, can instead become centres by themselves. At the same time, other places and other areas, will be redefined to the status of defined or experienced peripherality or marginality. Meaning that, methodologically, policy-orientated analysis has to look out for relative changes in places and spaces, changes in the substance of the periphery, and therefore, a need for a longer view on methodology and measurements.

Experience

A fundamental difference, already touched upon, appears between a geography representing a material/physical representation of the periphery and an immaterial experienced dimension. Distance-defined peripheralisation (remoteness) encompasses a dimension of relativeness, meaning aspects and combinations of aspects of distance (physical, transport-time, transport cost) creating a situation where some locations are experienced as less peripheral, while others (where the train does not stop) become more. The choice of material variables creating a pattern and degrees of peripheral experience, with changes in distance, time and cost also create, formed by experienced, new peripheries, projected identities and self images. The whole concept of geography is viewed through aspects of experienced communication, participation in relevant and important networks and possible realisation of expectations and outcome (Herrschel, 2011, p. 88).[9] Generalising in two manifestations of peripherality, spatial and social-communicative, which could, but do not always, combine in different appearances, creating patterns of further complexity. Other types of experiences or 'feelings' connected with distance-defined peripherality consider the idea of 'far away' using distance but also indicating 'backwards', implicating other types of backwardness. The last point was built on by Fimreite and Selle (2006), who further refined it into aspects of cultural distance.

Continuing down the same track, a functional administrative regulation/power/control could be both far away and backwards. A discussion emerges around functional regions where relevant variables become highlighted, in terms of centre and periphery. Functional regions describe a common trait, which simplifies and enhances the analytical possibility. Within the concept of a functional region, classical entrances of centre/core and periphery/hinterland, are integrated in distance terms, distinguishing specific aspects of impact/influence. Another kind of functionality of relevance distinguishes attributes like problem and border regions indicating a deepened peripheral interpretation.

> The condition experienced by individuals, firms and regions at the edge of a communication system, where they are away from the core of controlling centre of the economy.
>
> (Goodall, 1987, p. 350)

Experience plays havoc on some fields of scientific analysis. Peripheral or rural comes in many differentiated and fragmented versions. Actors and participants, functioning within any statistical category of rural, peripheral, non-urban etc., are not always aware or noting their categorisation. The spaces, experienced and categorised, do not coincide with these actors' experience, defined by different combinations of cultural constructs and creating and formed by an elastic dynamic lifeform, "the question of whether people are 'truly rural' in their lived worlds and whether there is an 'essence' in the emerging place of a village" (Johnston, 2000, p. 718) . . . and last, but not least, the rural experience also appears as a potential commodity. This brings us to a range of those seeking a 'rural experience' or reaching out for a specified quality of life. The question is if there could be found a continuous scale of QOL, where ingredients of absolute urban and rural are simultaneously considered.

Rural and rurality

The substance of 'rural' stands, to a large degree, for empirically definable structures and processes. General and popular utilisation of the concept refers to a category of settlements or for special types of landscapes. These general references are and cannot be useful for any formal and exact delimitation of rural areas "not imbued with power to explain geographical differences in socio-economic conditions" (Hoggart, 1988, p. 35). To answer the question of what constitutes the rural, the non-urban or the countryside is that a final definition is hard to come by. Evidently, they encompass quite numerous variations of formal appearances,[10] translated by way of far-reaching, subjectively constructed understandings (Anderson, 2000). Important, even crucial aspects lead us further into the functional and experiential approaches. Definition and further conceptualisation of the rural take place at different geographical scales, changing the profile depending on levels chosen, in turn, of relevance for attitudes, behaviours, practices and decisions, where rural behaviour compares with urban distinctions. Further alternatives are found in Haugen and Lysgård (2006).

Extensive land uses, where functional characteristics described in economic terms, are associated with agriculture, forestry and other natural resources, and finally ecological aspects, in terms of the natural environment (Fuduric, 2012, p. 166) that includes the presence of large areas of undeveloped and unexploited land where settlements are small and architecture is adapted (experienced as rural). Altogether this kind of land-use promotes a special identity, a type where "respect for nature and environment are defining characteristics" (Johnston, 2000, p. 718). This description, fascinating in its richness, defines types of activities, development levels and organisation of settlement patterns in interaction with landscape and aspects of experience, ranging the totality to questions of identity; it has

> ingredients as harmony, consensus, healthiness, simplicity, peace, safety, tradition, community, domesticity, aesthetic quality (nice landscapes), and pastoralism in common.
>
> (Berg and Forsberg, 2003, p. 176)

An alternate approach is found in the more systematic counter-positioning from the urban. Positive qualities of tradition, authenticity and serenity stand out in importance, linked with nature and landscape. They are especially brought forward in social/settlement categories like holiday destinations or suburban/rural living. Distance to or from the centre is a low-order variable (Eriksson, 2008).

The definition of rural is, however, not limited in a static, traditional construct. Rural as in change, in progress highlighted, in more general terms of social theory, aspects of production, consumption and changes in patterns of interaction. What once was a natural resource base for urban development is today a continuous function, complemented by the utilisation, exploitation of the rural in alternative types of consumption. This means that human aspects, the process and progress of humanity and culture follow in the footsteps of this progression, as does the images of what constitutes the rural. Diversity of the rural becomes more and more prominent. Finally linking rural with marginal Dahlgren (1989) contributes some qualifications, emphasising a tendency to use 'rural' instead of 'marginal' due to an implied negative connotation by the latter. He also refers to a practice where rural is used for agricultural policies and marginal for regional.

> In terms of uniqueness, for analytical purposes this is a devastating blow: ". . . if you have seen one rural place, you have seen one rural place."
>
> (OECD, 2006a, p. 37)

Connecting with the preceding discussion, one of the most frequently appearing dichotomous distinctions in the present area, is that of the urban and the rural.[11] "'[R]ural' and 'urban' as two poles of a dichotomy was soon found to be unrepresentative of the real world situation" (Cloke, 1977, p. 31). Arguments around the latter are still in the crossfire: "all too frequently, writers have implied that the urban and the rural are essentially discrete and separate entities" (Potter et al., 2008, p. 405). In terms of the complexity of patterns, variables and interactions, the possibility of an absolute dichotomy, as such, seems disqualified. A real-life continuum simplified via thresholds and boundaries takes it far enough.

A number of different representations, reinforce the two as defining poles, but include a continuum, reaching from the utmost urban parts of the city or megapolis to the most rural parts of the countryside (Almaas and Elden, 1997, p. 8). The continuum is quite simplistic in other distinctions.

The theme of urban-rural is continuously present in the history of mankind. It appears as a fundamental form of societal presentation and representation and in many societal profiles. It is evident that constructs of rural and urban are intimately interlinked and define each other. They remain strong and distinct attributes, perceived as separate modes of spatiality. They are also used as pawns in the game of identity building and definitions of the 'other':

> inhabitants of areas where town and country seem nearly indistinguishable may nevertheless elaborate a difference through extensive cultural discourse.
> (Creed and Ching, 1997, pp. 2–3)

Social, cultural, economic and other changes in the city and countryside seem to eliminate, or at least weaken, some of the former categorical differences (Hoggart, 1988), "increasing functional integration in the era of cognitive-cultural capitalism" (Scott, 2013, p. 41). A social and cultural process takes place where elements from the stereotyped entities of the bipolar converges – a process of 'rurbanisation'. "Local nationalisation and local heterogenization are two other concepts that are being used for this development" (Strøksnes, 2006, p. 102, my translation). The first one covers the process of a reducing or disappearing difference, the second emphasises national coherence and local differentiation. It includes phenomenon like 'rurbanity', or commuting between rural residential areas and urban workplaces or 'urban farming' (that is, in daily life). Processes within the information society "lead to obliteration of the dichotomy between urban and rural areas" (Smetkowski et al., 2011, p. 19), although the nature of the impact, or the extent of it, has to be qualified. Opening the door to another conceptually relevant dimension carries differences, the distinctions towards other dichotomies like core/periphery, centre/periphery are clearly not identical with urban/rural. An important example emphasised already is the role of small and medium-sized towns with possibly more limited extent of centre functions, integrated into the concept of 'rural'.

Debates and controversies have led to a major refocusing of the research orientation from "processes that construct and reproduce geographies of difference within western nations" to a research and debate much more focused on the intricate complexities of what constitutes rural identity – or, should one say, ruralities:

> rural and urban identities . . . (urban and rural) masculinity, intersectionality, and research on 'invisible' rural populations . . . gradually concern 'rural otherness' – divisions and difference in the countryside. . . . Similarly, the focus has shifted from studying singular identities to research on the intersection of multiple identities, such as class, gender, race, sexuality and so forth.
> (Eriksson, 2010, p. 96)

This discussion of the urban will be taken further in Chapter 5, where a deconstruction highlights the necessity, also, at least partly, of disqualifying the simplified continuum approach, as much of the descriptions of the rural are defined in terms of negative reflections of the urban. The following statement is still relevant:

> Given the pervasiveness of the rural/urban opposition and its related significance in the construction of identity, it is remarkable that the explosion of scholarly interest in identity politics has generally failed to address the rural/urban axis.
>
> (Creed and Ching, 1997, p. 3)

Traditionally rural has been conceptually defined in terms of its economic profiles, and historically defined in terms of more detailed preconditions for agricultural activities, creating quite clearly defined cultural patterns and processes (Hegrenes, 2004, p. 45). This refers both to delimitations of where human activity has been at all possible, but also in different directions and levels of agricultural activity. Agriculture and forestry represents a lot of explanatory power in describing the traditional. In many countries, the idea of rural was and still is connected with agriculture and with the production systems: "agriculture is a central mechanism for delivering sustainable rural development" (Marsden, Banks and Bristow, 2002, p. 809). Things change and the economic profile of the traditional rural is complex in new and alternative ways. High-quality production, nature conservation and landscape management, agro-tourism, part-time farming, short food-supply chains, cooperative management are relevant new concepts with a lot of substantiating changes to the original concept. Modern rural spaces today are heterogeneous and differentiated. "Farm businesses are now increasingly located in highly complex sets of institutional, market, and regulatory relationships" (Marsden et al., 2002, p. 812).

The overarching idea of agriculture dominates the description of rural and peripherality when, in fact, traditional agriculture is a declining activity in most peripheries in Europe and is analytically problematic in taken-for-granted trajectories into the future. The economic patterns and processes that are linked to the 'rural' are so much more, so much different, that even terms like 'agriculture' have changed in substance. Going outside of the traditional, the main characteristic of the rural is its definition of being more orientated to consumption than production (Berg and Lysgård, 2004, p. 61). However, it notably does not take place everywhere. Policies and mindsets establish limits, at least in short-term perspectives.

In order not to repeat what already been said, an example is found in the 1960s' and 1970s' migratory patterns, described as the Green Wave. Something similar is found today but carries different ambitions and culture, based on new contextual preconditions. Migrants living a dream of rural bliss hold on to conservative values, their traditional ways and recreation of past times, compared to the hippie culture, longing for clean air, clean food and ideas of a simpler life.

> As in-migrant middle classes have exerted greater influence, so studies of the interrelations between new class fractions and rural communities have become increasingly important.
>
> (Johnston, 2000, p. 718)

Rurality enters with and into soft, qualitative aspects. The rural experienced, is interpreted, in perspectives of mental images, social and cultural constructs. What kind of myths or preconceptions that characterise the rural. Encompassing the range, all the way from what the word inspires, to how it is locally communicated and defined as correct/legitimate.

> that rural people, whether long-term residents or in-migrants, will have strong cultural and geographical imaginations of what rural life should be like, and that these imaginations will be associated with particular practices of social relations.
>
> (Cloke, Goodwin, & Milbourne, 1998, p. 134)

To understand rurality is, partly, to take a step away from the economic-geographical interpretation – the way the rural is experienced by those who find themselves actively engaged in interpreting it into their lives (Berg and Forsberg, 2003, p. 175), something that will eventually be returned to. Rurality as a cultural category is also, in one part, mentally and unconsciously associated/interpreted with rusticity, in the urban-defined sense of being backward and outdated or in a rural sense of belonging or being someone from somewhere. To live in the countryside is the base for the experience. Through this path one can also find positive and negative connotations where the rural and rurality are linked to concepts like security, safety, commonness and identity (Forsberg et al., 2006, p. 52). Migrating is then founded on much more than rational, logical decisions. Instead, it is planted with the seeds of growing up, of identifying cultural values not always linked to rural in general or rurality as a sentiment, but as on a specific place within the rural, representing an individual reflection of the nature of rurality.

The multidimensionality in the concept reflects diversity and variety. This is reflected in many ways, not in the least in the large variation of social relations and a wide scope of cultural variety. It is also reflected in the use of plural – "ruralities/countrysides" (Berg and Forsberg, 2003, p. 174). Today, as has been mentioned, diversity is considerable. It is defined in space as is done by Johnston (2000, p. 718):

> from those which may still be defined functionally (by land use and geographical location) to those closer to urban centers where 'rural' is more of a socially and culturally constructed and therefore contested category.

Rurality here touches upon a return to the rural as a social construct. It is notable that rurality and urbanity are determining each other in this process (Berg and Lysgård, 2004) in

> a series of socio-cultural constructs, with 'rural' thus being increasingly interpreted as a world of social, moral and cultural values in which both rural dwellers and others participate.
>
> (Johnston, 2000, p. 720)

Age is among those background variables that define expected or probable values. Changes in the rural primarily characterised and induced by exogenous forces. Today the power of tradition, heritage, etc., is partly being replaced by education, easier travel, etc., leading to a higher number of alternative individualised trajectories. A future as a farmer is not as self-evident as it once was and constitutes "[a] weakening of the identity as a farmer, and the ties between the farm and the person" (Forsberg et al., 2006, p. 35). The importance of gender distinctions in the socially constructed rurality, both in the image of the rural and how the rurality is expected to appear, is highly recommended but seldom analytically executed. This includes a reorientation from generalisations of categories of urban/rural and women/men "to focusing on diversity and variety. This is reflected in the use of plural – ruralities/countrysides, masculinities and femininities" (Berg and Forsberg, 2003, p. 174). For instance, identifying gender-based patterns in social networks is larger/extended for women (Forsberg et al., 2006). To be a farmer he (and she) is to be several things and variations in the nature and substance of the living-style. Combinations of occupations and roles are tried, discarded or changed (Forsberg et al., 2006, p. 39).

Inspired by this diversity and many interpretations of the rural, policy development demands – and the academic community happily complies and loves to promote – different typologies to simplify or to legitimate their own activities. This fails, however, to reach a general acceptance from their communities or in the field of study. This is part of the inspiration also behind the present approach.

Somewhat concluding

It is time to consider some of the conceptually interactive implications. A process that has, actually, taken place continuously in this chapter. Practice in literature seems, when discussed quite superficially, to be an identity between the words/concepts, pairing them off, or making one a part of the other. This includes examples where peripheral and marginal could be major characteristics of certain geographical or functional dimensions of the rural area/countryside. This increasing in complexity as the dichotomies carry the burden of other qualifications and ingredients of the qualitative continuum.

The basic question, raised earlier, is when rural turns to peripheral or marginal and the rural dimension of periphery or the peripheral dimension of the rural. This requires looking for the most important variables, structures etc., where differences are indicated, but also, consideration of the idea that these differences bring meaning. Rural brings functional meaning to peripheral or marginal depending upon which part of the substantiated rural we bring into the equation. Or turning the argument around, the "periphery is defined by rural, non-urbanized areas with a certain geographical distance from the center" (Fimreite and Selle, 2006, p. 10).

Periphery and margin are more about distance and relations, geography and function. Rural is more about structures; countryside is more about landscape and culture. Rurality is found within the soft dimensions of culture. Still, changes in distance have an impact on aspects of the peripheral and change structures in the medium- to long-term, and also on aspects of culture.

Entering the door of experience brings the actor her or his role and a special dimension of relative positions defined by interests (individual, organisational, collective). Sitting in the centre makes the periphery less important, i.e. contributing to the process of peripheralisation, in itself. Sitting in the periphery makes its status a question of perspectives, and through this prism, we see all other actors in the same kind of processual analysis. It is possible to exemplify *in extenso.*

Notes

1 A term appearing frequently in the literature is 'remote'. It is the present author's opinion that this term in all necessary aspects is identical with the term 'peripheral'. It will therefore not be analysed on its own.
2 A *term* is a word or phrase used to describe a thing or to express a concept, especially in a particular kind of language or branch of study. A *concept* is an abstract idea representing the fundamental characteristics of what it represents.
3 More systematic approaches relating to the concept of 'sparsity' will be found in Chapter 6.
4 An aspect covered more extensively in Chapter 4 on methodological considerations.
5 Returning to the notion of marginal as a more functional concept.
6 There is an intellectual history in geography and sociology of discussing 'the other', drawn upon to examine the interactions between place, people and status/power.
7 The status today is unknown.
8 'Local' and 'place' will appear as quite prominent in the upcoming pages with discussions and interpretations of EU-defined policies described in terms of 'place-based' and 'smart'.
9 The author brings forward the notion of peripherality appearing in the core, or in between closely located cores.
10 Using attributive distinctions, within the vicinity of earlier concept we could find 'remote' (commented upon earlier) and 'accessible' rural.
11 Further developed discussions on the 'urban' are found in Chapter 5.

3 Theory

Limits and potentials

The basic objective in this chapter is to gain insight into the status of established theory, relative to the terms/concepts of periphery,[1] rural, etc., as objects and processes. The approach is twofold, first whether we can be satisfied with the way theory is used in the analytical approach. This chapter starts out with identifying the relevant basic theories and if they are sufficient for their task and suitable for the problem area approached. Second, whether some aspects of modern theoretical endeavours could improve our understanding of the periphery. The position of the bridge from theory to practice on the theoretical side over to the technicalities provided by general methodological considerations should provide a platform.

This chapter begins with a hesitant, although challenging, 'no' to some questions and a 'do we know?' to others. Many theories take the urban/centre dimension/priority as a given. Others do not cover the whole problem area and are not used in an extent to be expected. What is described here is a still unsubstantiated fact, that what happens in the periphery is neither examined or explored with the same emphasis as urban, high-tech structures and processes. Some essential parts of the case for 'economic' reality are missing, which makes the overall picture severely handicapped, even, in some cases, false. This makes the discussion of the designated areas less assertive, compared with dominating approaches. What ought to be the case is a much broader and more penetrative inter- and intra-communicating holistic approach within and from the whole arsenal of theoretical contributions. There remains a general concern for limits, in shedding "light on the different social phenomena and structures that explain regional development and policy" (Moulaert and Mehmood, 2010, p. 104).

Development manifests change over time, encompassing a number of dynamic social processes interacting directly or indirectly with economic ones, resulting in and with non-economic consequences (Gibson-Graham, 2011). For example, Tomaney et al. (2010) widen the argumentative scope, pointing at the issue of unequal growth fostering unequal health through disparate living conditions, in turn impairing the overall growth and therefore development potential. They turn from a general focus on economic growth as such to a more widely encompassing dimension of reducing levels of inequality and prioritising lagging, peripheral, marginal areas and, through this achieving strategic and sustainable objectives of development, including the potential for economic growth.

Socio-economic processes taking place in societies are not fully explained by the dominating economic paradigm. Encompassing aspects of large fundamental changes are generated by globalisation, individualisation, self-reflection, fragmentation, mobility and uncertainty (Mangset and Røyseng, 2009). They refer to Ulrich Beck (1992) who spoke of risks to society including "the spread of temporary and insecure employment, discontinuity and loose informality". Also "flexibility, part-time jobs, job combinations, short-termism and risk" (Mangset and Røyseng, 2009, p. 13) seem pertinent.

Some relevant classical theory

The route travelled identifies classical theoretical contributions, sorting them into growth and structural categories. Be aware, however, of how interlocked they are and the way they contribute to each other. Growth mechanisms – traditionally explained by a focus on the accumulation of factors of production and relevant technological progress and a relation between these – are supported by descriptions of efficient redistributive functions, such as financial and labour markets. Classical economic and economic-geographical theoretical constructs and examples of their modern adaptation focus on urbanisation, cities and economic growth rather than on general, geographic and functional, qualitatively oriented development processes.

This general and partly negative starting point seems seldom reflected upon in the form of a coherent and conscientious effort. Results in this direction and sphere are primarily indirect, residual and sometimes only fortunate analytical coincidences. There still remains a fast track to understanding aspects of the peripheral entrance in and of these approaches.

Industrialisation includes, in its different stages and appearances, *verlag* capitalism, industrial capitalism and centrally planned economies (read state intervention or administrative variants). Mobilisation of raw materials, energy and labour creates and continuously defines and redefines peripheries and marginalisation by the results of ongoing concentration, centralisation and, therefore, urbanisation processes.[2] All this takes place with a preconditional background based on an agricultural surplus and agriculture with impetus to technological development. Agriculture continues to fill this role through food production, etc., enabling urbanisation. Development and growth mechanisms have, in a long tradition, been connected or explained primarily by the accumulation of the factors of production mentioned above. The relation between these is supported by descriptions of an improved transport infrastructure. On this very simplified level, it is still pertinent to question the basic preconditions. The simplicity of the ongoing processes are not analytically questioned although complexity seems limited, while explanations do not really consider "different conditions of growth that apply to specific economies at varying stages of economic development" (Mitra, 2012, p. 4).[3] Just to exemplify: this includes age composition of population, availability of natural resources and regional topography, factor markets and densities in terms of economic actors. Classical growth strategies and factors extend the basic analysis – enter markets, import substitution, export incentives, and also identify the entrepreneur and entrepreneurship.

We can find in the Growth Pole Theory, based on revisited classical work, an important addition to identifying factors and processes contributing to the theoretical framework by François Perroux (1949) and his *pôle de croissance*. It connects us with the issue of conditional economic agglomerations and their interaction/contribution to societal development at large. Specific types of growth centres (large and dense, i.e. urban) promote unevenness in economic relations (Moulaert and Mehmood, 2010). The special dimension of government intervention relates to the urban advantage with a pertinent theoretical consequence. Starting out with the concept of 'propellant industries', where one or more major enterprise stimulates relying 'impelled industries', which, in turn, can be identified as a regional growth effect. The overarching culture of the 'growth pole theory' is defined as an influence from a centre towards its hinterland/surroundings, based primarily on the idea of centrifugal and centripetal forces in society. Relations between different centres (poles) include, in their most simplified version, gravitation, where the strongest entity formed the largest hinterland, with competitive impact from what was on offer in the nearest alternative poles. The Perrouxian platform develops into different types of discussions, among which 'trickling down' and 'cumulative causation' mechanisms appear as prominent. Alonso (1964) and Myrdal (1957) and on a more general scale Wallerstein (1976) – World System Theory – and Massey's discussion on the spatial divisions of labour (1984) make substantial contributions.

Although with roots in Alfred Marshall's book on *Principles of Economics* (1920), agglomerations as a theoretical platform return to policy with strength, focusing on resources in locations characterised by high density and diversity. Assumptions of market forces, being conducive for and through agglomerations, and through this, economic growth, included in New Economic Geography (NEG) models bringing us forward to the present phase. Agglomerations have generally remained within static presentations and homogeneous populations and forwarded as a theoretical concept, without much concern for actual processes and functionings.

> However, current research explains little about how exactly these come to play, or about the critical thresholds of different elements making the concept difficult to operationalize.
>
> (European Union, 2011a, p. 4)

Neither does it dwell on the intricacies of dynamism, composition, the economic contextual preconditions and the force of their eventual contributions (Kogler, 2015). Although, possible contributive mechanisms are mentioned, as for example different types of 'external economies of scale' effects, exemplified by interconnections between suppliers and purchasers of intermediate inputs and outputs, labour pools, and the transfer of information (Copus, 2001). Economies of agglomeration enumerate advantages bringing in cost reductions in generalised terms (Fontes, Sousa and Videira, 2009).

Taken-for-granted implications are substantial. A policy trying to even out regional differences assumes to threaten national economic growth. Ambitions to support sparsely populated areas will in this conclusion, end up in a category of threats to that growth. However, "the view that big cities are the most productive places may seem much too simplistic" (OECD, 2011a, p. 196). Other arguments reflect on this tangle of causalities, noting that the substance of agglomerative development is a product, where delimitations and definitions of agglomerations includes analytical biases in different stages of the development process (Gruber and Soci, 2010). The argument is highlighted in an OECD analysis where the following figures: "the sample of 78 OECD metro regions, only 45% grew faster than their respective national averages over the past decade" (2009a, p. 3), questions the generalisations.

Regionally defined applications, in terms of trickle-down and back-wash both with a combined ideological and theoretical basis, include a controversy in terms of advantages and disadvantages. Albert Hirschman distinguished between positive trickling-down effects and negative polarisation effects. The idea of the trickle-down means that production factors should be exploited where they supposedly do most good for the economy in general (Hirschman, 1958). In Myrdal's and Hirschmann's arguments, regional disparities, defined in terms of agglomerations, were focused on the essence of cumulatively draining some regions (read sparsely populated, peripheral ones), of capital and labour, in favour of expanding growth regions. A positive economic process emanates, according to Myrdal, from one or a few economic initiatives (sometimes random), and that these, by the logic of their own development and dominance over other centres/regions, start a spiral effect to their own advantage. Other entities reproduce patterns on lower levels. Absence of value-adding front-line elements drains attractive opportunities indicating and accelerating this downward spiral "creating decline in the rural economic and social fabric" (Anderson, 2000, p. 94). Cultural and political processes contribute and lead to an increased inequality between regions and places, only to be solved by political means (Moulaert and Mehmood, 2010, p. 109). An ideological profile, including state interventionism, where ultimate effects would hypothetically reduce disparities, are also discussed.

Another theoretical platform, within the family of growth-related approaches, emanates from The German Historical School, mentioned as a starting point for the 'stage theory of economic development', later popularised (with no known connection) by Rostow in his book *Stages of Economic Growth – A Non-Communist Manifesto* (1960). This approach identifies what is supposed to be necessary thresholds in order to commence a sustainable growth. The presumed ideological dimension has to do with the experiences emanating from the ideological orientation of the state-planned development in the Soviet Union, originating in the founding GOELRO-plan (de Souza, 1989).[4]

Discussing economic growth and development with classical and neoclassical perspectives is clearly manifest in the following contribution:

> Growing cities, ever more mobile people, and increasingly specialized products are integral to development . . . such transformations will remain essential for economic success in other parts of the developing world and should be encouraged.
>
> (World Bank, 2009, p. xix)

There are doubts thrown at these basically neo-liberal fragments. There are dangers of biased, too-simplified presentations, where complex interaction is replaced by government in action (ideologically based), simplification, return to the urban bias, or uninformed intervention. This results in long-term implications: "and will continue to shape the prospects for local and regional development" (Tomaney et al., 2010, pp. 618–619). They do fit into an economic-geographic tradition. The 'economic-base theory' (Hoyt, 1954) refers to the status of the internal 'local' economy and base trade/economic interaction, with the geographical environment defined, as well as the interconnections between these (Smetkowski et al., 2011). The main principles in traditional economic-base theories imply that the incomes to the local 'manufacturers' and communities are generated and based upon the external market. Other sources of contribution and income are produced by complementary, supporting local business services, as necessary preconditions and consequences. Although not explicit, local, in policy, implies centres, core, urban. Identifying factors of economic growth and which sectors and locations of society that are most important for it recognises innovation, high technology – meaning R&D – and ultimately indicates where further financial resources should be allocated (Wicken, 2008).

Sectors most often mentioned are ICT, biotechnology and nanotechnology, although hard empirical evidence for their degree of importance and contributions seems scarce. A traditional updated historical simplification roaming in the background is the notion of the 'curse of resource economies', the idea being one of adaptation and need to restructure such an economy for modern conditions, or otherwise remain poor. Wicken (2008, p. 26) emphatically concludes that there is no relation between raw material resources and weak development tendencies necessary for long-term economic growth. The well-argued importance of the role of low technology sectors in the world economy is a similar case in point, standing up for a major share of world production and labour markets (Potter et al., 2008).

Development perspectives in the projection of innovation are a crucial theme in modern discussions, where innovation, in a broad sense, is described as important for all types of regions (Tödtling and Trippl, 2005, p. 1204). Even some specific aspects of innovative development are hesitantly defined as possibly better suited for rural/peripheral areas. Aspects like incremental innovations are workable in characteristics of institutional thinness and local networks with lack of investors, SMB-dominance, etc. "[T]he unique feature of innovation practices in rural areas" (Fløysand and Jakobsen, 2010, p. 108) is mostly ignored or methodologically lost. This will be returned to later.

Entering through the huge portal of development economics, an important distinction identifies dimensions of exploitation based on structures and processes of colonialism, imperialism, 'civilisation', i.e. unequal patterns of economic exchange, notably defined and creating a specific category of the peripherality and peripheralisation through exploitation. The description of this explicit 'exploitative' period resulting in a transformation (i.e. peripheral to the centre of civilisation in European terms), recreating its peripheral status into the popularised category of the 'third world'.

Theories of localisation, structures and spatial interaction

From what creates growth, the distance is not so far to structural patterns defining preconditions and outcomes. Johann Heinrich von Thünen devoted a lifetime defining the economic rationale for land-intensive activities in agriculture, where distance to the market varied, in specific relations to land utilisation for various productions and products, matching this with transport costs in absolute and relative terms. In his main work *Der isolierte Staat: in Beziehung auf Landwirtschaft und Nationalökonomie (The Insulated State in Terms of Agriculture and Economics)* (1966), he examined and answered the question about the economical land-use system. He created a theory of land rent consistent with David Ricardo (2001) but put more emphasis on the relative location of the land. Von Thünen's theory was primarily about areas suitable for various branches of the farming economy, different farming systems and different methods of operation. Around the city in the hypothetical isolated state, he defined a number of concentric circles, within which different branches were situated based on the rule. The model generated four concentric rings of agricultural activity. Dairying and intensive farming first, timber and firewood, then extensive field crops such as grain. Ranching was located in the final, outer, ring. The analytical consequences have much wider implications. In the 1960 to 1970s, the bid-rent principle was developed and applied to both rural and urban land-use, and for agriculture and industry (Copus, 2001). This theoretical approach, although extremely simplified and general, has the 'urban' or, more poignant, 'market' as its main precondition.

In 1909, Alfred Weber (1971) presented a localisation theory for industrial activity in order to explain patterns of industrial location. It was a deductive construct based on the premise of economic rationality. In it he assumed that industry was looking for a location where the total production cost was as low as possible (least-cost theory), primarily focusing on transports for raw materials, energy and manufactured goods that were ultimately important for financial performance. Given which of these transport costs were the greatest, the industry became raw-material, energy- or market-oriented in its location. Weber's original place or location theory was later developed, including the impact of and on labour markets, impact on the product market, and the development of more complex presentations with behavioural aspects. The urban was not taken for granted, but implicit through aspects of consumption, ubiquitous resources and where complementary input factors with high weight impact were found in or near the market/urban centre.

Walter Christaller contributed with a theory around the appearance of hierarchies of service nodes/points/centres. He considered the provision of services related to a user-defined hinterland (1933). The Central Place Theory, founded the idea of system of centres/cities. In modern terms, the thresholds are positive and negative, but in sum create patterns of relations. Interestingly the market is defined by centres, but the consumer is supposed to be mobile, which still makes distance, time and cost important variables. The point being that the mobility of the service user defines the patterns of the system. As a framework for interpretation it is still noted as valid, and Jonsson (2013) suggests a renaissance, in terms of modern approaches of polycentrism. An important theoretical dimension is its logical link with the concept of the 'functional region', where variables defining specific functionalities are relevant in discussing centre and periphery. A functional region, linked to a chosen variable describing a common trait, enhances a conditional quality. The classical entrances of centre/core and periphery/hinterland where the relation of a centre through a specific distance-related attribute make a forceful contribution. This distinguishes the impact where a number of characteristics change nature, based on quantity and quality within absolute and relative distances, substantiating and through this strengthening the argument for an 'alternative logic' in itself.

A somewhat similar approach identified central places in the economic landscape. August Lösch recognised (1940) relations between the number of urban centres and occurrence of sectors. His is a localisation theory where enterprises aim for maximum profits, consider product price and costs, and in this way find places with similar results but different cost-inducing processes. Lösch also noted that it was not necessary to search for locations that resulted in 'maximum' profits as long as profits were achieved. Some of these ideas are found in variants, focusing on the way economic structures are identified as the earlier-mentioned economic base, and then further interpreted and translated into urban/rural. The types of functions and transactions include administrative, culture, health care, trade and finance. Economic functions serving the rural register the labour market, transportation or telecommunication services. The urban is the nucleus, the node.

These classical entrances to modern economic geography was already discussed, as noted, by Alfred Marshall, but then with an orientation towards agglomeration perspectives. Marshall explained, indirectly, that urbanisation, through a concentration of economic activities, creates a kind of snowball effect, where new players are taking advantage of greater diversification and specialisation of production. Co-location of actors with similar profiles in output provides accumulating opportunities. Locational advantages are the benefits that companies get through collective elements of the production system locating in the same area. The optimal location is found where the production entity refines or assembles inputs on a least-cost basis, including economies of scale; this is not achieved if the entities are located far from each other, i.e. "sparsely populated areas tend to be sup-optimal in this respect" (Gløersen et al., 2006, p. 24). However, this source also notes that the impact of transport costs have, through the years, decreased, and the impact on the periphery should, therefore, be substantially less. The causality could, however, become a Darwinian selection of businesses "less sensitive to transport costs in peripheral or sparsely populated areas" (Gløersen et al., 2006, p. 24). Marshall extends the economic analysis to social and geographical interaction, abandoning "the pure logic of economic mechanisms and introduces a sociological approach in his analysis" (Asheim, 2007, p. 73). Asheim also forwards the notion that Marshall's approach includes penetrating aspects of interaction, in terms of 'mutual knowledge and trust' and the industrial atmosphere – linked to the much-quoted sentence that "there is something in the air" (Asheim, 2007, p. 73). Also Marshall included informal 'tacit' knowledge and perspectives linked to the workplace and the locally 'profiled' labour markets.

Providing external competitive advantages for the individual company and internal benefits for the group in general or the district, created in this way an alternative to the benefits that are expected within a much larger company. The dynamic implies sector-defined concentrations that promote creativity, learning and knowledge transfer (knowledge spillovers) and through this a greater innovative capacity. The mechanisms underlying the interaction on learning and innovation are, however, far from clear (Crowley, 2011). There is, for instance, an ongoing debate whether specialised or diversified agglomerations are most conducive for innovation. This discussion will be returned to when approaching some of the more up-to-date models and variants, like clusters and innovation systems. The necessity for agglomerations being present does not explain the presence of innovation elsewhere (Tomaney et al., 2010, p. 625).

Localisation theory implies alternate patterns and processes for economically peripheral regions. But, is it possible to generalise? The patterns are different; does this lead to different behaviour? The characteristics are precisely that the peripheral region's nodes are not properly connected, the supporting structures are not strong or full-bodied, but weak and undeveloped. In modern aspects, the concept of geographical proximity (further developed under a separate heading) has appeared and placed its mark on theoretical development. The basic proposition is that most types of innovative and entrepreneurial practices appear as parts of networks, systems and in social terms, collective processes. Co-location creates advantages for this (Fontes et al., 2009). These positive concepts register externalities through aspects of geographically concentrated demand based on available or potential services and products (private or public). A labour market with access to specialists, flexible mobilisation and demobilisation of skilled labour, is often used as an example. Social institutions contribute to the dissemination of knowledge and shared commitments. The key elements in these modern interpretations of districts/agglomerations are the presence of structural phenomena like social capital, trust, complementarities, functional and relational proximity, networks and knowledge spillovers (Jonsson, 2013). Social and institutional patterns and processes encompass collaboration, specialisation and intangible assets

(Birch, 2005).[5] Short transport links lead to lower transaction costs. The realms of savings are achieved through collective functions of scale both internally (for the entity), and for the agglomeration as a whole. Aspects of the agglomerative idea also attract more participants.

Agglomerative practices and their relative importance change through time and in constitutive elements. Arriving at their later manifestations, spatial entities experience substantial structural changes in efforts of economic renewal and reorientation (Parr, Hewings, Sohn and Nazara, 2002). The focus on agglomeration opens the door to a collection of concepts, which together form a:

> foundation for several strands of research and a very large combined literature, including the Italian 'industrial districts' school, 'milieu innovateur', clusters, local/regional innovation systems, and 'learning regions'
>
> (Gløersen et al., 2006, p. 26)

There is still a way to go before analytical clarity is achieved and thereby potential operationalisation. Discussions on agglomerations explain some of the growth potential but not all; Walter Isard showed that this potential is specific for different branches, developed conceptually into 'regional science', with location and spatial economic analysis as generalised methodology (1956). At Massachusetts Institute of Technology the name 'regional science' was instituted and solidified for the new research field.

Before concluding this general framework, there is also a specific dimension, when analytically identifying the agglomerative forces as urban. Arguing for the urban advantages, Cheshire and Magrini say,

> As was noted above, cities generate the basis for the division of labour and there is increasing evidence of both a theoretical and an empirical nature as to the importance of agglomeration economies in cities.
>
> (Cheshire and Magrini, 2008, p. 3)

Urban areas, by definition, concentrating people and firms, and sometimes resources can, by nature of a mathematical logic, potentially generate more matchmaking per areal unit than less dense entities. This is until density ceilings are reached, accepted or passed, introducing congestion (Delfmann, Koster, McCann and van Dijk, 2014). The authors also note that definitions of agglomeration and urban manifestations vary greatly across countries and do not usefully translate into others.

Among classic models of urban spatiality, we have Ullman's triad and a group of gravity potential models (1956). Complementarity, intervening opportunity and transferability determine the quality of the ties. With these as building blocks and analytical steppingstones to the complexity of agglomeration, its theoretical underpinnings and outcrops reappear. But, also appearing are its opposites of deglomeration and disglomeration. Still, words of caution: research is and remains totally focused on agglomeration and not the latter two.

Most evidence suggests that regional concentration (read specialisation) will produce growth on a national level, i.e. when the main advantages of agglomeration are, in some form or other, realised and not out-classed by congestion costs. A theoretical starting point in density (population or labour market) is taken for granted in its beneficial properties. "Indeed population or employment density have been used in the literature as variables to proxy for potential agglomeration economies" (Cheshire and Magrini, 2008, pp. 14–15). Complementing theories and policy prescriptions of the last quarter century have continuously stressed agglomeration and geographical clustering, necessarily complemented by overall concentration and, recently, also in terms of proximity. This returns to the repeated qualification that the prerequisites for growth among all regions stand opposite to the generalised growth objective, not accepting propositions that networking and clustering, like in urbanisation, are actually draining a functional countryside of its potentials (Danson, 2009).

As the economic and societal benefits are cited to be generated or extracted from agglomerations, the fact is that they are, at least, not limitless, and can, as noted above, be replaced by internal negative processes. The nature of those ought to be of much more interest: "Once agglomeration economies are controlled for with city size, cities with higher density will have higher costs of space and greater congestion" (Cheshire and Magrini, 2008, pp. 14–15). Deglomeration effects, appearing in a number of different forms, result in increased costs (salaries, transportation, supplies, rents, land values and congestion). Contributions to overall economic growth do not provide further positive total or per capita effects at certain levels. Fascinatingly, market participants recognise this and, if it hurts enough, relocate, but seemingly not the urban politicians and not theorists, at least not to the same extent.

Aspects of spatial policy are promoted as a partial solution, directed at offsetting some of the pertinent costs. However, political authorities "shy away from policies which could certainly reduce the costs of city size and so allow us to benefit more from agglomeration economies. The most obvious policy is to introduce congestion pricing" (OECD, 2011a, p. 192).

In the traditions emanating from von Thünen, Isard and later Alonso, theorisation on land-use and industrial location, in the framework of urban patterns (city structure), saw its roots with Anthony Burgess, already in his empirical description of Chicago. Relevant themes are the functional presence of different types of public goods, like public transportation, police and fire departments, water and sewage handling, complemented by a developed framework also of private services. Continued discussion also includes Jane Jacobs, interested in communities, urban decay and planning. She is best known for *The Death and Life of Great American Cities* (1961), a powerful critique of the urban renewal policies of the 1950s, enlarging on qualitative aspects of the urban structure with modern theoretical propositions, especially in social interaction as a necessary path for a future research agenda. The stand against the urban renewal policies of the 1950s was based on defining cities as engines of growth and in turn, market-driven land-use as optimal for city social culture, advocating the abolition of zoning laws, resulting in dense, mixed-use neighbourhoods. Her contribution has been quite influential, but still debated.

People in large cities have noticeably less 'close friends'. The theory here is that increased mobility reduces the 'bonding' being replaced by the exploitation of the moment as found in Morrison (2011, p. 1053). There is much to know about how density affects network functionalities. Theories of social capital are closely linked and claim that other congestion effects as population growth, high house prices (relative and absolute), traffic and decreased availability of service facilities can reduce 'happiness'. The potential commercial benefits and creative dimensions have an impact on employees' happiness and satisfaction (Morrison, 2011, p. 1055).

Looking at the range of formalised models giving some explanatory substance to the peripheral disadvantages, these are, primarily found in categories of land economy and regional science. Economic phenomena manifests itself with a clear distance variable defined from the centre/urban nuclei, starting from the concept of spatial disparities (encompassed by Nobel laureate Paul Krugman) under the heading 'New Economic Geography' already referred to. This economic-geographic focus identifies spatial forms and patterns in cities, industrial districts, clusters, centre-peripheries – spontaneous or planned defined in the sum of micro activities (Martin and Sunley, 2012).

Some further perspectives on modern theoretical approaches

A starting point for discussion of theory in terms of clusters, innovation systems, triple helixes, learning regions, etc., is whether these actually are theoretical constructs in themselves, parts of a larger one with a background in general agglomerative considerations, or primarily a policy development/offensive given an aura of academic polish. The question raised in the preceding chapters identifies them as parts of a paradigmatic mantra and a kind of self-reinforcing theoretical spiral, both in substance and form. And if so, if this, in itself, has a biased impact on the focus or outcome in peripheral territorial dimensions. Modern variants of agglomeration theories emphasise a functional and territorial integration leading to benefits for those involved and an expected growth for society (Rehfeld and Terstriep, 2013). It is clear that buzzwords like networks, clusters and innovation systems have become part of a daily rhetoric among policymakers and planners. The differences – compared with earlier regional development programmes and plans, together with the consideration of uniqueness of the region or locality in question, with impacts in defining a general strategy – are emphasised. The urban bias is one of the taken-for-granted generalities.

The relations between the terms/concepts are complex, in all their simplicity. Networks are used to emphasise the value of links or cooperation between different kinds of actors and activities, primarily in the economic sector. On an abstract level this notion does not have to be defined in terms of sectors or branches, but could easily stretch over or cover traditional statistical and organisational or functional barriers, diving into each other's conceptual substance, appearing in different consigned designations. A huge number of networks, when functioning, relate to societal development in dimensions of social interaction. Networks, carrying specific attributes and defined sometimes clearly, sometimes in more fuzzy directions, and sometimes, given names like the above designations:

> suffer from ontological and epistemological reductionism: they use idealized categories of design strategies for future development also as key categories in the analysis of the structural and institutional dynamics of the past, hence short-cutting the causality.
>
> (Moulaert and Mehmood, 2010, p. 108)

As regards clusters, they are much discussed, but seemingly with few hard and systematic facts in regard to their internal functions/activities. Michael Porter's (1990) cluster analysis and strategy – which has had a significant impact in regional, national and EU approaches to development – favour the core and especially metropolitan centres. This more or less avoids design strategies considering the internal dynamics benefiting all parts and partners, as they have different demands on the region/cluster as an environment for resources and cooperation (Jonsson, 2013, pp. 126–127). It needs a more detailed strategic approach emphasising a focus on the nature of the participation/membership. Size and impact of smaller players vs. larger; advantageous opportunities for early entrants; issues related to the distance from the fleshpots and decision-making authority and nodes; and a focus on what happens in the shadow of, or in the tail end of the cluster, and its actual dynamism. "'Cluster periphery' is defined with respect to the geographical location of the cluster in relation to major successful clusters as well as its reputation" (Kasabov, 2011, p. 828). Companies already in place have a higher survival rate and impact on future processes and industrial dynamics (Ter Wal and Boschma, 2011, pp. 925–926). That this has a distinct geographic appearance is quite obvious. What is happening outside among the rest, in the periphery – the small, traditional craft – and the way this impacts on the general development should be a natural analytical stepping stone as well.

Kasabov (2011, p. 828) registers that, peripherally defined negative characteristics in terms of weak interaction, ineffective contextual features, i.e. infrastructure and public service/sector, strategic concerns and general weaknesses, are linked to cluster branding. There is no analytical and policy priority to non-economic factors and institutions. System-defined competitive analysis is available, but neglected. Lack of interest is evident, because taken-for-granted results' lack of measurability are possibly an explanation. "Can efforts to establish clusters in regional dimensions become dysfunctional in the meaning that other forms, relations and networks are hidden?" (Jonsson, 2013, p. 125, my translation). The eventual potential is very little studied, but imbalances are clearly identifiable in the context of the process of cluster-system development: "small or medium sized ones (SMEs) – increasingly rely on innovation-related cooperation with a variety of partners such as customers, competitors, suppliers and universities" (Uyarra, 2011, p. 171).

Returning to networks, the issue is in what way they relate and how their internal processes are designed (Lind, 2002). There is still a long way to go, empirically, defining the structures and processes for claimed benefits of these theories *cum* policy packages. Whether the cluster is a product of context, an innovative environment or innovative people remains unanswered. A tentative response, in the form of a definition that suits all, is a common denominator in the focus on urban, high-tech and export-oriented. Porter (1990) describes the contents of clusters and how they are created. However, operationalisation has to include some principles for delimitation, whether it is the number of entities included or the degree of specialisation achieved, which often are lacking. The quality of the home base for a company is a fundament for the notion of competitiveness: factors/inputs, demands, competition, related activities. The nature of the networks described as clusters is the potential interlinkage and the concentration (primarily spatial) of these activities.

A major effort in reporting on the cluster literature is made by Cruz and Teixeira (2010). First, the backward linkage to traditional Marshallian agglomeration theory is discussed in the preceding section. The notion here is of added quality. When clustering occurs and develops, fuzziness in regard to the concept opens up for a quagmire of policies – like new infrastructure –which are defined by increasing demand, knowledge spillovers and a labour market with specialisation and supportive institutions (Ter Wal and Boschma, 2011) all interacting and promoting each other. Mitra considers, as an example, the up-to-date frequency of ideas around sharing knowledge, technologies, and the talent and services registered and linked to notions of proximity (Mitra, 2012). In spite of clusters' popularity policy-wise the debate still rages, whether they actually exist, whether they produce the hypothesised outcome and whether society and policy have any role to play (Mitze, 2011).

Agglomerations in a system-defined conceptual dimension are also the network versions of innovation systems and their theoretical qualifications. As explained in Andersson (2002, p. 13), a step towards including innovation systems notes interactive dimensions, but not primarily in aspects emphasised in the present theoretical orientation towards spatial effects. "[C]ongestion or negative path-dependent factors such as 'lock-in' . . . prevents firms from seeking new knowledge from elsewhere" (Mitra, 2012, p. 12).

Cluster theory links up with innovation processes focusing the regional dimension. It is also where the rural or peripheral qualifications should enter the picture. With a similar theoretical starting point, innovation and innovation systems forward the Marshallian agglomeration concept (co-location, interaction, dynamics). This is no surprise, as the relation between clusters and innovation systems includes the notion of the former being qualitatively part and precondition of the latter. This discussion is also valid for concepts like triple helixes, learning regions, knowledge regions, leading to more holistic approaches of the innovation systems. The differentiation within the field of regional development issues spans from the identification of national innovation systems to the notion of regional innovation systems (RIS).

A conceptual nucleus for innovation rests on the processual and dynamic properties and the outcome of interrelated actors (Uyarra, 2011, p. 182). The same author also indicates system characteristics on a higher level, including self-organisation and emergent properties, making system formation unpredictable, and less prone to policy operationalisation. The radical leaps in high tech are nowadays combined and complemented by incremental changes in production systems but also in organisation, marketing, etc. On the agenda is the inclusion of the public sector and public institutions implementing innovative practices.

The noted outcrop from the innovation system field, i.e. the regional innovation, brings us back closer to the cluster, geography and region. The distinction between the cluster and the RIS is not self-evident. When talking about the RIS, the primary concerns are with the knowledge infrastructure, the production and distribution of knowledge. Around this, there is an institutional framework with support and subsidies, investment resources, etc., and even more, an institutional context defined by laws and regulations, policy and implementation, a matter of what Jonsson (2013) calls 'innovation culture'.

Richard Florida (2002) has in his work focused on major urban regions, although the popularity of his approach has included efforts to fit or use his concepts on other entities (administrative, functional or socio-cultural) as well, which has been conceptually problematic. The 'creative capital' has been noted as essential for modern and front-line growth processes. Jonsson (2013) links this with other, more traditional regional growth theories (commented on earlier). In studies applied outside the urban, the impact seems, if there, hard to measure (Hauge and Thulemark, 2012, p. 169). Florida's focus on the four Ts (technology, talent, tolerance and territorial resources), in this orientation needs substantial qualifications (Hauge, 2012). Diving into the intricacies of empirical investigation, there are clear tendencies of an urban bias. The unstated understanding is that peripheral regions are lagging, uncompetitive and not or less attractive to mobile and creative labour, thereby losing talent and failing to benefit from migratory intellectual labour.

In the learning or knowledge of regional concepts, a dominance of agglomeration theories indicates the benefits of density in its agglomerative sense for knowledge accumulation. However, "In both academic and policy circles the mechanisms underlying the learning and innovation benefits of agglomeration remain poorly understood" (Crowley, 2011, p. 18).

Participating in these kind of constructs supposedly provides benefits to the economic actors to join up, mainly focusing on being part of a doctrine of profit maximisation, where economies of scale, quality of inputs, subsidies or other connotations are identified advantages. The role of the market provides cooperation in the framework of a cluster's or innovation system's privileged status. There is nothing particularly new about this. This way of reasoning was present already in connection with the 'staple towns' and trading privileges of the 19th century, or reappearing in the example of Perroux (already referred to) and his growth centre theory of the 1960s. These taken-for-granted analytical entrances and objectives are supposedly preconditions. Here enter the unique and good practices, i.e. considerations, in important complementary directions. The historical pastimes of a place or local community, wherever it is found, have their specific history and natural conditions, creating profiled culture/s and dimensions of accumulated knowledge, sometimes in versions of tacit knowledge. The generalities combined with the uniqueness places economic actors and activities in situations that are conducive to economic and social activities formed in order to handle and adapt also to "act as driving forces in wider social development processes" (Virkkala and Niemi, 2006, pp. 6–7). Connections with the accumulation of knowledge and competence specific for this line of work and production and defining the cooperation as such, are crucial. Similarly localised labour pools, sharing aspects of the potentials of localised skills, etc., increase adaptability and potential development processes.

The discussion around the peripheries within networks in the aforementioned consignations of clusters, innovations systems, learning regions, etc., includes the distance factor in the transfer of information, cooperative frameworks/networks, sources, channels and personal links. All being preconditions for local/regional capacity and interaction links with the outside, world-at-large. Looking at the openness of the system – i.e. the nature of the global pipelines emanating from members of the system or members in cooperation – could be noted as compensatory. The strength of these outreaching links, is where the analysis should be heading in terms of complementarity. When it comes to peripheral regions, the taken-for-granted opinion of them is that they are less innovative than agglomerations. The process and stock of R&D is notably lower as is the share of product innovations.[6] However, not only that, the elements also have to interact in a manner qualitatively conducive to innovation. A wider definition questions these taken-for-granted arguments. Incremental changes and process-related innovation presents more complex pictures, which indicate an evidence of innovation, even in different forms of innovative clustering and elements in the periphery – as well as problems hindering innovative processes and change in urban and other agglomerative contexts (Tödtling and Trippl, 2005). Structural prerequisites promoting or hindering the development of RIS are found in underdeveloped organisational and institutional settings, which are part of the characteristics of the periphery. Elements in the limited RIS can, for example, refer to the inadequacy of the knowledge infrastructure's width and depth. A lock-in behavioural pattern is possibly also at work (Tödtling and Trippl, 2005). Compensatory efforts are further approached in upcoming chapters, but efforts of institutional formation in the form of competence building are one of the keys. Centralisation and concentration in this latter sector act contrary to the strategic potentials with severe consequences for long-term strategies.

Theoretical fragments with implications towards the periphery

The entrepreneur

Theoretical endeavours in the field of entrepreneurship in general and its role and reflection of the way biases in the urban/rural dichotomy could appear, will just be introduced here. Part of the exercise is, of course, on the level of definitions: what is in the functions that are specific, and what they encompass. Entrepreneurship is a way of being, behaving within different sectors and activities. Just the process of sorting-out carries a dimension of priorities. Placing an emphasis on business in economic terms could range, but seldom does, from establishing new firms and registering them, to developing and diversifying ongoing economic activities. Functional activities in the economic field range from productive to unproductive (e.g. rentseeker, moneylender, portfolio manager) or even destructive entrepreneurs (Mitra, 2012, p. 52). Aspects of contribution to and relative importance in societal development stand in line for discussion.

The traditional theoretical view assumes positioning of the entrepreneur in the centre, thriving core, often the capital. High skills and research capabilities combine with the centripetal effects of high income markets and thriving socio-cultural communities. There are many reasons to question those kinds of qualifications. "Peripheral regions now provide fertile breeding grounds for entrepreneurs who are skilled and connected (Saxenian, 2006)" (Mitra, 2012, p. 68). This is not exclusively a matter of definitions; the behavioural quality means its individual possibility and potential. It is much more the context of allowing, promoting and recognising its presence and values.

Social capital, economy and social entrepreneurship

Part of the picture of differentiation in society is concerned with questions pertaining to why some localities or regions seem to be more successful than others. Among the explanatory factors are the presence and quality of social interaction, interpreted in terms of social capital, where interpersonal trust between citizens and cultural forms of reciprocity are reflected in organisations, in terms of membership and participatory levels. All of this is considered from the viewpoint of facilitating both social and economic benefits (Kawachi, Kennedy and Glass, 1999)[7] Social capital is interpreted in different directions among its founding identifiers. Bourdieu (1977) emphasises the benefits of participation in groups. Coleman (1990) discusses advantages for the individual, and Putnam (1993) (2000) writes on reciprocity. Its substance is interpreted:

> To some degree, it hinges on mutual respect, trust and civic-mindedness. Declining social capital means that society becomes less trustful and less civic-minded.
>
> (Florida, 2002, p. 268)

Empirical evidence, on a regional level, is scarce (Echebarria and Barrutia, 2013, p. 1002). Social capital as an analytical concept has developed primarily into studies of networks and interaction (norms) and the nature of benefits and eventual sanctions. The level of analysis is, in the present context, focused on group and community characteristics, but also on individual and family relational attributes on a micro level. The nature and substance of links/ties/relations are of primary concern. 'Bonding' refers to the quality of social interaction, indicating strong ties, while 'bridging' refers to weak (Granovetter, 1983), where promotion of social interaction is more on the level of facilitation. "The line of reasoning is consistent with the thinking of regional researchers who have emphasized the relevance of weak ties for growth . . . and have shown the limits of trust and strong ties" (Echebarria and Barrutia, 2013, p. 1002). Finally, we find 'linking', identifying the presence of contacts, analytically distinguishing vertical interactions, including degrees of power and resource control.

In economics this all means that the nature of cooperation and complementarity between enterprises is defined by the degree of trust between the individuals participating. This in turn opens the door for information flows, and qualitatively, to dimensions of knowledge sharing and providing. The quality of the relationships has been noted to be of substantial importance.

Florida (2002, p. 269) argues that a shift from strong to weak ties characterises prosperous localities and territories. "Our evolving communities and emerging society are marked by a greater diversity of friendships, more individualistic pursuits and weaker ties within the community. People want diversity, low entry barriers and the ability to be themselves."

The nature of these processes, interpreted into their preconditions in rural or peripheral environments is hard to find, due to the range of biased preconditions. The debate is about the nature of its presence. Intensively argued is that social capital is an important part of rurality. It has also been argued (Putnam, 2000) that social capital is higher in rural areas. OECD notes, in its rural policy document, that social capital is a key asset of rural areas (2006a, p. 3) Sørensen presents evidence in the other direction, although identifies the notion that rural areas often seem rich in social capital based on: "the transition from rural to urban societies as a transition from high levels of social life in small groups to low levels of social life in large groups" (2012, p. 874).

A dimension of the discussion penetrating the cultural dimensions of society in regard to social capital is where rural and urban areas are intertwined with (semi)urban jobs (commuting), while remaining rural in settlements at a distance from the urban. It does not say anything outright about the quality or the consequences of this on the presence of social capital.

> Social capital is a complex construct, which . . . has a structural, a relational and a cognitive dimension (and various sub-constructs may also exist inside these dimensions).
>
> (Echebarria and Barrutia, 2013, p. 1002)

Proximity[8]

A general and popular theme for what promotes growth and development within modern theoretical considerations takes a complementary route via the concept of proximity. It is considered, partly, as a reflection of discussions on density. A theoretical link also exists to the concept of agglomerations, where reduction of transport work, where the presence of a support infrastructure, where individual interaction on a 'daily' basis, where knowledge spillovers and learning between actors, where the presence of a labour force with suitable training and skills all describe a type of economic interaction. It does, however, follow a more qualitative track. Early approaches emphasised aspects of spatial proximity, with its impact on innovation and interactive learning. Through the works of Boschma (2005) and others this approach has extended into a number of variants where functional attributes are differentiated.

The important point is a substantiated proximity relevant for the present discussion, in the presence of tacit and/or local knowledge. Tacit also encompasses possible exchange/relations over longer distances appearing in non-spatial interpretations of proximity. A further development in this field is the approach of 'relational advantage' where knowledge spillover effects appear in the interaction between firms in their process of information processing, deepening the impact of the spatial parameters (Cooke, 2012). Spatial proximity can compensate for cognitive distance as it probably defines a common dimension of norms and values. The quality of spillover impact increases in this pattern. Proximic approaches ease transfer of knowledge. The spatial variant is within localised clusters but complemented by social and team dynamics.

Focusing on knowledge and learning

Leading into a brief excursion of the intricacies of the knowledge economy, knowledge defined as a major force drives productivity and contributes to economic advances (Benneworth, 2007). Deducing from the preceding section the idea of a landscape where physical knowledge infrastructure appears, together with immaterial flows and presences, is a *sine qua non*. Quality in depth and width, and sometimes also quantity, are requisites. The notion of innovation is defined both as a prerequisite and result of the presence of this complex and nebulous feature. Innovation systems and processes, in their dynamic, are most often collective and interactive manifestations relying on continuous learning and teaching (Uyarra, 2011). The discussion is and, could be, even more specific, dwelling on elements and features deemed necessary for a degree of dynamism. Specifically looking at organisations . . .

> universities can play this role and have a broader systemic effect on the regional economic environment, by plugging gaps in the local regional innovation system.
>
> (Benneworth, 2007, p. 487)

This aspect of theoretical development links up with more general discussions on the conscious use of institutions of higher learning, as drivers in regional development pertinent in a discussion of the peripheral dimension. The case is that universities have a more or less taken-for-granted role and have a suggested essential need to develop in a receptive context, i.e. a city of some size. The role of universities and colleges to become an embodiment of regional dynamics is constantly under attack from centralistic forces. Questioning the limits focuses on the existence or need for a more fully developed knowledge society, where the periphery is an analytical object.

Path dependency

Looking at different aspects of development trajectories there is a very well-argued analytical theoretical metaphor in the concept of 'path dependency'. Its explanatory power refers to actions and processes that have a tendency to follow existing travelling paths. For instance, behavioural patterns of firm development and localisation, and in aggregated terms, in sectors and industry evolution in general (Uyarra, 2011). The argument here is the urban is definitely an intellectual version of dependency, being the allocated highway for the periphery or the rural. An alternative logic is, however, partly hidden, due to the principles at work. Pointing to the impossible, non-existence of agglomeration economies restricts the policy search for alternative solutions or scenarios. In more fine-grained studies, the absolute necessity of distant, extra-regional sources for knowledge and economic solutions strengthens the path. Isaksen and Onsager (2010, p. 232) point in this direction even though they acknowledge the possibility of other local sources. The purpose of this short reference is the notion of path dependency, substantiated by the urban dominance, from theory all the way to policy.

Institutionalism

Based on North (1990) and Scott (1995) the idea of institutionalism, not as organisations or actors, but the rules of the game and its preconditions, has developed. What governs the economic and social activities of society are its actors and therefore its processes. According to North, there are three types of institutions – regulating, normative and cognitive. Rules and regulations (recognised in terms of place and level) formally define societal activities. The strongest of these institutions are issues around ownership. Regulations like the tax system and labour market characteristics have a high impact and the eventual morale around these regulations do as well. Our values, norms and conduct are normative. The final, cognitive, variant is where the experience of reality is based on the type of culture that is defining the context (Jonsson, 2013). North uses the Enclosure movement (18th-century England) as an example of an institution defining long-run growth and development (World Bank, 2009). The example is pertinent as it was a major contribution to the industrialisation process, stimulating the exodus of rural labour into the cities and at the same time, preconditioning and increasing productivity in the countryside. The totality of the institutional system is, partly, described in the concept of 'institutional thickness' which tries to interpret a kind of culture into business-promoting conditions outside of market relations and analytically relevant traditional economic relations. Within the public sector, institutional theory can also be applied when studying how different activities are executed. Quality could be much more than quantity in this pattern, which makes us return to variants of a decentralised institutional system. The ideas of Elinor Ostrom (1990) identify the in-between market and state intervention where local actors defined in collective form can exploit resources in clearly defined areas and functions, through self-organisation. This appears more clearly in small local communities. Issues of a sustainable development, based on local interest rather than market forces or inefficient subsidy structures, link it quite heavily to aspects of social economy and social capital. The institutional dominance of urbanism has a substantial impact on "the conditions for sustainable societal development" (Johansson, 2012, p. 10, my translation).

Its analytical role is the focus on the long-term successive adaptation – deeply entrenched and therefore hard to change – on the verge of culture. It is empirically very difficult to identify or measure (Bristow, 2010). Of special interest in this book are the institutions that define the urban bias paradigm as well as peripheral/rural preconditions.

This theoretical approach should and, certainly does, identify the specificity of local, geographical regimes. Fostering local culture expands legitimacy or suppression in regard to aspects of interaction in the social *cum* economic structures. But also, to what degree there exist regional and local preparedness for learning and change indicates how well business and society in general is placed to pursue targeted development. Prerequisites and opportunities lie in a consciously created ability to handle the 'informal' in the form of unconscious rules, norms and behaviour patterns.

Notes

1 'Periphery' is used here as a collective word, based on the conceptual discussion in the preceding chapter, but somewhat simplifying the flow of writing.
2 Discussed more extensively in Chapter 5.
3 Although it is noted that this refers to macroeconomic conditions on a state/national level, it could be argued for regional comparisons as well.
4 As it is not framed in an urban, centralised context, it is not further elaborated here.
5 Notably present in a peripheral/rural context as well.
6 Product innovations as this is important in an analysis of volumes and flows.
7 The article also includes a discussion on methods – in this case connected with health-related factors.
8 An extended discussion in this field takes place in Chapter 6.

4 Measure what, with what and what does it represent?

This chapter starts from the proposition raised in the introductory chapter that issues connected with the core, centre, capital, urban dimension define the rules of the game in analytical as well as policy and implementation terms. This paradigm encompasses even 'the' model for development and growth, which has consequences for choices of theory and methodology. These presumptions are strategically quite severe, in that the periphery often, on the basis of the biased results, is coerced into adopting inappropriate approaches to its local and regional solutions, and qualitative aspects of more fundamental and general objectives for society tend to be excluded. This reflecting, directly or indirectly, consciously or not, a political choice. This chapter looks at some aspects of methods and methodological substances, the beginning of a process in need of further elaboration by others.

It is a well-known and worldwide trend that authorities desperately need to have more and better researched indicators to assess development processes, i.e. they still are primarily designed within the spectrum of pure economic growth. Comparisons among the plethora are not considered enough.

> a United Nations Development Programme (UNDP) report from 2008 shows that, at the time, some 178 indices and rankings were actively produced and maintained in relation to global governance and the general performance of states.
>
> (Öjehag-Pettersson, 2015, p. 245)

The understanding that economic change is not always representative for assessing the full spectrum of development, especially not its immaterial aspects, is a matter of concern. Issues triggering this qualification were originally substantial differences in country-to-country comparisons, while sub-national differences, the focus in this book, also promote the quest. An OECD report (2006b, p. 6) notes the complexity of place-based rural development as a case-in-point where lack of research – due to fundamental difficulties in evaluating cross-sectoral, integrated, policies – identifies representative indicators within the need for medium- and long-term approaches. "Among the shortcomings have been the use of very broad and varying rural definitions and the predominant use of bivariate instead of multivariate comparisons" (Sørensen, 2016, p. 392). The complex substance of the concept demands a multifactor analytical approach:

> it is hoped that we can better appreciate the complex, multifaceted nature of rural development and the way that any response to rural development problems (whether from a network standpoint or not) must alert to this complexity.
>
> (Murdoch, 2000, p. 409)

There is, as stated, a reliance on the core as a role model/ideal for the rural/periphery, rather than the reality of actual change, i.e. where and how things are actually happening. The definition of the periphery and what is happening is based on the choice of the studied variables, the quality of this choice and the identification of what each actually represents, and, taking a step further, the nature of how the results are guiding policy, policy change and evaluations to ultimate implementation. There is a discourse on rural development in that improved conditions can be achieved or, at least, a clear direction for an organised process. It is here that the crucial nature of the analysis enters. An extensive development, covering a wide range of natural and social conditions within a community, aims to capture the quality of life in an area, usually measured only indirectly and in a limited, though complicated, way. When policy enters through the door, it is conditioned by differences in a huge number of aspects and because of that, interpreted, implemented, in quite different ways and with substantial differences as to results. Bristow (2010) discusses the issues of regional competitiveness, where each and every one of the included indicators represent a high degree of complexity:

> The nature of these indicators and their inevitable use in regional benchmarking also help to perpetuate the notion that regions are engaged in fierce and direct competition with one another over these key resources and in respect of outcomes.
>
> (Bristow, 2010, p. 24)

In this case, questioning the validity and by that the usefulness makes this whole exercise questionable for operationalisation.

> [R]egions, their competitive performance or success and what this 'success' actually means – [are] questions which today have received only limited critical interrogation .
>
> (Bristow, 2010, p. 68)

After this broad entrance, the ambition will be to discuss different elements, variables and indicators related to the choice of entities, of qualitative and quantitative data, availability, representation and presentation. Finally, I also offer some words about combined indicators and contextual analysis.

The choice of the entities studied

A fundamental methodological problem is identifying the geographical areas that should be the basis of definition, and why? Since the definition of remote areas, localities and regions could be a product of the analytical approach itself, the question of what comes first seems relevant, and also the nature of the contextual analysis. As the periphery, or other designations, are complex concepts, simplified statistical definitions and categories will create problems all the way into regulations, management and practice. The combination of already existing administrative categories makes the path-dependent character of the existing statistical material a case in point. "[D]ifferent classifications of rural areas will lead to different conclusions about economic performance" (Curry and Webber, 2012, p. 280). Functionality also enters through another gate, regions, where variables defining functionality are relevant when discussing centre and periphery. This rationale enforces the analytical range. Within the concept of a functional region we have the classical entrance of centre/core and periphery/hinterland where relation with distance distinguishes the impact. A variation of functionality also distinguishes attributes like problem and border regions indicating explicit complex peripheralities.

Size is an example of considerable concern. Successful regions are usually described in categories as large labour markets, strong enterprises and well-developed R&D sectors. Geographical entities enter into the problem area in different disguises, based on dimensions of aggregation, which is a classical methodological approach where results and focus change, depending upon method and methodological selection. Large aggregates indicate and simulate homogeneous regions, although a disaggregation discloses large internal variations, both in disaggregated unnamed entities or distinctions of places/settlement on a specific geographical level. Large labour markets are supposedly developing better than small, but wide variations exist within the small groups. To introduce regional results, distribution factors and spatial irregularities in the statistical outcomes should be requirements. The periphery could in that way come to appear in completely new perspectives.

The same kind of argument appears when reporting on net flows. A net flow reduces the analytical substance significantly. Gross flows are usually of much further interest. Evidence of a high leakage (read migration) out of the periphery is a net result, which implicates the future of the entities. This flow is the result of at least two aggregate flows, in and out. Making detailed analysis of each one is necessary as, when policy enters, the need for a differentiation of measures becomes evident. Evidence of the benefits of disaggregating even more are very convincing.

The map and cartography as a measure and manifestation

Before we go further in this direction, there exists a special analytical dimension in connection with the geographical approach and that is 'the map' and 'mapping' or 'cartography'. To start out with a kind of exotic example:

> In Russia, too, the unabashedly local maps made during litigation over property represent the authority of the central state in the provinces. They exhibit the skill of the central state apparatus at extending its influence and bringing its routinized practices and language to the local area. The interests of center and periphery intersect in the use of the maps.
>
> (Wood et al., 2010, p. 33)

What is expected in mapping and in interpreting a map is its status as a model of reduced reality. The map illustrates many things, sometimes interpreted in the legend (i.e. the table of explanatory symbols printed on the map somewhere). The content of that legend is by matter of choice – the choice of a centre defining, teaching, explaining a structure, a function, an interpretation. There is imbedded ideology and politics translating 'facts'. Borders and boundaries distinguishing administrative entities are cases in point. Realities sometimes found out in real nature, sometimes as signs along the road, sometimes as barbed wire.

> But most are not . . . the utility of most map propositions: generally they take the form of linkages among conditions, states, processes, and behaviours conjoined in the territory that the map brings into being.
>
> (Wood et al., 2010, p. 52)

The map offers many opportunities to present ideas as stated facts, using the full arsenal of mapping techniques, projections, centring, relations, hierarchies, etc. It reflects different authoritative, administrative ideas and by this transforms ideas, ideology and interests to factual propositions. At the same time the map and legend also outline the political hierarchy, and indirectly, institutions.

Time and categories

Time and change are not only items for philosophical considerations. Development paths can highlight past, present and future potentials/determinants. "Accordingly, the best way to improve competitiveness of a more developed region may not be the same as for a less developed one" (Breska, 2010, p. 68). Dimensions of time contribute in a number of ways in finding substance to the entities or processes investigated. A dynamic approach recognises the status of areas/regions and processes within those and any defined context – analytically by way of combined linear, cyclical and complex systems' interactive progressions.

Time is also included as an available resource or a limiting obstacle. Travelling, as an example (commuting, tourism, service trips), considering time spent, strengthens the basic definitional arguments. This means that the discussion on methodology is brought further than simplified causality. Discussions should complement what is mentioned in relation to dynamics and process, with a discussion on the complexity of the 'dynamic' periphery in its interaction with the centre. Many analytical efforts describe future potentials and possibilities.

Distant time, in the future or past, has a connotation of being less secure, less relevant and therefore less explored.

There are a number of attempts to develop typologies in order to capture dimensions of non-urban space within primarily rural connotations. Peripheral still remains scarce. The fact is that the same terms for differentiation are seldom used. Approaches and results argued are case-specific, a reason why they are seldom used for planning and strategy purposes. The ambition is to catch the scientific object through classification within different types of hierarchies or typologies. An important distinction is found where the implied hierarchy is either a subcategory or positioned in some kind of ranking. For the typologies, being thematically construed, the hierarchies chosen have something – by way of categorisation and/or simplification – to do with centralisation and concentration. Policy-defined ambitions work with it all the time and when policy (geographical coverage) is used, ladders or scales of peripherality and marginality are simultaneously accepted.

Here is a diversion to a definition of analytical practice. The idea of using politically defined districts, i.e. subsidiary definitions, etc. (Johansen et al., 2006) is a case in point. Peripherality is identified by administratively defined borders encompassing areas recognised for special (primarily subsidising) policies. Calculating delimitations based on specified criteria – and weighing the importance among those based on political expediency or some combinations thereof– dominates. This naturally demands a continuous dynamic approach and introduces changing impacts of contextually recognised delimitations. Level-defined decision-making is, by way of its functionality, important when recognising this outcome. For instance, solutions – when it comes to extended welfare services proclaimed by central authorities and applicable to local communities – could limit local initiatives, as to variation, multifunctionality and choice. The impact of a system definition is clearly manifest (Fimreite and Selle, 2006, p. 15).

The negative argument is the potential dependence on urban/core perspectives. Examples are quite frequent and the scientific legitimation comes out of habit; conscious efforts of discussing any eventual biases are lacking. Distinctions like remote rural, accessible rural, non-rural are representative and quite frequent. This includes different countrysides as well. Periphery is found in many appearances, ending up with a large variation induced by attributive demographic, political, economic, social and cultural categories. By itself it is a proof for the argument that choice has to be highly qualified.

Lorentzen (2012a, pp. 8–9) presents an interesting index for rural communities/entities defined by 14 parameters, resulting in 16 peripheral, 29 rural and 18 in between (*mellemkommuner*). The English government provides two definitions. One is based primarily on population density, another on commuting patterns, and through that, they define city-regions. The peripheral is identified on specific notions of economic performance (Curry and Webber, 2012). What we are suggesting here is that any index of rural or rurality has to be argued quite carefully, as there are "fundamental questions about the nature and causal importance of 'rural'" (Hoggart, 1988, p. 35).

The region and the local

A discussion on the production of value in a given place and territory is a complex endeavour, and should be approached finding out how the production is performed and with what, simultaneously with qualifying, in depth, that choice. It should distinguish the important variables in a change and in contextual preconditions. It is self-evident that a wide definition of value should be used, whatever the implications for increasing complexity in the comparative exercises. Wahlström (1989, p. 79) identifies exchange, utility and symbolic.

To be more specific, take the example of innovation. This is a theme covered in the section on distance and accessibility as well. The regional perspective becomes more accentuated when the innovation process is disaggregated in its parts and derives different spatial and functional structures from this (Breska, 2010). Making a mirror analysis, in terms of regional structures, identifies the composition and the ability to respond to different phases of innovative processes, i.e. a profiled inventory of the economic (branch) geographical structure of the summarised production cycles. The nucleus of the argument is found in the selection of variables that urban actors, and primarily institutionalised knowledge processing and development, has identified. Rural innovative practices are downgraded in that comparison (Fløysand and Jakobsen, 2010).

Region- and local-specific conditions could, and should be, considered in a much more explicit way. The classic methodological dilemma, the unique versus the generalisable, does not diminish the importance of this statement. A qualitative analysis cannot merely be a question of disaggregation of national-regional totals. Decomposition of data for regional growth is often represented in the reality of points, nodes or locations within the regional landscape rather than in the region as a territory/landscape. Authorities need better and more qualified indicators to assess development processes (i.e. those primarily designed to describe results within the spectrum of economic growth, but preferably wider) in all their complexities. There is no 'optimal' design for performance indicator systems in regional development policy. The problems focus on the choice of area-based accounting, combined with analysis of gross flows, complicated by the choice of background variables. Problems associated with an area-approach are in measuring differences in productivity at the local level, whether one should use the workplace or residential-based information, and how to integrate revenue and profits in the results. The alternative proposed by Rizov and Walsh (2011, p. 642) is to estimate productivity from firm or plant data and then aggregate this into land-based units.

Taking the rural, the estimates used are density, centrality and number of workers in the primary sector, numbers of self-employed, etc., creating a kind of index, with cutoff points, called rural, in different appearances. The same types of relations consider other categories like, settlement structures linked to different social, economic, etc., categories, specified in more detailed delimitations. 'Weak population densities' is an example of a basic indicator for both obstacles and compensatory conditions. Substantiating 'weakness' is not always done. What we get are measures for analysis, which is not an exact, but stimulating exercise, throwing light on aspects of economic development, culture and changes in social patterns. By nature of the input, outcomes range from inspiring, through informative to disinformative.

Choice between variables – defining the outcome?

General remarks

The first and most common proposition when choosing a variable, or between variables, is that this leads to 'somewhat biased' results. This is defined, among other things, basically, by actors and situations (time and place). The choice, in itself, indicates importance or necessity –availability or voluntarism, i.e. a wished-for projection. This can be an argument in the direction of relations between freedoms of choice or given as mandatory. Examples could be found in the regulations of the EU structural funds, or INTERREG, in the form of political ambitions and showcase adaptation. This is the nature of the beast, as there is no way to enquire, in quality, into place-based conditions in depth and in the present. In practice, these variables can be further rigged to follow the old advice MNI (minimum necessary input) for control or follow-up considerations. Also relevant are the interpretations that take place, even with defined mandatory policies, with adapting as far as possible to local conditions or personal ambitions or prejudices. The evaluation includes a discussion of aspects of choice, also when it comes to the position of the variable in the analysis. Is it categorised as dependent or independent? Is it a matter of substance or contextual?

An interesting example, with impact on defining general territorial principles, based on quite far-reaching ideological/theoretical grounds is found in the following that is:

> represented in the World Development Report entitled Reshaping Economic Geography (World Bank, 2009). In this document places are located on a developmental continuum determined by their distance (to markets), density (of market activity) and divisions (preventing freedom of trade and migration).
>
> (Gibson-Graham, 2011, p. 227)

Quantity and quality

A common position is that what is quantifiable will get a more prominent position and role, outclassing the quest for more substantive, qualitative, representations. Hard statistics have a way of strengthening an argument, carrying a cloak of neutrality/objectivity in relation to the object studied. There is often a dimension of self-defined objectivity, evading questions about substance, about representation. Indexes found where numerical legitimation carries a brunt of ideological or political ambition worked into their hard, sometimes categorical, manifestations.

> In this sense, the Reglab index is an example that serves to illustrate a more general point concerning the ways that politics is enacted through techniques of measuring, ranking and ordering in advanced liberal societies.
> (Öjehag-Pettersson, 2015, p. 246)

A substantial part of the investigative reality is problems pertaining to difficulties in methods of quantifiable analysis, where the properties of the variable are problematic to verify by empirical, quantifiable means. The need to approach it through the field of qualitative exploration, extending the possible understanding, could be a special peripheral prerequisite. Methods exist for the transfer of qualitative data into quantitative, but usually identified as, in many respects, less reliable. Whether qualitative studies are more frequently used in the periphery and why are relevant questions. The affirmative answer is explained by deficiencies in the collection phase. Disadvantages appear when comparing meaning (qualitative) and results (quantitative), and are highlighted in the centre-periphery dichotomy. What happens to qualitative approaches in the analysis when quantities are available? How should they be evaluated? With their direct dimension of readability and the interpretation of black and white pictures, numbers and a thousand words? What is available in existing sources, and, what has to be compiled in a developed, traditional research process? It is not only absolute categories. It is also a matter of the existing sources and the quality of these. It is about time limits and expediency. Partly, it is about blaming practices rooted in the past and noticeable as path dependencies in the methodological world.

How does one measure and evaluate relevance under these conditions? We have to qualify the analytical material in dimensions of quantities, static/dynamic, time series, time-scale. It requires a regular examination of the selection of variables and weighing, problematic also for comparability over time. Weights should be defined in a substantiated theoretical framework, according to clearly defined overall importance, at least presented with a how and why (Bristow, 2010). To continuously question the principles of selection and the selection in itself, stands against cost- and time-efficient considerations.

Examples, with a focus on performance indicators in EU structural fund programme operating plans and deliverables and in other forms of assessments dependent upon scoring and quantification (e.g. the approaches of the World Bank, IMF, OECD, Scottish Enterprise), are all problematic for peripheral northern regions in two respects. There is a greater variety of experiences and higher costs of identifying and collecting data than for communities and economies in the core, which undermines the eventual efficiency and effectiveness of standardised applied analysis. Second, objectives are captured by measures and data based on the norms, processes, relationships and input-output linkages of the mainstream economy – the periphery evaluated as if it is like the core, implicitly competing with the core. In specific cases, such as the Highlands and Islands of

Scotland, 'national' surveys may not even cover their area and population, biasing the aggregate in hidden ways and with consequences for reliability and validity.

Demographic variables and examples

General descriptions of demographic characteristics covering the periphery, normally present a picture of a shrinking population. What defines this process is, first, fertility rates, also used as a general illustration of the peripheral status. This is a rough and indirect measure and historically problematic. Fertility rates were used to classify development levels, indicating diminishing rates with increasing industrialisation, education, etc. Fertility rates are important, together with migratory flows, in the long-term dimensions of local or regional demographic status, linking children and qualities of growing up, defining attitudes/identities and relations to the local/regional community. These are quite distinct consequences than moving in as a grown-up: "[T]he link with the periphery will be weakened when fewer have their roots there" (Fimreite and Selle, 2006, p. 12). Therefore, fertility rates are a start, but not enough to evaluate the totality of the demographic process in a local community. Causality and future implications should be in focus for the analysis.

A population decrease takes, as its starting point, an already relatively low population level, and usually indications are that population changes are primarily defined by migration. But this is a representation, as noted, where only the final net sum is considered, hiding the qualities of important flows in both directions. Taking migration, or rather urbanisation, changes focus when we go behind the short-term aggregates. Note that the rationale in this section is to question or at least increase our attention to the methodological problems.

The sum total does not represent a draining of the countryside or promoting of the urban increase. Disaggregating the urban, its growth is the combined effect of fertility rates and numbers and inflows of migrants, especially foreign. Also, not all demographic cohorts show similar patterns of out- or in-migration (see, for example, Berg (2004). Young women have a higher migration rate than young men, This applies to both out- and in-migration. Young women, will to a higher degree than men return to the rural districts on the completion of their education (Fimreite and Selle, 2006). This is, however, not the case in the international refugee and economic migrant categories.

What is important are the causalities. The first recognised emergence of a rural-urban exodus in the United Kingdom, in the middle of the 19th century, was defined by the industrialisation process. The main causes at that time were employment opportunities in industry and over-population in the countryside. The employment factor has been a major stimulant in explaining this process over time. However, the general tendency has changed into something much more complex, demanding more qualitative in-depth studies. Today a notable counter-flow is also taking place. The explanation encompasses a number of different categories. Suburbanisation is easing the pressure of congested centres, stimulating the notion of city-regions. The quality-of-life explanation is another. Several types of such migration – green, retirement, commuter and expatriate – are qualified in the literature. Impact analysis has a lot to do with characteristics and motivations in different migrant groups. As in traditional migratory analysis, we will find both push and pull factors. "Champion (1989) identified seventeen different explanations for counter-urbanization based on studies of nine countries" (Akgün et al., 2011, p. 1209).

International inward migration and the internal migration of foreign-born have become increasingly important (Halfacree, 2008). Reflections on the inward flows are usually described in positive terms. There are, however, aspects lurking behind the curtain. As to internal rural-oriented migration, there are tendencies of conflict between local development interests and the conserving ambitions of the migrants. Increasing housing costs, due to increased demand from a well-to-do cohort, makes young local people look in vain for cheap accommodation. As to international flows, social and cultural issues are prominently impacting flows to outskirts of major urban centres. International migration with ethnical and racial implications is gaining populistic ground.

Commuting and leisure become another complexity in migratory processes studied in the long term. Potential contributions indicate aspects with far-reaching impact on age structure, service demands and so on. A special example of this is found in Arnesen, Overvåg, Skjeggedal and Ericsson's (2012) arguments on the concept of multi-house homes. The definition distinguishes between a home in the city for daily household functions and a recreational house in rural hinterlands. Dispositions and actions influence the local economy, where demand for public and private service production, planning and politics appear in both ends of the construct, most notably in the rural communities.

The concept of sparsity is a demographic feature touched upon earlier. In Sweden the term in translation is '*glesbygd*', defined as those areas not distinguished as '*tätort*' (settlement), in turn, clusters of housing with more than 200 inhabitants and less than 200 metres between. A number of ways to measure sparsity exists, interacting in substance with other indicators or aspects. See, for instance Haugen (2012b, pp. 7–11) who delimits areas using the proportion of population for each region below a certain threshold, rather than average population densities. Following these kind of qualifications analytically could disclose qualitative alternative aspects of consequential development. Different measurements/thresholds values found in international comparisons speak about other priorities. It can and has been argued that population density is a too-rough instrument to distinguish the nature of a sparse area. Instead, it represents a combined effect of densities and patterns, together with specific aspects of the economy. Definitions of villages, hamlets and smaller urban centres vary, where village is a 'collection of farms and houses in the countryside'. Solving one issue, however, raises another. The research interest into this issue was raised by the discovered disappearance of an existing population under the statistical radar of 3,100 small villages (15 percent – 800,000 of the Danish population), i.e. with less than 200 inhabitants they are now categorised as 'rural areas' (Møller, Staunstrup and Winter Johansen, 2010, p. 1).

Discussing population densities on a regional level could be problematic when scale and delimitation, as already noted, have a substantial impact on the result. Perspectives on periphery or sparsity will never be absolutes. Sparsity could be defined by numbers in different dimensions, by density (inhabitants per square kilometre) and by distance to density (travelling time to settlement with a minimum level of inhabitants), etc., but the summarised experiences of density, distance, etc., could be something totally different. Problems appear when variables and indicators are still interpreted in general statements. For instance, how would one go about interpreting the following: "Sparsity . . . less prosperous . . . habitually suffering from a lack of business and social services and with a poor basic infrastructure endowment" (Gløersen et al., 2006, p. 2)? Causalities are not linear or straightforward.

The quotes here define variables classified through describing a problem, such as looking for areas where people de facto settle and live but also analytically including where they have decided they do not want to go. Of the part of the total land mass of Norway (306,000 square km), 57,325 square km are inhabited to varying degrees, while in measures of peripherality based on sparse population, some 250,000 square km are not inhabited at all (Johansen et al., 2006, p. 15). Reservations, of course, pertain to inhabitable areas. Sparsely populated areas are a combination of more and less populated places/areas on a relatively low population level. Average and area-defined densities used, i.e. in the Norwegian North, a measure of 12.5 inhabitants per square kilometre, including water,[1] the latter important in itself defining necessary travelling distance, i.e. around real-life barriers. In EU, there is a differentiation between NUTS 2 and 3, where the former have eight inhabitants per square kilometre and the latter 12.5 as norms. The basic approach here is defined by the physical distance between settlements, houses, people, workplaces and service facilities of different types. It is the distance between inhabitants – i.e. the average distance between people in an area (see below).

The examples represent alternate approaches where basic political and ideological – i.e. not always scientific – platforms create a structure of cost-definitions versus welfare/equity, complemented by functionally defined categories. It is a version of the old saying: 'The way you ask is the answer you get'. Sparsity can be a problem or a resource, an obstacle or challenge, as part of the whole or as a heavy, to-be-discarded rucksack. Sparsity is sometimes also described in terms of 'thinness', which also "prove[s] notoriously difficult empirically and results have been mixed" (Bristow, 2010, p. 21). This author notes that there is very little research into issues of degrees of density and regional economic space, a supposedly anti-polar approach. Part of the perspective includes aspects of where the population lives in relation to where they work. These factors, in turn, relate to where different types of services are provided. The categories, at first of geographical connotations (settlement structures) and later linked to different collective categories (social, economic, etc.), specify in more detail any arguments regarding delimitations/categories, or are defined by these delimitations.

Density varies from place to place, from time to time. Density is the basis for the urban logic, in its organisational and functional but also symbolic appearance.

How does one measure the expected processes emanating from this? How density is processed in quantity and quality is far from clear. Density as a precondition describes a way of life and a form of expected potential, all the way from simple bilateral connections/relations to images and cultures, springing from systemic consequences. Another popular analytical approach is the so-called population potential, i.e. people living at a certain distance from a specified point. 'Weak population densities' is then an example of a basic result, both for compensating and hindering conditions and structures. The mirror image is the numbers of persons reached. A 50 km radius is an accepted maximum commuting-to-work standard in the Northern countries. Distance to services or other types of consumption also have a comfort zone, but this depends on the characteristics of the product/provision or the characteristics of the demand as such. Different densities have different bearings on the issues at stake. Relations between experienced and factual distances are also an important variable with lasting impact (Hermelin and Rusten, 2007).

A kind of malpractice in this direction is found:

> Nearly all empirical approaches in the recent literature use overall employment data to measure geographical concentration, . . . we will not be able to assess the true underlying distribution of economic activity if we 'blindly' use inappropriate empirical identification strategies.
>
> (Mitze, 2011, p. 14)

A complementary demographic, qualitative aspect is that the population in the designated areas is supposedly growing older (Gløersen et al., 2006). This is most often described as a burden on a diminished share of the working-age cohorts, i.e. a dependency ratio, a measure often used in spite of its weak relevance. It presupposes that age groups have generalised exclusive functions (consumers/producers, needing/providing). Furthermore, it presupposes that specified age groups do actually work and vice versa. It does not consider any further variations within the working group, as part-time or the extent of leisure time. Relevance between countries, regions and time contexts are weak due, for instance, to more general contextual or, more specifically, cultural factors. This includes increased average age through improved health covering the whole life cycle; better health/sounder labour force providing a higher income with more energy, less sick leave, higher productivity, higher education due to longer time horizon; larger total life income; etc. If a deficit appears on the supply side in the labour market, increased income, technical boosting etc., could compensate.

Distance and accessibility

Distance is quite a complicated dimension when entering into exact measurements in multifunctional space. What is measured (i.e. relations to area, place, person) creates increasingly complex calculations. Sometimes turning the analysis on its head – starting out with more generalised and complex characteristics and then venturing into the field of empirical substantiation – clarifies issues. Regions with low densities, dispersed settlements, challenging economic activity patterns and service provisions, return this back to the continuous dynamic processes. Distance and accessibility are natural parameters when discussing peripheries, sparsely populated areas and remoteness. Distance could, at the same time, be a quite simple and straightforward dimension; accessibility, a reflection of it, a complex process and becoming even more complex when turning into policy. The impact of congestion levels and travel speed are aspects when these have "strong methodological disadvantages" (Geurs and Wee, 2004, p. 127).

An interesting dimension of the distance factor, when talking periphery, is that measures are, when increasing, more or less automatically negatively interpreted, needing to be tackled, corrected, by decreasing measures (infrastructure, communication, etc.). As the periphery is located, at best, at the ends of the centre's complementary spokes, it is disadvantaged in several aspects of location and transportation. Physical distance is an analytical approach on its own and reinforced by introducing time and costs as complementary or alternative factors. However, distance-defined peripheralisation also encompasses the idea of relativity, meaning combinations of aspects of distance (physical, transport-time, transport cost) create a situation where some locations appear or become less peripheral while others (where the train does not stop) become more. Infrastructurally based measures analyse the quality of the transportation system, for example average travelling speed on the road network, which could be included in elaborations with a more penetrating analytical ambition. Measures in travel-distance cost calculations most frequently used in core-periphery perspectives. What is noted is that the choice has a direct impact on policy direction and selection (Copus, 2001).

The network (spider web pattern as a metaphor) has a higher density the closer to the core/centre you find yourself. The tendency of the analysis defined by the position of the observer, consumer is guided by a number of essential prerequisites, like the ultimate pattern of the network and intensity of the flows in linkages, defined by timetables (public traffic frequency) or traffic flows (private transport). Using network theory clarifies some of the more intricate patterns exemplified:

> air transport very significantly improves the relative accessibility of areas in the immediate vicinity of an airport, but not for the rest of the regions.
> (Gløersen et al., 2006, p. 10)

The basic pattern, spider web or spokes, does not do much for transversal relations, instead strengthens the dependence on the infrastructural nodes. The significantly longer travel times and expenditures incurred in contacts among the peripheral localities themselves are

> the weakest transport connections with the metropolitan centre – that is, those situated between transport corridors or in the region's periphery.
> (Smetkowski et al., 2011, p. 277)

Structural changes (due to budgetary constraints or reductions) reinforce these patterns. Many other complementary, indirect changes also make an impact on the result. Discussing peripherality through this prism is, of course, self-evident. The relation being the more peripheral, the less accessible. An example found is when environmentally friendly carbon taxes on fuel consumption impose distance-related increased costs, changing the substance of the status of peripherality. Another, the subsidised structures of agriculture overcoming distance to market and other differences in conditions of production, and changes in subsidiary structure create conditions having a far-reaching impact (Hegrenes, 2004, p. 52). However,

> transport costs (reduction) does not outweigh the distant geographical location of these areas.
>
> (Gløersen et al., 2006, p. 2)

This approach does not cover all consequences. The relativity towards competitive advantages between the dimensions of peripheral locations has to be considered. Different ways to go about it indicate different principles for consideration.

Different explanatory factors present different interpretations of access. The concept of accessibility could be defined as to how much effort people use in order to reach a certain function, place or activity. A more practical definition is presented by Elldér and Larsson (2011, p. 2) as "the ease that societal demand and activities can be reached, elsewhere bothering citizens as business and public organizations needs are intended." Accessibility is, apart from modes of transport also, a result of structures and patterns of settlements, and provisions of different types, in themselves. "[A]ssess the usability of accessibility measures in evaluation of both land-use and transport changes, and related social and economic impacts" (Geurs and Wee, 2004, p. 127).

Technical changes will have an impact on centre-peripheral relations, adapting the essence of the concepts, questioning the validity of conventional (spatial) models:

> Technical changes in the field of transport, communication and information technology, together with long-term structural shifts will, in the new century, allow a degree of spatial reorganization of European economic activity.
>
> (Copus, 2001, p. 539)

Sought are "more appropriate 'aspatial' concepts" as defined by Copus. What is noted is their potential for peripheral regions, and, notably a "relief from 'overheating' at the core."

Measures of accessibility could possibly be acceptable as rough social indicators, when evaluating quality of life aspects in society (access as availability). The same pertains to social equity by way of social impact assessments, evaluated if accessibility measures are spatial, if the empirical foundation is differentiated and disaggregated enough. One can identify such categories as:

jobs, food, health and social services, along with the potential for social interaction with family and friends.

(Geurs and Wee, 2004, p. 131)

These down-to-earth aspects could appear in, for instance, distance to school and school bus transports in sparsely and densely populated areas. Compare the municipality of Vilhelmina (SE) with an area of 870 square kilometres and 700 kids in primary school with, for example, the outskirts of Stockholm (Sundbyberg) with 1/1,000 of the area and five times the population. Distance in the periphery demands a choice between very long transports or smaller schools and classes (Hörnlund, 2009). Unfortunately this is also an economic issue.

A reason to activate the accessibility concept in policy contexts is that its improvement stimulates integration between regions and, by this, leads to qualitative development and enhanced and more effective labour market regions (Elldér and Larsson, 2011). However, what kind of characteristics are pertinent, and how should consequences of leaking by linking (drainage effect) be integrated, when the centre, with cheapening transports makes access go two ways and change the centre/periphery relation? Labour markets are a case in point when complementary activities in neighbouring rural regions change the prerequisites for local development. The ultimate and total socio-economic effects of the establishment of transport linkages seems hard to prognosticate. A reversal effect of increased access is also when the local economy opens up for external competition.

Accessibility-indicators measuring the degree of distance/remoteness/market potential are therefore a methodologically central issue, but what they actually measure demands careful consideration. Being remote implies that some valuable quality, asset, resource is far away, in terms of a core, centre. Could being remote be measured by population mass, industrial activity and how does the dimension of distance impact, and when does it appear (Gløersen et al., 2006)? In another contribution, the nature of a market determines the degree, necessity or counterproductive aspects of accessibility. A direct link is found between rural areas and the global arena, where area-specific aspects of tourism, brand food, etc., are competitive assets (ESPON, 2013, p. 40). An important caveat indicated by Elldér and Larsson (2011, p. 16) is the notion of being identified as more or less accessible, i.e. identifying a series of problems pertaining to the areas in question rather than their possibilities, potentials. Using 28 different measures from all over the literature Cheshire and Magrini conclude that "Test statistic value[s] for spatial dependence were highly sensitive to how distance was measured" (2008, p. 19). As discussed and noted, measures of distance and accessibility are complicated when the analysis enters into the nature of the estimated (i.e. points of departure and arrival relations to area, place and person).

If the analysis of the service sector is included, defined to the notion of accessibility, the choice relies on its implications for the present book. The starting points are simple enough, provision and consumption of services. On the personal side, this is based on welfare ideology and policies important for living conditions. Regionally defined solutions in the periphery have been on the public side, private ones being not usually cost-efficient (Edvardsen, 2004). On the organisational side, defined in an alternative and, primarily economically orientated direction, this present in both public and private entities and activities.

Definitions cannot remain on that kind of aggregation. What kind of services in terms of private/public and their nature – face-to-face, online (telephone or net-based) or infrastructural – should be considered? What does quality indicate in terms of continuous, on demand or standby? What is the quality of the demand? Is a critical population mass a good indicator for minimal delivery or optimal efficiency? Definitions on peripherality could and should make a basis for comparisons in at least two directions. Necessary thresholds, as in a population base, or service per thousand, should be based on the substance of consumption or provision.

A large amount of complex and alternative solutions exist. Alternatives are more emphasised in peripheral locations and sparsely populated areas. Frequent solutions are found in unequal relations between the urban levels of supply and local/peripheral needs. In an advanced welfare state, dependency is closely related to the availability of services provided by the centre, making it possible to live in the periphery (Fimreite and Selle, 2006). Basic is where different types of services, etc., are provided. The same types of relations but considered different categories – at first of geographical connotations (settlement structures) and later linked to different collective categories (social, economic etc.) – specify in more detail arguments around methodological delimitations. In general the status (which does include a number of analytical entrances) of the infrastructure (for this discussion read 'transport') range analytically from the non-existence of linkage possibilities to the provision of intensive, high-quality, low-cost networks, creating for the latter the possibility of optimal (given the technical potential) accessibility at a given point in time.

A special aspect in labour statistics notes that the public service sector is more dominant in peripheral labour markets. A more disaggregated analysis will find that this does not reflect all types of services. Some sub-sectors are distinguished by urban locations and urban contexts. For analytical purposes, it would have been valuable to penetrate these dimensions in relation to relevance for general development purposes in alternative contexts.

Information technology and flows have been used and defined as the panacea for aspects of distance and sparsity. At the same time, information has everything to do with interaction. The ICT provides, among other things, a foundation for the creation of new working patterns, appearing in terms of distance work and distance studies. Capacity and intensity, in these kinds of networks, have a tendency of developing from the centre outwards, increasing accessibility in core regions, more than in the peripheral locations focused here. Of interest is the changing pattern of an overall increased accessibility, complemented by new structures and new relations, which do make the jump, passing defined and natural thresholds and prerequisites and by this, creating new opportunities. The market takes care of some of it but sparsity also defines a need for public support:

> the key issue is likely to be human capital (i.e., informing local entrepreneurs of the opportunities, and the training of the local workforce).
>
> (Gløersen et al., 2006, p. 18)

The gap has more to do with qualitative aspects than quantitative. A general description of knowledge as an analytical factor in peripheral and/or sparsely populated areas identifies a lower average level of formal education and lacking complementarity between jobs and job seekers as to education and competence. A general lack of educational opportunities and migratory patterns relating to achieving higher education (brain drain), exacerbates the situation. Formal evaluation and educational aspects are quite straightforward. Educational levels and number of dropouts are measurable. A wider approach, referring to a cultural climate, promoting or demoting educational or general knowledge-driven processes, is argued but seldom analytically approached. The system, the qualifications (pedagogic and social) of the teachers, their organisational priorities and inventories of extracurricular institutions and activities are analytically unreachable. Identifying the crucial role of knowledge makes it remarkable how little qualitative attention is focused on the workings of this parameter in society.

The lack of localised institutional capacity in higher education and research is further exacerbated by budgetary considerations in cutbacks, closures and questionable fusions. Discussions about population levels and other thresholds are necessary to create preconditions for knowledge spillover effects, especially in reference to aspects of centres and centrality of the major part of 'valuable' knowledge caches, seem lacking in substance. The arguments should be qualified, at least, into general and specialised knowledge. It has also possible in-built qualification in regards to distance effects.

> Conversely, dispersed or peripheral organisations are said to be deprived of the advantages of knowledge spillovers because of the costs of overcoming distance barriers.
>
> (Whittam and Danson, 2001, p. 1)

Compensatory patterns of local knowhow, competence or – as it is sometimes called – 'tacit knowledge' are noted, although empirically difficult to qualify or quantify. Their impact on the definitional exercise is intriguing.

The mix of variables – indicators – defining the outcome?

Arguments behind choices of what should or should not be considered in a mixture of variables is a start-up for an investigation into the complicated world of indicators. What is a good indicator? What should it reflect? Definitions, according to the rules of the game, and statistically measurable? Is there a hidden agenda in what is included and what is not? Not only the choices, but also how the choices are interpreted is important. Indicators are a form of presentation where the process and results of comparing is in focus. This is done with an orientation towards different entities in time series, between functional units, often between areas. The indicator as an analytical tool requires a self-analytical approach, and an acceptance that the substance of the method affects the objects compared. Looking for a potential basis for the existence and construction of bias is important, as the results, most often, are far-reaching foundations for policies and practices. This depends on the conscious use of information, how and by whom or using hard-to-identify causalities and giving room for distortions in implementation. How the impact of some types of indicators are affected and interpreted and discussed having the 'periphery' as a thematic approach is a necessity.

There is a lot of politics and future image building taking place within the development process, where state or regional resources are available, with specific connotations and conditions attached and with indirect guidance in the substance of performance indicators and reporting variables. In addition, local, regional political ambitions are defined in general and/or party-related preferences, within the local community. Popular aspects are also participation in the ranking games, preferably position on the high end or advancing upwards.

General and general economic indicators

Basic among these categories are GNP, GDP, GNP/cap and GDP/cap[2] found in arguments linked to economic achievement, and/or the idea of economic growth reflecting development. They are not only popular but also heavily and increasingly disputed. Economic gaps between European regions are, as reported, affecting the assessment of 'improvement' and the 'success' of policy initiatives, the discussion of what kind of value for money (EU cohesion reports) is received (Tarschys, 2011). In many cities, the GDP is being inflated by commuting, and by this, it's deflating surrounding areas. Other examples found in the balance are affected by under-reporting actual production and results in areas with sizeable informal economies.

Differences between metropolitan areas and other regions do not appear the same in varying phases and stages of economic development. This exemplifies a need for evaluating measures used, and here, in and for the periphery. Aggregated values hide important societal processes; using more exact information for the present, the locality or the function is a *sine qua non*. For example, noting a decline in GDP per cap in rural regions between 1995 and 2000, the economic performance is supposedly driven by

> people moving away to urban areas and ageing, lower educational attainment, lower average labour productivity, and overall low levels of public service.
>
> (OECD, 2006b, p. 2)

Or, that income growth on a regional level has a complementary explanation. Migrants have on average higher incomes than those who stay put.

> Since the average income levels are higher in central areas than in the peripheries, centralization through migration contributes to increasing the regional income gap.
>
> (Johansen, 2009, p. 19)

Or, as stated by Hudson (2007), GDP/cap as an indicator of growth, interpreted as development, does not recognise considerations of socio-economic approaches, i.e. aspects, in a more detailed approach with greater impact, in the periphery, than in urban/core areas.

Authorities involved in finance and decision-making evaluate performance on a macro level of aggregation, losing distinctions for different results in different sectors, branches and spatial entities. A focus, as an alternative, on actors, creates a tendency to register or take for granted a smaller number of industries and technologies as motors for economic growth, already from the start. Much of modern economic history seems to be written in such terms. These noted representations have close links with the liberal approach in economy and economic theory. Value, exclusively linked to economic results, is hard to handle without a normative bias. A lot of economic statistics and presentations derives or defines these concepts, making their presence self-reinforcing. Another approach describes the relation between generalised indicators and qualitative aspects of growth. "[H]ealthy or unhealthy growth, temporary or sustainable growth . . . what is required to actually improve the quality of our life?" (Bristow, 2010, p. 94).

The complexity registered in the following, where differences between authorities using different performance indicators, shows up with differentiated impacts. Examples given are well-being, endogenous development, income support, productivity. The choices are ultimately important, as:

> There is research evidence to suggest that rural areas tend to perform more successfully in economic terms against measurements of wellbeing, for example than those of productivity.
>
> (Curry & Webber, 2012, p. 280)

Exemplifying, a major argument that, partly disqualifies these general economic indicators, are that they do not reflect interactions between growth and welfare. Arguments should be considered concerning, changes in wealth, distribution, productivity, incomes, purchasing power etc.

From the sideline enter efforts to consider and evaluate aspects of sustainability and subsidiarity (NUTEK, 2004, p. 11). A need for geographical, social and institutional analysis through reflections of the structure of the economy in spatial/geographical categories is also pertinent. Paul Krugman (1991) and his colleagues introduce a limited spatial dimension into the framework of macroeconomic modelling and the institutional theory of North (1990) that is an ingredient in such orientations.

This is pertinent as the creation of value is supposedly taking place in the centre, especially when it comes to new economic branches, suggesting, that in order to 'catch up' or not 'lose ground', the districts or peripherality has to rely on the ability of the centre or link up with support points in the centre (Onsager and Selstad, 2004, p. 298). On another side of the same discussion, related to cost levels, it is often noted that 'weak' (read peripheral) regions have higher costs for production than necessary (Hegrenes, 2004, p. 48). Thoughts in this direction also develop in EU policy, indicating special qualities in a regional context:

> Our current accounting measure is GNP but this does not effectively cater for the notion of well-being. We need a new way to calculate performance, particularly in the regional context.
>
> (European Commission, 2012, p. 5)

New perspectives cannot, however, be evaluated with traditional methods or measures.

> We cannot move towards a model which caters for . . . leisure time and for nature and resources without changing our method of calculation . . . then regional policy will appear much more useful.
>
> (European Commission, 2012, p. 5)

A theme where perspectives of innovative and related practices are discussed includes the evaluation of how this dimension of development is treated. Why does Norway have such a good performance in productivity growth and value creation, even excluding the oil sector, while R&D expenditures are on such a low level? This could be the result of biased indicators already referred to, of innovation such as patents and sales based on branding, design, high-tech exports, etc. This 'Norwegian paradox', contrasts the Swedish one, characterised by a high R&D investment level, relatively high volume of patents, trademarks, etc., but with seemingly weaker levels of productivity and value creation.

The argument here is that there is still a tendency for manufacturing to stand in the forefront when measuring innovation. Evaluating variables, like patents, scientific publications and investments in R&D enforces this tendency, in spite of the fact that they "have more (and more severe) weaknesses than is often assumed . . . little correlation between the various indicators" (Kleinknecht, Monfort and Brouwer, 2002, p. 109). Having said that, the availability of comparable data estimates innovative development, when R&D and patents only cover a limited aspect of this development. Davies, Michie and Vironen (2012) and Roper, Bryson, Hales and Love (2008) write that this is an analytical problem of crucial importance. Regional differentiation of measured innovation discloses in a Danish investigation a 23 percent stake in the Copenhagen region, 17 percent in northern Jutland and 16 percent of Denmark's southern regions, while in the middle of Jutland and southwestern Själland regions show shares of 11 to 14 percent. Denmark's average total is 18 percent (Lindegaard, 2012, p. 81). This, in itself seems hardly notable, actually quite normal. What it indirectly emphasises is the presence of alternative sources of knowledge inputs to innovation than research. This highlights the relation between one of the major variables used indicating innovation, i.e. R&D, where Copenhagen takes the brunt of capital investment, but does not deliver the same proportionate share.

On the level of the firm, the average level of innovation is not always directly related to the volume of resources spent on R&D. The innovation system processes capture the role of different sources and institutions harvesting also in open innovation processes. An explanation of the Danish innovation paradox found in the peripheral patterns of cooperation compensate for R&D investment. One of the drawbacks, mentioned in the literature, is how rough variables like R&D act as defining variables when operationalising policy. Explanatory power is weak with so many other relevant inputs, although hard to measure, making an innovation process successful: learning, educational mobility, machines and technology. This proposition also includes the need for alternatives. It is reinforced with the doubt of whether, as noted in *The Urban and Regional Dimension of Europe 2020* (European Commission, 2011), patenting really is representative of the diversity of ongoing innovation processes and results. Not all innovations need or qualify as patentable. When it comes to patents, they are probably worse in their coverage and impact, as they do not consider all innovative activities outside the formal span. Unrealised patents are by basic definitions not innovations. Shelved patents or those scheduled for future processing, etc., are the same. Un-patentable changes or products enacted or developed are not registered at all. Can the variable be representative, i.e. "be assumed to be constant across branches or firm size classes" (Kleinknecht et al., 2002, p. 112)? When categorising innovations with technology, non-technological aspects are registered. Extending the picture further to where the level of innovation occurs in the regions and cities identified in Community Innovation Statistics (CIS)[3] statistics, compared with similar information on municipalities and parishes based on where business is conducted and where patents are recorded, the former provides a much more accurate description of spatial distribution. Mitra notes that innovation is important for a majority of small firms, although details are not available for type and value or market impact (Mitra, 2012). "We overestimate innovative activity among firms that collaborate on R&D . . . we underestimate the rate of small firms that innovate. . . . We overestimate the innovation intensity of small-sized patent holders" (Kleinknecht et al., 2002, pp. 112–113).

Breska (2010, pp. 49, 53) states that evaluative practice neglects informal innovative activities in smaller firms. Disaggregation on a regional level is also biased, as reporting is done by the head office. Geographical distinctions are not disclosed, as most of the processes around incremental innovations – small-scale, local – will usually not be considered.

> Rural areas are at the best seen to develop incremental innovations since such areas are associated with institutional thinness, local networks, a lack of investors, SMB-dominance, etc.
>
> (Fløysand and Jakobsen, 2010, p. 109)

There are efforts to improve evaluative methods in order to extend the statistical coverage of innovations, and that from different angles. OECD tries to catch innovation processes by finding indicators describing preconditions in dimensions of the creative climate and structures promoting creative activities. Patents and R&D are only two among a multitude of input factors like product design, trial production, market analysis, training of employees or investment in fixed assets that could be analytically applied (Kleinknecht et al., 2002, p. 110; OECD, 2011a). Branding, patterns and immaterial protection are other ways. Standards could help in another sense as well. Findings recognise different cultures and practices, identifying the concept of innovation. Departments involved in rural development in the regional administration approach the concept with a more down-to-earth approach, partly in conflict with the dominating knowledge status, which has an impact on practice, in interpreting what kind of progression is taking place (Høyer, 2013, p. 216). Noted is that these latter departments seem to be more positive to what is achievable in the periphery.

Indices are also prominent in identifying and describing results within different types of clustering. To exemplify, the following quotation seems significant:

> the author proposes an index that builds upon the actual distance among sample firms in order to detect clusters . . . [and] propose . . . improvements to account for intersectoral linkages and the criteria needed for statistical threshold values in cluster identification.
>
> (Mitze, 2011, p. 14)

He is careful to emphasise that exercises like this should be considered in terms of what we want to learn or measure and why "so that it can be a relevant input for policy-making and evaluation" (Mitze, 2011, p. 14). An example used is different outcomes identifying the existence of clusters using employment or R&D employment information in a number of branches and sectors, where, in regional distribution, high-tech comes out better with the latter. Other combined indicators measuring professional activity, productivity, training, R&D investment, number of patents, etc., are frequent. When entered into combinations, they result, supposedly, in emergent properties.

A definite and alternative step away from the mechanistic approach of different economic indicators is the Human Development Index (HDI). Here variables like life expectancy, analphabetism and relative share of age cohorts in education, etc., provide information of relative development, not, however, covering, future potential. The HPI – Human Poverty Index – includes life expectancy, analphabetism, long-term unemployment and number of people under the poverty level. Approaching aspects of deepening qualitative evaluations – the HPI[4] – the Happy Planet Index, combines an evaluation of how much non-renewable resources of earth that a country exploits and makes this a basis for evaluation of happiness, further identified in questionnaires. The index focuses its attention on quality-of-life aspects combined with resource exploitation.

Contextual considerations

The nature of peripherality changes over time. Places and areas defined as peripheral do not necessarily remain so. Specific policies (long and short term) and exogenously given processes create, for instance, 'limited' functional centres. At the same time, other places and areas, by way of similar processes, become redefined to a status of peripherality or marginality. Change is not a linear projection or causality but also a consequence of complex and cyclical processes. This means that relative changes in places and spaces, changes in the substance of the periphery therefore need longer perspectives on methodology and measurements. Peripherality in time-specific dimensions contributes in a number of different ways to these efforts, finding the substance to the concept in general terms, but also to its uniqueness.

Contextual approaches are found in several directions, and peripherality, sparsity, etc., do or ought to change the rules of the analytical game. Approaches used in regard to phenomena, structures and processes in the European periphery are not automatically relevant for Northern Europe, where sparsity is so much more pronounced and demands other considerations (Jönsson et al., 2007, p. 237).

On the first steps of the Maslowian pyramid are found the basic necessities. Arguments around the lack of direct links between productivity and living standards seems, as mentioned, hard to establish with any certainty; other indicators like prosperity, infrastructure and labour market performance, together with productivity bring possibly an improved understanding. What is noted is the extent of elaborations necessary for analytical quality. Promotions of the idea of a middle-class climbing the pyramid and economic prosperity being replaced by the demands and desires for quality of life are becoming more frequent. This path has a weak scientific frame of reference.

> We have continued implicitly to assume that urban growth will continue to raise our subjective well-being – how we feel about living in cities.
>
> (Morrison, 2011, p. 1040)

Going from material satisfaction to well-being demands different types of progress-indicating standards. Morrison's (2011, pp. 1040–1041) example in this context is excellent:

> The research question is whether one can establish empirically the contribution of place at the city scale and identify those characteristics of the city that contribute positively or negatively to one's level of happiness, satisfaction, and quality of life.

Notes

1 12.5 excluding water has also been found.
2 The remarks about GNP and GDP exemplifying some of the question marks around the concepts does not restrain me from using these designations in descriptive material in Chapters 5 and 8.
3 The Community Innovation Survey (CIS)-based innovation statistics are part of the EU science and technology statistics.
4 Note the similar abbreviations.

5 The urban deconstructed

Introduction

This chapter continues the effort of defining the rural, peripheral and other relevant concepts, started out in Chapter 2. This time the focus is in the discussion of their 'opposites'. The major elements of substance defining the concepts of rural and peripheral are their distinctions as reflections and/or antonyms of other concepts like urban, central, core, etc., here principally through a focus on the urban.

The outline of urban deconstruction is meant to question the nature of the aspect of the generalised urban, especially in its role of qualifying the definition of development (in positive terms), by encompassing agglomerative aspects that form the basis for advanced processes of innovation. A disaggregation of the urban in districts, quartiers, etc., is a direction made with emphasis. An argument around the lack of information distinguishes what lies in the advantages of the city in general – innovation, entrepreneurship, etc. – is highlighted. This chapter favours the idea that disaggregation points to the benefits of certain sub-areas of the city, but, at the same time questions the way to find them. The fact that the frequency of entrepreneurship does vary within the framework of the city is a case in point (Percoco, 2012, p. 343). This chapter searches for a deconstruction that identifies those parts, functions, relations, that actively contribute. At the same time it does not leave the negative, the obstacles to the same processes, outside the analysis. It disqualifies the idea of a generalised concept of 'urban' as containing any explanatory power to an analytical approach towards 'non-urban' qualities, and points a finger towards similar conceptual processes as to core and centre/periphery.

Other concepts, within the wider meta-version of urban is the 'city' and/or 'town'. They are and contain nuances, some of them quite important in a dichotomous presentation. For example, as administrative entities distinguished by measures of population density, towns sometimes are categorised as smaller than cities. The city sometimes describes the centre of the urban, as a place of economic activity or exchange, or a place/way of life, symbolic for the urban culture.

> For analytical purposes, a city definition based on a minimum density and number of inhabitants has been developed jointly by the European Commission and the OECD.
>
> (European Union, 2011a, p. 1)

This exercise will make it possible to search further for another developmental logic and for rules of the game in that endeavour of being able to avoid the limitations of the undefined urban.

Being peripheral or rural relates to something that is central, according to certain – but not explicit – specifications of the centre/urban/core. Comparisons of the former are done through the expectation of simultaneously substantiating their common opposite. In order to do this, however, it is necessary to qualify the urban/town/city, as it is many things, and not all of them true. Counterparts are also complemented by their unequal relations (read also impact). The periphery, and especially the agricultural periphery, explicitly serve the core/urban. The very complex interaction is rooted in historical processes voiced in terms from conceptual interdependence to policy implications. This chapter argues for ideas, presented later, on the holism of complementarity against the uneconomic and antisocial aspects of the bipolarity, where one 'governs' the other. The present:

> forc[es] a gap between existing forms of knowledge and the creative contexts out of which new imaginaries can emerge.
>
> (Le Heron, 2013, p. 1195)

The nature of the former approach is exploited in policy development all the time and uses policy (geographical coverage), simultaneously accepting ladders or scales of centrality and peripherality. Methodologically, this is of interest as it accepts the concepts/terms as elements also in continuities, qualifying the analysis. Among others, a major argument already in the start-up of Chapter 2, appears in the often sloppy day-to-day simplifications of the dichotomies. An example is the relation to other peripheries or categories of peripheral functions on a scale that could redefine the nature of the periphery as such.

It is also important, in the practical application of the concepts, that the substance is built by actors/groups (read interests, roles, etc.) differently, with subtleties and nuances in interpretation. It is of analytical consequence whether the functional and spatial periphery is simultaneously defined. The conceptual problem then appears as a functional consequence of the behaviour of and in the core. An example of this, with an increased focus on dynamic interpretation, is discussed in terms of dependency and qualified in the ways to operationalise it. Generalising a phenomena disclosed in the New Zealand, agricultural sector.

> little is known about the processes whereby actors and interests politicize decisions-making in these domains.
>
> (Le Heron, 2013, p. 1192)

Is there any proof of conscious analytical endeavours in defining the core, from the peripheral perspective? "As a consequence, within urban research, urban spaces are taken for granted and need no explanation" (Stenbacka, 2011, p. 237). The periphery then tends to be the opposite of the main focus of attention, although its dichotomous reflection lacks analytical substance. The periphery also possibly lacks any attention at all – so the economic/social system defines, analyses, establishes policies for the centre or core and the periphery as 'the other', the rest, the remainder, a reflection. An example is the concept of 'core cities' or 'core regions', where the antonym 'peripheral' refers to a subordinate conceptual relationship with and within categories like cities, hinterland, region, which are undetermined or instinctively defined as residuals. The intellectual history in geography and sociology behind 'the other' can be drawn upon to examine relations between places, people/s and status/power. Prominent in this discourse was the late Edward Said (1979).

As noted, a major argument behind the focus on the urban and urbanity[1] is the role it is supposed to play in economic development (read growth) in society. Extensively approached elsewhere, highlighting the stereotypes of rural/agricultural profiles and provisions of surplus labour for the centres, historical realities are somehow modified in modern interpretations. Potter et al. (2008, p. 393) refer to Lipton's (1977) argument about the rich exploiting their core position to provide for their further enrichment by denigrating the rural poor. Consequences sought have been unequal trading relationships and direct control, which are in themselves also instruments for a continuing urban bias. A representative collection of some of the main arguments found is based on the concentration of population (labour) and consequential higher per capita income levels, a more efficient labour market, flows of workers, scale economies in the provisions of public service and similar amenities (OECD, 2011b).

It is natural to investigate the nature of these general propositions. Smetkowski et al. (2011) refers to theories (Chapter 3) on polarised growth encompassing centrifugal and centripetal forces. Cities/cores/centres are continuously discussed as defining economic growth on both a regional and national level as, they do in the international economy. These kinds of statements are very common, but there are grounds to doubt some of the claims of an altogether too-close relation between economic growth and centralisation/urbanisation *per se* and to highlight the more multifaceted role of the urban/centre and economic growth (Danson and de Souza, 2013) and "A concentration of activity is neither a necessary nor a sufficient condition for high growth" (European Union, 2011a, p. 4).

Another approach that relates to what is written above is a definition of periphery and marginality based on what these functions do not have, what they are lacking or what they are deprived of. An interesting entrance to the discussion here is the dichotomy of urban/non-urban, i.e. not having the characteristics or features of that core. The idealised 'urban' described, for example, in terms of the *robust* region enumerating a number of qualities as described in Chapter 2, is not present in the periphery. A preliminary conclusion is that the situation in the periphery, when not identified with assertiveness, and using the dominant tradition when approaching the theory of development, particularly in its growth and urban orientation, defined as a role model lacks relevant and important analytical aspects.[2] The 'urban', being generalised to such a degree, is hiding that urban is many things and not all of them beneficial (Danson and de Souza, 2013).

> Urban areas are places where the economy grows, jobs are created, pollution is generated and scarce resources are used.
>
> (European Commission, 2014)

The urban-rural dichotomy

In order to deepen and visualise the complexity in the discussion – at the same time excluding that stage and version of the analysis – the possible outer extensions of the bipolarity are exemplified here. On the one hand, there are numerous examples where the periphery extends into increasingly extreme representations, exemplified by the following quote:

> a *marginalised rural periphery* with problems of relative poverty, social anomie and decay [stands] in contrast with the mainstream vital and creative, renewed, rich and high-tech, global post-industrial urban centres.
>
> (Lindegaard, 2012, p. 78, my emphasis)

The Eurostat's more strict definition of 'outermost' (synonyms: outmost, extreme, ultimate, utmost, farthest), appears in EU statistics describing primarily insular regions lying outside of the European delimitation of administrative regions. On the other side, distinctions of megapolis and metropolitan are defined in population and territorial coverage, urban entities in special categories, sometimes marked by 'unique' positions.

To continue with the basic argument, within the demographic structure, there is an image of the urban as compared with the rural, based on major urbanities. To question that: when looking at Sweden's ten million people, about 75 percent of the population lives in small towns and in what is statistically described as rural areas. So, what is the urban? In statistical descriptions and characterisations, definitions of the urban vary considerably across countries and do not usefully translate into each other, so systematic comparative coverage is not immediately available. France identified 'agglomerations' back in 1831. The concept resembles something of the present concept of city-region. Taking this as a starting point and applying it (for comparative purposes) on other geographical entities or contexts creates problems (Magrini and Cheshire, 2008). The other end of the bipolarity does not clarify the issues. Take, for instance, notions of authenticity, serenity and order, with ingredients of nature and landscape. The rural here, includes areas close the urban, while remote and 'genuine' rural has by definition "rural populations as traditional and stagnant" (Eriksson, 2008, p. 372). Part of the earlier discussion also noted the urban and rural interactive influences as problematic within a dichotomous presentation.

> The geographic, economic and human dynamics of rural areas are increasingly influenced by urban development (i.e. urban or semi-urban economic activities, infrastructure and habitat, patterns of human and material flows).
>
> (Dax, 2014, p. 61)

What is indicated here and before in Chapter 2, is that there is no simple rural-urban dichotomy, but a continuum between them, where 'urban influences diminish with distance' (Monsson, 2013, p. 6), and where there are many designations of the rural, not all of them linked to distance. However, note the wording used – 'urban influences' – what about the other way?

In the research programme 'Regional development' launched by the Research Council in Norway about ten years ago, the 'Distriktsnorge' (District Norway) comprised those parts of the country that were not included in the large city areas around Oslo, Bergen, Trondheim and Stavanger. The policy was focused by this category, had a lot in common with what other countries call 'rural' (Berg and Lysgård, 2004, p. 63). This reference avoids one of the problematic issues though, i.e. the definition of in-betweens of some categories of suburban spaces, villages or small towns. Creed and Ching (1997) refer to a concept of 'shallow' rural as something in between 'deep rural' and the city. The problem was, and still remains, whether there is any one-dimensional polarity exemplified in the change within the urban, reaching for defined positive elements of the rural and vice versa – "a hyperpreservationist suburban culture which needs to redefine itself in relation to nature in a highly particularistic and exclusive way" (Marsden et al., 2002, p. 810). Although gradual descriptions have had to include discrete elements, "the politico-administrative need to define hamlets, villages, towns and cities has involved the imposition of clear thresholds and boundaries" (Potter et al., 2008, p. 405).

Different representations still reinforce the two as defining poles, sometimes on a simplified continuum that reaches from the most urban parts of the city, in a continuity, to the most rural parts of the countryside (Almaas and Elden, 1997, p. 8). The scientific controversy of the idea of the continuum is highlighted by Johnston (2000, p. 721) "demolishing the concept of rural-urban continuum". Although, in a positive ambition, statements point out the need for differentiated policies (Ølberg, 2012, p. 45), venturing in the right direction but not in the extent and, partly, manner needed. Categorical thinking prevails and affects decision-making and policy definitions. It is evident that constructions of rurality and urbanity are intimately interlinked and defining each other. Social, cultural, economic, etc., changes in the city and in the countryside seem to eliminate some of the former, sometimes stigmatised, categorical differences. "'Rural' localities share causal processes with 'urban' places, with substantial (intra-'rural') dissimilarities in socio-economic determinants" (Hoggart, 1988, p. 36). A concept of 'rurbanisation' developed where a mutual influence creates a hybrid or structural change on both sides (Strøksnes, 2006). But it does also recreate conflicting attributes as a highly cultural phenomenon.

> Consequently, the rural/urban distinction signifies far more powerfully than physical appearances suggest; inhabitants of areas where town and country seem nearly indistinguishable may nevertheless elaborate a difference through extensive cultural discourse.
>
> (Creed and Ching, 1997, pp. 2–3)

The substance of the continuum has provoked very little scientific attention, in spite of its significance, connotations and important ingredients in the construction of the categories. A good example is the category of peri-urban appearing in the outer fringes of the suburbs, continuously moving outwards as the functional urban region extends (Monsson, 2013). The material and immaterial are constantly tested also through the job market:

> In fact, with the severe decrease in employment within agriculture, rural areas have increasingly become settlement communities for people who reside in rural areas and work in urban areas.
>
> (Sørensen, 2012, p. 885)

It is also argued that technical development is removing practical obstacles by reducing defining differences and attitudes. How far this process will go has a clear spatial distinction and no immediate bearings on issues where the continuum of urban/rural links with degrees of peripherality. The importance of it is the argument in itself, raising the point of where a general qualitative change in experienced space appears as important enough to have implications on analysis and therefore on policy and policy implementation.

The dichotomy is multifaceted, both in a functional and geographical sense, and contains a number of interesting and consequential variables in both their structural/static and their process/dynamic versions. Approaching it from a societal/social analysis, a general contextual framework with historical connotations seems necessary. Such an approach discloses some taken-for-granted preconditions and results. A classical power and control definition is found in the nucleus. The state is at the centre with agenda-setting powers, the prerogative of legitimate violence, control of knowledge production and transfer, and the economy, with its distinctions of structure, of control of income generation and distribution. Locating this in the abstract, a functional and possibly geographical centre of a specified society is analytically feasible, and interesting from the present, structural point of view.

Aspects of urban size and economic growth

Another approach refers to the simplified connection between urbanisation, the urban, economic growth and development and needs some further elaboration. It is taken for granted that there is a causality! Large cities are the centre and the norm. Growing cities an indication of positive societal change, simply defined in terms of economic productivity and therefore in the forefront of economic growth:

> cities are critical drivers of national and aggregate growth. The contribution to aggregate growth of just the 2% 'hub' regions – mainly composed of the largest OECD urban regions – is approximately one-third. Their large and critical contribution largely reflects agglomeration economies.
>
> (OECD, 2011a, p. 129)

In policy and ideological terms, this usually appears in arguments against attempts to hinder further urbanisation or the spontaneous and continuing growth of large cities, as this stands counter to the continuation of economic growth. A lot of arguments and facts are emphasising the need to qualify and question this generalised proposition. It is, as a start, notable that countries and regions being on the top of the list in terms of population and urbanisation (increase) are not necessarily in the same division in terms of economic growth or welfare.

> Despite the strong overall performance of metro regions, over three out of five saw their GDP per head drop between 2007 and 2010 relative to the national level. Smaller metros lost most ground with 74% of them declining relative their country. Also second-tier metros suffered with 54% losing ground. Only capital metro showed a stronger performance with only 30% losing ground.
>
> (European Commission, 2011, p. 15)

Noting this fact implies that EU Framework Programs and Horizon 2020 are missing the major target for changes in the sphere of innovation processes, at the same time as combatting high unemployment, which ultimately so far has had consequences with territorial impact and in the urban structures. They have been directed to existing growth or 'excellence' centres, at present found in a somewhat dated quote:

> 'islands of innovation', namely Greater London, Rotterdam/Amsterdam, Ile de France, Frankfurt, Stuttgart, Munich, Lyon/Grenoble, Turin and Milan. By default rather than design the Framework Programme serves to reproduce the gap between poor and prosperous regions.
>
> (Morgan, 1997, p. 496)

Cities are reaching points that are no longer providing increasing returns and thus are becoming less competitive. Demographic concentration, not always the most desirable outcome, and external economies of scale overtaken by external diseconomies with congestion play a major role. The argument focused for the agglomeration economies and for funding their further development is questioned, payoffs are not always self-evident, while policies focusing on downsizing or limiting population growth, could, if implemented, actually realise positive agglomerative economies (OECD, 2011a). When discussing volumes in terms of general economic effects, national perspectives and capacity limitations, generalised conceptions do not consider the details of who, when, where and especially not how. The assumption of higher productivity in big cities brought about by economies of scale being a 'primary' basis for economic growth, should be questioned, or at least qualified (Potter et al., 2008). For instance, a catalytic element is the establishment of smaller firms, an outcome not necessarily better in an environment where costs and prices are normally higher, discouraging new entrances (Delfmann et al., 2014).

How then is urban size and growth measured?[3] Is it a rate of increase? Is there an optimal size? Are there any quality considerations? In the centre of the argument stands the question – what drives economic growth? A causality is generally present, where general population growth sets conditions for both relative and general growth (ACANALYS, 2011). A much better answer is found in the statement of not all cities and not forever. Cities (large or small) do not coincide automatically with innovation and entrepreneurship, the present formula for successful development. Not all cities are good for innovation and entrepreneurship. It also means that not even the 'good' ones are always good. One of six cities in the world are decreasing in population. Size is not always an automatic answer.

> [U]rban regions beyond a certain level of GDP per capita tend to experience a deceleration of growth rates. Nonetheless, one may also observe the divergence among a group of urban regions recording fast growth with higher-than-average levels of GDP per capita.
>
> (OECD, 2011a, p. 38)

There is no doubt, that urban growth defines a kind of competitive status, an attraction, which can be short-lived or stretch out through centuries. An interesting phenomenon is that "small urban regions and the rural regions have a higher share of innovating, knowledge-intensive firms than the large urban regions" (Isaksen and Onsager, 2010, p. 227). The authors note a partial explanation in a higher rate of funding in the former, a proposal that could and should be investigated further. They also note that quality of innovation differs as well as firm foundation rates, to the advantage of the latter.

Two 'geographies' may exemplify this claim. The city's relative position in specific economic-geographic structures defines much of the city's process and progress. It also serves as an interactive element in the formation of this structure and process. The explanatory value of the general geographical context of, for instance, the EU and NAFTA, analytically compared with other designated environments, such as the European Banana or cities in countries such as Kenya, Ethiopia and Argentine, all have their, not always prosperous, unique logic.

The other explanatory complex of factors refers to the city logic of growth, promoted under the noted catch-all phrase of 'agglomerative economies', extended to 'urban economies', is not always substantiated. For example, categorising cities with in-migration and economic growth, cities with growth and shrinking population and "Cities within urban areas of complex shrinkage, where both demographic and economic decline can be experienced" (European Union, 2011a, p. 17).

It could be argued as Ølberg (2012) does, that it is not the resources as such, but the level and form of their combination that is important. The logic also encompasses break-off points "as when congestion and other diseconomies begin to outweigh the advantages of agglomeration)" (OECD, 2011a, pp. 35–36). Cities reach a point where they no longer provide increasing returns-to-scale and thus become less competitive. Further concentration is not always the optimal outcome. External economies of scale not always present. "[V]ery large urban areas such as Mexico City, Istanbul or Seoul, but also more advanced cities like Milan, are unable to fully exploit the benefits of concentration" (OECD, 2009b, pp. 31–32).

Encouraging more concentration (i.e. higher density) evidently seems to be a policy with some questions marks at best. In urban areas with more than 1.5 million inhabitants within OECD with averages noting higher per capita GDP, there is not higher than average national annual growth rates (OECD, 2009b, pp. 29–30). Approaching the same issue from another angle, the global 'South' annual growth rates of urban population are well in excess of 2 percent per annum. Both Africa and Asia are characterised by urban growth rates higher than 4 and even up to 8 percent. This is a concept of population surplus or over-urbanisation appearing. Push factors in the countryside are starvation and escape from a general hard life, migrating just for the glimmer of hope, for some better opportunities. Urbanisation does not automatically indicate that jobs and resources develop in a needed pace. Very few countries are able to handle the massive migratory flows that this type of modern urbanisation encompasses, and those that possibly could, do not have to. Among the results are the huge (numbers and scale) of squatter areas. This gives rise to the connected idea that increasing population densities are often associated with cities in the developing world, whereas population is often declining in the core cities in the 'developed world'. Central is the fundamental change in the nature of urbanisation in the present day, compared with historical variants. The nature of the urbanisation processes should be considered in much more detail and on a basis of contextual, temporal, spatial and functional characteristics. Then talk about a drain from the periphery and its supposed value for society in a more comprehensive, inclusive, societal development, will be severely questioned. In such discussions and collaborative research, participants outside the capitals and metropolitan areas are more likely to question whether the unchallenged and constant claim for success of economic growth where centralisation/urbanisation takes place, is consistent with reality. Related to this is whether the urban/centre is a consequence of or is a prerequisite to economic growth as there are opportunity costs to the attendant decisions over public expenditure and investment financing. The important thing in this challenge, scratching the surface, is what is measured and why, with the proposition that conclusions are far from self-evident.

As to economic growth, expanding urban regions are achieving faster than the rural average. What is not explicitly noted is the fact that a large number of rural regions grow faster than the average urban region. Higher income levels are a fact, but not economic growth:

> there is no consistent relationship between urban concentration and economic performance.
>
> (OECD, 2009b, p. 17)

Absolut and relative numbers can also play games. Garcilazo, Martins, and Tompson (2010) argue that production capabilities of lagging regions are just as important as in big cities, and aggregate growth for a national economy depends also, on maximising the growth potential of lagging regions. The impact of regions with high GDP levels does, in many cases (over half), contribute a smaller share (<25%) to the national wealth, while lagging regions contribute significantly more (85% of OECD countries) (OECD, 2009b, p. 32). Noting further:

> Between 2000 and 2008, only two out of five metropolitan areas experienced higher productivity growth than the other regions in their country.
>
> (European Commission, 2011, p. 9)

Metropolitan regions seem, in general terms, under-performing, showing a slowdown in growth rates, a condition far from investigated enough. Turning the coin, the fastest growing are not necessarily those most densely inhabited. There are a number of cases that indicate that existing growth is an effect of efficient and long-term mobilisation, defined in terms of the specificities and uniqueness of a specific urbanity. Success for a development process emanates from many sources, not value creation and innovation alone. Within the flows of global ups and downs, the future of the single, unique, city is ultimately following people, resources and activities (Ølberg, 2012).

There are also some connected aspects frequently returned to that have to do with negative implications: congestion, pollution, etc. Considering this as indirect economic, long-term effects, a comprehensive societal analysis should be done. The point where no further net contribution is achieved and analytically disaggregated should be of strategic interest. Other effects, on the cost side, are reflections linked to arguments about the environmental footprint. In a more encompassing approach, the nucleus of production and consumption is also a reflection of resource utilisation. This questioning the geographic capacity to accommodate, and definitely not compensate, for environmental impact.

> Natural ecocycles, especially those for waters, are being disrupted by a lack of natural soil and wetlands. The scarcity of land within cities creates pressure for an uncontrolled expansion outside the city cores driven by price rather than environmental considerations. Water generation leads to land being used for landfills. The concentration of fine particles in the air has adverse effects on health. Noise pollution is amplified by concentrations of activities, in particular transport, and the use of hard, sound-reflecting materials, causing health problems.
>
> (European Union, 2011a, p. 27)

Another approach of interest is to evaluate to what degree major cities have a structural impact on land utilisation/exploitation in general. The exploitation of a growing city in the way of water demand, quarrying and pollution, to loss of valuable soil resources extends much further than the city-region (Potter et al., 2008, p. 439). In a study on the ecological footprint of cities, the resource consumption and waste assimilation estimated for areas serving the 29 largest cities in the Baltic area, ranged from 565 to 1,130 times the cities themselves.

The urbanites in the city require supportive ecosystems outside the city (Folke, Jansson, Larsson and Costanza, 1997). The hinterlands appear here in a picture of exploitation, social and economic inequalities in relation to the proper 'city' (Tomaney et al., 2010, p. 620). There is a counter approach where urbanisation, in general, and the overwhelming growth of megacities with nearly 500 cities with over one million people and several with more than 20, forwards an argument for a positive impact towards a transition to a green economy, by way of increased density and consumption of less energy being achievable in synergies not available in more sparsely populated areas (OECD, 2011a). The dense city stands then as a role model when combatting climate change or forwarding a green economy. Describing a change in the nature of urbanisation and its likely outcome in 2050, the OECD report (2011a, p. 128) argues for the advantage of density in creating efficient logistical solutions for electricity and transportation, because the synergies found in an urban solution are "more likely to deliver green growth than a wide economic approach only" (OECD, 2011a, p. 128). The likelihood of such a scale of restructuring is questionable.

Some examples of deconstructing the urban

The historical perspective develops and describes another part of the present approach, i.e. the relation between cities through synergies, competition, hierarchies, etc. This contributes to the specific identities of individual towns and their involvement in the distributional patterns of and in economic, political and social processes and structures. The hierarchy of places and their relations and dependence upon each other and, on the appearance of these within a geographical and functional context has an important impact on the analysis. The positioning of a specific place is a historical consequence and dependent on the preconditions that formerly existed, differentiating in many instances the focus of analysis. Further discerned are the pull-effects and analytical products resulting from identifying the specificities of attraction of power, control and resources. As these, in turn, mobilise investment capital and create the potential of an international market for products and services, thus both demand and create potentials in a kind of spiral evolutionary process. As a further caveat, the rank is and, continuous to be, relative to forces of economy, politics, etc., on a global level, not guaranteeing the node its position, as the competition is severe. They "may well already be in the problematic situation which its periphery has already long been in, namely that their population is too small to achieve critical thresholds for a self-generating economic development" (Westlund, 1998, p. 57, my translation). Whatever that is?

World cities, in loose terms, have become control centres for information, cultural production and financial decision-making and flows, and function policy-wise as role models for aspiring and specialised cities, for activities and organisations, for resources, etc., lower down the urban hierarchy, although not too low. The position is a combination of several aspects of presence: the presence of large-scale enterprises or conglomerates, organisations of international repute and importance (public, private and institutional), results of the physical concentration of decision-making in large-scale strategic terms and, not the least – where sub-processes are combined with historical timing – crucial decision-making. Capitals (found within the mentioned category) play a special role in this. Something to be qualified as well, is the relativity of their position:

> The comparative advantage of metro regions is strongest in the Member States of Central and Eastern Europe, where metropolitan areas often have a level of productivity more than 50% higher than in the rest of the country. However, this often only applies to the capital region.
>
> (European Commission, 2011, p. 9)

The awareness, or should one say priority, is self-reinforcing, as the government/state strengthens these tendencies with out-of-proportion allotments of extra finance in crucial areas of the capital's development. "Barca and McCann (2010) argue that 'agglomerations are the effect of billions of dollars-rupees-euros-renminbi of taxpayers' money used by governments to boost agglomerations'" (OECD, 2011a, pp. 196–197). Of functional importance in this concern are international airports, high-speed railways, subways, special investments in place-enhancing activities like investments for major cultural and sport activities like the Olympics and World Cup. I turn to essential public services, financed to a large degree by the state and through tax-based budgets, the view presented and excuse given is that big cities in themselves are positive seedbeds for economic growth, which is one of the issues being questioned in this chapter:

> The cumulative effect of the central government's direct investments in primary cities often dwarfs that of the subsidies provided to politically less important regions.
>
> (OECD, 2011a, pp. 196–197)

The role of smaller and medium-sized cities, constantly referred to, but far from defined in detail or meticulously analysed, act as rural centres and small-town networks function as hubs for services, trade and administration.

> The urban hierarchy is a very well established empirical fact for which we have no satisfactory explanation.
>
> (Cheshire, 2006, p. 1240)

Another dimension of importance for the present discussion is the interrelationships between different cities, within the national contexts concerning connections between the capital and other major centres. This also embraces mono- versus polycentrism, and includes aspects of functional differentiation and degrees of complementarity. Such issues appear in the symbolism of growth engines – the capital dominating secondary towns in its hinterland – or in the multiplication of diversified structures. These arguments appear from the reading of Fimreite and Selle (2006).

Urbanisation and reflections on sub- and counter-urbanisation

Urbanisation, in general historical terms, is identified as an inevitable, fundamental and positive process and a logical part and consequence of the industrialisation process, and later as a backbone to the process of further modernisation. Of importance is, as already described, the interlinkage between this process and issues associated with the productivity in the rural sector. The successive mechanisation of the countryside increased the momentum of change and created preconditions for the urban exodus. The modern phase, in comparison with the old classical exploitation and utilisation of an agricultural surplus, turns to an accumulation of profits based on trade and the increased specialisation of production and the ultimate control over resources and decision-making.

Two outlining processes could be apparent: historical-descriptive and process-analytical. To understand a specific urban constellation, there is a need to know reasons for its appearance and the conditions for its early development, i.e. the specific processes, in their generalisable perspectives. The processes have changed in nature and the sources of the flows are no longer found in the countryside, but in smaller and medium-sized cities and on the international arena, and further provoked by other factors than industrialisation and the transfer of labour power to the manufacturing industry (Johansson, 2012, p. 11). Still, the nature of the beast is an appearing dominance of the urban entities, in 1900 comprising 13 percent, in 1950 29 percent and in 2009 passing the mark of half of the earth's population. Disaggregating that, European urbanisation reached almost three-quarters in 2015. Population increases and redistribution led to the consequential absolute, physical growth of urban areas. There are a number of ways to technically describe, define and substantiate urbanisation. Exemplified here are three:

- Demographically – as the share of the population who live in urban communities. An analytical complication could be the rationale for giving city privileges.[4]
- Behaviourally – or ways of living as a basis for definition.
- Structurally – definitions refer to manners of relations between functions, branches, activities.[5]

The definition of what actually appears – forming physical and material patterns – and the complexity of the interactive sub-processes all need to be considered. This is exemplified through powers to take tribute/tax, control of labour, forceful means via religious and military acquisitions, specialisation and work differentiation, cultural and civilisational processes, necessary complementary changes in the social fabric, development and increasing numbers of everything, growing concentration, popularisation of sustenance other than agriculture: 'city culture'. Based on the appearance of an integrated world system, the organisation of the origins of trade and more traditional aspects of economic interchange are administered through colonial, imperial and geopolitical strategies.

In a presentation like this, it is of value to extend the description to major historical urbanities like Rome, Venice, etc., in order to enlarge on the multifaceted aspects of urbanisation as process/es in all its/their complexities.[6] In the 17th century, the most important cities were London, Amsterdam, Antwerp, Genoa, Lisbon and Venice. In the 18th century, it was Paris, Rome and Vienna; in the 19th century names like Berlin, Chicago, Manchester, New York and St Petersburg took a step forward. Cities developed on the locations of delegated state powers: churches, military establishments, marketplaces and production sites, which all later came to produce their own intra- and interconnected logic(s). All of this was developed within a framework of societal elites associated with relative freedom from feudal lordships and the establishment of professional groups, crafts and guilds. The development of different service facilities included banking of central prominence. Banks representing a fundamental link between functions and gatherings of people. Instrumental to the urbanisation process were also different aspects of colonialisation, creating, among other things, political-administrative structures through technological networks and transports, which started out through staple towns and markets. At a certain stage of production development, waterways (temporarily channels) were the main thoroughfares and urbanities along those were temporarily important, the changed technology making them disappear into the backwaters in the shadow of the restructuring economic growth process. Logistical patterns of different characters remain important. The process related to changes in functional importance and today a logic – less based on trade and more on financial functions like head offices, international banks, administration – functions on an international level with international organisations in general.

The point is that as the nature of the urbanisation process changed, the pattern of the outcome in city/urban structures changed. In terms of the theme covered in this book, the nature of the ongoing migration processes are considered in much more detail and because of temporal, spatial and functional characteristics an important new motor and also a new kind were developed.

Differentiated entrances will be used as approaches to urbanisation. Some of those relate to different categorisations in production or economic systems. For example, the extent of the geographical labour market influences the spatial inertia of production, the organisation of production, the separation of production and consumption, the spatial differentiation of consumption. All aspects include in the circulation process goods, money, labour with the necessity of some kinds of spatial transfers in time. The rationale is to reduce the impact of time and space fundamental cost-saving ambitions.

In order to describe more than define the advantageous – or, maybe more neutral – processes taking place in the urban context, functional descriptions (as the agglomerations are continuously referred to) are used. Alternative processes appear in modern, industrial societies developing in terms of urban sprawl and/or counter-urbanisation. Issues around urban sprawl are numerous, like attractiveness, infrastructure, resource efficiency, level-defined service provisions, quality of agricultural land exploited, planning regulations (European Union, 2011a).

Part of the structural patterns and processes in this movement are identified as a middle-class exodus (Andersson, 2007).

A different and contrary picture promoted, is where the link with the hinterland is reduced in importance, marginalised, although still providing the inputs crucial for the urban/regional development found elsewhere. This suggestion is forwarded with a question mark as the labour market region, defined by the centre, and the infrastructure integrate even more territories. At the same time seemingly controversial voices are raised, referring to severed metropolitan ties with the *rurban* hinterland, becoming itself self-sufficient. A viewpoint ignoring the dependence on behalf of the peripheral parts of the hinterland in terms of services provided by the city and the dimensions of sub-urbanities links with a wider labour market. An asymmetry could possibly be recognised, but in the reduced reliance of the city core specifically. Analysis and discussion are ongoing.

This links to the upcoming section on theoretical contributions, where the bipolar relations between the city and its surroundings are scrutinised in their impact on growth in general and uneven growth in particular. Here, one of the doctrinal ideas through decades and even centuries has changed focus but not attention, i.e. the hinterland around the city, first feeding, providing labour and then being part of a suburbanisation process, sometimes defined in terms of counter-urbanisation "whether counter-urbanisation is a retreat from urban life or whether it is in fact the spread of urban lifestyles into rural areas" (Bosworth, 2010, p. 969). This simultaneously pushes the hinterland frontier further out from the centre.

In the post-war period, the forces of agglomeration have weakened, while those of dispersal have gained strength. The centre as a prominent structural characteristic was replaced by new emerging metropolitan areas, where suburban development appeared as prominent parts of a process of decongestion when the industrial cities reached too high population densities. The quality of the suburb is still a matter of contention. The fact that it is included in the concept of urban and even more so, the city-region, needs qualifications. Röe (2009, p. 43) has studied the suburbs as places in themselves, noting differences among them.

> We call these in-between cities. These spaces now appear as the most dynamic and problematic forms of (sub)urbanization . . . a wild and often unexplainable mix of uses untypical for either the inner city or the classical suburb, they present landscapes of extreme spatial and social segregation.
>
> (Young, Wood and Keil, 2011)

Referring to examples of cities earlier in decline, there is another picture needing a visit, the revitalisation or resurgence of some cities: "Intra-urban dynamics, i.e. the relative decline or growth of core or inner cities compared to their larger functional areas, are as important to consider and understand as overall growth or decline" (European Union, 2011a, p. 18). Reasons for the decline are one-sidedness or specialisation, not keeping up with contemporary technology and other processes, losing out in the continuous battle for market shares. The fact is that technical conservatism is permeating power structures and cultures characteristic from early days of development, making efforts to change and revitalise a complex one, turning out 'new' agglomerations, gathering new competitiveness, attracting front-line and growing activities. This phenomenon of agglomeration appears in different contexts and in different variants, not easily adapted to dominant urban theory making it

> a hard concept to define precisely and the evidence suggested that . . . far from universal, even uncommon, and – more significantly – its causes [are] not clearly understood.
>
> (Cheshire, 2006, p. 1231)

So the notion of former industrial urban decline should be qualified by noting fundamentally changed characteristics of and in, for example, Dublin, Glasgow, Madrid, Birmingham, Leeds and London, among several others.

Aspects of the urban structure

Structural change is often described in abstract terms, their urban, regional or distant outcomes vary fundamentally and substantially in terms of time, place and function. An important characteristic pertains to the nature of the development in itself. It introduces dimensions of structural preconditions and fragments of generalised processes. It is possible to visualise in models generalising centrifugal and centripetal forces or transitionary phases of such distinctions. Specialisation of city sectors in geographical and functional terms is clearly distinguishable.

A nucleus for the discussion here is what it is, in the urban structure that creates the 'good growth' in an economic sense, i.e. an innovative and entrepreneurial environment. A number of potentially interesting excursions, as well as necessary explorations of the city's internal structure and structural flows, could be considered. Basic structural and institutional conditions provide little or no basis for predicting either the rise of such dimensions or the way they function. Despite similar circumstances of cities in general, the ability to forecast their future positions is not really possible, although efforts in this direction could be found. Examples like Kogler (2015, p. 708) are found, noting that creative industries are located in 'dense, mixed-use neighbourhoods' close to the city core, while 'science-based' ones are located in the 'suburbs', in turn characterised by low-density, single-use neighbourhoods.

There is a tradition of establishing theoretical principles for the internal organisation of the city. Park, Burgess and McKenzie (1925) outlined a simple model of concentric zones based on principles of functionality: competition, dominance, invasion and succession. In the centre is the CBD (Central Business District) and the out-going spokes are transport routes, defining secondary centres with commercial and social hubs. Outside of the centre, a transition zone, expecting to become part of the centre through changed profit margins is realised by the invasion of the centre and so defined. These zones are made temporary by a lack of interest in investment in something that will anyhow be taken down. The working-class zone, with small enterprises, large entrepôts and working-class facilities comes next. Further out there is space for the middle class while working in the centre and then a zone for commuters. There are factors that have an impact on this general pattern, like differences in topography, heavy industry, etc. Criticism has primarily been concerned with activities defined by the analytical simplification of a first-floor definition. Concentric circles register clear-cut boundaries too rigidly, not being internally homogeneous. Path dependency, as a theoretical endeavour, was not invented at the time of this construct, although ideas on factors of inertia were present. Another approach, presented by Homer Hoyt (1939) (land economist and real estate evaluator), based on structural development along main transport routes, created a star-like pattern. This was complementary to or replacing the preceding model, a reflection of the importance of the main explanatory variable, accessibility, defined through the cost of land. Land-use in different sectors appeared homogenous and expanded outwards in historically established patterns. Another model described as the multiple nucleus model identified different nuclei with different kinds of functions (Harris and Ullman, 1945). An early cluster-theoretical approach showed functional links between different activities. Complementary to this were a number of planning concepts where the green belt approach stood out in importance. Land-use planning used to retain areas of largely undeveloped, wild or agricultural land surrounding or neighbouring urban areas. The structural pattern of these approaches were derived through physical divisions of the city.

Defining the heritage of older patterns decided the future. An important aspect of this were distinctions about major roles played by the urban centres in the past. In general they were presented in one or a few profiles, like military-administrative, economic, cultural and legislative/judicial, which defined earlier stages of development and still put their impact on structures and patterns. Combining concentric models with sectoral variants when using empirical material on weather variables also exemplified impact and concentric forms based on age and function. Impact factors also found among topographical features and earlier defined dimensions of ownership was also relevant. Patterns were also discernible in reactions/consequences to the cyclic behaviour of economic highs and lows. They introduced ethno-centricity, showing evidence of sectoral patterns with different elements interacting and defining ideas of generalised urban structures. Another possible tendency/trend was the noted changes in the impact of the in-migrating rural population, now with an orientation towards international migrants replacing the rural exodus.

The continuing discussion circles around the possible degree of generalised structures of towns and urbanities. A relevant point is the presence of the internal centre/periphery structures. This was a pattern clearly found around centre and hinterland, the concentric zones developing according to some aspects of the ideal models presented. Certain activities/functions attract each other while others repel. Within the concept of concentric zones, manufacturing, storage and transports tend to collocate in working-class neighbourhoods. The number of higher middle-class inhabitants close to production with negative impacts on the natural environment is imaginably very small. In regard to stores and shopping, there are a number of spatial links where high fashion and shoe shops are found close to department stores and as far as possible from garden markets, porno and red light districts. Co-location of similar activities are also noted, such as the diamond districts in Antwerp and Amsterdam. Consumer technology in the centre of London. Co-location is a variable that is defining geography where different activities have different potentials to pay their way within these structures.

Social implications are found when we approach aspects on the back side of the growth orientation discussed earlier, in volatile and sometimes structural tendencies of labour markets. "Although cities are high generators of growth, the highest unemployment rates are found in cities" (European Union, 2011a, p. 5). Of in-migration:

> Many cities have a significant loss of inclusive power and cohesion and an increase in exclusion, segregation and polarization . . . problems of integration and increasing racist and xenophobic attitudes, which have amplified these problems.
>
> (European Union, 2011a, p. 5).

Hincks (2016, p. 8) argues that urban space does not allow for inclusiveness. He distinguishes between different urbanities – "whose urban and which urban are we concerned with". He also identifies different groups with different affiliations. In the kind of problem raising the issues of social expenditure and interregional, inter-urban cut-throat competition, there will be a considerable number of losers in aspects of regions, urbanities or localities, but even more in the population:

> polarization and segregation are increasing . . . of the poor getting poorer, concentration of inequality, poor housing, low-quality education, unemployment, difficulties and inabilities to access some services.
>
> (European Union, 2011a, p. 22)

Aspects of urban structure also combine with social class or levels. We find the poor pushed out from the centre. Explanations include increasing income gaps and hoarded riches, changes in the welfare system and reduced public involvement in policies concerning housing and structural effects in regard to renting and owning. The idea of exploitative practices is mentioned, where the well-to-do develop in splendid isolation, while presuming their right to the full diversity of the urbanity (ACANALYS, 2011). Structures of poverty and social exclusion are primarily urban, especially in northwestern Europe. "In 2011, people living in cities in the EU-15 were at a greater risk of poverty or social exclusion than those living outside cities" (European Commission, 2011, p. 15).

Density deconstructed

Trying to evaluate the positive – and sometimes substantiated evaluation given to agglomeration as an explanatory concept – one taken-for-granted quality, more or less, is aspects of density. In density and the urban, city, etc., one scarce resource is fully exploited – land. Considering time-specific factors (context), the basic principle always remains. "[D]ensity ha[s] been used in the literature as variables to proxy for potential agglomeration economies" (Magrini and Cheshire, 2008, pp. 14–15). Through this appear time-specific, time-dependent and functional patterns. Behind it stands topographical-*cum*-regulatory foundations limiting and delimiting change and appearances. Beneficial aspects of density are qualified by their sought-after rationality and translated into measurable variables. When looking on dimensions of consumption, the extent of the city marketplace is based on quantitative combinations of actual consumers, with implications of potential production levels and income benefits for the producers. "Conditions for entering a market are thought to be more favourable in more densely populated regions . . . because of closer proximity to the consumer market and the more developed business infrastructure" (Delfmann et al., 2014, p. 1037). When agglomerative benefits are conceived, regulations regarding urban land supply and use have to be considered. The implications regarding policy are, however, complicated. Taken-for-granted assumptions are frequently criticised. Density as a background variable creates increased differences between individuals, an increased complexity as to social structures, social segregation, differentiation between work and living, which also promote aspects of competition and exploitation.

Classic approaches to urban development in terms of density/agglomeration need a number of additions to reach a level of analytical justification. How to accommodate red light districts, dilapidated neighbourhoods, suburbs and central ghettos analytically highlights the point. There is a need for an increased deconstruction, including elements and relations between the parallel organic and planned processes. A starting point found in the self-evident recognition that the city/urban is a process with myriads of small decisions, individual households, organisations and institutions in continuous economic, social and political interaction. Former-day necessities of marketplaces and walls are today complemented with parks, green lungs, drive-throughs and public transport utilities were established:

> It is only in the past 100–150 years that human beings really decided to 'plan' cities in the modern sense.
>
> (Cheshire, 2006, p. 1233)

Examples of these kinds of culturally defined features of the urban landscape are Middle East towns/cities with basic homogeneous patterns that especially focus on the *medina* – the older parts. Central in these are the mosque, which by tradition is not only a centre for religious ceremony but also for educational, social and service functions. In the growing city a regular frequency of mosques and minarets are always within hearing distance of the population. Walls and defence-related installations and gates define other patterns. Palaces and baths are prominent historical relics with an impact. Privacy is central, which has an effect on architectural solutions. Dead-end streets are frequent, limiting the number of people approaching. Maximal shade is a necessary ingredient.

Based on aspects of economic forces is an alternative example, indicated in ACANALYS (2011), where the relative positions of districts within larger, major urbanities are exploited by resources (location as such linked to power in economic and other terms). A preference system exists for the advantaged citizens, exploiting the size (diversification) of the total city while defining their own homogeneous spaces under different degrees of exclusion (i.e. gated communities, etc.).

Another pertinent argument is around industrial composition. Many times the explanation for good or poor growth is primarily based on the combination of branches that characterise a specific urban economy. The eventual success of regions and sites has to do with the nature of the constituting industries and corporate behaviour. Its impact on urban structure is not discussed but seemingly taken for granted, disappearing in the flattened image of the positive urban 'environment'. At the same time, the simple fact is that industry is 'located' and there is a reason, coincidence or pattern. What about the fact that the percentage of industrial investments per capita in the northern parts of Sweden is higher than in Stockholm, the latter ranking third, from the end of the Swedish administrative regions (Müller and Segerstedt, 2015)? Geographical structure enters through the back door in regards to the business cycle arguments, where old industrial centres wait in line – this also includes a greater number of industrial 'ghost' or 'museum' towns to prove the point.

Another example with similar structural approaches is the argument about diversity as a general phenomenon. Urban areas, in general, are described in terms of diverse population. The causality from this is the existence of a more diverse demand, which in turn leads to new firm start-ups, fostering innovation. The suggestion is that the relation between the general process of urbanisation and its outcome, urban structure, is extremely complex and further connections with other societal processes like economic 'progress' are hard to substantiate. As the processes are changing in themselves, important efforts in that direction have been unsuccessful. An example in regard to agglomeration profiles is that they "have exhibited significant structural transformation over the last four decades" (Parr et al., 2002, pp. 675–676). The idea here is that when structural implications appear, the logic of agglomeration will change, resulting in among other things geographical patterns, possibly also including a reduction in the importance of the urban.

Processes of de-urbanisation, suburbanisation, counter-urbanisation discuss opposite flows. An important sideline in this discussion is how these processes, in turn, create other kinds of structural phenomena/patterns. Approaching the urban from the analysis of the city-region presents an interesting alternative and digression. It is possible to identify in terms of land rent/high value profiles.

> Whilst these rates have not changed much in the recent past, rural areas within city-regions are expected to grow more successfully than those outside. In terms of policy, whilst rural areas within city-regions perform better than those outside . . . they still retain typically rural characteristics such as low wages and low skills.
>
> (Curry and Webber, 2012, p. 284)

So far, the discussion has not included people apart from some demographic statistic. It is self-evident that in order to bring the discussion forward, people with different characteristics (poverty levels, etc.) appear complementary to basic demographic and urban structural data. Exemplifying theoretical concerns, Florida emphatically points to 'creativity' as the "principal driving force in the growth and development of cities, regions, and nations" (2005, p. 1).

Cities encompass a large range of lifestyles: family orientated, career orientated, sport and event focused, educational, old age. Lifestyles that benefit from short distances to sponsored cultural events and a high variety of means of private consumption. At the same time this means high-intensity consumption and life pressure. High levels of social polarisation are present as well: income differentials, ethnically defined exclusion, poverty, deprivation, neighbourhood decay, homelessness, violence, criminality – within the static structure of incomplete labour markets. An analytical mosaic can be placed on top of the physical, the functional, etc. Development can be discussed simultaneously with identifying areas where exclusionary practices are evident, where the feeling of being left outside of society is a connecting characteristic. These kinds of spatial islands can be identified in any middle-sized or large town and even be declared a presence in smaller ones.

The extracted urban of the innovative environment

Among the processes considered to take advantage of the urban context, the ones most often mentioned are included in the innovation and entrepreneurial processes. Innovative processes are, as discussed in general, supposed to be favoured in areas where industries are concentrated geographically, and this is by exchanging experiences, information and knowledge. Conducive to these processes are also ideas and findings on the social, cultural and structural potential, also found in an urban environment. The classic presentation of the urban-*cum*-innovation link is made via the research-defined orientation and by investment and organisational capacity of R&D and thus geographically linked to research centres and institutions of different magnitudes. Another promoting argument refers to the general positive prerequisites pertaining to knowledge: "urbanization also increases the likelihood of the presence of a more skilled workforce and facilitates a freer flow and exchange of ideas and knowledge" (Delfmann et al., 2014, p. 1037). Studies of the innovation process that have, as noted, explained this type of fundamental link far from cover the essentials. "Some large cities (New York, London) are also known to be globally important as knowledge centres, but relatively weak as innovation locations" (Cooke, 2012, p. 14).

Transfer of knowledge, as a basic ingredient in innovation activities, often needs face-to-face contacts categorised in time between the haphazard to the conscious search for specific 'faces'. Whether this is random or planned is an important analytical aspect. The process behind ideas of new combinations of knowledge, referring to specialised financial services created by haphazard meeting seems farfetched when looking into the intricacies of it. In this category, a question often left unanswered is how the random meetings occur and what conditions are needed to create a constructive output. There is a certain kind of probability, of the one and only, but the journey to realise it is long. The question is whether the 'first time' and the second time are realised. One needs to take a step back to conclude that the innovation process requires many different kinds of meetings, meaning different forms of agglomerative effects in urban areas, possibly statistically more likely there than in the sparse periphery.

Part of the knowledge-transfer condition is the presence of academic facilities, including education. The question of the role of higher education, especially its geographical location and priorities has generated an intense debate through the years. The role of higher educational institutions (HEI) as knowledge engines of regional development and the contribution of academic research to economic development are one dimension. The establishment and/or localisation of HEIs were earlier a conscious ingredient in regional development policies. The causality was questioned in terms of the polarity defining its optimal structure, critical mass and distribution. The discussion is brought to a wider and deeper level than in terms of location, funding and distribution. Issues of location are reduced in importance, the regional policy dimension disappearing in favour of concentration, centralisation and university wannabee attitudes. This has resulted in a reorientation from their roles as regional growth engines to classical academic profiles.

The urban positive is taken for granted, in spite of the fact that some urban centres lack dynamic clusters of innovative firms even when individual technology companies, R&D activities and research organisations are present. Even when a high degree of high-quality organisational infrastructure and developed knowledge-transfer services of different kinds are present. One of the catalytic problems refer to degrees of integration, interaction or as said by Tödtling and Trippl (2005, p. 1211), referring to peripheral regions,

> the problem of fragmentation, i.e., the lack of networks and interactive learning seems to represent an important innovation barrier in such regions.

Knowledge will only 'spillover' when there exist mechanisms (networks, checkpoints, physical space) that are appropriate for their purpose. Where are these conditions met, within the urban? Could it be that in the urban there is an overload? Where the transfer of knowledge is identified as taking place in a dynamic manner, there are other necessary qualifying factors. The presence of mechanisms for knowledge spillovers is said to be a robust indicator, but how? The choice of product- and production-process innovation seems common and natural as a result of indicators for this kind of development although it is summarised in terms of critical mass and similar abstractions, and very rarely in more tangible terms or in explicit causal relations. Other types and categories of innovation demands other kinds of preconditions. It is far from clear what the causal links are and even less how they are created/formed although aspects of knowledge concentration and organised and spontaneous meetings are used in some descriptions. Density in itself, already disputed, is a qualified argument.

The question of what, in this context, is exclusive to the cities remains and demands necessary qualification in terms of the different patterns in different functions and branches. What works for biotech and financial services in Frankfurt seems not to be in place for chemical and automobile industries (Tödtling and Trippl, 2005, p. 1211). Cities or city-regions that are, at present, quite successful will find themselves in trouble if the nature of their specialisation or one-sidedness loses out in competition with other regions with more advantageous compositions of activities. Advantages, due to natural resources, new technologies, competitive housing and real estate in general or an HR potential-creating attractiveness, point to possible future lock-ins and eventual downturns, if not consciously approached (ACANALYS, 2011).

Notes

1 Characteristics and personality traits defined in the urban communities are describing the urbanity and viewpoints associated with cities and urban areas. It is loaded with connotations of refinement and elegance, the opposite of *rusticus*, which is associated with the countryside.

2 A notable counterpoint to the concept of urban is the lack of rural/peripheral understanding.

3 The definition of the urban is a methodological problem with far-reaching analytical implications. In Australia and Canada the breakpoint is at 1,000, in Italy at 10,000 and in Japan 50,000. Numbers are necessary in order to define urbanisation.

4 This has to be somewhat qualified as reasons to grant city privileges can have different rationales, and these privileges are a minimalistic way of defining the urban.

5 It is important to note that functional change in this perspective has to be qualified. For instance, some changes in functional distributions of occupations in local communities do not represent a process of urbanisation. A local community in the periphery, going from primary to secondary and tertiary sectors, represents a shift but not a qualitative leap into stages of modernisation.

6 The logic of this is, of course, the urban being many different things in different contexts. What will then appear as non-urban in such an exercise?

6 Geographic and demographic structures and processes

General introduction

Among the preconditions for the continuing discussion stand the nature of decision-making processes and decisions in themselves having an impact on the rules of the game. Structural tendencies run deep, as do mindsets, summed up in images – this has already been approached but is important enough to repeat. The rural periphery is ascribed with poor developmental capacities; absence of physical infrastructure (road, rail, telecommunications); lack of qualified labour, research and technological development; lack of social capital; low institutional capacity; low quality and ambition/power of the political establishment; and a general passive attitude towards problem solving (Morgan, 2007). The linking of peripheral, sparsity and deprivation is notable. However:

> Economically deprived regions, for instance, also exist in the core areas of central Europe and, simultaneously, economically dynamic, innovative regions can be found in geographically peripheral areas.
>
> (Eskelinen and Fritsch, 2006, p. 54)

It also includes a discussion on societal values of resources and sources, linked to perspectives on development and economic growth. Putting people, groups and categories, in this equation, different kinds of systematic patterns emanate, where some are or become disadvantaged/marginalised, not fitting into the general framework of the dominant ideology with its theoretical and practical implications. Their resources, and them as sources, are not possible to evaluate in a traditional manner or in a traditional economic context. The ambition for the present effort and following chapters is to bring together bits and pieces of empirical information with theoretical fragments in an effort to initiate a presentation and representation of the positive and/or the definable extent of an alternative peripheral/rural logic. The book questions the general framework, also enforced by the nature of the modern, new processes taking place in different aspects of the economy. For example:

> Peripheral space seems to be moving from an outlying zone of primary production to become an area that is a consumption zone; one where the very qualities which made it peripheral are consumed in their own right.
> (Anderson, 2000, p. 97)

The general idea of the market economy is still prominent in the debate and in theoretical considerations and mostly analysed in categories invalidating aspects of state intervention or neglecting public and voluntary sectors. In the centralising market-determined economy, the urban/core/centre identifies agglomerative effects together with concentrations of economic control and similar aspects of ownership and spatial patterns based on that. Part of the overall picture or conscious efforts is supposedly cost saving and rational – via regulations as to geographical size and thresholds – while draining peripheral resources and potential is taking place under an umbrella of modernisation and rationalisation.

In the public sector within the framework of policy, other priorities than costs are primarily considered. In public-choice theory, analysis of centralisation and decentralising tendencies highlights defined results. Informal processes roam in the shadows, maximising, for instance, not general welfare but the personal and organisational interests of the central/urban elite in terms of bureaucracy or politicians. A general acceptance of the fact that the concept of welfare is historically determined and redefined with changes in the historical preconditions. It is, however, possible, at these historical constructs to define and operationalise the concept for earlier periods, encompassing a substance today with multidimensional ingredients and appearances. Having its foundation in aspects of the material, in complementarity to the concept of quality of life, it appears as representing the fact that humans do not live on bread alone. Satisfaction is not defined by material resources. The generalised welfare state is questioned in, among other tendencies, aspects regarding geographical coverage.

To exemplify, in budgetary considerations, large organisations with a lot of hired help have higher salaries for the top echelons and even more direct and indirect power conditioned by and benefiting from their larger economic flexibility. Benefits for organisations appear, or seem to appear, where a location close to others is supposed to be necessary in order to get influence and power and ultimately an even larger share of the golden pie. This also takes place in electoral structures and voting processes, both in the manner of prerequisites in the process itself and in its short- and long-term outcomes. Large centres with large populations continuously get priorities.

At the same time, centralisation and concentration processes are stimulating their own counter-tendencies – for example, increasing the value of land in core locations and by this reframing the picture, creating effects where simple activities are feasible everywhere – and these businesses tend to be pushed to low-cost locations. Relevant aspects even in market theory are also place- and price-driven international market effects on mining[1] (Pajala, SE) and on demand profiles within sectors of leisure and tourism.

Fragments from the other side of the picture bring us structural changes, reframed by processes developing in the rural/peripheral influencing the urban. The interactive private, public, social processes are suggestively, as noted, changing the rules of the game. Occupation and form of living becoming more diversified, turning from agriculture still defining land control and substantial dimensions of activity and identity (Potter et al., 2008).

Leaving the hard core of official economic patterns and economic social behaviour to later, there is also a field of theoretical challenge in holistic considerations of interactions between the formal and informal sectors of society. Another type of analytical approach is the presence of processes driven by non-economic forces in strong motivations for local and communal practices and socio-economic aspects. The entrepreneurial spirit – on alternative foundations, and forces of change and status – is not explainable in traditional terms, finding itself in the murky waters of the residual in economic analysis. Ronny Svensson (2012) wonders in an interview in *Dagens Samhälle* (2012) how it is that little Bjurholm (2,400 inhabitants) up north in Sweden functions well, while Karlskoga in the middle, with ten times the population, does not.

> In the zones of contact between the legal periphery and autonomous social sectors, an arena for a plurality.
>
> (Mezzandra and Neilson, 2013, p. 185)

Geography, location, distance, identity and culture

Geographies

While discussing (in the first section) a positive starting point for a presentation and operationalisation of an alternative logic of the periphery, in this section we enter into the framework of 'different' and 'differentiating' geographies that could and will enhance the discussion. The 'alternative' geographical presentation means geography as both a precondition and outcome. Geographic representation is seen as a complementary dimension to other complexities of society and development, complementary to aspects of demography, economics, politics, culture, etc. The intellectual definition of a designated area and/or the definitions of what is becomes place-based. There is more to space and place than formal and traditional geography and geographies. It's a content that exists in daily activities, dreaming and planning, shaping the order of things and their spatial representations in cities, countrysides, districts and clusters (Martin and Sunley, 2012).

A kind of natural starting point to get out of the way is the supposedly identified dimension of empty space. Sparsity and periphery partially carry this image. This is an issue recognised for considerable territories, especially in the Nordic countries. Being an illusion, an area lacking people is empty only of people. At every specific point in time, specific types of conditions are always full with other things, conditions, etc. Also of people, on a temporary basis.

Here the focus will be on other aspects of the definition of the periphery and related concepts, already extensively approached. As noted, the main words in themselves do appear in a range from pejorative to affirmative/positive. In general, however, peripherality and marginality have, in their popular/general appearances, mainly derogatory attributive values, which are significant for more conscious analysis and sometimes wished-for developmental processes. Here shall, however, be presented an extension of some of the conceptual discussion based on a number of specific geographical terms in order to elaborate a little more on substantiation, towards a discussion of relevance.

> Subjective . . . experienced region . . . a region does not exist as an objective or physical entity, but instead as a socially constructed one, and is thus an important term for the social sciences (Lysgård, 2001).
>
> (Higdem, 2007, pp. 2–3)

Especially the verb 'sees' in the following quote has a strong relation with the verb 'experience':

> a constructivist approach sees a region as created by individuals and their ways of acting, which would include certain institutions and the impact of science and technology.
>
> (Higdem, 2007, p. 2)

The idea that regions are social constructs is transferable to peripheral, marginal areas or locations in the way that these designations are prisms through which the status of peripheral is defined, described or analysed – the function (or often enough dysfunction) of being peripheral. The picture of peripherality and/or marginality is used as a metaphor or translator for the totality of the different facets of this prism. But the picture goes also the other way; it allows/gives a dweller or an inhabitant a part, a role, an identity defined by some collective mark, bearing a name and a set of characteristics – whether the periphery or margin is positive or not.

An approach that brings us into a much more intricate theoretical excursion is the potential nature of emergent properties. In their excellent seminal paper, Martin and Sunley (2012) present a framework for these kinds of properties. They note the fact that different geographical forms (urban, regional and local) are not the results of conscious efforts or policy interventions, but develop as they progress – "appear as self-organising . . . from the behaviours of myriad economic agents" (p. 339). "Contextual combinations of processes in particular places can be said to have emergent effects that produce particular spatial forms which then feedback to shape the operation of those same processes" (Martin and Sunley, 2012, p. 339). The authors refer to Paul Krugman also being quite emphatic about these properties, which are implied and not apparent among the agents as a systemic outcome. And, from the pencil of another distinguished and authoritative geographer (Massey) the causality shaping geography creates a precondition for the future and reshaping:

> One way of thinking of all this is to say that the spatial is integral to the production of history. . . . Just as the temporal is to geography.
>
> (Massey, 1992, p. 84)

The complexity carries an analytical burden, making the scientific process more than difficult, hindering meaningful conclusions and effective policies, as we know very little of the interaction of scale and localisation economies due to lack of research and "whether they can be developed equally across all parts of a regional economic space (Kitson, Martin and Tyler (2004)" (Bristow, 2010, p. 21). Complexity develops further when we find ourselves in the intricate web of 'uniqueness', eliminating generalisable aspects of the 'alternative'. The argument is that the road to peripheral uniqueness in these geographical connotations is linked with attributes that bring forward alternative logics. The picture of the rural, as in agriculture and forestry, is complemented by other dominant sectors like tourism, etc. but in varying forms and sectoral combinations and in successful and unsuccessful processes and outcomes. As an empirically based development in between the unique and the generalisable, categories like mountain regions, coastal regions, islands and EU-defined 'outermost regions' are appearing. Variants of relevant functionality distinguish attributes like problem and border regions indicating special peripheral variants. The 'outermost' territories recognised in the Treaty of Amsterdam (1997) and carried over to the Treaty of Lisbon (2007) are a case in point. Uniqueness appears as local adaptations where this quality is continued in processes of conditional change.

> [W]orld-wide flows of capital, people and knowledge, enforcing economic actors in rural capitalism to be creative to survive increased international competition.
>
> (Fløysand and Jakobsen, 2010, p. 106)

The rural has a huge number of unique and special manifestations and therefore meanings both on local and regional levels. These are partly, but only partly, possible to identify, decode or deconstruct. The special attributes of 'peripherality' and 'marginality' are usable as part of the contents or defining a framework where this is constructed, and also the other way around. An appearance of general phenomena in diverse forms identifiable in this 'diversity' is possible: "entrepreneurial activities can enact rurality in a variety of different ways" (Korsgaard, Müller and Tanvig, 2015, p. 6).

Loading the argument with further direction, sparsity, its logic and consequences create a number of intricate hypothetical landscapes possible to put on top of each other, arguing against the undergrowth of some of the pejorative definitions, painting the rural/peripheral/sparse as a handicap to development or 'survival'. This representation is not only an illusion, it is false; on the other hand it is a reality in need for a qualified substantiation of negative and positive impacts. For example, introducing the 'rules of the game' for 'survival'. For instance, when comparing population densities combined with travelling patterns. Travelling distances for young pupils to school centres in Vilhelmina (SE area = 870 square km and ~3,650 in population) and Sundbyberg (SE 877 square kilometres and ~46,000 in population) indicate a generalisable functional problem of service levels and costs that cut substantially different tolls on the municipal budgets. Pointing in the other direction, sparsity and large territories make room for functionality in the form of water preserves, and through this the production of hydropower. Further examples of this are nature protection areas and other geographically delimited measures in a modern land-use regime, defining a number of different interests, like biodiversity, tourism, etc.

A more generalisable and basic structural phenomenon starts out from the perspective of gender relations and gendered patterns. Stenbacka (2011, p. 238) argues that within the counter-urbanisations process a popular image is the traditional division of labour and accompanying patterns. Women in the countryside are more politically active than their city sisters, without giving up their careers. The nature of the 'female' part of the 'going-back-to-nature' or 'going home' including countryside security, etc., is clearly not in the dimension of 'women's sacrifice', as rural areas provide women with new and different opportunities – 'a higher degree of freedom' (Stenbacka, 2011).

A geographical space, be it a region, somewhere local, a locality, a place or wherever – with an accompanying attribute of periphery, rural, sparse or countryside – brings forward a lot of fascinating alternatives and extras together with ruralities and other cultural attributes. It is both a potential and a troublesome reality. In an era of continuous communication, speech and traffic being the pacemakers of the urbanites' lifestyle, there is an increased need, a craving for counterbalance. Rurality, and the notions of silence and tranquillity in general, represent some taken-for-granted diffuse forms of answer to this. The counterbalance becomes valuable, as the rural (or others) are expected to contain a potential to heal, to refresh, to be secure, which in turn ultimately indicates a complementary possibility of entrepreneurship in many different forms. What comes first is not the important question, identifying trends in cultural traits are. There are clear indications of a longing or seeking for rusticity, with sub-trends exemplified for instance by slow culture, slow food, etc. How permanent or temporary these are as traits could be questioned, but the impact on individuals and collectives of different categories is today of strategic relevance.

Conceptually 'local' is at the bottom of a hierarchy of geographical entities, slightly above or on the same level as place and subordinated to the region. It also appears as an antonym to global, which, in turn, has placed the former prominently in development theory and development practices of today. Local is not only to be interpreted in a geographical sense but also functional, encompassing a number of social, economic and political practices/meanings. It is primarily in this sense we will find a possibility of its use in dimensions of the peripheral and marginal. This is based on a hypothesised proposition that the substantiated local is of quite a substantial relevance in peripheral, marginal and general geographical situations.

Local development (in its dominating perspective and simplest form) is a continuing process of adaptation, serving to support an acceptable day-to-day situation. It also encompass a dimension of survival or continuation of the local community, and in analytical and practical terms an everlasting interaction with and under influences from the surrounding world. What actually constitutes inner and outer is by this a crucial aspect of the definition. The impact of the local could even explain itself, taken as a starting point, formed by the mobilisation of local resources to satisfy local needs and strengthen local control over these resources (Wahlström, 1989).

The 'rationality' of the local appears in a number of configurations. Even a notion of a future status (individual or collective) often carries this attribute. Among other things, describing the local 'absolute' – there is always a local representation. Also describing a local 'necessity' is pertinent. The meaning sought here is that the need for most human activities and human artefacts to be geographically situated or located is important.

> For those who have grown up in the Swedish countryside, agriculture can, however, represent something more than a technical process to produce food. Agriculture can for them appear as the very foundation of their existence. It is doubtful that agriculture has this status for the generations born after 1970.
>
> (Malmberg, 2011, p. 111)

In a discussion on local 'contents' we can find another important contribution. Paths for analysis can take many forms. Ownership of land and real estate discussed as a process combining selling, buying, taxing, networking and interacting and by this realising value changes in structures of living, nature of population and distribution of wealth. Values function to create local and regional spatial pockets and patterns in terms of behaviour of attraction. This exemplifies local as in 'precondition'. Positions and characteristics of the local define, through absolute and relative causality, the nature of social, economic and political processes. A good example is found in the situation for islands. A high degree of structural openness to trade and high dependence upon exports may lead to export-led growth strategies. This example of causality is just one among many.

Local often has a name. The name is analytically a kind of first step in defining, describing a place. Position, distance, size, spirit and identity are some of the constituents. The geographical concept of place is brought forward with other concepts like the psychology of an individual, the sociology of day-to-day practices in groups of different kinds. The local is understood in terms of where we live and work, i.e. places where we (as individuals and groups) are giving contents, meaning, roles and degrees of identities. A place is more than different cultural essences. It is a high-powered mixture of meaningful ingredients, formed by different people, social and natural forces. The culture is represented, in a system of collectivism, by the people that inhabit the area, the same landscape, community, and taking on parts of and constituting and interpreting different groups and nations. Sharing a feeling of cultural belonging contributes by strengthening common traits and forming the identity, declared or just there. It is also a foundation for interpreting the surrounding world.

The local culture, as indicated above is continuously created by a fundamental precondition, one found in the concept of relative proximity. This bringing the concept of local another dimension, not really increasing the possibility of operationalisation. The difficulty is found in identifying what the proximity is in relation to. To find the proximity within or to a group of individuals that are described under common characteristics could be a solution or a starting point, but then what? Take, for instance, aspects of cognitive distance: how to catch the depth of the concept. Proximity has also to do with shared norms, values, identities. Parts of these are place specific and become important when influencing dispersed individuals or multi-local firms.

Belonging and identity define at the same time value-loaded ambitions linked to future development perspectives. It often enough contains patterns, constructs within the domains of culture(s). Culture plays a role in the development trajectories for a place, locality and region. Degrees of importance could not be evaluated but could be conceptualised as to different (economic, community, etc.) profiles and taken-for-granted interactions (Huggins and Thompson, 2015). It becomes accentuated when it comes to threats and possibilities and described as compensatory.

> In essence, Wales as a whole can be characterized by a community culture based on social cohesion, caring, femininity, collective action and a general desire for fairness and equality. . . . In many ways, however, they are values contrary to those of regions that are more successful in economic terms, and which have advanced through more entrepreneurial economic cultures.
>
> (Huggins and Thompson, 2015, p. 147)

Possibilities for the alternative logic are found when the process contains elements of coming to terms with common objectives. It is not decided exclusively by the local space of competence or resource control. In situations or conditions where the preconditions for local achievements are dependent upon the relations with the surrounding world, a subordination defines the outer limits of room for action and changes. Among all the facets of this, some strengthen, some weaken the role of the local community for the individual or group or its identification. There are substantial lessons in the historical textbooks, where identity-forming and defining interests shape the long-term institutional formations:

> Politics, economy and culture on the contrary influence each other reciprocally within various geographic centre-periphery areas, thus giving rise to the well-known mosaic of European regions.
>
> (Knudsen, 2011, p. 320)

There is a geographical distinction that is not satisfactorily touched upon, and that is where aspects of the local and local development in marginal and peripheral geographical dimensions have tendencies of becoming increasingly important and developing on the basis of more general characteristics. With an orientation towards marginality, periphery and border issues programmatically approached here, the combination with the preconditions for the local specifically appears.

> [D]ependent on value structures and on descriptive models and rule system derived from them . . . changing material structures but also changing value structures. . . . With this approach interest is focused on the way we value, describe and use the resources rather than on the resources themselves.
>
> (Wahlström, 1989, p. 79)

Entering the door of experience brings in the actor, the role and special dimensions of relative positions defined by interests. Complementing a relative position in the periphery makes its nature quite often an important presence and question. The subject matter brings us into the conception of geographical proximity, defined in simple physical terms and complicated normative dimensions. However, widening the approach into cognitive perception, there are dimensions of shared norms and values where distances are overcome by the substantiated idea of belonging. Where also workplaces in a region become defined in terms of common cultural denominators.

Looking first at the 'material/physical' aspects, when these variables are directly and positively correlated their distinction has no importance. In most cases it is not really relevant: "there is only little hope that this will outweigh the distant geographical location of these areas" (Gløersen et al., 2005, p. 2). In 1960 the daily average travelling distance in Norway was about 8 km, including holidays. Forty years later, this measure has increased fivefold. There has also been a parallel increase in regional transport volumes. More frequent and longer work-related mobility in search of combinations of work and good living are part of the explanation (Selstad, 2004).

Another example, earlier noted, is where environmentally friendly carbon taxes increase the 'reality' of peripherality. Agriculture is subsidised in order to overcome distance to market and other differences in conditions of production (Hegrenes, 2004, p. 52). This leads to questions where perspectives and perceptions have different impacts and logics, socially, politically and economically. In a simplified manner: access between places and personal access to reaching places (Haugen, 2012a, 2012b). If one takes the perspective of distance with a focus on the centre, the normative position of a location in the centre makes the periphery less important, i.e. reinforcing a process of peripheralisation and marginalisation. At the same time sitting in the designated periphery makes the centre something much more than distant. Different normative dimensions intermingle and promote/provoke each other. In general, the status (which does include a number of analytical entrances) of the infrastructure ranges analytically from non-existence to the provision of intensive, high-quality, low-cost networks. What could also be considered is the combination of varying transport means and potentials and thresholds linked to traffic intensity. The latter creates the possibility of optimal (given the technical potential) accessibility to a given point in time.[2] Time is also a matter of timing (interpreted as timetables or office hours for service centres of different kinds or other complicated and complicating logistical patterns). The classical conceptual entrances of centre/core and periphery/hinterland – where the relation of a centre through a specific distance attribute makes a forceful contribution, and where a number of other characteristics therefore change nature based on quantity and quality of absolute and relative distance from the chosen centre – are used as an analytical starting point. Finally, the individual component includes extensive needs, capabilities and the potential of the individual. Accessibility is a variable that has developed substantially through time; at the same time it has provoked a process of "regional concentration of services and workplaces. People who do not own cars do not benefit from increased accessibility" (Johansen, 2009, p. 18).

As the periphery is located, at best, at the ends of some defined centres complementary spokes, it is disadvantaged in notable aspects of location and transportation, whether places, localities found on routes passing between major centres or distinguished by being at 'the end of the line'. Hard borders, like for instance the one that used to be between Finland and the Soviet Union, created regions characterised by a *cul-de-sac* (Eskelinen and Fritsch, 2006, p. 58).

> [A] number of associated symptoms of disadvantage . . . mutually reinforce . . . not necessarily connected in a causal sense . . . a very substantial cumulative barrier to regional development.
>
> (Gløersen et al., 2005, p. 17)

An example of physical/material dispersion/sparsity is characterised or defined by the physical distance between houses, people, workplaces and service facilities of different types. These factors relate to different types of services needed and provided. The same types of relations – but considered different categories at first of geographical connotations (settlement structures) and later linked to different collective categories (social, economic, etc.) – specify in more detail. Physical distance is an analytical approach on its own and is, as earlier noted, reinforced or accentuated by introducing time and costs. As long as distance/time/costs are directly and positively correlated this has not any major analytical importance. A turn away (for example with subsidised tariffs) makes the approach more complicated, although transport costs (reduction) does not outweigh the distant geographical location of these areas (Gløersen et al., 2005). Furthermore, there are social restrictions like perceptions and culture acting as reinforcing limitations (Haugen, 2012a).

Even this entrance is not enough to interpret all spatial consequences in the picture; the relativity towards competitive advantages between the analytical dimensions of peripheral locations has also to be considered in view of the alternatives. What is emphasised here is that accessibility is central in individual decision-making every day and in the long term, from logistical complexities in travel to work to fundamental quality of life issues.

> [I]t is also a crucial aspect of the functioning of society more generally in terms of welfare and social policy and in the planning and development of cities and regions, including localization policy, for instance.
>
> (Haugen, 2012a, p. 1)

Overcoming distance is the basic parameter defining a travel limit (see above) and registering what is within the scope. Decreasing distance (see above) is the deciding instrument and therefore also a key for policies. Being in a certain place means certain advantages/disadvantages when it comes to availability/accessibility to other places and functions.

The distance dimension is not only an ingredient of different geographies, it substantiates and through this strengthens the argument for an 'alternative logic in itself', further approached in the upcoming sections. The periphery could create a specific form or structures of opportunities that have a positive impact on, for instance, the entrepreneurial foundation rate. Particular characteristics create a 'window of opportunity', matching particular entrepreneurs and specific local structures. 'The proof of the pudding is in the eating' and the successful combinations not empirically identified, at least not in terms of generalisable characteristics. This considers role models, norms or local culture that are 'loose' or 'soft' factors, rather than age, gender or educational levels.

Changes in substance and significance of the accessibility complexity have a long-term impact on structural patterns of dwelling and workplace, an impact difficult to substantiate or estimate. Cultural change is, through structural change and difference, ultimately realised. Structural change of transport is particularly evident in relation to its cost aspects, but also reinforced directly and indirectly through temporal logistics. This appears in connection with the mobility of factors of production and business (to keep in mind. the local market, the cost of production, the philosophy of the owner, etc.). The patterns of availability/accessibility and the generally lower cost in the periphery provide an output with a positive return, compared with a city/urban or town centre location. In certain circumstances, upgraded physical infrastructure possibly removes the 'natural protection' of poor accessibility and opens up for competitive actions based on agglomerative advantages in other locations. "At every level this means that peripherality can be seen as relative in terms of cost and time of transportation and communication" (Lorentzen, 2012b, p. 17).

A discussion of factors that possibly shorten distance are found or rediscovered also outside of the normal, traditional geographical discussion – although limited by the physical denomination of 'as the crow flies', it returns with full force in temporal and economic categories. Information flows are used and defined as the panacea for aspects of distance and sparsity, primarily as a foundation for new working patterns. Distance work, distance studies are notable as part of the solution for the periphery.

> The advent of information highways is one of the aspects that has raised greatest hopes in the peripheries. The entry into the century of the immaterial world at last make it possible to do away with disparities linked to geographic distance.
>
> (Copus, 2001, p. 544)

The question of the quality and extent of the mobile broadband network in Sweden is a good example of where the main economic actors are bringing down their physical networks, limiting availability and reliability in parts of the rural/remote with lower connection qualities. Coverage is generally an issue on both a macro and micro scale. The Swedish Post and Telecom Authority (PTS) took special action for broadband in rural areas (www.pts.se 08/02/2011) and in a campaign asked people to register their grievances. Commercial alternatives do appear. Net4Mobility has undertaken extending broadband for 300 million Swedish crowns in areas where no other telephone companies offer services. The logic of the market, however, prevails.

At the same time, information has a lot to do with interaction. This means that the ICT provides new and alternative types of interaction that encompass the whole of society, in areas that we could not plausibly identify 20–30 years ago. With ICT and improved infrastructure in general, propositions as to the lack of qualities of the periphery seem dated, instead becoming substantially diverse and in constant transformation with the peripherality becoming more related. Capacity and intensity of these networks has a tendency, however, of developing from the centre outwards, increasing accessibility, as a start, in regions already substantially better off. The changing pattern of an overall increased accessibility is complemented by new structures and new relations. The digital revolution is taking place with such a speed that part of society (the periphery), is constantly left behind; in spite of advancing, the nature of this 'peripheralisation' changes.

> Again, providing that basic cost differentials (due to differences in market size) can be overcome by public support, the key issue is likely to be human capital i.e., informing local entrepreneurs of the opportunities, and the training of the local workforce.
>
> (Gløersen et al., 2005, p. 18)

Defined by relative population decline and ageing, thresholds for upholding traditional forms of service facilities are deemed uneconomic. Alternative solutions are discussed and implemented, often based on the digital format. Distance appears in the removal of functions exemplified in the UK, where local libraries are closed and massive main town palaces with libraries are built. This perspective on service function availability and accessibility is discussed in other sections. Even measures to improve the situation do not always turn up as expected; reducing distances do not always lead to expected or sought after results. A bridge shortening travelling distance opens the door to increased competition partaking external actors. Increased labour market opportunities drain local opportunities for engaging in entrepreneurial activities, etc. Service functions become centralised due to economic rationality, i.e. in savings on budgetary spending for the local communities.

The analysis could also benefit from raising the issues of relative and absolute proximity. The basic idea here is as a start identifying the size and internal – qualified later – interconnectivity within the geographical entity having an impact on structure and process characteristics. The present debate/discussion concerning the size of local municipalities in Norway and the Norwegian and Swedish history of reforms on this administrative level could be an interesting in-depth study. The nature of the Norwegian 'district' policy defined a number of decades of regional planning practice, with important implications for the nature of the localities, their service structures, the implicated labour market (changing from agriculture, forestry and manufacturing towards public sector dominance). The networks of small communes combined with the general policy upholding a basis for a more distributed population base (Naustdalslid, 2012, p. 20) than in Sweden.

The investigation into the area of proximics started out as a way of defining local components appearing from social interconnections, where especially non-codified knowledge was present, transferred/exploited and scientifically highlighted. The empirical studies, answering questions like why some individuals or networks were better connected than others and whether this was defined by geographical distance or rather proximity, were, at this stage, still underdeveloped. The main argument is the proposed appearance/existence of agglomerative forces, especially in the form of different versions of prominent knowledge spillovers just at close quarters:

> to glean knowledge from intentional face-to-face contact as well as the more diffuse forms of knowledge acquisition that arises from chance or accidental meetings and the mere fact of being in the same location.
>
> (Bjarnar, 2008, p. 5)

It also approaches aspects for different actors in the way of active promotion and operation, to create 'proximity' effects in the sphere of general development, notably innovation and entrepreneurship. Döring and Schnellenbach (2006, p. 389) note that there did not really exist any literature for the ways and means through which knowledge transferred in geographically secluded areas. They also noted the existence of local innovation networks, where the specified role of knowledge transfer was not established or identified. For quite a long period, the approach appeared primarily within economic geography, developed a theoretical framework for understanding some basic aspects of economic, especially innovative processes. The most fundamental is a relational one. This understanding started out from a spatial dimension – geographical proximity, which, so far, has received most scientific attention and scrutiny. The basic question was whether there existed a reflection from physical, geographical proximity to human interaction, social activity and through this learning. Proximity has since then extended to other forms relevant for the learning and innovative processes, primarily compensating for an eventual lack in the analytical reach of the geographical variable. It is argued, that geographical proximity needs characteristics. From this, an identification of other proximal dimensions emerged. For instance:

> Torre and Rallet (2005) put forward a healthy 'disjunction' between geographical and organizational proximity, as a strong remedy against inherent tendencies in the territorialized innovation theories to spatial reification and the uncritical way in which the (tacit) transfer of knowledge is thought to be highly correlated with physical proximity.
>
> (Lagendijk and Lorentzen, 2007, p. 461)

Complementary within the framework of network theory and evolutionary geography, further dimensions were presented:

> other forms of proximity besides geographical proximity may facilitate interactive learning and innovation . . . geographical proximity is neither a necessary nor a sufficient condition for learning and innovation.
>
> (Boschma and Frenken, 2010, p. 120)

Since then the proximics approach has been complemented with organisational as well as with cognitive, cultural, physical and social, returning to complementary articulation of the issue of geographical 'proximics' (Lagendijk and Lorentzen, 2007), increasing the potential depth of the analysis. The general perspective to proximity dynamics does not explicitly focus on the context of interactions, but tries to understand the actual linkage in formation and substance. Through those mentioned: the same space (geographical proximity), the same formal group (organisational), the same institutions – i.e. norms and values – but also, with reference structures in the knowledge base (cognitive) and being part of a community of some kind (social) (Boschma and Frenken, 2010, pp. 122–123). "[P]roximity is required in some (but not necessarily all) dimensions to get firms connected and to enable interactive learning and innovation among them" (Balland, Boschma and Frenken, 2013, p. 191).

The theme of what proximity is good for returns to the issue of knowledge transfers. The idea of 'knowledge spillover' emphasises the significance of local linkages for a firm's creation and development of its own knowledge (substance and level). Operating in dimensions of proximity seems to introduce innovations at a faster rate than in comparable or competitive functionalities located elsewhere. This appears where there is a concentration of similar or related firms, as they can share knowledge, technologies, talent and services owing to the proximity as such (Mitra, 2012). The extension to other dimensions is relevant when the local buzz is complemented by the approach of global pipelines. Among the issues of analysis is the potential relation between intra-local knowledge assets and non-local knowledge sources for local firms (Bjarnar, 2008, p. 4). Another possibility is defined when external owners allocate a local representative in order to tap knowledge flows.

This approach makes the main theme more evident. Sparsely populated peripheral areas are lacking or are supposed to have some basic traits for the agglomerative processes mentioned. It is argued that interregional/inter-local knowledge spillovers as well as policy-defined public innovation funds cannot be absorbed in regions of this kind, as the low level of clustering and agglomeration imply a 'thin' or non-existent presence of relevant specialised structures of formal knowledge suppliers and educational institutions. This leading to questions like: "to what extent, if at all, can peripheral regions innovate?" (Morgan, 1997, p. 495). Special institutional frameworks do "not meet their demand well enough" (Tödtling and Trippl, 2005, pp. 1209–1210). "[W]ith a reliance on market forces, there is a real danger that peripheral rural areas will become increasingly disconnected from the opportunities presented by the new digital economy" (Grimes, 2003, p. 63).

The argument describing this relative position is, however, not relevant in all cases and does change through time. For instance, the degree of heterogeneity of infrastructural provisions and capacity and a remoteness that is changing with the development of the communication structures highlight the internal interdependence of forces at work (Edvardsen, 2004, p. 24). "[S]uch differences can be partly explained by the profile of rural businesses in these areas, and particularly by the degree of localization of business activity" (Grimes, 2003, p. 63).

The potential is discussed in a multitude of sources and found in identifying complementary contextual ingredients, compensating somewhat for what is lacking in terms of effective local business networks noted in the literature on regional competitiveness. Here 'flexible specialisation' is highlighted and combined to other local contextual variations. These networks are of interest as they are a modicum for a number of different interactive processes in (less tangible) 'untraded interdependencies'. They are an alternative to more conventional agglomerative economies as a stimulus for local development (Copus, 2001). This author also makes references to aspects of 'local embeddedness', referring to the way business networks are rooted in the localities, in soft dimensions of cultural traits and core functions of social interdependencies. Other authors develop this theme, popularly in categories of the 'social economy' and 'social capital'.

Returning to the knowledge theme, what is even more important is, as mentioned, the nature and the substance of the knowledge transferred. Distinctions are traditionally made and found in simplified categories like mode 1 and 2, of codified and tacit.

> Simple knowledge flows equally to actor near and far, while complex knowledge is unlikely to diffuse, no matter how proximate actors are. With knowledge of moderate complexity, however, the outcomes show that more

> close actors are in a better position to benefit from knowledge diffusion, in contrast to more distant recipients.
>
> (Boschma and Frenken, 2010, p. 125)

Demands for specifically profiled knowledge make an impact on the type and quality of channels used, meaning variants of all types of proximics identified. The demand raised by the locational and organisational structures of the entities varies. Proximity is, for instance, said to compensate for cognitive differences if there is a mutual understanding (read norms and values) among working places in the same region.

A major criticism concerning alternative proximics approaches – directed towards the reduced/downgraded explanatory emphasis of the geographical dimension, partly even hindering a discussion of the possibility of geographically distant alternatives – could be worthwhile. The interpretation of that in the territorial dimension makes aspects of the complementary spokes of long-distance connections a relevant approach. This pattern highlights and continues to develop, primarily in light of potential technical processes and given political priorities. Its relevance is qualified as the spatial prerequisites of the periphery sets definite limits to interaction. Finding contacts is problematic in general and the context does not make it easier:

> They have no choice but to establish linkages over space providing access to distant products, markets, and technologies developed elsewhere. F2F interaction in local context is often not an option for these firms.
>
> (Bathelt and Turib, 2011, p. 524)

Ending up with a complementary framework of network geography refers to local activities. Links and different flows provide a structure, automatically including an outreach activity of global potential. This introduces also the need to emphasise higher-order structural patterns, which is not new on the agenda. Structuralist theory – with its institutions and agencies, their interlinkage and the overall context – is defined in versions of dependency visited and revisited since its inception (Copus, 2001). International actors establish networks, where exclusivity in partners (nodes) and flows (linkages) are present. Patterns of behaviour of these actors within local or regional networks is imposed based on strength/importance. The ground rules for knowledge exchange limit the resonance of tacit knowledge flows (Bjarnar, 2008, p. 2).

A special example is where structural definitions – approached through the idea of random meetings demanding the quality of the organised, planned ones – are being defined by the sophistication of the product or production technology. The analytical entrance is dependent upon a first-order definition. "It often relies on a mixture of different types of more or less hierarchical network relations which are derived from existing ties, organisational bonds, or even repeated visits to international trade fairs" (Bathelt and Turib, 2011, p. 524). The locational decisions of the main functions to the specific demands of the production processes, R&D processes, market definitions, etc., are qualified in the proximics analysis. On top of this the variance of different inputs and outputs defined by distance distortions are also pertinent. "[W]e have to specify exactly which proximities are key and in which combination: i.e. proximity to market, production and/or knowledge pools" (Bathelt and Turib, 2011, p. 524).

Returning to accessibilities, meaning here potential proximities, brings the investigation into the analytical dimensions of geographical proximity assessed and complemented to provide innovative or alternative solutions. Potential opportunities for interaction bring us to define the prerequisites for improving the positive impacts of proximics, in whatever dimension, like the physical ones standing in the nexus of attention (Geurs and Wee, 2004, p. 128). It is not always a necessary ingredient or a sufficient condition but it appears among a number of important qualifications where degrees of coordination and structural obstacles are present. The spatial is complemented by local deficiencies and opened up to the potential of lock-in – i.e. too much proximity of any category (Boschma, 2005). By way of this 'new' dimension, we can differentiate between aggregates. A dynamic analysis could distinguish changes in geographical coverage. Negative path-dependent behaviour naturally has an impact on network quality and "may cause retention in the local network . . . local network retention might lead to regional lock-in" (Boschma and Frenken, 2010, p. 121).

A final geographical extension of the proxemic theme has to do with socio-economic features defined or accentuated by the geography of the local and/or the peripheral. Elinor Ostrom's (1990) research on local communities and the administration of collective resources is a case in point. This writer shows that decentralised institutional systems have advantages to the exploitation of common resources, especially when taking place in a well-defined group of users. Geographical delimitation for such a definition and the size of the group is another. The argument suggests that forms of organisation have a more prominent place than power and control in general. Taking the wrong way to organise could be a larger explanatory factor for market failures and blunt subsidising structures. This bring us back to the issue of proximity but from another angle.

> As such, geographic proximity has been found to facilitate the creation of social networks encouraging the interaction of agents and the spillover of knowledge and information within a locale. Singh (2005), provid[es] a feedback loop through which information of the potential effectiveness of a partner is gathered and moderat[es] the uncertainties faced in this process.
>
> (Johnston and Huggins, 2016, p. 1333)

Places, identities and cultures

Scientific elaborations about localism and environment suggest that certain aspects pertaining to the local strengthen the financial and therefore general standing of locally owned businesses and municipalities, by offering alternative economic development strategies. Products and services defined by and defining the notion of 'local' are a basis for old and new entrepreneurial activity creating opportunities for economic 'survival'. Frequently mentioned are 'place-specific' dimensions, specific contexts creating a milieu, an environment. Key words like quality, stability, resources, institutions, identity and image keep popping up in this discourse.

> This, in turn, tends to encourage regions to invest in upgrading those natural and man-made amenities which differentiate them and which provide the foundations for a range of economic activities, such as local food production and tourism.
>
> (Bristow, 2010, p. 64)

Noted here are ingredients in a countertrend, happening simultaneously with and in relation to concurrent processes of 'globalisation' and increasing mobility of people, things and ideas. As such, the argument also includes the notion that localism fosters environmental benefits by reducing transport needs, the dependence on exports and increasing environmental awareness. 'Buy local' is a popular slogan in this context, making a travesty of the old Marshallian saying, – 'there is something in the rural/local air!' This is implemented through strengthening measures and mechanisms to support independent dealers, businesses and farms. A decreasing role of the public sector is complemented or recombined when a new era starts for the resource economies and culture is refound as a resource on its own.

What is local has, however, to be qualified. There is nothing like a 'pure' local. An individual or any somewhat functionally or geographically defined identity functions parallel or integrated with other designated identities. Identity and especially regional identity are used primarily to relate to natural and cultural features collectively interpreted from some kind of spatial entity. With this as a platform, new attributes can and have complemented this internally dynamic concept, like landscapes, foods, dialects/language, traditions. A special orientation is found where identity is promoted and created in the naming of places and firms. Part of the identity is also what others say about you and the eventual named collective or place:

> Regional identities are now regarded as vital in planning and marketing as a means of mobilizing human resources and strengthening regional competitiveness.
>
> (Paasi, 2013, p. 1207)

This kind of argument has to do with the interactive concepts of place, community and identity. It is emphasised through place identity or identification of places, regions, enterprises, etc., and the role played by complementary aspects of development in functional and/or geographical localisation and locational preconditions. One of the strongly held arguments in theory and methodology has to do with an increase in importance of the local in connection with the general process of globalisation. Where the local in its multifaceted appearance stands as a counterpoint or materialised reflection. In the local community in all its appearances, local entrepreneurs and managers and their firms exploit and contribute to continuing processes of forming and invigorating aspects of community:

> emerging strategies through day to day practice and face to face contact; and field dynamics stimulating hybrid forms of capitalism balancing internal and external resources (people, knowledge and economic capital).
>
> (Fløysand and Jakobsen, 2010, pp. 116–117)

This is a special strengthening aspect related to the potential of a kind of collective self-awareness and/or self-confidence (Strøksnes, 2006). The approach, encompassing a Pandora box of complexity and open-ended analysis as the object of study, never stands still, neither in its geographical, functional or temporal senses. There will therefore never be one, there will be many and contested identities and meanings, not always marching in the same direction (Hudson, 2000). The concept does remain murky in applications of analysis and measurement and therefore hard to operationalise (Paasi, 2013).

Interpretation as a process is taken for granted and the combination of attitudes and the substance of meaning itself have clear implications for policy and politics. "It is generally believed that rural people possess a strong sense of community and a marked feeling of belonging to their village" (Akgün et al., 2011, p. 1210). Defining, defending and promoting this identity is a matter of local pride, instinct and partly conservatism, all appearing with the substantiation of the identity as such, or as a self-chosen profile. Now we turn to policies directed to empowering and enforcing the substantiation of the local, in its effort to create, recreate or conserve the identities and differences concerned (Hardt and Negri, 2003). Conservatism or preservationism appear both in 'remaining the same' and 'promoting' for the future and bigger picture (Bosworth and Willett, 2011).

Another kind of tendency is possible where a transformation of the local identity is immanent. The rural/urban dichotomy, sometimes with reduced emphasis on physical appearances, still maintains an immaterial difference, a cultural discourse. When the physical attributes are noticeable, they tend to be exaggerated, cultural trends or stigmas being notable. "[I]nhabitants of areas where town and country seem nearly indistinguishable may nevertheless elaborate a difference through extensive cultural discourse. Where visible differences do exist, cultural oppositions may exaggerate them and erase countervailing similarities" (Creed and Ching, 1997, pp. 2–3). What is apparent, however, is that identity is not static – it is continuous and continuously changing.

> The representations of Norrland discussed in this text are both old and new; they have time and again been reproduced, reworked and reshaped with shifting contexts.
>
> (Eriksson, 2010, p. 96)

With ongoing changes, there are formed new substantiated foundations where the outcome is not imaginable. The role of agriculture and forestry plays a less significant role and the rural inhabitant is, as a first, no more a farmer:

> most of the inhabitants of our smaller urban centres have bound their gainful employment and economic outcome outside the agricultural sector – and thus away from the rural villages and hamlets often in larger metropolitan areas.
>
> (Møller et al., 2010, p. 4)

References to place identity and community appear frequently although Creed and Ching (1997) emphasise that scholarly interest is dominated by studies of identity in connections with race, class and gender in social, economic and institutional contexts, not primarily on spatial (Korsgaard et al., 2015). "[T]he focus has shifted from studying singular identities to research on the intersection of multiple identities, such as class, gender, race, sexuality and so forth (Valentine, 2007)" (Eriksson, 2010, p. 96). The linked nature of rural-class, rural-race and especially rural-gender experiences and forms is not really disclosed.

> For example, social theorists generally fail to acknowledge that a rural woman's experience of gender inequality may be quite different from that of an urban woman, or that racial oppression in the city can take a different form from that in the countryside.
>
> (Creed and Ching, 1997, p. 3)

As references to identity and community appear frequently and is a substance in concepts like social economy and social capital, this orientation should be self-evident.

Another aspect of interest and potential ingredients in the future of specific regions and localities is defined by the approach to policies of marketability, of branding. The term identity, differently used among sociologists and market economists, is incorporated in other disciplines as well. Marketing regions and rural spaces also discussing the idea of self-appreciated definitions of those who live, act, etc. in these areas is problematic. Sociological perspectives are about belonging, indicating not belonging somewhere else. The dimension of self relates to the physical circumstances passed through an intricate interaction of conscious and instinctive ideas, beliefs, etc. that seem and/or are relevant to these circumstances. The ultimate goal is to create a foundation of attractiveness in a differentiated focus on a future labour market, economic structure, population and visitors. This is still not any kind of branding:

> Spatial cognition studies demonstrate that the extent to which a region is known positively influences the place image, simply because of the human attitude of not trusting and not liking the unknown (Hospers, 2004). At the same time, visibility – especially in the long run – depends upon the degree of communicated place distinctiveness.
>
> (Pasquinelli and Teräs, 2011, p. 9)

If the picture or image is consciously strengthened, the way this happens is of importance. In Norway, a project including an educational programme in qualitative branding took place in 2008 through the initiative of the Ministry of Local Government and Modernisation. The intention was to increase the conscious work on profiling, qualitative branding and place development (Follo and Villa, 2010). A matter of substantial evidence noted was that what is identified as promotable has to satisfy two types of objectives: delivering messages that make the place stand apart from other places, and being successful as a concept should not be possible to copy. The necessity of conflicts of interests enters into the question of how the local/regional is presented, is experienced. Which audiences are considered, especially in the meeting between the local and the visitor/outsider? Here the distinction of place branding and community is crucial. Branding/marketing/belonging could be three distinct worlds – often competing for resources in time and space (Giles, Bosworth and Willett, 2013). The number of trendy promotion campaigns of places or regions is substantially more than the creativity of the profiles. Similarities dominate the outcomes, as imagination and risks connected with projection failures stand as pertinent obstacles.

Returning to the concept of identity and belonging – 'who' is closely connected with 'where'. Spatiality identifies relationships turning into networks, while still maintaining different roles, positions, etc. (Cabras, 2014). Discussion is usually found in marketing aspects of business strategies, and, primarily, in a terminology of internal culture. The substance of the local community has to do with creating meaning in and with that community. It is home and the meaning is loaded with experiences and memories. It is a 'sense of place' or 'spirit of place'. It encompasses going away, maintaining partial meaning in origin, and potentially returning. The type of identity/meaning has a lot to do with physical environment, activities in connection with this, with traditions, with economic structures. Primary economic activities and linkages to these profiles constitute part of this inheritance of belonging. Shops, libraries, schools, etc. provide a framework for performing "important social, economic and community functions in maintaining village life" (Cabras, 2014, p. 7). Another part of the substance of belonging is the presence and activities of social organisations, sporting teams, interest organisations, collective formations related to the rural and or the defined area – as in agriculture, impacts – which possibly/hopefully strengthen aspects of community identification (Smailes, 2002). This bringing us to the perspective of social capital, where sense of community and interpersonal trust are basic ingredients. "Both play a major role in modifying subjective well-being" (Morrison, 2011, p. 1053).

The nature of peripherality could change over time and place, and areas defined as peripheral do not necessarily remain so and could – by and through specific policies (long and short term) and, exogenously given processes – become centres for both this and that. The point made is the mixture of remaining and changing meaning and substance of identities. Methodologically, a need exists to look for relative changes in places and spaces, changes in the substance of the periphery and a longer view on methodology and measurement, where identity is one of the outcomes but also a starting point.

A possible approach is where remoteness becomes a benefit and present solution – special bottom-up projects, etc. where bottom-line arguments seem less valid. What matters is the factual or mental distance to the relevant centre in relation to the feeling of belonging, in one way and form or another. Nowadays, instead of physical distances that earlier hampered the environmental qualities of a place, mental and social distances appear as more important due to the conditions of a continuously increasing physical and virtual mobility. A potential line of thinking – where local adaptation (emphasising uniqueness) brings alternative solutions and approaches – is developing. Considering the quite heterogeneous quality of the localities, some are found close to the urban, others are more remote, and even the quality of the remote is qualifying (Akgün et al., 2011).

Bringing all these themes together means that the inhabitants, in the rural peripherality of whatever version, increasingly define the advantages rather than the disadvantages, giving tribute to the unique subjective worth of their culture and location. The combinations of local traditions, landscapes and livelihoods being resources in themselves, enacting a recreation and continuation of patterns of revitalisation of local cultural traditions. 'Traditional' is a platform for what distinguishes the 'unique' rural from the stereotyped urban. The traditional is combined with the 'place specific', emphasising the otherness in quality and style.

Quality of life (QOL)

A basic perspective in the analysis on growth and development has been, and still is, the claim that material welfare primarily secured in the city enhances the subjective experience of well-being/improvement (Morrison, 2011). What will be discussed in this small section is primarily how and if the rural/peripheral dimension has something specific, alternative to contribute within the rural/urban or peripheral/centre continuum. An interpretation of success is usually an interpretation of material standards. It is counter-argued that, in the middle of the material welfare, happiness is not, or at least should not be, taken for granted. Suggested is a change in perspectives, where immaterial needs are more important in these countries of top development ranking, where material development could result in overindulgence. This can be a change in perspective to the importance of roof-over-our-heads from house-with-a-view, and where life is culture and free time is personal development.

The substance of what constitutes the QOL varies. An ongoing process is taking place to be able to show some trends of identifying particular measures of QOL (Stimson, Stough and Roberts, 2006). From the general abstract mentioned above this varies from aspects of longing for and belonging to traditional ways to being highbrow or potentially a snob. 'Authenticity' represents the sum total of a kind of megatrend, where a location to the rural seems needed, encompassing anti-commercialism, co-creation, handicraft, wisdom, ecology and solidarity.

Making QOL-perspectives a research area is quite problematic, and efforts to sort things out – by trying to deconstruct the concept and its contextual features – proliferate. Starting from the contextual and defining perspectives, QOL has to be identified in both its objective and subjective appearances – with the first one measurable, and the latter indicating personal assessments made as part of a personal track record and prognosis (life satisfaction, happiness, moods and emotions like joy, contentment, affection, anger, anxiety and sadness and, not least, expectations for the future) (J.F.L. Sørensen, 2014). Other authors also reflect on some of the depth and complexities of an operationalisation of different terms, where happiness "turn[s] out to reflect relatively short-term situation-dependent expressions of mood, whereas self-ratings of life satisfactions appear to measure longer-term, more stable evaluations" (Helliwell and Putnam, 2004). Life satisfaction encompasses material standards as well as aspects of happiness.

One of the complex dimensions of whatever locality we are talking about is the nature of object of study in itself, what is usually the comparison of predisposed areas or communities described as poor, in terms of material standards, social relations, etc. Social indicators created on backgrounds of poverty, natural disasters, migration, commuting, secularisation and some multicultural patterns are linked to a concept of disintegration (T. Sørensen, 2011) and found in both city and countryside. Lack of social integration correlates with higher frequencies of depression and anxiety. Aspects of experienced high quality of life will be found where interaction, identity, security and belonging make for a good diagnosis and prognosis.

Structural conditions and patterns-of-life formations are backbones for different demands and needs, aggregated in different categories within the population. The existence of different cultures within and between different countries delimits culturally homogeneous entities where attitudes to what constitutes the good life are different, in terms of attitudes towards knowledge, wisdom and education, attitudes towards what constitutes development and especially good development. What is good in one construct can appear as secondary or negative in another.

Another kind of approach defines different platforms for good living, where a dichotomy of material standard and belonging is distinguished through different accessibilities. This is where material has direct implications of QOL. The following example describes quality-of-life disadvantages in areas studied: "living in rural areas is associated with lower household income, lower employment, more housing problems and a lower access to private as well as public services, such as stores, banks, cinemas, public transport facilities and medical care" (J.F.L. Sørensen, 2014, p. 1452). One of the problems with this kind of perspective is classic. If 'happiness' drops as the material welfare increases, when we crowd more and more, population aggregates and material indicators cannot constitute a measuring unit. It is, however, not that simple as it is also a reflection of a need to clearly define the entities. Rural dwellers have a higher positive well-being than urban, in rich countries. While the opposite is true in less rich (J.F.L. Sørensen, 2014).

If the material benefits in dimensions of health increase due to the presence of immaterial conditions, this should be considered. Time spent in nature may reflect on stress reduction and a long-term impact on aspects of fatigue in general. To raise the question of measurement is probably getting too far in the exploration, although efforts are made. An investigation in the EU12 noted the presence of higher satisfaction in rural life than in the cities, with higher levels of insecurity about the future among the urban dwellers (J.F.L. Sørensen, 2014, pp. 1457, 1460). We still have not identified the nexus of the research question, which is whether there are definable, measureable quality-of-life (QOL) aspects in the increasingly mobile population, and if that is qualified in the local/rural. Questions pertaining to the presence of different complementary labour/life careers are answered in terms of whether it is possible to measure partial explanations behind the aggregate, mobility statistics with an impact on happiness, satisfaction and quality of life. "One example of this change is the growth in the value attributed to 'quality of life'" (Anderson, 2000, p. 91). Definitions of silence are brought forward as aspects of rurality and rural spaces, places and cultures. Senses of space, fresh air, wilderness activities, fitness training, contemplation and pilgrimage events. Peace and quiet – an established cultural categorisation of rurality – are, of course, impossible to grasp in a methodological approach. Subjective evaluation is, however, not out of line. "[Y]et also, as a positive association, 'unspoiltness' and 'escape' and respite from urban hectic and overcrowding" (Herrschel, 2011, p. 86).

Rural lifestyles associated with traditions and nostalgia with simplicity are defined by the context, but not primarily as a focus of entrepreneurial activities (Korsgaard et al., 2015, p. 12). The argument is that the realisation of the entrepreneurial process still maintains the realisation of quite basic ambitions which do constitute a dimension of QOL identification, but are maybe a wider and more fundamental reflection of the self, solving the logistics of combining aspects of material standard of living with QOL. "Consequently, entrepreneurial perceptions of value are not limited to financial profits but reflect their own, and wider generalized value systems" (Anderson, 1998, p. 134).

The kind of entrepreneurship should and could, however, be differentiated and Korsgaard, et al. outline two categories. One is described as above and another is also identified in a peripheral context and version with an orientation towards exploiting rural structures and processes. The front line, based on the aesthetic and experiential consumption of the urbanites, creates "a multi-functional place of leisure and heritage consumption (Mitchell, 2013)" (Korsgaard et al., 2015, p. 14). QOL is exploited in business ventures with the peripheral and remote as attractions – creating a workplace while at the same time living the dream.

Turning the argument around, there is a process that goes in two geographical directions. On the one hand, and on an aggregate level, we find arguments about moving to the city (with a number of attributes referring to jobs, quality of jobs, hotspots, melting pots, service and culture provisions, partner-seeking, etc.). Resources are present but are not always produced and consumed here, whereas the kinds of individual and collective profiles to a large degree are defined and realised by where they live. On the other hand is moving to the countryside where peace and quiet, security, serenity, nature, a slow pace, cheap accommodations, etc. are rural attributes. In this rough classification, we have also generational perspectives, discussed more in the upcoming section.

Location complemented with size of the communities studied seems to matter as well, where smaller categorised communities noticeably neglect variables like income and employment with clear implications for aspects of the discussion on social capital and social economy. Where social capital consequences appear in terms of belonging and trust have also implications on well-being (Morrison, 2011).

> Thus rural dwellers are often held to have a higher social interaction among each other and to possess a higher community feeling than their urban counterparts. Phrased differently, strong social cohesion is often mentioned as a trademark of rural areas.
>
> (J.F.L. Sørensen, 2014, p. 1452)

A relevant and maybe more complex point is the acceptance of the reality in a moving target. QOL is a changing concept or, eventually, several, where rurality appears as social constructs going from consumption to encompassing social, moral and cultural values (Johnston, 2000, p. 720). Trends are identified in marking culturally different analytical and decision-making frameworks both on an individual and collective level. Finally, the dimensions of QOL manageable for decision-making: "still need to be discussed, conceptualized in theoretical models, researched, validated empirically and widely applied practically" (Stimson et al., 2006). Maybe this can be accomplished through priorities defined by thematic conduits like alternative entrepreneurship, social economy and sought-after social capital, just to mention a few or by reducing differences in regional disparities or ingredients in general formulations about the right to similar living conditions wherever you will find people or populations. If this takes place in achieving or providing room for regional competitiveness among social actors or entrepreneurs with ideas where social implications are considered, that is even better.

Demographic patterns and processes

This section choses some, from a peripheral, rural perspective, important demographic aspects. Those most often mentioned in generalised terms are age and ageing, interregional migration and international immigration. Especially the first two outline the interactive processes of gentrification and youth exodus, usually described in highly negative terms and linked to other so-called negative aspects. Regions that experience sustained net outmigration "also display other indicators of economic distress" (OECD, 2011a, p. 50). The notion of context, in terms of cultural traits, sentiments, etc., reflects on settlement and migratory patterns and processes. The absolute volumes are not covered; the simplified general argument is that volumes and areas play a substantial societal role. The example highlighted through the Finnish situation:

> The types of areas that are counted as countryside cover 95 percent of Finland and within them live 1.66 million people (31 percent of the population).
>
> (Landsbygdspolitiska samarbetsgruppen, 2014, p. 16, my translation)

> Sparsely populated areas cover 68.3 percent of Finland's total area, but only about 308,000, i.e. 6 percent of the population lives in rural areas.
>
> (p. 18)

Already at this very preliminary stage, the picture is multifaceted. Sparsely populated regions – found with both decreasing and increasing populations, with age distributions extended from youth dominance to gentrification – are identified as existing, upcoming or non-existent problems. The consequential effects or problems cover a range of possible and plausible scenarios from negative causalities or what is described in terms of nonsense correlations. The demographic 'situation', described in net results, is awkward for analytical purposes, as it hides analytically interesting movements among, for example, the generalised cohorts of the migrating population. As earlier noted, net out- or in-migration does not in itself consider qualitative aspects within the flows. Relevant aspects with notable impacts today are found in increasing climate awareness, of traits of solidarity, of a transfer of well-being going from material to service demand and an urge for the small-scale. These exemplify things/trends that could have implications and activate a longing or increased interest in links with the countryside (Ulver, 2012). In a micro-orientated, directly relevant approach, the following exemplifying quotations seem pertinent:

> More specifically, both commuting and migration patterns are influenced by the extent of locally available jobs appropriate to the types of residents attracted by the distinctive mix of housing and other conditions in that area.
>
> (Coombes and Champion, 2010, p. 184)

Or qualitative aspects:

> Whether the better-off are tending to move in or out will relate to local characteristics such as:
>
> - housing types and conditions
> - reputation of schools, secondary-level ones in particular
> - levels of crime or antisocial behavior
> - retail and leisure facilities
> - access to open space and the quality of the local environment including the public realm.
>
> (Coombes and Champion, 2010, p. 188)

Discussing territorial aspects to the general projections are important. In absolute terms, this means defining threshold values and in relative terms outlining interactive processes with other areas, with centres, etc. (Arnesen, Overvåg, Gløersen, Schurman and Riise, 2010, p. 73).

Among the approaches studying peripheral and sparsely populated areas, policy dimensions are in the nexus. How should the situation be defined and what should be done about it? Niedomysl and Amcoff (2011a, 2011b) recommend an increasingly important although inopportune approach where a diminishing population leads to efforts of reducing the impact, trying to avoid or reduce the level of emanating problems, rather than trying the impossible, i.e. to stop the process in itself (Ulver, 2012, p. 6).

Fertility

Fertility rates, as a measure for defining or describing characteristics in outlying areas with peripheral status or with other entities with similar connotations, describe a specific contribution to the demographic process with a time-specific status. Together with migration and mortality, it outlines the long-term potential of absolute changes in the population of a specific area. Fertility rates have been used to indicate development levels, where diminishing rates have been connected with processes of modernisation, industrialisation, education, etc., forming the theoretical backbone to the demographic transition curve. In a qualitative analysis it has much further implications, one being a relation between absolute levels, future progression and the dimension of being born or at least raised in a specific locality. Fertility rates encapsulate flows in the long-term aspects of local or regional demographic status relatively seen as more important than migration. This proposition is qualified, for instance, when there is a need to look at specificities of families, parents, mothers and fathers, brothers and sisters, cousins – and venturing into the idea of growing up and connecting this with future parenthood. It is argued that this is part of forming an attitude/identity in relation to the local/regional community, compared with moving in, as a grown-up, does (Fimreite and Selle, 2006). There is also a kind of loop in the causal chain in this regard. Living close to and in families or extended families is more likely in rural and small-town settlements, a profile that also includes higher fertility rates "and possibly the migration of (some) families with small children from large cities to rural areas and small towns" (Kulu, 2013, p. 898).

The variable does not of course stand alone; there are a number of causality chains at work, where fertility also contributes and reacts. For instance it varies with educational levels, i.e. different communities have different educational profiles, *ergo* different fertility levels (Kulu, 2013). Higher fertility rates are linked with other demographic factors like total numbers or share of married people in the population – thus indicating a higher likelihood for child-related family formations. This includes or indicates more traditional attitudes and lifestyles, pertaining to rural areas and small towns and also encompasses values regarding size and extension. The modern city lifestyles include individualism, self-realisation. Young people migrate to the city for jobs, fun and tempo.

When decisions to raise a child in a quality-of-life defined neighbourhood take place it does have an impact on the rates as such. There is a noted difference between urban and rural fertility rates, although differences are reduced (Kulu, 2013). Why is far from clear. The quoted author indicates socio-economic factors in general as an explanation. A possible complement is the domain of cost-of-living combined with economic opportunities. "[C]hildren are more expensive in cities" (Kulu, 2013, p. 897). The author argues about costly attractions found in the city. Compared with less peer pressure and even helping out on the farm or other natural, economically related activities, living in the rural can have a more direct impact on bottom-line economic aspects. Migratory aspects and the nature and quality of housing define complementary dimensions of decision-making or culture surrounding a collective higher fertility rate: and "explain a significant portion of fertility differences between family houses and apartments, as expected" (Kulu, 2013, p. 898).

Age, gender and education

'Demographic concern' is a concept attached to absolute relations between specific age groups. This is often called a ratio of provision (provider), the dependency ratio, the burden of 'xxxx' and similar more or less formal designations. This ratio is used quite frequently in spite of its often weak analytical relevance. It presupposes that age groups have different, interdependently exclusive functions (consumers/producers, needing/providing). It presupposes that 'those who work' do work (and pay taxes), and that the needing do not. A great variation in professional frequency and free time is hidden behind simplified categories. Comparison between countries and over time is questionable as the status is culturally designated. It is used here only to open a door to specific kinds of demographic processes and structures relating to age and gender in a rural/sparse context. Identified changes in peripheral and/or rural demographic processes and patterns indicate that gentrification as a sum total, will, in the future be accentuated, 'implying' an unidentified and unsubstantiated situation with 'negative' connotations. The range from 'burden' to policy and market urges a development of the argument. Take for instance the following quotation (one among many): "encourage older persons to continue to be competitive assets for regional development (Poot, 2008)" (OECD, 2011a, p. 48).

Age as a basic demographic trait/contribution to the process of modernisation describes relations between age cohorts. Increased life expectancy, promoted by improved health, covers the whole life cycle. In other parts of the world, young population cohorts are very large and growing. Examples from the EU-defined category of 'outermost region' states that the population growth for young people (<15 years) is substantial. Fertility and age as variables create special and varying pictures and profiles where: "Between 1995 and 2008, the elderly population (e.g. over 65 years) in OECD countries grew more than 1.5 times faster than the total population" (OECD, 2011a, p. 48). There is a notable difference in the way peripheries appear in regard to these variables. "Population ageing has been more pronounced in rural and intermediate regions than urban areas" (OECD, 2011a, p. 48). Cabras elaborates on the situation a little more in detail:

> less than half of those living in rural areas today are aged below 45 years . . . about 60% in urban areas . . . larger in sparse and isolated areas where there are proportionately fewer younger people overall; about 21 of the

> population in urban areas are aged 15 to 29 years, whereas in rural areas this proportion falls to 14.6% of the population – about one person out of seven.
> (2014, p. 6)

Within the framework of the general demographic process, the impacts of the after-war baby boom have led to structural implications concerning ultimate economic and social service provisions. The baby-boom generation becoming pensioners will lead to a nominal lack of labour (defined by working-age limits, etc.), increased salaries and (at least in theory) increased supplies of working opportunities. The post-baby boom generation, considered in a wider framework, carries the burdens of climate change, health programmes, etc., possibly also becoming a new wave, or ripple, in the migration process to the countryside.

Avoiding sheer numbers, there is a clearly needed and crucial discussion on qualitative aspects of these patterns, as to how the wave of elderly will actually behave in the future. Also, a better health/sounder labour force may provide higher average incomes, have more energy and less time off, create higher productivity, and have higher education due to longer time horizons, etc. Similar arguments are raised by Lunde (2012). Approach to life and its necessities is a changing and complex demand. The complexity of the demographic issues could also be noted in analysing age cohorts, where for instance, patterns of commuting in connection with advancing age also become patterns of preparing for retirement, *inter alia*, migration. Whatever the case, the picture is as already noted not the same everywhere. Demographic profiles include the specificities of the Sami and also those in northern Finland and Norway where forced outmigration during the Second World War combined with no return after the war.

Another pattern of historical significance is aspects related to education and socialisation, where the countryside/rural with its large families used to have an impact on the formation of cultural values and norms for the next generation. Malmberg notes that policies towards the rural were created not only by economic demand but for their role in qualitative aspects of these qualities (2011, p. 111), registering a difference where the socio-economics of agriculture and the rural changed from being pillars in society to being substantially reduced in importance for the generation born after 1970.

With young adults, i.e. those most prone to migrate, there are a number of factors around push and pull in the countryside versus the urban apart from the recognised need for further education and work – that is the urban temptations are linked closely with the idea of remaining behind creates a stigma for being a loser (P. Möller, 2012). The rural mixture, with educational patterns as an observation point, is defined by a number of different trends although primarily not really a change in substance. Outmigration dominates certain cohorts looking for education and work, while the slightly older in-migrate, where work is possibly not a primary issue. This trend reinforces gentrification through the share of migrants defined above, marking a special strata, even possibly a segregated one (Smailes, 2002).

A different approach as to rural/sparse is becoming a part of the socialisation of youth, where seasonal and part-time work in environments like ski and beach resorts introduce measures of urban culture and norms into the countryside and to the country youth.

> [This] could simplify young grown-ups establishing themselves in the grown-up phase of life, but positions within the tourism branches are, in certain cases temporary, unqualified and low paid . . . which makes the impact of the tourism trade on becoming grown-up not self-evident.
> (P. Möller, 2012, p. 215, my translation)

The discussion under the section on fertility rates refers to issues where birth and growing up indicate a future attitude towards the place as such and, how it is established in memories and culture of the individual. The process is closely identified by aspects and demographic attributes of gender. Some groups, especially younger women, experience/participate and migrate to a higher degree, compared with young men (Berg and Forsberg, 2003), i.e. migration from rural to urban/central districts, but also the other way around. Young women return to the rural districts more frequently than young men on completion of their education (Fimreite and Selle, 2006, p. 7). The mentioned interaction between migratory patterns and the role of establishing a family and the cultural traits has important implications on the demographic structure of the future local community. Issues here are, however, much more complex. Traditional and conservative cultural traits, including gender-defined inequalities are a case in point. This is combined with the dynamics of, or rather the lack of, the labour market.

Qualitative aspects in demography cover an important range of different and complementary issues noted in terms of education and competence. The question raised here is what kind of aspects are of special concern in sparsely populated communities. A life cycle perspective presents a progression from upbringing and socialisation related to quality and actual availability of educational facilities. It also includes advancing in age, sparsity of necessary transport solutions, even weekly commuting – the beginning of severing links with home and the defined locality. Aspects of potential local competence building (handicraft, nature, etc.) have an impact. Exiting high school results eventually in a choice for further and other formal educational opportunities. The pattern of educational localities and functions are of long-term importance (Baltzopoulos and Broström, 2013).

Part of the youth exodus will also and, sometimes simultaneously, be triggered by urban dimensions of culture and party life, by the token of greener grass on the other side, etc. In the sparsely populated areas, this will as a first stage mean, long-term commuting or outmigration. It is described as an early phase of a brain drain (a concept usually reserved for other, more global, flows), but with an active decision from the side of the educated – taking a formal exam, for instance, to stay on in another location, realises this. Distance learning and similar activities seem linked primarily to age cohorts in, on average, older brackets. All these aspects stand in relation to dimensions of societal needs, where the background of an increasing demand for higher competence levels – primarily for higher education – has implications on the provisions of learning and educational facilities on all levels, and also on the quality of their services and staffs, i.e. demands on and from jobs (Kompetansearbeidsplassutvalget, 2011).

The processes described produce an idea, a structure of the potential supply side of the labour market in a local community and its commuting space. Disaggregation of the supply side provides a picture where labour markets' functions and potential are based on a degree of matchmaking between the presence of individuals, educational profiles, competence and demand. An individual returning with an exam and/or definitely with experience, sometimes in the category of competence, will face a labour market with a demand side. An interesting special dimension of this is the discussion on the availability of so-called profiled competence and tacit knowledge in specific sparsely inhabited geographies. As noted, there are structures in this where the males are less inclined to return, while the females, to a higher degree, do. This phase of life includes establishing a family and the individual and collective preferences turn to quality of life, security, a return to social contexts, etc. When matchmaking in the labour market does not take place, adaptation will appear, with indications of downgrading formal aspects of the earlier achieved education. Migration has, however, a result in that newcomers increase the average level of education on both sides, the rural impact possibly becoming more strategic for development purposes (Akgün et al., 2011).

To be considered are also other migratory consequences. There is some scientific support for the notion of stimulating in-migration of small businesses, and by this challenging local practices and redressing some of the brain drain aspects resulting from youth outmigration. Skill levels among in-migrating entrepreneurs are higher than the local averages. The question mark is around the reasons to migrate. Bosworth and Willett (2011) suggest careful consideration, as these entrepreneurs do not necessarily bring improved economic performance, as entrepreneurial skills 'need' to be imported to get results.

Mobility

The specific theme of mobility includes a number of tracks worth following. On one hand, general aspects of distance and accessibility, discussed earlier, on the other, different distinctions like commuting, migration and leisure. Part of the common ground for these flows or processes are the notion of place, place quality, identity, etc., discussed in other sections as well.

> Demographic trends are determined not only by birth rates and life expectancies, but also by mobility and migration. The finer the unit of analysis, the more important mobility and migration become.
>
> (European Union, 2011a, p. 15)

Mobility as a concept is much too aggregated, its potential subcategories or processes identified as analytical entities that are also scrutinised in their interaction. Migrating, commuting, leisure travelling, etc. have important things to say for places, acting as origins and destinations and in-betweens. Mobility in spatial aggregates and international/global frameworks with important implications are discussed in terms of international divisions of labour. Details on a regional/local dimension interlink with dimensions of the labour market (with migration) extending beyond the region and nation. A dimension of environmental concern is part of the modern picture (Coombes and Champion, 2010).

The special population cohort, the inhabitants of the areas/localities studied – and their connections with the locality and place, as an ingredient – and the notion of push and pull factors are part of the picture of a 'good' community having to do with identity composed of ingredients of solidarity, communality. This starting point has a rather complicated and complicating appearance. Although vital in its repercussions on the potential 'inflow', the visitor – the temporary, potentially future inhabitant – turns to commuting, leisure-seeking. Though premature, the specific aspect of the result, the relation between the 'inhabitants' and properties of the 'in-migrants', is that the former could be offset by the risings numbers of the latter, the point being different roles and different interests (Smailes, 2002, p. 79). It is, as noted, a common proposition that in-migrants change the sense of community among the existing residents (Akgün et al., 2011) and the 'old' community is destroyed (Bosworth and Willett, 2011).

It is not self-evident that this flow means better living conditions for the already resident population. A first argument is that the migrants/urbanites do not primarily move to those rural areas where the population decline is most drastic: "one should ask not only if rural areas are invaded by the urban middle class or hampered by depopulation, but also where" (Hedlund, 2016, p. 461). Another is a reference to the concept of 'dilution', where integrated dimensions of home and work stand with different social platforms as in the category of home and going away for work (Smailes, 2002). Pressures in the housing market may mean increasing housing costs to groups of local people (primarily young, with small wages and savings). An impact could also be registered on local provisions of public service, as they are already pushed/rationalised to lower numerical population levels, so the way upward is much harder (Cabras, 2014). Staying on the theme, in terms of increases in short-term daily mobility, Haugen emphasises "the continued importance of immobility, although this issue is perhaps somewhat obscured by the main focus of population geography on mobility in general and migration in particular" (Haugen, 2012a, p. 26).

Although low birth rates are described as having a larger impact in forming the demographic process and structure of the periphery/rural at any point or period in time, the issue of migration is important enough for further consideration. Migratory patterns are recognisable in long-term historical trajectories. Basic aspects of climate change, warfare, nomadism, crop failures are significant triggers and nowadays more relevant in aspects of international migratory patterns. The first noticeable aspect of a significant and consequent rural-urban migration appeared in the United Kingdom around the middle of the 19th century and then spread all around the world. The primary reason for the latter (which is also one of the crucial points for a discussion on present and future tendencies) was the appearance of employment opportunities within the industrialisation process, matched by poverty and lack of alternative opportunities in the countryside (Akgün et al., 2011).

Modern aspects of the migratory process appear in a number of ways.

> It has been suggested that instead of stressing the purposeful and calculating character of migration, one should emphasise its location with the individual migrant's entire biography . . . the complexity . . . migration is a cultural experience making concepts as cultural identity, sense of place and dislocation central to the analysis.
>
> (Berg and Forsberg, 2003, p. 176)

For the purpose of this book, rural-urban and rural-capital city have already been discussed. Furthermore, intraregional and international aspects have important implications for the present situation/position of the variants and places of the countryside. Migration from rural to urban areas has been a well-known development throughout the Western world, and is still recognised as a factor, although less so. Disaggregating this process into distinctions related to chain migration and geographical patterns, it is noted that the flows encompassing centralisation processes include a successive progression, the move to communal centres and then regional centres and further to the major cities and the capital city. Outmigration from the countryside/periphery plays an important role in defining fundamental policy problems, primarily on threshold levels for service provisions relative to age cohorts, but should also be considered on issues in a wider range.

> Further, social ties are disrupted by continuous outmigration, causing a decrease in support systems and social capital, which can have detrimental effects on liveability.
>
> (Delfmann et al., 2014, p. 1035)

As a special and at the same time crucial contribution to the picture we find aspects of the international migration/refugee processes, where the dominant tendency is for new immigrants to settle in the three metropolitan counties – in Sweden 62 percent, 35 percent in the Oslo region (Norway), and the same tendencies are found in Denmark and Finland.

Evidently, the definition of the mobile population (migrants, commuters or leisure-seekers) also needs qualifications as to their complex motives to where they want to live, motives for their mobility and the impact of where they find themselves in the life cycle (Overvaag, 2012). Taking a long-term perspective, commuting can be a valid strategy for a combined future job and a potential place to live.

The analysis should investigate the issues of commuting *cum* migration in three general directions. The focus should be on how commuting encompasses day-to-day functions from the home or working place and in connections within the mobile population. There are different processes at work in the home and in the labour market, whilst the interlinkage physically carries a number of qualifications. A framework discussion on these perspectives is needed.

Defining the starting point from the viewpoint of home-living conditions and quality-of-life dimensions does highlight a number of qualifications. As in all area definitions, homogeneity in categories of the population in working-age cohorts is too limited, as the creation and location of a home in a locality have – in a more penetrating analysis – different logics. The same kind of general qualifications pertains to aspects of the labour market activity, depending upon or creating commuting behaviour. This includes local conditions in the periphery; identifying changes in the local labour market; creating, for example, conditions to reduce commuting. An interesting variable although in a number of not only positive consequences.

Remaining on the same level of abstraction but approaching a less intricate dimension, the commuting link – in terms of distance, cost and time, separately or all brought together – creates some generalisable patterns of behaviour: general thresholds in regard to distances, and optimal times and costs are also differentiated into categories like the ones discussed above. When the migration inflow remains commuting, this does not only lead to positive impacts. Effects on the level and demand for local services and public transport are a case in point. It upholds a local demand for retailing, financial and other services as the commuters preferably use services close to their workplace. The same refers to the consumption of public transport as the commuting in-migrants use the household car. Residents without these means are put at a further disadvantage, where the public alternatives are under cost pressures (ESPON, 2013).

Commuting varies within the urban-rural dichotomy in the simple dimension of higher density, lower levels of commuting. "Analysing UK National Travel Survey data, Bannister (1997) shows a clear correlation between increasing settlement size and decreasing commuting distance" (Coombes and Champion, 2010, p. 189). Pertinent questions in the same category of argumentation refer to in-migrating (i.e. to the countryside): "do long-distance commuters actually gain the well-being they expected from a rural lifestyle if much of their time is in, or travelling to, a city? . . . [P]eople's moves may not match with their motivations (Halliday and Coombes, 1995)" (Coombes and Champion, 2010, p. 189).

People may re-evaluate the impact of long-distance commuting or decide to stay on in a possible down-shift employment in order to achieve home-related qualities (Coombes and Champion, 2010). As noted by the authors, trends in the composite processes have "eroded this apparently straightforward distinction between migration and commuting", and the authors go on to exemplify this proposal (Coombes and Champion, 2010, p. 183). For instance, approaching aspects of ageing, the implications of the ageing process includes a preparation for alternative settling via a phase of commuting, a phase with a relative short time-span.

Major decision-making complexes could be summarised into a dominance of certain variables within those. A crucial part of the picture is the unmeasurable end result, whether possible trends or tendencies are discernible or not. For example, labour market qualitative input/output aspects referenced to here include structural tendencies behind migration "such as risk management or entrepreneurial spirit" (OECD, 2011a, p. 50). The latter has necessary implications for local and regional societies, where the labour market is just one dimension. The composition of immigrant categories makes for a mosaic of regional and local profiles. Regional skill composition among migrants is a crucial aspect in local labour markets. Some indications of changing patterns appearing today. "[T]he net immigration rate from urban to rural areas has been constantly growing over the past decade, particularly in sparse villages and isolated hamlets, outpacing the population growth in urban and suburban areas" (Cabras, 2014, p. 6).

Intraregional mobility in terms of urban-rural movement includes significant structural effects with long-term and still unknown ultimate consequences. Changes in the composition of the labour market are found in this field. Despite a substantial decline in employment in agriculture and forestry, increases are found for employment in the service and industry sectors, noted for rural areas in the OECD area, with declines in urban areas (OECD, 2009b, p. 86).

Future projections are, however, an open affair. A study by SIFO referred to by the then Minister for Rural Affairs, Eskil Erlandsson showed that 45 percent of Swedish people are willing to move to the countryside. A dominance of factors produces a quality of the place/locality, emphasising pull factors such as the availability of areas for natural experiences, leisure time and culture (Overvaag, 2012). Of all women aged between 15 and 29 years, 70 percent are willing to relocate to rural areas, 44 percent saying they want a slower pace, 36 percent closeness to nature. However, in the category of people who cannot imagine moving to rural areas, reasons like poorer communications and access to jobs were prominent. Modern pull factors seem, however, mixed/complicated. Ulver (2012) with reference to Niedomysl (2008, 2010) notes that social factors are prominent, while work opportunities come in second.

Returning to family constellations is, however, complicated, especially in that a household is defined by two incomes, two careers. A possible relocation has to solve that equation simultaneously. Families with two higher incomes, based on advanced education and well documented, special competence is difficult to place in an incomplete labour market. The digital society cannot always compensate for this (Ulver, 2012, p. 6). Still, aspects on the labour market analysed in more detail present more complexities.

> But at the same time we see that large international companies are headquartered in greater degrees in big cities, and that these require the physical presence of the employees in spite of digital solutions.
>
> (Ulver, 2012, p. 6, my translation)

The process of suburbanisation and what was once called 'the green wave' should also be covered here. Several types of such migratory processes – green, retirement, commuter, expatriate and international inward migration and the internal migration of foreign-born – have become more important (Halfacree, 2008). "Suburbanization eased the migration flow to urban centres, but generated new settlements close to, and well-connected to urban areas (Woods, 2005)" (Akgün et al., 2011, p. 1208). Connecting arguments are: looking for work, seeking aspects of quality of life by the Dutch and German and looking for the bliss of nature and countryside (open space) (Overvaag, 2012). Defining the nature of motivation in the rural-urban migration pull is noted in the spheres of education, work, tempo, leisure, partner-seeking and systematically analysed in a large number of sources, and only touched upon here.

A final comment regarding patterns of migration refers to the complexities of large-scale refugee movements, characterising the present-day European agenda. As noted in earlier comments, this aspect of mobility has two prominent sides. Expectations of and from the rural peripheral as being a solution to the continuing reduction of its population, and the other, consequent establishment of a major share of these migrants in the major cities.

As humans, given the opportunity, changes in behaviour during different regimes of qualifications, do create/implicate fundamental differences in behavioural patterns. Looking at migration, commuting and travelling when considering leisure and free time shows quite interesting implications for staying and living, of using space and time linked to availability. This includes control of means needed to 'be able to' have leisure, in terms of time, 'surplus' income, opportunity, consumption patterns based on the tourist/in-migrants' income brackets and therefore demand profiles. This gives implications on competition for the property market, landscape preservation and landscaping, frameworked by tax rules and population markers in taxing and budget distribution. Consequential causalities are quite complex. An example of leisure infrastructure consequences in material and immaterial dimensions includes:

> The accessibility of leisure destinations, and a well-developed tourist infrastructure means there is less pressure to own holiday homes than is the case e.g. in northern European countries. Cultural factors also seems to play a certain role in this regard.
>
> (Smetkowski et al., 2011, p. 180)

The northern regime of sparse territories and uninhabited space is linked to an increasingly well-to-do population and presents other tendencies. Bringing this together in a spatial dimension creates a foundation for alternatives, including multi-house homes, i.e. one house/apartment in the city for daily household and labour market functions and another recreational house in the countryside. The examples given – just to highlight an approach of leisure regimes – are necessary to evaluate the nature of differences appearing in connection with differences in the implications of sparsity, remoteness, etc.

First, in the opportunity itself, its causes, rationalities, etc.; second, the impact on the role of city dwellings, financing, labour, etc. seen from a perspective of the attraction of the rural. The urban, standing for a place for non-leisure activity and the non-urban activity appearing as complementary, is defined by different motivations, i.e. logics.

This brings forward an increasing (by numbers) part of the population connected with implications on the nature of the economy, investments, consumption, land values, service demand on both ends, but primarily in the rural areas (Overvaag, Arnesen and Hagen, 2009). The numbers are not of primary importance, but the systematic construction of high-quality dwellings has an impact on prices, on the nature of land utilisation and leisure time, or leisure combined with work (Gløersen, Riise, Schurman, Arnesen and Overvåg, 2010, p. 27). The latter appears, as in the discussion on migration, where the local community is broken up or redefined under the pressure of the newcomers, guests, etc.

A complementary consequence is where the rural/peripheral population itself consumes leisure or leisure combined with service and product consumption. Notions of public service consumption are similar as in the case of migration and commuting. Special profiles/combinations are considered in this case. Travelling, hunting, fishing, scootering, playing sports, watching wildlife, beer drinking. Although this has naturally varying implications related to gender profiles.

Seasonal variations and their impact on the labour market are also a case in point and put special demands on opportunities for the local economy. Leisure infrastructure defined by different social and economic profiles is the result of different kinds of marketing. Seasonal variations are more noticeable in locations in the periphery, i.e. outside major market areas and with limited marketing segments (C. Möller, Ericsson and Overvåg, 2012, p. 199).

The possible chains of events leading up to more definitive settling down has sometimes been argued for: starting out, trying out through leisure trips, becoming regular, becoming extended, successively severing links to the urban. This is the case where social impact reverses trends of a middle class defining one of its positions as urbanites and complementing the 'proletarians' in the rural exodus. There is proof of in-migratory patterns and eventual population growth closely linked to leisure-related triggers (C. Möller et al., 2012, p. 199). Studies of regional development and linked tourism or leisure-related structures have a focus on the functional use of amenities, where some destinations provide these on a level comparable with urban areas. For instance, in the provision of restaurants, bars and cultural events, organisations, etc. But also, their presence contributes to attract people from the creative class, and by that, in the end, stimulates different forms of chain migration (Hauge, 2012).

The argument, could, however, be turned around. In a newspaper article Nordström (2014) points out the lack of cultural activities, events, etc. in the countryside, with included distance impacts weakening accessibility, having a definite and severe consequence on consumption levels but also on structural effects. In the urban areas the most active and diversifying consumers are to be found, strengthened by higher average incomes, higher formal educational levels. All variables contribute to a picture of low cultural activities and levels, i.e. depending, of course, on the definition of what constitutes culture. Culture has a different meaning in the smaller localities and societies, as it exists in being a part of defining your identity. The questions then lead to migratory processes, their role and end result.

Notes

1 Northland Resource Mining.
2 This discussion has been approached on methodological grounds already in Chapter 4.

7 Extended definitions

An alternative way to re-analyse

A prominent factor with analytical consequences, partly approached in Chapter 4, is formed by the way terminological definitions and conceptual analysis have impacts on results. In order to exemplify and enlarge on this basic theme, a discussion about three strategic concepts – innovation, entrepreneurship and context – and the way these are and could be interpreted is done here. Entrepreneurship and innovation are terms described as crucial to explain economic, social, personal and collective values and include a variety of means, disciplines and methods to reach that. However, to this day, these approaches are quite singular in their interpretation in spite of their complexity. Contextual analysis is an approach where the results in a very direct way are defined and interpreted by their definition and exemplifications. A mentionable example for this is the returning mantra within economics of the importance of economies of scale, where advantages of efficiency and effectiveness are supposed to be reaped in larger entities with in-built tendencies of concentration and therefore, usually, also of centralisation. Nothing new, but necessary and relevant to systematically reconsider within the spatial aspects covered. This final concept appears in three approaches essential in and for politics, research and practice, each with different consequences for different categories of actors, action fields and policy formulations. The primary terms above, when reaching implementation, are interpreted based on the prevailing culture in the organisation and area in question. So this will mean that returning to evaluating the presence and results of innovative and entrepreneurial practices and preconditions remains an open exercise for final execution.

Innovation

The starting point is based on a common interpretation of innovative practices. That peripheral regions are less innovative is continuously noted (Tödtling and Trippl, 2005, pp. 1207–1208). The argument is based on having, as said earlier, fewer R&D investments and less patenting. This starts from a description/definition of innovation in its most common taken-for-granted, appearance. Innovations are products, results of production processes and R&D and registered as patents.

> As in the EU, innovative capacity varied markedly across the OECD regions. Only 13% of regions account for over half of R&D expenditure in the OECD area, and the top 10% of regions generate on average around 280 patents per million inhabitants, while 40% are responsible for fewer than 20.
> (Breska, 2010, p. 53)

Cooking down to statistically verifiable variables: 'patents' are products and production-process related, while generalised geography and functions are taken for granted, i.e. not investigating any potential bias. The chosen variables also indirectly assume/define as self-evident a culture or a competence level necessary for receiving and absorbing new knowledge taking place in larger agglomerations. What is questioned here is the taken-for-granted causality – no R&D, alas, no innovation. However, in order not to oversimplify causalities it is noted that alternative paths do also register needed potential levels of absorption where R&D maturity is a facilitator.

The argument raised here is that there is more to innovations than this kind of representation. At least, "the characteristics of a remote rural location influence innovation in different aspects" (Dimitris, 2004, p. 87, with reference to North and Smallbone, 2000). Traditional innovation definitions do not catch variants of incrementalism and other more nuanced variations. "As such, conventional innovation studies are not adjusted to capture the specific characteristics of innovation processes that take place in rural areas" (Fløysand and Jakobsen, 2010, p. 105). The knowledge base lacks coverage and substance, a conclusion that makes measurement and evaluation problematic, not low activity in itself (Rønningen, 2012). That is, when the issue of rural, sparsity or peripherality is considered at all, it is in terms of small changes and changes in processes and procedures, and statistically much harder – on the verge of impossible – to verify. Status descriptions usually end up with low innovation activity, which, in this light, could be correct, although wrong in substance. In that, the common alternative, the interpretation of the scope, broadness and depth of the definition, has a fundamental bias.

Analytical ambitions widen the application to incremental as well as radical, external/internal, public, organisational, social and the multitude aspects of 'open'. In regard to the rural, its identified characteristics include institutional thinness, special types of local networks, lack of financing opportunities/institutions, a lack of clear leadership (Morgan, 1997, p. 497) and a business profile dominated by small entities. This makes a policy process defined by the indicated form of urban bias, more or less, impossible for rural circumstances as "they overlook the unique feature of innovation practices in rural areas" (Fløysand and Jakobsen, 2010, p. 108). In regard to new firm formation rates and firms with more radically orientated profiles, the large urban regions do predominate (Isaksen and Onsager, 2010, p. 227). Causalities behind this are, however, not presented. The authors enter a discussion on the potential preconditions for more qualitative aspects of innovation in peripheral and sparsely populated regions. Here a necessity of external information and knowledge resources increase in importance, and the geographically induced isolation enforces an adaptive behaviour (Isaksen and Onsager, 2010, p. 232). When efforts are actually made for alternative analytical approaches the evidence discloses some hidden empirical findings. "[S]mall urban regions and the rural regions have a higher share of innovating, knowledge-intensive firms than the large urban regions," explanations possibly found in public funding.

Studies of innovations outside of the so-called growth centres or high-tech locations have been and continue to be quite limited (Aarsæther and Nyseth, 2007). Fragments indicating presence of innovative activities can be found, and as a complementary perspective, everything is not that cosy in the major centres, as Tödtling and Trippl indicate "of innovation problems in large agglomerations" (2005, pp. 1207–1208). Empirical results in a discussion are defined by the size of the locality where small municipalities in the periphery do not to a substantial degree differ from larger or mid-sized ones. It is even so that the frequency is higher in smaller entities than in larger, on a per capita basis (Aarsæther, 2014, p. 27). That this could be linked to the frequency of smaller firms is suggested. Smaller management structures and smaller decision-making teams conducive for a positive innovation culture are qualitative interpretations (Mitra, 2012). Could it be a reflection of the presence of a specific local culture? In regard to embeddedness, it could be noted that the prerequisites for technological innovation are found connected to the ability for qualitative social innovation processes and social entrepreneurship in general (Christensen and Kempinsky, 2004). The logic of this promoted by a constant need for integrative and supportive aspects of the surrounding society. This leads into more general discussions of social structures and norms.

As a basic analytical variable, size – noted above – and possibly the choice of branch profiles matter as: "The role of innovation for small firms operating in low technology industries has received very little attention in the literature on innovation" (Crowley, 2011, p. 18). Combining small size with low technology, no real research base has scrutinised this connection, which is unfortunate as the "development intensive manufacturing may be especially important for sustaining rural economies" (Crowley, 2011, p. 18).

Notably, it is not only geographics that are treated differently. Some actors, organisations and functions are not included in mainline exercises as well. There is a 'common knowledge' of where innovation is a result, who is involved and who is entrepreneurial, excluding specific categories in the labour market. It seems they are automatically defined as not innovative or entrepreneurial. This is unfortunate as they do represent substantial categories. This concerns a long line of functions, organisations and certain types of economic or semi-economic activities. Categories like lower occupational levels in nursing, cleaning personnel and people working in larger kitchens are notable examples. That these are primarily female occupations is no coincidence.

> There are, therefore, reasons to discuss how the concept of innovation could include more categories of labour, be loaded with more substance and used in other circumstances, in other activities that are driven by other logics than

> the knowledge-driven, research-strong innovation environments in the borders between natural science and technical research and high-tech industry.
>
> (Scholten, 2013, p. 91, my translation)

Another concept that, due to its specific qualities, covers initiatives focused on improving where society (as in state/public) is incomplete in its service to individuals and collectives, are different categories of social capital. Starting out with the discussion on rural, peripheral/remote and sparsely populated, this aspect of societal development has become quite prominent. It straddles the border between public/private/social, financial and utility values, making it of even further interest. Trends of positive evaluations of societal efforts in matters concerning climate, sustainability, solidarity, quality-of-life are all functions in pushing forward the social innovator.

A further variant is in how and with what to evaluate results of the process studied – starting with what, fundamentally, is a necessary substance of innovation as such. However, disaggregating the innovative process as such will also disclose important aspects. There is evidence as to innovative practices and innovative results, where 'special' types of innovative activities are presented.

> [P]eripheral regions may develop a form of 'innovative milieu' based upon horizontal networks . . . which, it is assumed, perform the role of 'carriers' of innovation activity.
>
> (Dimitris, 2004, p. 101)

There is no proven direct relationship between networking and business performance, in terms of employment, turnover, market share, profits margins or investments – the quote indicates a need for information. The argument is that there is an indirect relation in these terms, through different kinds of innovative behaviour. Another result, mentioned by Mitra (2012), argues that as smaller firms interact much more than larger, their share in the periphery is relatively more important, networking as indicated above a self-evident necessity.

> Given their traditional internal resource constraints, smaller firms are more likely to use external sources including individual firms, personal contacts and social networks to provide leads for developing new products and services.
>
> (Mitra, 2012, p. 96)

Networking and clustering seem beneficial, even though developing and growth firms can choose to migrate in search for new opportunities and resources. Or, as an alternative, exploiting knowledge and other transfers in terms of 'global pipelines', are stressed as complementary qualities (Calignano and Hassink, 2016). Another process-related point is the need for creativity and the preconditions identifying what kinds of environment are conducive for this. Dominant in present-day mainline analysis is Richard Florida (2002), who ends up identifying that it is most often major cities that are necessary frameworks. Usually, small places are said not to have the critical mass and combined social and economic structures necessary to see these processes through. Arguing against this, Follo and Villa (2010, p. 134) note that these instead have always been creative – 'things happen' – and there is no special need for artists or the presence of a cultural class, or specialists in creativity. Joas (1996, p. 4) writes that there is "a creative dimension to all human action". Creativity in day-to-day situations is not always evident for passers-by or visitors and not necessarily linked to the size of the place. Among the consequences in widening the definition of substance of the original concept is the possibility of achieving a larger range of change/innovation. This brings us into philosophical and political issues, where the phases or ingredients of the process find their local, general outcome:

> but rather to develop a fine-grained view that takes into consideration the type of actors involved, the nature of knowledge relationships and the specificities of the industry.
>
> (Martin, 2012, p. 45)

Describing or defining what kind of region or functional entities are conducive for promoting innovation processes brings us back into the basic conditions on which there is still no agreement. This represents the ongoing debate whether specialised or diversified agglomerations are more conducive for innovation. The question of thresholds or presence of diversity also remains. An argument around possible population and other levels is necessary in order to create preconditions for knowledge spillover effects. The argumentation also has aspects of distance variables.

> The concentrating force in this arises from the idea that successful knowledge transfer decays with distance. Conversely, dispersed or peripheral organisations are said to be deprived of the advantages of knowledge spillovers because of the costs of overcoming distance barriers.
>
> (Simmie, 2002, p. 889)

This connects to the classical thesis of agglomerative tendencies. Sparse, meaning thin, indicates "a lower chance to form regional networks between firms, universities and other research organisations" (Martin, 2012, p. 46).

This argument is raised in spite of the existence of compensatory patterns of local knowhow, competence, or, as it is sometimes called, 'tacit knowledge'. The consequences of these are multifaceted. Their impact on the definitional exercise is intriguing. The analytical extension of substantiation involves non-codified knowledge and distinguishes a wider range/type of innovation. Crowley (2011, p. 20) suggests improved advice-seeking ties to overcome eventual distances: "The results of this study support the view that even when firms are widely dispersed, geography matters for inter-firm learning."

A follow-up differentiation discussing the nature of the innovation process is the special role of interaction of rural firms "belonging to the value chain of the information and communication technology (ICT) cluster" (Virkkala, 2007,

p. 512). This interaction in a wider market within a value-producing chain is positioned in larger chains' networks that specifically service the countryside/locality.

> The lack of local networking opportunities in more peripheral regions need not, by itself, hold back innovations in SMEs. The question is rather, what kinds of innovations are possible.
>
> (Virkkala, 2007, p. 514)

The author refers to the woodworking and electronics industries. The point made, 'going on their own' defined by sheer necessity, do not refrain them from innovating. The question is rather one of possibilities. It could be that the special nature of sparsity/rural/peripheral is creating a breeding ground for survival, alas innovation. There is a need for additional efforts to communicate this potential finding, where the image of backwardness dominates. Arguing a definition in a hostile environment encourages more rather than less innovativeness.

Another approach, widening the scope, is the appearance of different designations and categorisations where the substantiation of the innovation process – taking it as a whole, or specific aspects of it – is qualified. As an example, Isaksen (in a presentation in September 21, 2011) referred to three general avenues for innovation: science-based (science, technology and innovation – STI) learning processes; processes based on experience (doing, using, interacting – DUI); and finally complex and combined innovation (CCI). Also defining the level, the result, the outcome and changing emphasis and structure depend upon this. The argument is that the types of categorisation will find a differentiated geographical representation. The specificity of the areas, in question, create a demand for special solutions,

> broader kinds of innovativeness and adaptability in firms throughout the region, which are only partly linked to R&D activities. It also argues that business innovation in this region often draws on local resources and strengths, but is sometimes also stimulated by the need to mitigate the constraints of peripherality.
>
> (Davies et al., 2012, p. 119)

There is complementary evidence where locations provide preconditions for R&D not found elsewhere. Within EU 'outermost' designated areas, strengths and potentials for research and innovation are based on geographical location and geomorphological characteristics, especially renewable energy, marine research, tropical health; biodiversity further developed as agricultural and agro-food research; mitigation of climate change effects; and astrophysics, aerospace, volcanology and seismology (European Union, 2012, p. 13). In a contribution to the public consultation on the Vth Cohesion Report, 28 January 2011, p. 4, Euromontana identified the presence of specific kinds of service sectors linked to the mountain regions. Actors, consumers and producers could be found in combinations on both sides but were physically located in the mountainous/rural areas (Marcon, 2011).

> This is the case for services, telemedicine, for alternative sources of energies, for operators of short supply chains, for centres of excellence in research on materials used for sports equipment or technologies requiring clean natural resources.

The emphasis is on the potential, hidden behind the generalised urban bias. Morgan (1997, p. 497) refers to the more generalised aspects of policy elaborations within regional economic development, where place-based innovative practices in themselves provide new opportunities. Aarsæther and Nyseth (2007, p. 8) exemplify this, by discussing service production and planning and also innovations within civil society. The borderlines between the public, private and civilian sectors are easy to transit, involving individual actors from each of these. Defining the future potential in improving and enhancing structural advantages is prominent to

> a greater degree than before, becoming part of the innovation activity. . . . [N]ew technology . . . expanded information technology . . . better opportunities to enter larger markets.
>
> (Landsbygdspolitiska samarbetsgruppen, 2014, p. 20, my translation)

Entrepreneurship

This section follows the same kind of reasoning – redefining or, alternately, dissecting the concept of entrepreneurship and new categorisations with special emphasis – in respect to its impact on individual, collective and societal results (in general and with focus also on the financial perspectives). What should be considered in the discussion is the fact that 'rural', 'peripheral' – indicating uniqueness – create an environment where the characteristics of locational windows of opportunities are exploited due to the nature of this 'special, generalised, uniqueness'. The kind of approach needed proposes the interconnection of entrepreneurship and qualities designated by that spatial context. In terms of peripheral, this includes distance; in terms of rural, this could include real sparsity, including variants of empty space. It could also be a counteracting definition, by being impossible to locate, to core/centre/urban. Peripherality does present challenges, as local markets may be smaller, transaction costs may be larger and financial and human resources may be limited. Which only means that the solutions have to go down the track of being 'really' or 'much more' or 'different', in terms of entrepreneurial/innovative.

Working with a widened definition still demands an analysis as to the intricacies of the development process at work on more detailed levels. The working hypothesis is that entrepreneurship should be analytically much more differentiated, but at the same time possible to aggregate to relevant geographical and functional orientations. Rural, as in a territorial definition, needs to substantiate what specific connotations the concept carries.[1] Suggested here is the presence of an alternative palette of objectives, where profit maximisation in neoclassical orthodoxy is replaced and/or complemented by other drivers. For example, emanating from the idea of farming households are self-organised sites of production, not 'scaled-down capitalist enterprises', the former possibly more frequent in the countryside (Sæther, 2015).

Entrepreneurship as a scientific object has developed substantially from personality, psychology references and demographic traits – extended by more holistic approaches linked to socio-economic processes (Fontes et al., 2009). In spite of that, research on entrepreneurship is, in comparison with other fields of social science, surprisingly little developed, although, in the last couple of decades, gathering momentum. In regard to the focus in the present book, it could be said that entrepreneurial activity at the regional level is also not thoroughly researched but it is still, noted to have an uneven spread.

> [B]ut the impact of regional location, or spatial factors, on an individual´s decision to become an entrepreneur is still unclear.
>
> (Mitra, 2012, p. 271)

Even more, eventual links between the periphery and entrepreneurship are not identified and possibly also sometimes believed to be non-existent, following that explanations, in this regard "are absent or theoretically under-explored" (Anderson, 2000). The reason is practical/logical. It is presented as lacking any contribution of substance to societal development in general and especially in regard to economic growth and structural change (Veidal, 2011) being a product of the formal institutional regimes, which do not evaluate potential alternative aspects of entrepreneurial activities and attitudes.

The question appears if the discussion presented here makes a case for rural/peripheral entrepreneurship being different, in such a way, that alternative and/or complementary scientific techniques should be used in order to investigate it. In a wider sense, i.e. social, moral and political, they are described as fundamental ingredients in any kind of development process, mostly noted, however, in connection with economic activities. A somewhat disqualifying issue is finding differences that are important enough in order to discard standard procedures for their special dimensions of entrepreneurship. Generally, the variations of conditions are tremendous and this point should at least be seriously approached. Rules and means for different categorisations have, however, to be applied. We need differentiated approaches even for the methodologies used, complementing by far the following:

> The heterogeneity and uniqueness of rural areas has often encouraged researchers to study rural entrepreneurship by means of qualitative research based on a relatively small numbers of in-depth interviews.
>
> (Akgün et al., 2011, p. 1211)

A central issue is also who and what the entrepreneurs are. Sæther (2015) exemplifies quite astonishing results with data on educational backgrounds among members of a network focused on eco-production, with a substantial share of academic backgrounds. Entrepreneurs are focusing on finding opportunities, of mining resources, whatever and wherever they are to be found – exploiting traditional opportunities, but also disadvantages or weaknesses, and turning them into business or development assets. The essence of being entrepreneurial in this sphere is trapping the difference of peripherality, sparsity and rurality compared with core, centre, urban and making it contribute (Anderson, 2000) or discovering alternative usages for classical resources. It could also be possible to identify a category of urban disadvantage forming an ideological/philosophical backbone among local/rural entrepreneurs.

Different contexts, in this case outlined by geographical references, create different priorities and different knowledge and makes way for culture and competition. This leads to a wider understanding of entrepreneurship, where business is culturally a corner stone but also a part of change in organisational structures, institutional designs and feedback loops – the symbolic representation for changed values and social interactions. Specific, unique contextual dimensions demand specific reactions, habits, attitudes. Mentioned in the literature are partnership-based and negotiated local development, informal economic solutions halfway or outside the official economy. Looking at the process from different angles makes the aspect of results prominent – start-ups and dropouts, temporal distinctions. Anderson (2000) mentions empirical evidence to support the idea of new value formations within the periphery. In another, more eclectic approach, general attitudes and ambitions parallel to local adaptability and necessities are discussed by Johannisson (2005), who also promotes a widened definition.

Changing the track a little, different analytical entrances could also be based on certain kinds of enterprises and activities. Studies and comparisons between them focus on differences as to average size, scope, etc. Clear-cut categories of entrepreneurship defined by the framework of a rural/peripheral dichotomy/alternative in itself is not expected, but aspects or themes bring nuances to the discussion. They can vary in size in terms of frequencies on a territorial basis and ambitions, orientations. Rural firms in remote locations are, on average, small and have a hard time overcoming distance, through this primarily serves close-by markets. On an EU level, SMEs in peripheral regions have an over-proportional share of labour intensive industries. Based on its traditional branches, taking the periphery as a special category within the rural or a special facet of the rural creates a specific branch-related entrepreneurship.

The metaphor of the construction of a brick wall where every brick plays a role or every grain of sand is necessary to form a pile comes to mind. The existence of an integrated local society, with alternative arsenals of specialities or multi-specialities are evident. The appearance of new value chains are among the possible end results. Statistical definitions seem at a loss to catch this kind of complexity, where special human resources of the farm and the farmer, the rural worker, the rural entrepreneur are not considered in evaluating the economic activity in total. If it does not create a statistical entity it does not exist.

Among the approaches indicating and promoting a wider definitional framework, Mitra (2012), describes the connecting link between social change and the need for social, moral and political entrepreneurship, which in turn widens the scope for a context where cultural, social and organisational preconditions are included. "Local social structures . . . 'entrepreneurship facilitating' form of local social capital" (Westlund and Bolton, 2003, p. 94). These interactive processes create changes in the understanding, promoting exploration and construction of entrepreneurship: "different social connections and links between people, organization and cultures" (Mitra, 2012, p. 61). Different characteristics and characterisations pertaining to entrepreneurship in rural/peripheral areas should focus on the entrepreneurs themselves. What is indicated is a search for combinations where different entrepreneurial categories appear together with common traits defined by the area in question. The entrepreneur is defined by the activities involved in and through this by behaviour, actions, judgements and situations. This indicates that differentiation comes before generalisations. The 'local' should capture "the imagination of the curious researcher, the policy maker and even the entrepreneur" (Mitra, 2012, p. 3).

The local, in a rural context, represents special appearances of entrepreneurship, where dimensions of special social characteristics play a fundamental role. Why some communities seem to excel while others do not is a returning question (Kawachi et al., 1999). Differentiation between the political, public, social and private economy orientates towards new roles, new approaches and new targets approached in redefining the context. Veidal (2011) exemplifies this with reference to Rønning (2008), linking social capital to farm-based entrepreneurship and local development in general. The extent of trust, norms of reciprocity, density of relevant organisations, intensity of social interaction and mutual beneficial activities are relevant (Kawachi et al., 1999). An interactive effect of social capital – promoting networks with unique, while sometimes generalisable characteristics – is a pertinent feature (Korsgaard et al., 2015). This source notes the importance of multi-objective ambitions, making one-dimensional, profit-orientated motives an, analytically speaking, dead-end, as "the concepts of space and place to rural entrepreneurship is important for establishing a more fine-grained and contextualized understanding of entrepreneurship in rural settings" (Korsgaard et al., 2015, p. 6).

Another differentiating approach with far-reaching implications is the notion of gender. Arguments raised about remoteness, distance, educational levels are, among other aspects, differentiating and differentiated quite substantially, both when it comes to distinguishing the potential entrepreneurs and the nature of their activity. However, being a female entrepreneur in the periphery defines crucial prerequisites in approaching the total situation, on both the supply and demand sides, in areas where these prerequisites are in short supply. Preconditions are noted as women "are even more strongly affected than men by specific infrastructural weaknesses in rural areas" (Margarian, 2013, p. 16). The same author notes, quoting the European Commission, in conflict with other sources, that due to these specific circumstances, women are "least prepared to take advantage of the specific opportunities that the rural industry structures and resource endowments provide. In many rural areas, this situation results in a low and below-qualification labour market integration of women who are "least prepared" (Margarian, 2013, p. 16). The argument is actually missing the point. It does not consider that women are also a highly differentiated group in entrepreneurial terms. Riding on this, support for women's entrepreneurship in these areas has been put forward as a policy measure to assist women to remaining or migrating back. Limited employment opportunities point instead to a self-employment policy, considering the dominating migratory flows by young women, "A policy model for supporting women's entrepreneurship – with a focus on sparsely populated areas" (Pettersson, 2012, p. 3). On the other hand, it is noted that "While the participating women's resource endowment is probably higher than that of 'typical' rural women it can still be shown to be significantly lower than that of participating men" (Margarian, 2013, p. 16) which indicates a realisation potential that is already evident, but severely under-researched.

Another one of these potential extended definitional categories is found in a range of acceptable levels of profit or non-profit – complementary or standing on their own. As already quoted: "the peripheral new businesses are often craft based, resource or tourist related and are not growth orientated" (Anderson, 2000, pp. 94–95). These businesses do not renege on profits but accept the realism of reduced profits in light of other individually defined objectives based on moral values, personal, societal and cultural aspirations and aspects of quality of life, which in turn mean that growth of the firm, in itself, does not stand in the front line of self-realisation, making activities "more viable in the long run" (Anderson, 1998, no page, downloaded). The argument leads to the tentative conclusion that development in rural areas depends to a much higher degree on a combination of entrepreneurial choice and personal life preferences (Akgün et al., 2011). For example, emanating from the idea of farming households, self-organised sites of production are not 'scaled-down capitalist enterprises'. This is phenomena more frequent in the countryside than in towns (Sæther, 2015).

Rural economic entrepreneurs face the same difficulties as entrepreneurs elsewhere, accessing resources and overcoming the liabilities of newness and smallness. The rural dimension also refers to specificities in how to make use/exploit these specific resources and how to create opportunities and value. Does this make a difference in the nature of processes and activities as such or in the demands on and of the individual, how the 'selection' process takes place, being the survival of the fittest or some special advantages? One aspect, among several, is the rural-traditional approach where aspects of conservation appear in modern variants. Being more specific, Veidal (2011) argues that on the farm there are no restrictions, rather opportunities. The relationship between entrepreneurship and farming is described as complex. Primarily farming is described without entrepreneurial connotations. Whatever the case, certain types of farming activities are still highly entrepreneurial. Alternative production processes adding new business activities are referred to sometimes as pluriactivity: "different ways in which entrepreneurial related to farming interact (or not) with the spatial context in which it unfolds" (Korsgaard et al., 2015, pp. 11–12). 'Combined or complementary entrepreneurship', based on the resource-based 'infrastructure' of the farm, is – at least in regard to medium and small-sized farming – a necessity for economic survival. Is the entrepreneur a jack of all trades, is problem solving of this kind an entrepreneurial skill? Identifying the words 'combined', 'complementary' and 'economic survival' in the rural dimension there can be found further traditional branch activities with add-on capabilities in forestry, hunting, fishing and gathering. Bringing the argument even further, there is business in the new qualitative ways of living. References could also be found in small-scale home-based activities, providing an extra income and carried out in a rural household by non-farmers. Examples are found in service and facility provision, tourism and recreation, crafts and arts, sale of home-grown products. The direct economic impact could, often, be quite small, but the potential seen in a wider context is not. We do not really know! There is a clear lack of research and eventually policy agendas for this.

Another analytical possibility is through the entrance of expectations from the potential consumers, where personal consumption as a motor for enterprise development is stimulated by on-average rising upper strata societal incomes. This does not bring us any further from the general, classical definitions, but it identifies a room of potentials, similar to the concept of 'windows of opportunity' in the world defined by business economics. If we approach the idea of multitasking and special operational combinations can this promote an idea of entrepreneurship as an alternative of categories? Are the frequency of these rural solutions higher than in urban environments?

This place-, area- and individually defined activity is specific for some of the existing branches in that they cannot appear anywhere else. Forestry, mining, farming, hunting, fishing are place defined. But not only that, there are also certain commodities, or 'commodified' resources like clean air, water, foundations for specific sectors of tourism, leisure and health-related activities[2] with similar qualities.

> Those very conditions that characterized the poverty and isolation of the periphery are turned on their head, the 'otherness' of the periphery has become a potential advantage.
>
> (Anderson, 2000, p. 101)

New economic branches appear today where the generalised uniqueness excludes the defined urban (cultural and leisure activities clearly defined). Partly included in this category is when the nature of the rural or peripheral entrepreneurship is able to redefine the essence of the rural. Interpretations of rurality offer alternative sources for competitive advantage and therefore uniqueness (as above) values for rural entrepreneurs. Rural landscapes, places and communities provide fertile settings for new ventures and entrepreneurial activities. New industries and new modes of entrepreneurship operating 'at the edge' revalorise local resources to be seen as keys to growth within rural economic and cultural life. Experiences and aesthetic consumption are cases in point. The conditions of the periphery becomes a potential advantage as it becomes a main, sometimes the only, source (Anderson, 2000). A case in point is also the possibility of place-based entrepreneurial and economic activity profiles linked to certain age groups. From jet-set hotspots to the 'silver economy'.

Another quality of the geographies in question has to do with the presence of integrated aspects of social economy and social capital. The conditional networks facilitate or avoid some of the constraints in the process and provide access to relevant resources (Fontes et al., 2009) included in strategic development, concerning a whole range of objectives. The combination of social missions and entrepreneurial creativity marks out social entrepreneurship as distinct from other public, private, or civilian sector activities (Nicholls, 2006).

> Obviously, this general interpretation of entrepreneurship transcends the traditional focus on market-oriented innovation and firm foundation.
>
> (Margarian, 2013, p. 16)

The discussion of the rural/peripheral being special in this dimension is still under scrutiny and will continue to be. Entrepreneurship with social objectives is initiated by both individuals and groups and often in forms of network mobilisation, realising social, economic and cultural values in the local community and possibly building bridges from that community into collective enterprises with links outside of the community (Follo and Villa, 2010). It concerns mobilising un-coordinated resources (Wagner, Strömqvist, Uppstad and Jakobsson, 2010, p. 145). For instance, compensatory activities for effects of state or local budgetary restrictions or reductions, or inadequacies or incompetence of state authorities or the market. This can range from creating minimal (or preferably acceptable) social service levels all the way to developing preconditions and prerequisites for quality of life improvement, identified by trends and findings, from recent shifts in regional socio-economic development. A wide range of stakeholders (e.g. private actors and non-profit organisations) have increased their importance in development planning, compared to approaches dominated by the central government, top-down initiatives. This concerns issues of efficiency and accountability arising from the modification of regional policy designs and responsibilities across administrative tiers, usually described in terms of partnerships and governance. This kind of entrepreneurship has also something else to offer:

> Entrepreneurship can also contribute to other aspects of quality of life, such as the level of social capital, in that it creates trust, maintains social relations and provides meeting places.
>
> (Delfmann et al., 2014, p. 1035)

Already considering new non-traditional forms of economic activity in the rural departing from the employment growth or profit orientation, the outcome of all these possibilities and potentials are notable, in spite of the often un-noted – the identified high rate of new firm formation *per capita* in rural areas in general. It is small communities of less than 150 inhabitants that show the largest growth in employment in the OECD countries. In the UK, these areas totaled 7.3 percentage points above the national average (Anderson, 2000, p. 96). Rural locations harbour a substantial degree of quality-of-life choices:

> Interestingly they (Keeble, Tyler, Broom and Lewis, 1992, p. 14) find that over 20% of this large sample moved to remote rurality to set up their firms, whilst a further 36,5% moved from urban areas before start-up. Remote rurality appeared to be a more attractive destination for these entrepreneurs than more accessible rural areas.
>
> (Anderson, 2000, p. 101)

Skilled labour is primarily provided by in-migrants, a category that also stands out in rates of entrepreneurial activities. Regional policies/ambitions are often linked to finding ways and means to tempt these individuals to relocate. Among migrant entrepreneurs it is possible to identify push factors emanating from urban structures and processes. Settling down and joining local networks, i.e. embedding in the local communities is, however, not self-evident. This type of entrepreneurship seems to have an impact also on local entrepreneurial actors. Promoting and provoking inhabitants by example or by competition, but also by focus. "lead the local entrepreneurs to be more concerned about the problems of their rural region" (Akgün et al., 2011, p. 1218). There is, however, a lack of knowledge in regard to the specificities of this category.

Making the case for the periphery should and could not include a panegyric exultation that stands up against all aspects of common sense and wisdom. Sparsity and remoteness do include aspects where lack or non-existence of infrastructural and other basic necessities makes life so much harder that economic and social activity are therefore marginal or non-existent. Awareness of existing opportunities are not always present. Limitations in this concern "within the periphery may perpetuate a lack of local enterprise" (Anderson, 2000, p. 94).

The case argued gives an indication towards policy issues. First, there is a need for more and better knowledge of what is actually there and happening. Second, there is a need to focus on the kind of bottom-up models that catch the culture of mobilisation in place-based investigation-*cum*-action, i.e. differentiation towards special prerequisites and conditions in order to improve understanding and identification of opportunities, implementation and value creation (Mitra, 2012). Subsidiarity is the EU *lingua franca* word in this context. Recent policy evolvement changes priorities from top-down subsidy-based blanket interventions designed to reduce regional disparities into broader policies designed to improve regional competitiveness and place-based initiatives. There is no universal panacea of entrepreneurship. Strategies should as far as possible be contextually defined and include a wider range of stakeholders (e.g. private actors and non-profit organisations) and a substantially increased importance attached to process planning.

> These environments are not necessarily points or stages in a single growth continuum, but a mix of cultural, social and economic trajectories informed by an incommensurable set of values, institutions and knowledge.
>
> (Mitra, 2012, p. 265)

The region-specific has a lot to do with a (still) undefined infrastructure, resource base, etc., and its composition is unique. When we speak of an entrepreneurial climate or context – a friendly environment – what does it actually include and mean? Do we go outside of the private business sector? Provide direct help to the company? What and which? Definitions could include everything from starting up businesses, to mastering difficult situations or providing collective services. The dynamics and disaggregation of the number of firms established and/or number of closures should be a natural (Johannisson, 2005).

Context(s)

What happens when we qualify, redefine or redesign the contextual preconditions for the development processes studied? They are analytically configured by a history of interactive processes whenever we take the departure into a modern framework. With references to Stein Rokkan (1997) social spheres with vested political, economic and cultural interests are a central heritage, with different implications on different geographical levels. His framework is articulated as changing results of hegemonic power relations. Activities and processes in each field of influence interact and infiltrate in dimensions of different centre-peripheral arenas (Knudsen, 2011, p. 320). Adaptation to changing circumstances is quite complicated, whether spontaneous or planned. Economic progress is intimately connected with social life, with politics and administration. Simple practical changes in working life lead to far-reaching consequences with important prerequisites for the specificities of consecutive futures. The contextual considerations carry a high degree of analytical importance, as societal activities take place within a home turf with mosaic-like complementary characteristics in combined unique and generalised appearances. "This implies that different forms of embeddedness are important for economic performance" (Fløysand and Jakobsen, 2010, p. 106). Furthermore, actors and reactors do not always behave in expected ways and any level of flexibility is quite demanding and sometimes unreachable. What is evident in the nexus of these perspectives is usually a continuous, and therefore limited, bipolar analysis for evaluating differences/uniqueness, sometimes looking and trying to improve the conditions to look for potential generalities from the general and at present prioritised terms, to the focus that has been chosen in this book.

Peripheries are heterogeneous, as has been discussed extensively in Danson and de Souza (2012, p. 413) and in the introductory chapters here. Identifying the point of intellectual departure is therefore of importance. Whether we locate or distinguish it as an individual, an enterprise, a place, an area, the process will create or define a range of preconditions/contexts with different scopes and priorities. The argument highlights the generalities, the rules of the game. Innovation takes on contexts with preferably economic processes and structures. These processes are embedded in social relations, turning to social structures and institutional frameworks – different mixtures on different geographical aggregates. Innovative practices develop in economic dynamics and produce it. The social infrastructure in the form of social capital is known to play an important role in the related processes, allowing for broader and deeper collaboration. The mechanisms, far from identified, also have interactions with other relevant concepts (Tura and Harmaakorpi, 2005). The latter authors take this point a step further, noting that the elements, composition and qualities change from the individual level and enter different constellations of collectives. At the latter it comes in the nexus of simultaneous qualitative processes and development (p. 1119). Diversity in itself forms a foundation for the process of innovation (p. 1120). Social interaction, the precondition of social capital and defined by the nature of trust and trust building, directly affects processes of knowledge transfer in regard to quantity and quality.

Before we actually make the jump, we have to qualify our argument with the general dimension of time and timing. Every moment has a constellation of contextual dimensions that is totally unique, never possible to repeat, and totally impossible to catch, or describe, in all its details and complexity. The analytical ambition is definitely not the full game-plan. Partly and/or sometimes substantially, it questions some of the taken-for-granted ingredients. Even further, it is noted that certain designations include quite wide and varied frameworks for analysis. Going outside of those, however, could deform the analysis. Aggregation of the unique can lead astray, as can disaggregation. The preceding sections on innovation and entrepreneurship function as springboards in this quest. The main presentation in analysing the results and these processes has been their complexity and, much more to the point, the complex interaction with different aspects of the context:

> a mix of cultural, social and economic trajectories informed by an incommensurable set of values, institutions and knowledge.
>
> (Mitra, 2012, p. 265)

There is also an analytical potential in defining processes within or enclosing where context provokes activities, which in turn, change context, creating another reality for the next cycle. Change, depending scale, brings notable effects in the local environment. New projects pave the way, decline, close opportunities in already ongoing activities. Business interaction is customer interaction. Ultimately the positive ends up with rising spirits, extended margins and better local service. The negative can be ultimately a loss of social cohesion and the sense of community (Giles et al., 2013). When the contextual approach is translated into proactive attitudes identifying necessary contextual changes or identification of different contextual properties as relevant, it eventually turns into policy (Wagner et al., 2010). From the macro level, we will simultaneously find always-present sets of micro- or meso-contextual elements and embryonic processes, where economic motives could represent examples of choices made:

> we might expect that clusters of new firms in a particular industry continuously evolve in regions, where human and other resources are abundantly present and where entrepreneurs are produced at a large scale in the incumbent firms of the industry. . . . But which factors determine where the initial activities of a new industry are located.
>
> (Dahl, Østergaard and Dalum, 2015, p. 10)

Discussing the complex consequences of redefining each of these variable structures, separately, only touches upon the outer fringes of the real, full picture. Starting out with the links – or should one say the highways – between the specificities of rural/peripheral entrepreneurship, it is motivated, inspired and capitalised in combinations where checks and balances are defined by the specific setting in itself.

Issues of nature, climate and sustainability

Behind a large amount of aggregated contextual features worthy of an analytical scrutiny, stands the totality of nature, climate and, eventually, the issue of sustainability. Nature and its impact on and in culture, as in cultivation, or maybe more, exploitation, defines an umbrella stretching from everyday necessities to the ultimate demise of mankind. The ecological footprint (read crisis) is today an important global phenomenon reconstituting local practices, reassembling meanings and redefining 'the center of the world' locally. From these stark colours appears an analytical step into strategic and tactical issues, of patterns and structures, of possibilities and problems. The crisis brings up different prospectives – locally as well as globally oriented – coping and livelihood strategies. A specific geography defines dimensions of problems and necessary impacts of development and spaces for eventual solutions. There are distinct patterns of potentials and responses to fundamental ecological questions in remote and rural areas. The issues at stake do have a considerable spatial dimension, often including a positive scenario or strategy where the periphery is the, or a part of a, solution. In the periphery, there exist clean air and water and extensive tracts of unspoiled land and soil; unexploited resources of place-based character affect mobility to (or non-mobility out of) remote and urban areas. Environmental pressures are problems that become competitive advantages. A link with historical patterns also includes the narratives of remote localities as a space for autonomy and self-sufficiency.

Climate change is a well-established, scientific fact though the causalities, direction and pace are disputed. Although, the generalised combination of short-term economic margins in production – combined with urbanisation, centralisation and lack of knowledge – seem like a presumed target area for a sawed-off shotgun ecological nightmare. Over half of the world's population lives in cities today and an increased share will create conurbations with 500 cities of more than a million inhabitants by 2050, of which a number will become megacities with over 20 million inhabitants. The contribution to the carbon monoxide footprint brings an estimated urban contribution of up to 75 percent of the emissions. In order to qualify the issues at stake, the impact does depend on aspects of urban density, which in itself is argued to reduce effects when planning and, actually, constructing higher densities, which implicate infrastructural efficiency, at least at a first stage.[3] Population and economy in the urban framework interact in relation to environmental degradation.

Green infrastructure refers to forests, rivers, coastal areas, parks, eco-corridors and other natural or semi-natural qualities essential for the provision of ecosystem services. The term 'ecosystem services' defined in the UN in 2004 in a policy document called the Millennium Ecosystem Assessment (2005) highlights the benefits that occur naturally and losses that may occur if not preserved. Air, water, land, species, soil and lakes are among the natural resources critical to our well-being and to our medium- and long-term economic prospects. Aspects of rural impact implicate the need for clean water and air, for space, for land and links with raw material resources.

There is a special case with strategic implications and that is the multifunctionality of energy production, transmission and consumption. In all aspects we have a clear pattern in the demand for space in already ongoing systems, where the provisions of production facilities are found in the rural/peripheral and transfer networks as well. Arguments for locations and demand for space could be natural preconditions (water flows, coal mining), security (nuclear energy), space (solar). At the same time, plans for future energy production show the same kind of patterns; most frequently referred to at present is onshore wind capacity.[4]

An interesting discussion already raised in other parts of this monograph is found in the geography of impact relative to control, decision-making and earnings. Substantial differences between the Norwegian and Swedish cases as to ownership and concessions are noted. Implications as to labour-market impact is also duly noted, although of more marginal importance. A presence of indirect effects but possibly of strategic importance is found in connection with an enlarged functional labour market and competence impacts. Although basic research and development is taking place elsewhere, there is a clear need for field studies in the neighbourhood, where try-outs and technical improvements are looking at local application and adaptation (OECD, 2011a).

Capitals in extension

Inspired by the concluded section, a comprehensive and enlarged definition of the widened concept of capital as a contextual phenomenon seems relevant for the present discussion, both in terms of stocks and flows. It highlights aspects of potential development not present in normal investment calculations or in classical descriptions of the role, organisation and status of financial instruments in a wider sense (here in the connotation of rural). The key argument is that the simultaneous presence of different forms of capital should be highlighted as well as the resulting cocktail of their combinations. Natural capital, based on quality-of-life investments contributing to human satisfaction both directly and indirectly (the man-created means the more traditional man-made capabilities) refers to the economic potential of the physical environment, sometimes in terms of 'resources or resource capital'. Human capital in turn, connected to the labour market, refers to size (and potential size) of the population combined with its abilities and capabilities in the present and future. Among the capitals, cultural capital is an offspring of different qualities of social capital (see below) among other ingredients taking its working/functioning into new levels of community, identity (Raunio, 2005), and returning to the identified qualitative contribution to social capital, giving it further depth or height. The World Bank has, for instance, noted the relative importance in Sweden of a combination of social, knowledge and cultural capitals, enumerating it to 87 percent of the total capital available. Capital invested in construction is mentioned at 11 percent and natural capital at the low end for 2^5 (ACANALYS, 2011, p. 8).[6]

Taking the lead from Granovetter (1973, 1983) the issue of social capital as an 'embeddedness' is a concept that carries a substantial portion of contextual content. A lot of controversy is found around the findings and interpretations but the basic proposition including social capital into a 'family' of 'different' capitals is clear (Tura and Harmaakorpi, 2005). As noted in Chapter 3, social capital is a notion of benefits within the interaction between human beings, having a consequence into their individual and collective socio-economic behaviour and life qualities. The argument provided in this discussion is the link between social interaction and trust, where trust, in general terms, is conducive to economic activities. Social capital refers to the importance of networking, trust, etc., in the community, fostering or blocking entrepreneurship and innovation: "social capital may influence the other forms of capital that affect growth . . . positive impact on human capital by increasing education" (Iyer, Kitson and Toh, 2005, p. 1017).

Before we go any further, it is necessary to make some fundamental distinctions or delimitations in regard to the concept. The theoretical background is found in two main directions: first, benefits from participation in collective endeavours, and second, individual advantages from social ties. The essence has to do with trust, respect and civic participation (Florida, 2002). To trust somebody saves a lot of energy in establishing economic, political or social agreements. It is substantiated in terms of reducing transaction costs. Increasing efficiency in a number of fields – like information gathering and distribution – and facilitating collective learning processes reduces the need for control and monitoring (Iyer et al., 2005).

Social capital refers to informal aspects of institutions and organisations in the form of networks and associations, with the explicit quality of sharing knowledge – based on mutual trust – norms and taken-for-granted ways of behaviour (Peiró-Palomino and Tortosa-Ausina, 2015, p. 103). This definitional extension appears in close connection with another more generalised concept, social economy, where the latter encloses the capitalised version. The concept of social economy concerns activities that have societal goals as their intention, organisationally separate from the public sector, based on non-profit and democratic values. A central characteristic of the social economy is based either on personal and/or collective involvement:

> the mainstream view defines substantial swathes of socially useful activity that can be summarized under rubrics such as the social economy, or Third Sector, as irrelevant to the development debate.
>
> (Hudson, 2007, p. 1156)

The discipline of economics has had a hard time encompassing and, even more so, integrating the concept. Of primary concern seems to be the lack of characteristics relevant for traditional economic rationality thinking, and also it being a complement to market-based processes and not a 'capital' on its own. Terms like GDP, as noted, exclude aspects of the social economy as dynamics – although of substantial social value – are not within the metrics of mainline economic considerations. A special feature, however, is where qualitative aspects of social capital are linked and created to and by specific forms of economic effects:

> The evidence shows that voluntary work in associations is significantly higher in rural areas, whereas passive association membership, social trust and institutional trust are equally high in rural and urban areas.
>
> (Sørensen, 2012, p. 875)

The role of social capital could also be approached, based on its integrated and enabling properties and/or indirect versions of economic capital, as a resource giving access to economic capital (Horlings and Marsden, 2010, p. 3). Social capital is a highly important contextual precondition when considering development processes. There has been and still are some doubts raised as to the validity of social capital being conducive to innovation in 'all' its phases and processes in its general role in the economy. Creativity for instance is not always a collective endeavour. With references to the importance of the creative 'class', the variants of social capital in traditional industrial societies are not sought for (T. Lundqvist, 2006). Social structures can, however, depending on time and place, both promote and hinder economic processes.

What is indicated is that social capital can be consciously created or strengthened. The caveat is that it remains quite hard, as it is subject to different perceptions, deeply penetrating aspects that have to do with historical experiences, cultural norms, traditions and religion. The answer to the proposition is somewhere within the claim that certain defined factors and processes may be generated or deliberately prevented, but the result is not guaranteed and sometimes undesirable.

A representation of an in-between approach is an attempt to link an overview of possible policy approaches with a liberal market mindset, exemplifying:

> the importance of viewing political struggles as conflicts over competing institutional and organizational arrangements that favour one type of indigenous social capital over another.
>
> (O'Brien, Phillips and Patsiorkovsky, 2005, p. 1042)

There are a number of differences noted, where the social capital is cultivated, being a 'product of intentional investment', but also just a consequence of beneficial social interaction. Hoarding of social capital is a type of capital accumulation with no 'ownership' at stake (Westlund and Nilsson, 2005). An interesting and important implication is its potential role in the theoretical and applied development of the cluster concept, where social networks, social capital and institutional formation are key aspects. Embeddedness represents the framework where economic and economically related structures develop. The argument in the periphery is, according to Hudson (2000), the presence of a higher share of these kinds of activities, when they are marginalised by the main functions of the economy. The concept, however, varies in scope between different cultures/countries. So will, consequently, the case for the ability to quantify any results. This part of the economy is described as complementary – i.e. where private or public actors, for various reasons, are not sufficient or, based on other normative criteria, discontinued or never initiated.

There are some basic qualities in the concept that catches one's attention. The mix is sometimes quite hard to identify as to its elements, and the kettle is continuously boiling. There have been queries as to why some communities prosper, in economic terms, and accordingly present a more economically healthy picture in regard to its institutions and inhabitants, while others do not. Social networks, and therefore social capital, are named as a framework. Firm formation and day-to-day practices are facilitated or constrained by the availability of personal and organisational links and resources, webs, etc. (Fontes et al., 2009). The impact of social capital has different emanations – as networking for resource control, personal networks (in terms of ethnic, migrant or other bonding characteristics) and business environments to name a few (Korsgaard et al., 2015). The common denominator includes aspects of trust and reciprocity. This brings forward the multidimensionality.

> Social capital is a complex construct, which, . . . has a structural, a relational and a cognitive dimension (and various sub-constructs may also exist inside these dimensions).
>
> (Echebarria and Barrutia, 2013, p. 1002)

It is in the interpretation of these networks as resources for society in general, its collectives, and within those (among its individual members) the essence is found. When we approach these dimensions, it is stipulated, intensively argued, that this is an important part of rurality. It has been indicated (Putnam, 2000) that social capital is higher in rural areas. In general network interaction is more intensive in rural than in urban structures.

> the rural entrepreneurs are required to invest more in local social capital. Given that the residents of such remote regions are usually in tight-knit communities, it is not surprising that successful entrepreneurship in such remote regions rely on connecting with these close networks.
>
> (Akgün et al., 2011, p. 1217)

Sørensen, however, argues that social trust is not significantly more present in rural settings. In social capital measures, factors like age, education and income have a higher explanatory value than the urban/rural distinction (Sørensen, 2012, p. 882). However,

> For several reasons, the voluntary work measure is probably the most valid of the four social capital measures used in this paper.
>
> (Sørensen, 2012, p. 886)

Attempts to measure social capital are many, complex and not always successful, the issue being the range of indicators within a social context in different aspects of the economy, across regions, countries and functionalities. Data, as such, are scarce and carry different meanings. "Typically, for narrow studies, social scientists have looked at civic associations; how and by whom they are created. In these studies, social capital is measured as membership of groups and networks" (Iyer et al., 2005, p. 1020). Mixing also means weighing, where interpretative norms and results will be found in different and opposing corners. In order to reach more clear-cut proof, there is a need for a methodology, and in that there is still a way to go.

The combination of a functioning social economy and capital suggests a positive influence for a new firm foundation. It is suggested that there is no absolute identity between entrepreneurship fostering organisations and a positive climate in this sense (Baumgartner and Schulz, 2010). Social capital has been presented as the beneficial glue of well-behaving communities, not only providing a still unsubstantiated foundation for economic progress, but also for a functioning local government and democratic processes that in themselves are conducive for economic advance. The quality of that glue is of central importance when the internal organisation and demarcation means that group cohesion can be shielded from the potential impact of interaction with the outside world. Apart from that, there are also indications of positive impact on crime rates and delinquency, and a direct impact measured by health indicators (Kawachi et al., 1999). As earlier noted, social capital in its different facets and its main appearances within (bonding), between (bridging) and connecting (linking) in communities can be especially important compensation for some of the real and experienced deficiencies defined in a peripheral status. Bonding, as in strong ties and relationships, is defined "for example, by special interest groups, families or based along ethnic lines, etc." (Cooke, Clifton, and Oleaga, 2005, p. 1066). Bonding social capital has been described as the most important one in rural areas. They "outperform urban areas with regard to localized trust, rate of passive and active participation in local civic associations, and various measures of local reciprocity" (Sørensen, 2016, p. 392).

The main characteristics of social capital networks are the relative strengths of their links (Granovetter, 1983) and the degree to which they include, cover and open up. Granovetter talks about weak and strong links affecting different aspects of society, for example, knowledge transfer as to extent, depth and cost (Fontes et al., 2009). Strong ties (more or less closed networks, too much social capital) are important for this and based on trust and cooperation and usually need geographical proximity (face-to-face) to maintain expediency. Strong ties are, however, not always for the good, as some of their special appearances could be detrimental both to their own qualitative development and to the environment, encouraging special and group interests, and costly for society in general (Iyer et al., 2005). Social capital in closed communities is associated with negative, criminal, corrupt, etc. behaviour. Strong ties could mean hard borders/closed communities, putting up restrictions, hindering new information and alternative ways, and ultimately "restrain[ing] innovativeness" (Iyer et al., 2005, p. 1116).

Bridging, as in "'weak ties' (Granovetter, 1973, 1983) concerns relations across rather than within groups. . . . Bridging social capital may be needed to improve economic and social performance" (Iyer et al., 2005, p. 1017). Bridging has, as noted by Sørensen, marginally higher presence in the urban context (2016, p. 392). Another complementary approach in the same thematic range is made by Florida, where he observes that the dimension of contextual process changes the quality of the network themselves. The kind of communities needed for economic and societal progress has turned from close and cohesive to

> evolving communities and emerging society are marked by a greater diversity of friendships, more individualistic pursuits and weaker ties within the community. People want diversity, low entry barriers and the ability to be themselves.
>
> (2002, p. 269)

It is notable that the substance of social capital is not just made up by horizontal networks. The vertical variation also includes different types of accepted power relations. The concept of linking identifies the existence of contacts, including degrees of power and resource control. This opens the door even wider for information flows to a dimension of knowledge sharing and provision.

> [C]ommunities that already possess a large stock of social capital are often in a better position to accumulate additional social capital than communities with a limited capital stock.
>
> (Raunio, 2005, p. 3)

A consequential and crucial aspect of social economy and capital is, however, that they are long-term products/projects. Comparisons are not in the volume but in the constitution of forms and dimensions of these forms. In each territorial context, social capital is a product of a number of factors and processes including historical experience, local cultural norms, traditions, religion and sometimes also politics. In spite of the fact that trust is an extremely valuable resource, you cannot go out into the market and buy it. "Rather trust has to be earned in and through repeated transactions" (Morgan, 2007, p. 104). Social capital serves as the glue between people in a society that both binds them together and lubricates the relationships between them. In rural areas where other structures often are sparse, personal contacts and business relationships often create dense networks.

Defining value, value production and value processes

This aspect of the contextual creates an argumentative framework around the breadth and substance of value-defining concepts, what kind of value concepts we use and should use. At the same time, this section provides a discussion on the relevance of these concepts, their content and their internal relationships. It is approached in close connection to the concept of development, i.e. what carries on as a central aspect of the substance of societal changes, in terms of growth and other related processes. The discussion focuses initially on economic value and utility and then slides into a more general material/immaterial orientation, towards their – comparatively speaking – broadest form with discussions of value concepts' potential and application in respect to such intangible expressions as joy, happiness, freedom, etc. This also includes categories of personal and collective values and evaluation. Values are described as fairly stable ingredients, defining what is worth fighting for, achieving and the ways to go about it (Hellevik, 2011).

The dominant – frequently occurring and 'simple' – definition/description is a monetary-defined value, broadening towards forms of benefits and alternative definitions with distinctions in material/immaterial categories. A side-track found in the form of reflections on quantifiable and qualitative perspectives. It is preferably a perspective on how the 'value concept' is defined and measured, how differentiated values are created and materialised. A pedagogical note appears here, being contextual encapsulates some of the basic arguments in this whole book, that of the alternative logic.

The concept of GDP and its offshoots is only one of several measures used and discussed earlier. As noted changing societal perspectives have required changes to more refined methods; levels and the rate of change of wealth, productivity, income and purchasing power are others. Traditionally, economists have in this respect a different formal value, a quite strict concept. The concept of value creation has, more and more, been taken over from terms like economic growth. Change and development in the ability to improve one's life that simultaneously opens the door to a broader value concept has also been introduced in the economic debate, considering, as in UNDP, factors such as health, literacy, life expectancy, gender-related considerations and qualities of democracy. Perhaps more important is a 'political' inclusion of everything described or defined as 'valuable' in society. The humanities extends the scope substantially. Another more technical reason requires concepts to include the micro level in macroeconomic perspectives. An underlying term that quite frequently recurs is the existence of and society's need for a value construct that also includes cultural aspects like pride of place, individuality, identity, solidarity, equality and sustainability, etc. It includes growth combined with objectives like resilience, sustainability and subsidiarity (NUTEK, 2004, p. 11). Emerging in the broad research perspective is the need for geographic, social and institutional analysis that includes the composition of the economy in spatial/geographical categories. Development will thus come in a broader perspective in terms of changes in structure, changes in and of the economic organisation, changes and access to technology and its applications. Finally, changes in the view of the role of knowledge in all parts of future progression including a shift of focus to other types of analytical units. This occurs especially in a societal perspective with an emphasis placed on differences between the public, private, collective and voluntary sectors.

In the extended discussion about value/s and benefits, a concept of cost becomes an element and often an argument in the ongoing debate. Optional application and opportunity costs are important for prioritisation between different processes or regarding assessments of development structures of a more fundamental nature. For example, Hegrenes noted that 'weak' regions have higher production costs than 'is necessary' (2004). The question pertains here to a defined value of necessity.

Before initiating the various interpretations of hidden and manifest values, it may be appropriate to identify the scope of the 'concept'. Already the use of the word concept implies something more than an etymological orientation or an absolute definition. Value as desirable, as important, as in quantity (and quantities for evaluating something else) and numerical. Each appears as complementary, or on its own. Values are complex compositions. Value can be: direct and/or indirect, material and/or intangible, profit or process (values in terms of absolute and dynamic categories). Equivalents in monetary terms are exchange value, profits, savings, GNP/GDP/capita Gross Regional Product (GRP). Other equivalents in a variety of forms are social, knowledge and competence, social capital, replenishment of emotional energy, personal development, contacts, and so on.

As an example, resource definitions are a category of value identifiers. Nature has value as a resource for aesthetic, contemplative, etc. enjoyment and experience, having a relation to utility and other indirect effects. At the same time, nature is a resource with what it contains in terms of timber, berries, mushrooms, carbon monoxide trap, etc. But the value in economic terms is also available in an exploitative perspective, distinguishing a differentiation between nature and natural resource, where resources are defined by man (Rees, 1990). Nature protection is a way of providing value to nature, for a benefit to an ultimate consumer (Brandtzæg and Haukeland, 2011). The transition between nature and natural resources includes a process in which knowledge, skills and technology are transferred and nature becomes through this a resource realised by demand (Wicken, 2008).

Values are contextually defined. Nature as a resource can change substance. An example is collected from the historical period when Finns migrated to Värmland, Dalarna and Hedmark forests, where slash and burn farming meant that timber standing did not have any direct value, as it hindered access to a cultivable area. The standing forest had, in this stage, as noted, a low value. Then came ironworks, and the demand for charcoal created a profitable alternative use of the forest (value), the wood use increased in general, and thus the value of the timber, which in turn forced slash-Finns away or into other occupations. The development of untamed rivers to regulated energy production shows the same basic process by which scientific breakthroughs and new technical equipment create processes of development from useless to useful, from valueless to rich. Indirect impact on other resources like fish etc. are duly noted. Electric energy production has spectacular usability (electrochemistry, electro-metallurgy, petrochemical, food), extending through this an indirect definition of a valuable nature (Wicken, 2008).

From these very down-to-earth examples, the distance is not that far to the identification or creation of fictitious values. The financial market derivatives, futures and stock market reactions to enterprise quarterly reports carry for the actors a high degree of reality in terms of value, whereas the financial market bubbles – railway speculation, real estate markets and the IT sector speculative capital growth – plummeted value levels under water.

Utilities/benefits are central concepts in social sciences and philosophy. In economics and business administration the term is used in several ways, and, as noted in the previous section, as reflections of how economic value could be created. The concept is central in most microeconomic models as part of the description of consumer behaviour and the economic models' introduction of marginal utility as a methodological elaboration. The rationality of the economic man is based on seeking benefits, often in hedonistic terms of pleasure and pain, modern variants defined in terms of preferences. Alternative utilities of the forest are an example, competing with the timber industry, relieving stress that: "cause pain, fatigue, elevated blood lipid levels and high blood pressure. This leads to diseases of type fatigue syndrome, diabetes, depression and atherosclerosis" (van den Bosch, 2014, p. 4, my translation). Cures found in healthy environments and the forest are identified as such.

The individual or household maximises its 'benefit' by successive choices. It weighs expected 'costs' and minimises these and/or maximises thereby the benefit/profit. When the consumer appreciates a certain product some benefit is obtained or realised. A benefit is a personal/subjective concept. This can also be done with more commercial intent through including or defining cultural experiences in dimensions of products and services (Aronsson and Braunerhielm, 2011).

Perspectives on perceived, realised and calculated benefits have obvious analytical problems. Based on a fairness perspective, including the first basic levels in Maslow's pyramid (1943, distribution issues and social indicators (such as literacy, infant mortality, etc.) illustrate the importance of composite performance indexes based on these categories of variables. The choice has to be legitimised and ordered in a preference sequence. When rigorous in its definition, prediction of choices could be made, however, far from qualifying for any eventual 'rationality' (Elander, 1978).

Hudson notes perspectives on development where socio-economic approaches, on a scale from 'near market' to the traditional voluntary sector, provides services/features usefully measured in terms of, for example, time consumption, or through other forms of mutual exchange. This could be taken further into the potential of alternative economics and alternative-to-economic solutions and transactions – "regions that have become peripheral to the main circuits of capital accumulation and the mainstream economy" (Hudson, 2007, p. 1156). Using an economic value concept as a core in a benefit-oriented development analysis indicates that the value/benefit considerations are more versatile tools for defining values in society, identifying the translation of quality, efficiency, productivity and satisfaction in the public sector (Hallén, 2013).

That the definition goes into the core of the social debate, i.e. about the economy's preconditions, functioning and distribution is obvious. What kind of measure could and should be acceptable? The choice of target defines the means. The choice of means defines the objectives. Where the conditions for certain goals lies in the achievement of others, achievement of given goals also gets second and unplanned/projected consequences. Formulation of goals and evaluation criteria force considerations that some actors perceive as constraints. Among the general EU priorities mentioned in this context, such objectives are found in the categories of gender, inclusion and sustainability. Analytical inputs are oriented towards and from cultural, psychological, technical, individual, collective, human, elitist values as well. Scaling in the already-referred-to Maslow's (1943) pyramid of needs means that in the developed (OECD) nations, the proportion of people who reach higher, who attach utility or value on culture and self-fulfilment on this scale, has increased. Immaterial needs as a beautiful environment, a rich cultural life and time off become increasingly important.

Another example related to the broad concept are effects of experiences and knowledge (health, quality of life, leisure, aesthetic, education, play, inspiration, identity and heritage) (Lundqvist and Johnson, 2014) that are difficult to measure but apparently exist. Measuring the impact of artists and art, how to compare? Values have to be scaled, but how? When a forest in the north of Sweden is evaluated for consumption, timber or recreation, the latter comes out one half the former, while in the south the outdoor experience is valued many times higher (Norman, 2014). This has to do with traditions and historical values. Partaking in the process of identity formation, definitions considered from a value perspective are intrinsic but also realise emergent results in larger structures and constructions. Other specific values, having to do with exclusivity, snobbery, etc., are open for alternative analytical inputs. What makes this type of argument interesting is that the analysis of society's more 'refined' economic values can, with such an approach, be brought to greater breadth and depth.

The terms 'value' and 'benefit' as departure points, each one individually and together, make it time to take the plunge into the processes – of value and benefit creation. But the road also diverges through another analytical input. Does the definition of value emanate from a value creator, the value broker, or a point where the value is realised and the value level is defined where the consumption, or the final consumption, takes place? "Value is always uniquely and phenomenologically determined by the beneficiary (. . . the customer)" (Grönroos, 2012, p. 281). An interesting discussion is the various actors' relation to different value aspects in the same process. To clarify – intermediaries are also consumers, and different individual players have different experiences. Grönroos exemplifies buying a car for the enjoyment of driving, for the possibility of meeting friends, or in realising a childhood dream of something fast and flashy.

A research and analytical process requires that we consciously identify what type of value/benefit and value creation process we are considering; second, that we discuss the methodological and theoretical implications for this; and, third, that we look further when it comes to finding methods to design and evaluate alternative concepts of value and their quantification or substantiation. The concept of value creation describes a process defined by a goal-setting – alternatively, evaluatory variables or perspectives – of what is created or to be created. It also provides a feedback and an indirect description of the potential for analytical inputs into the value-creation process. The most common use, as emphasised before, is the creation of economic value and its link to the processing of a product or its value interpretations or value chain. The increased value connected to the product at each stage of the production chain is its supplementary or added value. The process takes place in an organised manner, both outside and within different types of organisations. Sources of competitive advantage grow out of the way firms organise and carry out their specific activities and can be systematised and, through this, create opportunities for categorisations and reorganisation (Lean). That it creates value for customers through these activities and that this is recognised through how much customers are willing to pay is a major manifestation and for some, the exclusive one. If the sum of this value exceeds or falls below the cost of production is, of course, fundamental, when social objectives are excluded.

In the public sector, the combination of services and their goal orientation indicates values with different criteria, like efficiency, quality, satisfaction, utilisation, fairness, choice or variety. Ultimate objectives are measured in terms of cohesion, equality, wealth distribution, safety, poverty reduction, educational levels, health, trust, legitimacy, perception of service quality and levels, transparency (Bloch and Bugge, 2013, p. 135). Activities or objectives like these can be assigned a monetary value, or measured in categories defined on the basis of the activity. Training can for example be measured in its impact on knowledge and through this on educational production performance, or in the definition of summed (qualitative and quantitative) effects in terms of levels and skills – utilisation in terms of commercialisation and adaptation of approaches and methods. "The most common way for utilisation of research is education" (Nahnfeldt and Lindberg, 2013, p. 8, my translation).

Based on the consumer/user, etc., the basic question is, what is it that creates value for him or her? This identification must be done simultaneously with considerations that the processes that create value also include non-economic-value-adding activities. Thoughts that revolve around the production processes of various types (both physical products and services) will return in the processes as phenomena that do not add value or reduce it. The elimination (for example in the context of JIT [just-in-time] and Lean) by factors that are unnecessary is done by a (savings) process, which is an increase in value with conditional aspects. Sources to competitive advantage grow out of the way firms organise and carry out their specific activities and this also defines a potential value. Alternative perspectives that emerge here are concepts like Corporate Social Responsibility (CSR) and environmental and other beneficial certifications.

In the economic sphere value definition has also a clear spatial basis and outcome – a given territory, share and location. As is already evident, the analysis here becomes a very complex exercise, but when the value is given priority in society, the identification of the variables that constitute the value concept – that the prospective operator celebrates as central – also determines the identified dynamic of space, functioning and timing. What is also notable, not making the exercise any easier, is the fact that society processes and values (in terms of norms and ideals) change, which is no less important than basic values and norms (culture) differing fundamentally between different states and groups of states – and more distinctly, between nations or rather nationalities (Hofstede and Hofstede, 2005). Regional distinctions are, perhaps, not usually that eloquent.

In complex, composite products, structures, services, innovations, etc., the number of perspectives on what value can be are combined. The values represent different value-producing processes in or without defined objectives (Nahnfeldt and Lindberg, 2013). Mixed forms of value creation are frequent. The cultural sector can be said to have an activity that both delivers immediate value, realised in the form of sales and income, but due to its special character also values related to aspects of consumption without direct economic categories, as aesthetics, experience and memories. The normative here creates a field of tension with many interesting implications. Different types of value creation with different values produced can define one another, be each other's precondition. This dimension is, however, a socially summed dimension, making the whole discussion of the characteristics of value creation of even more strategic importance.

One discussion still remains and has to do with the earlier identification of whether value is created throughout the journey, or when the process of creation is realised in the consumption stage. Returning here to the service logic and user evaluation, where the value of an improvement in services, manifested through time savings, security, competence development, etc. must be experienced, integrated by the user – what the users need, not what is feasible (Kristensson, 2013). This includes both the physical utilisation, the mental process surrounding it and even with ownership as a specific phenomenon (Grönroos, 2012). At the same time the process has also an intrinsic value in itself. Value creation can, of course, be translated to a value-chain logic where function, production, consumption and geography make up analysable conditions and quantities. The actors involved in the value chain, suppliers, producers, supporters and consumers, here introduce the network as an analytical tool (Virkkala, 2007, p. 514) or, in a definition of values/benefits in terms of preconditions. With the value chain as a theoretical starting point, elements and processes are packaged for the analysis in different, interesting variations; all meetings, transfers, receptions in the process are articulated. Cluster theory exemplifies a declared approach which precedes this latter discussion of definition, in that a cluster is defined as a systemically defined value-creating chain, or a combination of chains. A firm's value chain is an interdependent system or network of activities, connected by linkages. These links and the substance and the quality of them is central (Porter, 1998). Different stakeholders' (suppliers, distributors and consumers) value chains are realised in the total.

Functional relationships that can be exemplified in terms of proximity in general and to the customer as a useful source for improvement in the efficiency of value creation are a similar example. The dependence on technological development, or rather the knowledge about the technical front-line displacement gives more opportunities. Access to business angels, *såkorn* and venture capital determine the pace, organisation and scope of value creation. Value chains are regarded as kinds of social and, sometimes, geographical force fields, where each element's (company, business, local community) position is dependent on the overall structural shifts. The presence or absence of important phases or moments of a functional value chain within a region or a local community create structural balances or imbalances in society, defined in categories of landscape, centre-periphery, urban-rural. The role of a specific 'territory', position and importance as a product of historical processes, transforms to the present and future. The definition of the value-chain elements and phases then are identifiable as strategic elements, reflected in the definitional exercise (Wahlström, 1989). A system perspective should/ought not to stay within the economically defined values. Its analytical potential may be an explosive force when the value concept, from the economic perspective, connects to the benefits, intangible and ultimate values and values in the role of cultural definitions. Which brings us into the vicinity of local, regional development in a holistic manner.

Notes

1 Look at the elaborations in Chapter 2 on definitions.
2 This is stated while trying to avoid a discussion on parks and the exoticism of inner-city tourism traps of clean streaming water, proving the point of created or recreated pure water regimes.
3 Its consecutive consequences of promoting further growth are considered elsewhere.
4 Its economic benefits are a case of concern on a detail level, not applicable in this monograph.
5 Noted in the secondary source is the fact that the provision of ecosystem services are not included.
6 Methodological considerations could and should be taken in the future.

8 Peripheral economics

Some alternative approaches

There is, when it comes to generalised socio-economic factors, no essential differences between the city and the countryside. Places and localities in the countryside are found in complex interactions with the international, national and regional and urban systems, providing their profiles of resources remains in compensation and combination, although distinct, still part of the same general socio-economic system. This statement, emanating from the realms of political economy, links the rural with the same kind of global and national forces and structures as the urban. Basically, however, the distinction of the rural and especially the rural periphery is found in situational and distance-determined catalytic effects and in the fact that most often triggers, causes and causalities, decision-making etc. for these processes are found in places far from the areas investigated.

What should also be noted are changes taking place in the urban construct where opportunities to be exploited are found in the interface of the urban-rural that "can function as a lubricant in rural development, stimulating eco-economical strategies which lead to a more multifunctional form of land-use" (Horlings and Marsden, 2010, p. 1). New market possibilities are found in niches where a general positive economic development generates a "growing affluence and can be exploited by remote rural firms. This is partially confirmed by the high orientation of remote rural firms towards personal consumers" (Anderson, 2000, pp. 100–101). Rural location combined with an urban consumer market could be optimised in reduced local internal competition and remaining forward urban marketing (Backman, 2013).

The forces appearing are, however, much more complex than these simple statements presume. The dimension of the national-regional-local tug-of-war – at present enclosed in different paths, from some hesitant devolution practices to direct and flagrant exploitation and control, seems, in spite of positive ambitions, to continuously disadvantage the periphery. Any public efforts to break the hegemony, if appearing, are working against a tide of underlying spontaneous or conscious centralisation. Decentralisation carries fiscal, political and administrative imbalances and therefore also explicit implied costs. However, focusing on the green growth agenda, the periphery-induced disproportionate costs for the supply of public services could and are already by far compensated by exploiting regional (rural, peripheral) specified assets. They are dominated by food, but also include a full spectra of natural and energy resources (OECD, 2011a).

In economic geography, a traditional management of localisation has focused on production-related, spatial decisions. Other types of corresponding decision-making structures are to be found within population or transportation geography, but decisions, theory and methods have kinship albeit, sometimes, a distant one. Their role in the argument that this book promotes is, in all respects, highly relevant. A single location decision affects the geographical starting point, the journey and the goal and is influenced by the specific characteristics of the same factors. Since the process studied and hopefully influenced has its core in their interaction, traditional scientific approaches come in the nexus of an attempt to understand what the substance is in a community, a region and its future development. It is the spatial dimension in the context of sociological, behavioural, economic, political, etc. dimensions. There are many possible dynamics at work here and purposefully stimulated. In-depth analysis can increase the reliability of the explanation and might serve for the development of societal policy. The very idea of development implies change over time. It is not always explained in terms of place, but place is always there. There are many examples of locations and localisations, which cannot be explained by purely financial and/or economic-geographical reasons: historical patterns and processes, innovation and diffusion processes, individual characteristics, achievements and idiosyncrasies, and the always present, random factors.

The chains, webs, etc., that link the rural and its places with the global in terms of cooperation and competition appear through filters defined by the domination of national and regional urbanities. Attached, with fundamental implications on the power of control, are issues of decision-making hierarchies, constantly defined and redefined. Among the more prominent modern structures are issues of subsidiarity within the EU and the mentioned, more academically defined discussions on devolution. The latter in terms of efficiency and expediency of decision-making bring in reality-based concerns, tailoring policies explicit for local needs. Aggregated efficiency and equity stand against institutional burdens. The bottom-line summarises gains and losses, dependent upon the level and organisational responsibilities (Rodríguez-Pose and Gill, 2005).

What has been argued is that the periphery should be analysed from its own preconditions and related to a possibility, or more strongly, a generalisable kind of uniqueness that has not, so far, systematically, been considered. An example of variation temporarily leading out of the peripheral domain notes that substantial changes are taking place both in the urban and the rural and possibly in the transit zones/areas or what is called the interstitial areas. For example:

> those more bucolic rural spaces that lend themselves to relatively informal types of economic activity and cultural economic expression in the guise of crafts, design traditions, environmental attractions, or specialized crop cultivation for discriminating markets.
>
> (Scott, 2013, p. 41)

The informal, however, pushed backwards when modernisation activated a state- and centralised-controlled development process. This meant that the importance of informality in the periphery was reduced and the impact of the waves of the primarily formal economy, became a problem for traditional dynamics (Wallentin, 1985). It is a range of economic activities that is not analysed in depth, due to general perceptions to what economy is and how people in the global periphery get by. Another example in the same category is the identification of economic activities being ignored.

> [I]n summary, even though many scholars and policy-makers have promoted small businesses as a means of rural economic and employment development, few have explored the growth expectations of side activities and their possible effect in regional development in general.
>
> (Markantoni, Koster and Strijker, 2013, p. 12)

A general need for diversification – heavily promoted by the local situation – individual drive and alternate ways of life lead to the construction of different activity portfolios and assets. Managing, diversifying, improvising – continuously entrepreneurial (Potter et al., 2008). Remaining in the field of economic aspects, the logic demands excursions into the socio-cultural fields. Still, the impact on and of peripherality, geographically considered, also accounts for systematic effects in cost structures for different factor contributions. Part of day-of-life considerations are also subsidiary schemes, a theme that has been and is questioned, creating a special kind of alternative and questionable culture.

Mentionable as a fundament is also a particular interpretation of localisation theory, with specific implications for economic peripheral regions. These areas are characterised in that regional nodes are not properly connected. Weak and undeveloped links and supporting structures are not strong, full-bodied, enough. The activity patterns differ considerably from the central regions in that the nodes, participants, to a limited extent or not at all, supply goods and services to each other or to their neighbourhood. The peripheral nodes are not bound together by mutual commuting flows. The social context is characterised by the same, so called, 'weakness'. A starting point, a process and an outcome put the periphery in a unique position in the grand total. But is it possible to generalise? The patterns are different, and hence, do they lead to different behaviour? The conclusion is that theory and its postulates must be tested in their most fundamental forms. For instance, it seems that the economy operating in peripheral regions is often export orientated. Contact patterns is another variable indicating structural differences (Johansson and Karlsson, 1991, partly my interpretation). For instance, the prerequisites for dynamic clusters in the top-of-the line production sphere, in the context of Regional Innovations Systems (RIS), lack the necessary support organisations and sometimes institutions. Public innovation funds cannot be absorbed to a sufficient extent. The same situation refers to the lack of aspects or elements of the innovation process leading to product and production process development, relying on developed R&D activities. As noted earlier, the statistics in these categories do not look good for the periphery compared to more 'advanced' (read selective urban) parts of the country.

Returning to a discussion on general economic prerequisites and structures, modern regional and local development strategies do not fit into the realities of the periphery/rural or have not been developed by, or bothered the scientific community to any major degree.

> People in places and regions are sustained by a vast array of non-capitalist and alternative capitalist enterprises, unpaid and alternatively paid labour, alternative private and open-access property, non-market and alternative market transactions and alternative and non-market finance.
>
> (Gibson-Graham, 2011, p. 229)

It could be argued that more penetrating long-term considerations, where the future of the society of the globe is considered – even the resources of the countryside being at stake, in terms of circulation, renewable energy and biological potentials – are crucial. The resilience of the rural, its 'survival' is a kind of reaction, a protest against some of the aspects of economic growth fostered in the urban environment. The existence of alternative objectives and other ways and means to organise life and choosing paths is discernible. Highlighting a holistic approach to the rural economy does contain a plethora of profiles where agriculture and forestry are not replaced by tourism but combined in different ways to open up other complementarities. "There are also both successful and unsuccessful rural areas in socioeconomic and demographic terms. This observation leads the OECD (2006a, p. 37) to conclude pointedly that 'if you have seen one rural place, you have seen one rural place'" (Hedlund, 2016, p. 461). There are further aspects of the economy where contextual aspects should be emphasised. This also includes considerations of the informal economy in terms of 'do-it-yourself', collective/communal and underground arenas (Wallentin, 1985).

Growth (maybe development)

Development is in societal terms a complex process with both positive and negative signs and most often described with elements of highly normative quality. Focusing on this term will bring us into a world of social philosophy – the basic political issues as others have filled books (current metres) with. The central question concerns the type of 'development' that is analysed and the type of change that is intended – encompassing a development where economic growth is one among possible ultimate consequences, but also a development where a socially used definition is particularly important. The definition revolves around the different configurations of goals that implicitly define a/the arsenal of means required.

In the Swedish National Encyclopedia, the word 'change' is supposed to be value-neutral, while 'development' presupposes a purpose. It is frequently assumed that development takes place from an essentially lower, undifferentiated state to a higher, better and more differentiated. The concept includes spontaneously a sense of optimism and expectations of success and a general improvement, all the way from the individual to conditions for humanity. It is customary, for example, to mention advances in medicine and education, as development. Economic performance is described as both means and ends. Contrary pictures emphasise the damage to our environment, disturbed and destroyed cultures and traditional economies, but the defined argumentation regarding these phenomena and tendencies depends upon the development of the normative contents of the concept – not as examples of development and growth opportunities, but rather as a 'temporary' negative development, or as spoils of modernity, which gives it a different charge.

In popular contexts development means, as already mentioned, a change for the better, going forward. The ambiguity and the popularity of these conceptual approaches are derived from and lead to a number of complex issues and problems: what values are good and which direction is, in different contexts, positive? Are different paths compatible? To what extent can we assume that values and 'benefits' of various developmental processes are universal? If not, from what perspectives should different development paths be valued? As a general abstraction and standing for itself, the idea of creating values requires a number of qualifying statements that, when the definition is pushed to its extreme, notes the who, when, where, how, for whom, etc. All these relativise the notion almost to inoperability. In value terms, there is, at the same time, a possible digression, sometimes a defined value also, in that nothing happens, i.e. no change, the lack of value creation preserves existing 'values'.

The issue of economic growth and prosperity is notably highly debated in social and economic research. This continuous debate is intense, as development perspectives rationalise the general thrust of the social fabric. In fact, the focus in the fundamental logic of the liberal economy (in both its practical and theoretical vintages) includes the multifaceted profit concepts and paradigmatic order. They are useful for communication and propaganda, but, perhaps less useful, for social construction. This kind of value relates exclusively to economic development, which by definition is difficult, and in some perspectives, impossible to manage without a strongly normative and reductionistic base. The financial difficulties over the past few decades have accentuated that the constructed goals/means have become strongly questioned from, for example, gender and green perspectives, as where the negative strategic consequences have become too obvious to ignore, related to issues of fundamental equality and climate change. That is, although the apparent complexity of the problem area, the analytically simplest form. Despite this the perspective continues to dominate the debate and political-economic practice. Much of societal basic information is sanitised to satisfy this kind of definitions and the practice which has subsequently developed.

In terms of the countryside, the general image linked to economic and demographic challenges, is popularly synonymous with decline or backwardness. Progress or what is more commonly called development is often described in a negative terminology. Eventual economic development is not necessarily development in other aspects. The emphasis on the economy implies that it encompasses strategic aspects of 'development' (Willis, 2011). The argument of what comes first, economy or development, has a way to be finalised before the explanation of interaction between economic growth and development is covered in a more profound way. Remaining however within the realms of economy, the track record varies among nations, regions, localities due to geography, demography, profiles and knowledge and other types of infrastructure. "Sometimes these factors reinforce each other; on other cases, they may counteract one another" (OECD, 2009a, p. 3). Another structural aspects of importance is the generalised types of activity. A pertinent example is the distinction of mobile and immobile resources and factors of production. Mobility of money, labour and information is promoted as crucial development factors in the modern ecocnomy, standing in contrast to established social, cultural, environmental and tacit structures. The taken-for-granted combination, without being questioned, defines rural space. Aspects of modernisation in these fields have their implications both in positive, traditional terms, but also with negative (technical development opening up for long-distance competition, reduced levels of working opportunities and competitive images of what constitutes the locality).

The dismal image of backwardness and lack of development is, in spite of its insistency, in its simplicity, false. There is no single/unique path to growth. Pictures based on an OECD report (see below) and also made in a presentation at Nordregio notes as a starting point that regions are different and hence perform differently. Growth measures note higher variation between regions than between countries (OECD, 2009a). This also meaning that they contribute differently. But most important are those that are mutually interdependent. The outstanding regions rely on the total complexity of the rest, the lagging, the tail, the rural and peripheral. However, the major players still contribute only one-third of the total (Webpage of Nordregio, 2013). Numbers show that the statistical tail plays a dominating role, as these regions "are so numerous that their contribution plays an important role in explaining aggregate growth" (OECD, 2011a, p. 39). Regions that are described as lagging behind contribute significantly more to overall growth than the best regions in more than 85 percent of the OECD countries and in sum more than the regions that produced more than average (OECD, 2009a, p. 32). From the same presentation we find the interesting remark that when comparing regions, lagging regions contribute 44 percent (1995–2007) of aggregate OECD growth; in eight OECD countries lagging regions contribute more than leading regions. There is also an ongoing 'debate' about the nourishing and debilitating aspects of society in which the periphery/margin/lagging without further reflection are included as subsidised. A major argument should instead be of maintaining the intricate and interdependent aspects of a holistic economic orientation. The basis of the argument is that all types of regions contribute to the sum total of national economic growth. Under the category 'rural remote' we find shares for Finland at 11.38 percent, Norway 25.53 percent, Sweden 12.31 percent and Denmark 13.68 percent.

There has been a convergence of regional growth patterns over time. More peripheral regions seem to present a growth potential. Here, peripheral regions close to cities are most efficient, followed by regions in the rural periphery. Over time, less populated regions are becoming more efficient. Strong growth can be achieved in different ways.

> [D]ata provide little support for the widely held belief that rural regions are necessarily in decline.
>
> (OECD, 2011a, p. 35)

What is also indicated is that, partial to general growth, peripheral and/or rural regions play a substantially more important role than is generally recognised. In the study quoted, a high growth among new firms in the periphery is shown. The activities taking place may, however, have motives and conditions making analytical sense outside direct economic factors. Locational preferences outside of income levels and profit margins are a case in point. When regions around capital cities tend to have higher growth than other regions and states, labour intensity/density is the deciding factor rather than the absolute population level. Another source identifies some rural regions having higher rates of growth than urban, when they are able to exploit their resource advantages and unique economic opportunities efficiently (OECD, 2009a).

> [N]o deterministic causal link between peripherality and reduced growth: the high growth levels achieved in e.g. southern Ireland and the Oulu region in northern Finland have shown that the constraints of peripherality can be overcome.
>
> (*Northern Peripheral, Sparsely Populated Regions in the European Union*, 2005, p. 79)

We are still only considering aspects of growth in terms of economic development. It dominates the picture, as the one and only way to supply humanity with expected means for survival and material progress. The questions raised about the costs of short-term perspectives in this field do not really make any impact. The burden for future generations of consuming today is not included or discounted into today's practices as to the environment and non-renewable resources. Short-term economic growth numbers play with people's minds. The rural/peripheral is part of the solution to this anomaly. Implications defined by local and/or sectoral reorganisation or rejuvenation have also quite substantial impacts on society at large: new methods, new productions, newness, changing the social fabric, work-related culture, institutions, behavioural codes, etc. These create innovative potential, but with in-built possibilities of stagnation and loss of power/empowerment. Human agency is here of crucial importance. Further examples, in regard to general growth, are found in the realms of inequality. "[M]obilizing resources in lagging and/or peripheral areas may constitute a valid recipe for both greater overall growth and lower territorial polarization" (Tomaney et al., 2010, pp. 626–627). Causality identifies levels of inequality and health range from individual impact, through different collectives all the way to general health indicators, ultimately returning to economic growth.

The case argued is that societal development is based on economic growth taking place everywhere and that everywhere is interdependent to realise the general growth, and, also, that identifying the winners is not that self-evident. Discussing differences in conditions conducive to growth, one of the major arguments already referred to, is linked to the assumed prominence of agglomerative forces. Causalities are, however, much more complex and not necessarily beneficial for "sustained high annual average growth rates" (OECD, 2009a, p. 3). This complexity of causalities in the general field also reflects on theoretical aspects in identifying economic weakness in different forms.

> Economically weak rural areas depend for their development on mechanisms and forms of economic development and growth that differ from those in industrial and urban-based service economies.
>
> (Bruckmeier and Höj Larsen, 2009, p. 39)

One possible and potentially interesting reflection in this context is that even if the concept of development in many respects has changed its social content, methods to measure, economic values, it remains an absolute imperative in the social development process in the public debate and in a variety of practical applications. Institutional structures have tendencies defined by centralising characteristics, even when optimal solutions are found in alternative projections.

Tracks to follow: knowledge

Entering into the discussion are potentials for innovation. This is a consequence of enterprise size and branch profiles of the areas discussed, traditionally dominated by SMEs and medium-size activities that are less mature, motivated or able to engage in classical R&D activities. A general low status for the knowledge infrastructure in the way of qualified research and education is also a case in point. The presence of innovative activities is recognised, but the identification of average frequency could benefit from distinguishing into more differentiated categories.

> If there are clusters they are often in traditional industries with little R&D and innovation activities. The emphasis is on incremental innovation and on process innovations.
>
> (Tödtling and Trippl, 2005, pp. 1209–1210)

The example motivates another argument, i.e. general descriptions of the knowledge and knowledge levels. Although low- and medium-level qualifications are readily available, more specialised qualifications are rare as are the positions to be filled. Accepting the educational status, one settles with second best, or dated technologies. The situation, defined as a knowledge imbalance, creates a reliance/dependence on the core providing special and extra services. There is also an argument raised around possible population thresholds and other more specific means – necessary in order to create the preconditions for knowledge spillover effects, a supposedly important ingredient in the innovative and entrepreneurial processes. This argument has an in-built distance variable.

> Conversely, dispersed or peripheral organisations are said to be deprived of the advantages of knowledge spillovers because of the costs of overcoming distance barriers.
>
> (Whittam and Danson, 2001, p. 1)

It is taken for granted that the 'spillover effect' is constrained to geographical distances from specified geographies; it is also taken for granted, noted before, that specialised or diversified agglomerations, in themselves, are necessary for an efficient innovation process. There are compensatory patterns in local knowhow, competence or dimension of 'tacit knowledge'. These consequences are multifaceted and hard to quantify. A major problem is that they do not provide policymaking with a defined objective. Their impact on the present definitional exercise is, however, intriguing.

> First, there is the question of how agents within peripheral areas can build and maintain links of knowledge exchange with 'core areas'. . . . Second, the question is what kinds of internal dynamics within peripheral areas can nurture the dissemination and absorption of knowledge.
>
> (Lagendijk and Lorentzen, 2007, p. 459)

Evidence tells us that knowledge transfer is taken care of in alternate ways. The combination of local buzz (localised knowledge spillovers) with input from the national or global arenas (popularly called global pipelines), does have an impact on choice of localisation, which is not always rational and therefore not taken for granted. What is described as pertinent is the formation of interactive learning, supporting the specific regional specialisation. In the rurally defined energy sector focusing on development in regard to renewable energy, one cannot expect any advanced scientific endeavours located in the countryside. An approach extending the analysis of these preconditions should include the nature of the learning processes defined by fieldwork in close connection with trials connected with prototyping. In general, this does not turn out in the form of regulated scientific procedures. Learning by searching or exploration are alternatives of knowledge transferal routes as are learning by using and interacting. Altogether a force to be counted with/for, especially in the countryside/periphery (OECD, 2011a).

Lacking local educational opportunities, migratory patterns relating to achieving higher education, complement the picture (Kosonen, 2005). What is even more important is the quality of the technological innovative processes, meaning that being in the backseat means a reduction of absorptive capacity, defined by both lack of knowledge and technological matching/adaptability. The technology level will be important. Low-tech industries, still play a major role in the international economy when it comes to volumes, value and employment (Smith, 2008). The main competitive factor is the cost of labour.

Global input via open sources is identified as a growing trend. Innovation processes defined by knowledge creation together with consumers and producers are a complementary alternative. Perspectives of innovation in their imitative and adaptive forms are possible (Lagendijk and Lorentzen, 2007) and more frequent. Strategies are chosen with pluriactivity as a necessity (in the periphery) and as a choice in other, more fortunate, regions (Sæther, 2015). The list could be further complemented, indicating the presence of innovative processes; however, hard facts are also hard to come by.

Tracks to follow: productivity

In explaining economic growth a lot of factors are included. Among those emphasised is the theme of productivity. In this book, the focus is through a filter of reasons and structures for differentiating geographies. There seems to be a general agreement that non-urban areas are defined, on average, by lower productivity levels. So far, there is no categorical evidence where this proposal is systematically qualified. It is also noted that there are situations, quite frequent examples, to the contrary. Taking labour productivity, the socio-economic context (level) describes structural disparities through levels of capital intensity, defining technological standards and extent (Smetkowski et al., 2011). Factors that, in themselves, have distinct geographical connotations and implications. In a specific example of technological development, the increased sale of chainsaws (Hjelm, 1991) shows an exponential increase in sale figures for this product in Sweden, starting out with a couple of thousand in 1953 and going straight up to 30,000 per year, indicating a productivity change in the forest industry, followed by an era of continuous technological development that ultimately restructured this part of the labour market to a very large extent.

Still, distinctions as to productivity continue to identify a lower rural one, although sparse urban areas stand out even worse. Differences, however, appear more prominently in inter-industry comparisons, industry composition being more diversified in an urban context (Rizov and Walsh, 2011). A differentiated sector-based productivity is, however, easy to recognise. The nature of productivity is possibly not less in rural districts due to rurality as such, but on distance and remoteness as explanatory variables and their specific sectoral impacts. "Rural remoteness, however does influence individual economic sectors outside of city-regions" (Curry and Webber, 2012, p. 280).

Identifying city-regions as a special category, rural parts, or activities within those are characterised by high productivity, higher than rural areas outside. This is not remarkable, when differences in skills, structures and other regional factors are considered. Earnings are on average higher, but not with any big margin, and primarily not explained by differences in productivity. The importance about these specially categorised regions is the simultaneous continuation of classical rural characteristics, which in general, are defined by low wages and low skills (Curry and Webber, 2012).

Another example found within the realms of ICT have simultaneous implications for productivity and innovativity. Aspects considered are the potential of unexploited resources, environmental considerations and the demographic profile, impacting on the future. "Innovative public service delivery plays a key role" (OECD, 2009b, p. 49), and structural, cultural preconditions are on a more general level and therefore, strategic perspectives in terms of productivity:

> Jämtland is often considered to be a pioneering area for rural development because of its strong traditions of regional culture and identity and close connections between local communities that are jointly struggling to survive economically and socially.
>
> (Bruckmeier and Höj Larsen, 2009, p. 41)

What should be qualified, however, are that sectoral advantages, as to productivitity increases, are sometimes quite hard to identify or evaluate. For the taken-for-granted growth brought about by ICT, biotechnology or nanotechnology, the jury is still out as to ways and means to measure both direct and indirect productivity effects. As a final open-ended conclusion or rather remark, the question of what we actually are measuring seems relevant. Bristow (2010) refers to the fact that the growth rates for productivity in London are based on growth in key sectors like the somewhat artificial measures of financial services.

Ignoring the comparative issues, the positive changes in productivity in the countryside is not really studied in depth, in spite of the presence of generalised comments like:

> From the late 1950s to the end of the century, there has been a shift of employment from urban to rural areas and a rise in rural wages which has arguably also been associated with a growth in productivity of all types of rural businesses in the United Kingdom.
>
> (Rizov and Walsh, 2011, p. 642)[1]

There are also references to productivity effects and drivers through general revenue generation based on occupational flows from the urban environment to the rural. According to Benneworth, Richardson, Gillespie and Coombes (2003), there are different productivity drivers in rural areas than in urban – employment and infrastructure are, for instance, more important than competition and investment. The influence of skill on productivity is not stable – low skills have an adverse effect on productivity in the periphery (Price, 2011).

Examples are found (singular yet) where certain types of activities are found to be more productive, noting localisation of ICT information offices where, due to the rigidities of the labour market, staff becomes more skilled in locations far from the urban hotspots. The former with a stable workforce with older, female and settled labourers, the latter with a temporary, student, mobile and therefore unreliable workforce. Could indirect quality-of-life aspects indicate lower levels of sickness, etc., issues eventually increasing aspects of long-term productivity?

Tracks to follow: labour market

The periphery is, as any other regional dimension, characterised by specific and varied patterns of production and work. This generalised fact need a more detailed level of analysis. It could possibly be hypothesised that specific elements of work and production are more suitable for the specific contexts (note the plural) of the rural and periphery. From this, an effort to generalise findings in such a context is a natural challenge. The characteristics of the labour market are not so much the total volume of it – i.e. the combined figures of people in and out of work, number of jobs, filled and unfilled, or potential numbers in working-age categories – but more on the type of jobs (quality and competence) and the matching labour available. The substantiation of peripheral, rural and sparsity is a starting point, while at the same time constitutes the argument. One of the pertinent issues found is in the relation between educational investment and economic returns, with a difference to the negative expected in the periphery. The local labour market in the periphery carries relevant distinctions in its economic profile, including lower incomes and wages. This varies somewhat as for instance in Finland the average incomes in the sparsely inhabited areas are significantly lower; in Sweden less so (Gløersen et al., 2006, p. 13).

In one way, this should be beneficial, a possible competitive edge for investments in the periphery, the back side being that low labour costs – combined with aspects of reliability and low turnover – makes productivity ambitions through new and better technology, i.e. labour-saving investments, less likely (Virkkala, 2007). The picture is less clear if combined with:

> The overall picture when comparing the educational levels in the regional categories is that lower levels of education, up to three years of higher education, is more rewarded in peripheral municipalities.
>
> (Backman, 2013, p. 52)

The dimension of distance in the peripheral and sparse are emphasised. "Rural labor markets are more likely to be 'contained' and poorly connected to larger labour markets" (Price, 2011). If matchmaking is a fundament for the efficiency in 'getting a job' and getting a labourer to do the job, this kind of geography is most often described in dismal terms.

> On the one side of the scale we find among the peripheral municipalities pairing of neighbouring ones. But there is a large number where every municipality form their own labour market.
>
> (Selstad, 2004, p. 25)

The situation being as it is, the dominant policy orientation is to increase the size of the labour market regions, i.e. the potential commuting area, provided through better and faster transport systems. A larger and therefore more dynamic labour market region increases the likelihood of separation between places to live and places to work (Gløtvold-Solbu and Ørbeck, 2012). The latter is an important analytical point in itself. Other factors than size also have implications. One of the more important ones is differences found in gender perspectives. In general and average terms remoteness and sparsity make for small labour market regions; however, social structural preconditions makes these for women even smaller as cultural dimensions in family structures make the labour market regions differ. That is, if labour markets' efficiency is determined by size and not considered together with other living conditions (settlement). The consequences of the unbalanced nature of male and female labour market regions are emphasised in the countryside. For instance, an "over-proportional share of SMEs in labour intensive industries" (Anderson, 2000, p. 95). Small labour market regions that function above average in regard to 'competence' labour power are, however, also found (Kompetansearbeidsplassutvalget, 2011). As mobility seems to be an issue of primary concern, this is not the case everywhere. If the peripherality is emphasised enough, including a definitional marginality, this impact is probably negligible. At least in the combination of peripheral centres and their immediate (read commutable) hinterland, preferences of work are combined with preferred 'rural' conditions for living-space (Selstad, 2004, p. 21). Small and peripheral labour markets seem to have structural impacts on the extent of possibilities.

As noted in the preceding sections, knowledge as an analytical factor identifies lower levels of formal educational; the lack of complementarity between jobs and job seekers; as to education and competence, lack of educational opportunities locally; migratory patterns relating to achieving higher education with a lower share of educated returnees in the peripheries. The process is further emphasised with cutbacks and/or concentration of the public institutional structure. The concept of competence is more wide-reaching and definitions are replicated in the need for specific types of working places, matching expertise with specialisations. Encompassing formal education, with other types of experience, promotes an understanding of specific fields. It does, however also encompass specific conditions where this kind of competence is promoted, empowered, distributed, indicating a variety of forms and environments. Thinking in terms of a specified labour market is not complete enough, it has to be flexible, inclusive etc., to be able to establish temporary, ad hoc solutions, in physical and virtual space. Centres of education and academic research have a proficiency in this regard, also shown in priorities and tendencies in development processes of modern society.

Modern theoretical representations identify economic development, focus on the agglomeration of specialised labour with the added qualifications of 'within the right context'. There is possibly an estimable threshold under which chances for a system to provide the right kind of local supply of the right kind of labour, is quite small (Gløersen et al., 2006). It could also include the promoting or initiation of specialised competencies defined by regional characteristics in themselves. A framework of regional specialisation can have important implications on local labour market dynamics and sometimes compensate for their relative size or institutional thinness (Eriksson, Lindgren and Malmberg, 2008). A note should be made in regard to skills that matter relatively more in the countryside; furthermore, combined skills, i.e. multiskilled labour, come at a premium. The present status is identified by: increased specialisation, legislative obstacles, demands for increasingly higher educational levels and a general qualitative orientation – all reasonable arguments, also to be found within the range of possible spheres of solutions. Working places with a clear competence profile trying to find competent labour locate to where a supply or surplus is expected to be found, which is, at the same time, where the supply is looking for the demand, in central positions with promising labour and living conditions (Kompetansearbeidsplassutvalget, 2011).

A complementary concern is the notion of a migrant when his or her competence is given a priority – although, in more limited labour markets, the focus should be on the family, i.e. two people seeking or getting new jobs. Potential jobs for accompanying partners are a *sine qua non*, for family migration. The public sector profile of gender-biased recruitment is, still, one of society's structural realities. Linking this with other settlement preferences is a natural investigative direction. But it is not only the labour market that should be suitable. As mentioned in earlier sections commuting and migration patterns are influenced by the extent of locally available jobs appropriate to the resident mix of the region/area in question (Coombes and Champion, 2010). This is complicated when it comes to specialists that are highly trained. Although it has been and still is assumed that they should be more geographically flexible, considering existing digital solutions. It seems, however, that the international standard among major players demands a high degree of physical presence in their location, usually a major conurbation (Ulver, 2012).

A self-evident differentiation between regions, as to the formation of existing economic activities, is necessary where the periphery has had a clear and remaining orientation towards the primary sector. However, the situation in the agricultural and forestry sectors no longer defines a dominating profile in the local labour market. Rural inhabitants are no longer primarily part of a farming community, but gainfully employed outside, with connecting physical links with metropolitan or city-region locations (Møller et al., 2010).

This is complemented and distinguished by a relatively high share of public servants in smaller municipalities and in the periphery. The public sector activities and workplaces play a significant role for aspects of residence preferences, employment, local services and economy. The increase in the public sector was formerly a basic part of general policy in Sweden, providing similar levels of service and other provisions, wherever the population was found, and through this, some of the service level differentiation between centre and periphery disappeared. This, in turn, contributed to the establishment of modernised and qualified labour market opportunities, especially for women outside of the major population settlements (Westlund, 1998). Although the policies have since then been changed by cuts in the state budget taking place in the 1990s leading to increased differences (Westlund, 1998), the impact does, partly, remain (Aarsæther and Nyseth, 2007, p. 7). In Norway the total share of public servants is about 30 percent of the working force. In the periphery this constitutes on the average 40 percent, i.e. a significant part of the local economies for these areas. A precondition for other activities, defining the positive and/or negative future development in the local area. Prominent are sectors like education, care and health services. These are also functions of increasing importance and a significant public responsibility. At the same time it contributes to the creation of place identity/ies in terms of a qualitative and quantitative provisions of services making the locality a good place to live, bring up children, grow older, guaranteed through the conscious development of competence and aspects of attractive work.

This all means that it is important to examine the contents and character of the kind of work taking place in the public service sector, and how it influences and reconciles with conditions for recruitment, for the impact on the establishment of a stable labour force in terms of change-over rates, matching of competence and competence requirements, etc. The most important problem is the recruitment of competence, versed in the intricacies of modern society. Often it ends up with inter-municipal agreements, limited variants of consultancy services. However, the importance opens the door also for structural effects of policy changes through state budget allocations and regulations. As noted, strategic concerns in this sector consider the total extension of the local economy and contributing/participating, so that the public workplace effectively contributes to a positive economic process. Arguments of the pros and cons of a large public sector will remain in the nexus of the debate on future labour market structures – dominated by the image of tax 'burdens' and on the other side statements like: "it is not the public sector that is too large in peripheral regions, but rather it is the private sector that is too small" (James et al., 2012, p. 448).

It is estimated that around 10 percent of the rural workforce is, on average, employed in agriculture today. Twenty-five EU members cultivating 96 percent of rural land. Considering the huge changes of improvements in productivity, the relative share of agriculture in gross value added for the economy remains low. The process to this stage has included a long-term "occupational adjustment, income-earning re-orientation, social identification and spatial relocation of rural dwellers away from strictly agricultural-based modes of livelihood" (Bryceson, 2002, p. 726; Potter et al., 2008, p. 448)[2] and also quite complicated adaptation processes in the interaction of economic and social life – which in turn stimulate permanent institutional changes in relations and cultural patterns, in consequences with a lasting impact on economic, political and social organisation.

The presentation in this section, should not be finalised without the notion that job creation, employment growth is not continuously facing a downturn. Although somewhat dated, Anderson (2000, p. 96) paints a brighter picture (with a lot of references) of above average small firms' formation in rural areas, and, at that time, small communities with less than 150 inhabitants having the greatest increase. This stands in contrast to general patterns usually described on a macro-regional level, through the prism of pros and cons of the urban labour markets.

> Seen together with the migratory outflow from the regional hinterland to the metropolis, this could testify to the backwashing of development resources (mostly human capital), from the periphery to the core.
>
> (Smetkowski et al., 2011, p. 298)

Future perspectives include widening the scope of potential labour market opportunities, including, for instance, measures for the preservation of the ecosystem, leading to the maintenance of jobs and socio-economic development. Today this makes up 16.8 percent of work opportunities linked to natural resources in Europe. Other describable niches are found in the production within the so-called green economy, horticulture, etc. Bioenergy and clean-tech could also be included. Future 'environmental services' or maintenance of the biosphere will be included in the definition (Gruber and Soci, 2010).

Important dimensions of technological change and its impact on the labour market have to do with efficient information flows. This projection has been used and defined as a panacea for aspects of distance and sparsity. It has also been described as a foundation for creation of new work patterns. Distance work, distance studies are frequently introduced into the analysis. Creating the opportunity of doing your business in or from distant locations has been the object of wishful thinking for decades now. But "Businesses based in the countryside can also hire remote employees based in cities" (Nieminen-Sundell, 2011, p. 15). At the same time information has a lot to do with interaction. This means that the ICT provides a new and changing type of interaction which encompasses the whole of society, in areas that could not be imagined, some decades ago. Still some of the expected consequences from the early '90s, are still slow in the making. Teleworking, homeworking has not developed as was expected. Net-based distribution activities are also a case in point although growth rates and absolute growth in the last 3–5 years have been quite dramatic. Further studies of processes in different aspects of the service sectors should be pertinent. The impact on the rural labour market in terms of volumes is, however, not self-evident or to be taken for granted, as potentially stricter climate-change technological regulations will impact sectors today present in the countryside, like coal mining, gas extraction, oil refining, electricity and natural gas utilities (OECD, 2011a).

Studying different sections of the labour market, seasonal work is also mentionable, primarily discussed in terms of the tourism sector, where impacts into the future are prognosticated to become of strategic importance, complemented by efforts to extend the seasonal impacts. What should be noted is that direct labour market effects are complemented by discussions on the influences of urban cultural interaction bringing young people into the labour market and paving the way into adulthood. However, working conditions are primarily temporary, unqualified and low paid, so the impact is not only positive (Möller, 2012, p. 215). Seasonality is also noted in the agricultural sector, in the form of organised berry and mushroom picking. Seasonal work should also be noted as a complementary activity. "More in-depth knowledge of these labour markets is lacking. The informal economy's importance in rural areas are also insufficiently illuminated" (Formas, 2007, p. 24, my translation).

Entrepreneurial processes and self-employment are also themes of interest. Capacity and intensity in these types of orientation has, however, a tendency of developing from the centre outwards increasing accessibility in regions where this, already in the start, is substantially better than in the peripheral locations. First stands the necessity, as rural, sparse locations have limited opportunities, and therefore the creation of a new firm does not replace employment, but is a means to avoiding unemployment, which, of course partly changes the rules of the game. On the other hand, ingredients in changing patterns emanate in an overall increased accessibility.

> [O]ffer new opportunities for the latter [sparsely populated, remote]. Again, providing that basic cost differentials (due to differences in market size) can be overcome by public support, the key issue is likely to be human capital i.e., informing local entrepreneurs of the opportunities, and the training of the local workforce.
>
> (Gløersen et al., 2006, p. 18)

Finance – as in savings, credits and investment

Important defined contextual aspects relate to the volumes and flows of high finance and finance in more general terms, not only in numbers, but also in regard to attention/focus. The following remarks seem pertinent, as a starting point. There is no need to dwell on the eventual relation between these two worlds, separated, on the one hand by the gulf between the logic of the global financial structures and flows and the day-to-day necessities of local communities on more material financial structures and flows, with the interdependence too farfetched to be analytically interesting. Maybe though, the down-to-earth necessities of economic survival and the availability of start-up and current capital should be considered in the fact that so much of the activities within the economic society are busy elsewhere.

> Overall, peripherality in the various cases can be attributed to rather weak financial capabilities of firms.
>
> (Lagendijk and Lorentzen, 2007, p. 465)

This has one huge exception, i.e. in relation to recent tendencies in the sector of natural and raw material resources, where global prices and, more or less temporarily, demand hikes have a direct impact on investments. Looking at the case of Sweden, Müller and Segerstedt (2015) note that the Northern parts of Sweden's peripheral regions have since 2006 taken a major share of total Swedish investment volumes, although the drop in the market the last years has had a negative impact.

The generalised weakness, referred to above, appears in the absence of financing institutions, in a wide sense of the term. The link between financial coverage or capacity and, economic development in less developed, rural areas, is crucial. The indicated structural imbalances need further investigation. The question whether there are generalised structural weaknesses defined in terms of spatial patterns is not possible to establish more unequivocally. There is a generally paucity of information, partly based on the flows of financial capital, influencing access. The situation and tendency within traditional banking is characterised with non-presence or exit strategies in regard to the periphery/rural. Explanations are found in long-term development strategies and expected low profit margins or profit-to-capital ratios. Banking organisational structures with decision-making authority are centralised, meaning lack of resources in regions close to financial centres' "availability of bank credits and local economic growth" (Özylildirim and Önder, 2008, p. 240) is not much better. Within the bank there is a lack of knowledge of local conditions. "[C]entralized large banks may have limited information about local investment opportunities" (p. 230). Small regional and locally owned banks behave differently (Meslier-Crouzille, Nys and Sauviat, 2012). Important aspects being superior access to local information, competitive advantage in the relationship between the lending segment of the market and a commitment to local prosperity, which enables qualitative monitoring and risk assessment of local firms. What could also be of importance/interest are possible variants as to localised interest rates, tariffs: "This evidence is consistent with distinct monetary conditions existing in UK regions" (Ashton and Gregoriou, 2014, p. 1467).

Making an inventory of the important services that could be provided by the presence of local banks, with enough financial and decision-making control is a first-hand issue. Reduction in the number of offices/branches indicates a reduction of different types of services badly needed:

- production of information on investments projects and capital allocation;
- monitoring and realising corporate governance;
- trading, diversification and management of risk;
- saving mobilisation;
- easing the exchange of goods and services.

Of further interest are, eventually, compensatory financial institutions like different types and flows of venture capital. The general picture here is also one of urban orientation. In certain states and regions this is compensated by public initiatives. Long-term commitment, in this regard, seems however, to be lacking.

Regularly, discussions on efficiency and risk taking are raised and the debate focuses on the nature of the viability of the funds in themselves. An example is in the county of Dalarna, in Sweden, where an amalgamation of two funds, is described in terms of a recentralisation (Joffer, 2015).

The important issue is availability, and then if rules, regulations are matching the local prerequisites. The preconditions for the public-financial economy is to a large degree defined by economic flows and structural ingredients outside of 'traditional' economic activities (agriculture, forestry, mining, energy production, etc.) and on the other hand, sectorally defined within 'modern', 'new' economic society (ICT, bio- and nanotechnology, etc.) sometimes also complemented by tourism and leisure-defined activities (possibly) and extended to aspects of the creative sector. Taking into consideration the input to the public local cash box and flows from the service economy by government transfers, client payments and tax contributions to the municipality, it would be reasonable to include these into an analysis of the economic potential mentioned. These are consecutively a source for making a living and also for doing business for many inhabitants.

The rural, peripheral communities are still expecting some benefits, not only from the recognised development towards a service society and with the emergence and present status of the welfare state, where the public sector is playing an increasingly important role, so also as part of the direct financial economy. The implications of this stands in contrast to the sometimes taken-for-granted viewpoint that having a large public sector in economic and employment implies a 'weak' economy.

Taxes, budgets, subsidies and ownership

Turning to taxes – public spending in the forms of budgetary grants and subsidies, price regulations, debt, exchange rate policies etc. – the potential for making a substantial difference is present. This section is just to touch upon some of the issues in question, without any ambition of detail and indicating areas for future research and discussion. What we have here are outcomes of ideology and culture, with different priorities in terms of regional and spatial economic preconditions and results.

There are many ways in which government taxes and tariffs have an impact. In general terms taxes are active policy instruments with a lot of sought-after implications and also a number of unwanted ones. Taxes are collected from individuals and enterprises and used to fund budgetary expenditures and instruments – in this connection, with implications on variations in the market seeking stability. They are also used, in order to level somewhat the differences between income brackets and income flows, socially or geographically defined. They could be classified all the way from blanket, i.e. uniform, to functionally, socially or territorially differentiated regimes. There are, however aspects where the discretionary impact of tax collection could be clearly defined. The spatial differentiation of personal and enterprise incomes is one, and most clearly related to the latter. Local communities in certain countries are not allowed to tax local enterprises at all, or where the enterprise structures formally bring general income, in reality the money goes to the headquarters or to some tax havens. The simplified picture given is formal and quite often distant from the active tax regimes, as these are in a continuous process of political haggling, of power games among different societal interests, of mending for loopholes, etc. Specified policy issues are often approached by different kinds of special taxes or tax reductions – levelling, macroeconomic ambitions, industrial policy, social policy, regulation of real estate and the construction of living quarters, entrepreneurial conditions and stimulation, environmental, efficiency in resource exploitation. The result often ends up in extra compensatory regimes with a high degree of complexity. Taxes are highly profiled, ideologically defined policy issues and one of the major problems, in this regard, is the identified ideological level of the tax 'burden'. Centralisation of private economic functions will increase the unbalance of the taxation in geographical terms. A geographical dimension is also where different tax regimes compete to attract financial flows and investment.

Different types of allocations – where generalised policies (popularly called the 'large') have different regional impacts and (small) – signify a direct regional allocation policy. The large is not defined by regional preconditions *per se*, but does have an outcome-input with regionally specified results. Different countries set up different budgetary allocations for their sub-entities, like municipalities, etc. Depending on the norms and quotas, the allocation principle has spatial effects. The combination of residency and per-head allocation in relation to that is found in Norway. Extra allocations are defined by different aspects of the demographic, social, etc. mix, which emphasise this point as well. Spatial patterns appear and in the Norwegian case, a tendency of redistribution to the detriment of the periphery seems to be the case (Berg, 2004). This takes place through a redefinition of the key of redistribution, where expenses for special social problems are given a larger weight, while sparsity, internal distances and small-scale current expenses are given less. Control over flows is an interesting dimension. Control over resources is another interesting entrance in terms of local/regional autonomy, whether they are tax or non-tax revenues or transfers with or without strings attached. Rural areas are usually described as clientilistic, that is, in order to maintain a specific standard of living, dependence on subsidies are dominating the agenda.

The change from classical regional policy with priorities based on a philosophy defining the right to live everywhere is further defined by the provision of general and specific services, later being replaced by a philosophy/ideology where territorial equality turns to an economic growth orientation, towards specialised functional and territorially defined priorities. One example being agricultural subsidies and, on the other side, EU structural funds. In regard to the periphery, of greatest importance is the large and heavy sector of service-providing units on the local level, which entails considerable and essential state economic transfers to municipalities and districts. Major sectors in this regard are social services and insurances, health issues and education. Complementary to this is a plethora of different issues and sectors and a borderland of public/private solutions (Eatwell, Newman and Milgate, 1998).

A fundamental contextual question, already touched upon, concerns who owns and controls what. Who does what? Profits? Implications? What about resources owned inside or outside a region or a locality. The rural/peripheral patterns of landownership are a huge stepping stone. It is, however, not only about monetary values. Structures like these are identity forming. This issue is raised here just because the link between location and control has an impact on the kind of decision-making and decisions taken. The argument is raised in ACANALYS (2011, p. 3) Resources found within an administrative entity do not automatically belong to the regional population, and it does not follow automatically that decision-making or revenues are received from or for that geographical location. Comprehensive planning and decision-making therefore becomes limited.

The question of ownership[3] is based on the basic code where the private is legitimate on the verge of holy. Private ownership is functionally and geographically decided and floating without any direct considerations for administrative or cultural regimes. Only administratively defined ownership is distinct in these geographical terms. A major category of ownership lies in the public system, where direct control is based on a range from general welfare functions to principles emanating from the private sector. A regime of complementary regulations imposed on the private could be relevant as well. A systematic discussion based on branches and sectors could be included here. The energy sector is a highlighting example in dimensions of ownership and control. This topic has to be left to the future.

Another kind of ownership with implications on regional and local development is that of land. This type of ownership is sometimes linked to state or absentee owners, where resources defined by these structures are an interesting extra dimension. The nature of the types of relation should be disaggregated into private and public terms, where an identification of ownership objectives and variants of control is pertinent. A Scottish dimension to this is found with Callaghan, Danson and Whittam (2012). The basic variable is, however one of centre-periphery, found in a combination of legislative rights and obligations, and location of the prerogative.

Discussing the role of ownership, one has also to consider alternative forms. Cabras (2014) notes the potential with cooperative forms in initiating, or rather, preserving facilities and services in rural areas; the functional impact will also have a direct effect in terms of social capital issues. This ownership carries significant characteristics in prioritising. References to Mondragón[4] are linked to

> ethical principles including open admission, democratic organization, the sovereignty of labour, the instrumental and subordinate nature of capital, participatory management, payment solidarity and intercooperation.
>
> (Gibson-Graham, 2011, p. 230)

Without really knowing the general situation in this functional type of ownership, the inspired guess is that there is an increase, and it is primarily small- or medium scale, and it is maybe/probably more rural than urban. This is evidently the case in the UK: "The number of cooperative members in the UK has also been constantly increasing since the late 2000's, reaching 13,5 million in 2012" (Cabras, 2014, p. 7). The potential coverage is quite extensive with the agricultural sector as a focal point, but with clear tendencies in energy (wind and hydroelectric), retailing, aspects of ICT and services. In the form of local social amenities like preserving "their local pubs from closure" (Cabras, 2014, p. 8).

Issues of more general collectivism could also be raised here. Landscape and shared resources found in the, already referred to, Swedish principle of the 'commons' (*allemansrätt*). "The use of land outside urban areas is largely determined by informal agreements that are made between people" (Formas, 2007, p. 25, my translation).

Notes

1 Note the problem of measuring area-related productivity on the same side.
2 The specific case is empirically based in Africa; the consequences are quite general.
3 Exemplified further in Chapter 9.
4 The Mondragón Corporation is a corporation and federation of worker cooperatives based in the Basque region of Spain. Founded in 1956, today it is one of the largest companies in Spain. Based on Wikipedia 10.06.2017.

9 Economic structures and structural changes

General reflections

The basic argument in this section is the proposition that economic growth could be identified, going in depth into the composition and spatial reflection of a branch structure and profile. The composition, whether it is urban or peripheral tells the tale of success, muddling through or phasing out, or most probably a combination of all three. It also tells a story about what to expect, in a not-to-distant future. The composition is the combined result of external and internal processes, all over the range of micro, meso and macro. The composition of structure and process will also address and/or create a scope of policies, hopefully relevant for change and achievement, including the vision "of rural regions as areas with substantive assets; and a focus on investment measures, instead of compensation payments" (Dax, 2014, p. 60).

Examples are found in a multitude of directions. In the continuation of traditional agriculture and forestry. In the changes of and in the development of the service industry, replacing manufacturing in its relative impact. In remaining manufacturing itself. Today, the productive element of knowledge in an economy's geographical position and contents dominates the picture, bringing university towns to the forefront. Another example in the same direction is the so-called experience economy/industry based on cultural profiles with a more general geographical coverage and with often unique potentials disclosed in analytical disaggregation. The differences appear in large amounts of still 'anonymous' (potential) sites and regions.

Relating to the issue of productivity in earlier sections, here is favoured an analytical and presentation form of value chains, emphasising, in a simplified manner, where extraction, production, refinement and assembling take place, where decisions are made and the riches hoarded. A future study has to consider a larger number of different chains, with a more penetrating approach into different territorial patterns. Taking the example of agriculture, the value chain in terms of ownership, production and sales in niches of agricultural production, penetrated and disclosed in disaggregated approaches of the countryside. Aspects of outcomes in the form of dependencies and centralisation appear in different disguises. Advantages of large scale, but also disadvantages, are considered. In forest production, experiences of a development of technological advancement could have a severe impact and reductions on the labour market although with positive impacts on productivity. The preconditions of the local, public-financial economy, defined to a large degree on gross economic flows and regulations for their spending. On one hand, there are outside-of-'traditional' economic activities (agriculture, forestry, mining, energy production, etc.) and on another sectoral processes characterised by the 'modern', 'new' economic society, tourism and leisure-defined activities (possibly) extended to aspects of the creative sector,[1] with the bio-economy looming in the background. Another important structural argument is related to the public-private dichotomy, where the 'disadvantage' of a dominating public sector is prominent and promoted in the ideological approach of the market.

Economic and more generalised structures within the centre and the periphery and in the relationship between them, are all dimensions of basic importance when analysing differences in the comparisons. The historical dimension of the constitution of the centre is worth considering further. With that concern, the centre was only highlighted when needed for the analysis, and then as reflections of the periphery, an innovative approach on its own.

Peculiarities or specificities in the countryside/rural – structural conditions and changes and thus the place of the change, i.e. growth, is the primary focus here. Local traditions, landscapes and livelihoods constitute valuable resources and structural implications. Local identities are, or at least should be, consciously maintained and recreated. At the same time, products and services based on the notions of 'local', 'peripheral' or 'remote' forms increasingly act as a backbone of entrepreneurial activities allowing people to plan for and make a sustainable living. Emerging new value process formations are found in changing structures of private and public consumption as such.

> [M]arket niches are generated by growing affluence and can be exploited by remote rural firms. This is partially confirmed by the high orientation of remote rural firms towards personal consumers.
>
> (Anderson, 2000, pp. 100–101)

The economic and development possibilities and potentials are also seen in dimensions of quality of life, in the supposed therapeutic rural, especially in the countryside offering multi-sensory, corporeal and mental experiences sought after in the modern, post-materialistic agenda of the urbanites – alas in the so-called developed world. This is described in terms of a move from production to consumption, where the characteristics of peripheralities sought 'in their own right' (Anderson, 2000).

Approaching the issue of general preconditions forming the backbone of society and, specifically, a fundament for economy and living the presence or non-presence of a school constitutes a fundamental part of that fabric, a basic, logical parameter. A process where the school closes does not only mean that the educational opportunity disappears, the school also stood as a symbol for the strength of the local community and contributed to local identity. The physical building is exploited for other purposes as well when it was sold to private actors not contributing to communality any longer (Landsbygdspolitiska samarbetsgruppen, 2014, p. 23).

In exemplifying issues of the presence, disappearance or (re)appearance of general structural elements, we find nature and its projections into dimensions of eco-'service' provisions a case in point. Production, in terms of nutrition, clean water, air, wood, fuel, building materials, etc. Maintenance of natural balances, i.e. photosynthesis and nutrient cycles. Regulations in terms of the atmosphere, water bodies and aspects of biodiversity and biological chains, and, finally, cultural production in terms of aesthetic experience, recreation, knowledge, inspiration and creativity (Landsbygdspolitiska samarbetsgruppen, 2014). Increasingly, policy development is focusing on place-specific externalities. Creating or re-establishing is described as a favourable environment for improving accessibility and attractiveness. What will it take to get mobile capital and workforce to settle? Noticeable today are environmental quality, cultural resources, educational institutions, QOL aspects of the environment – complemented by enhancing aspects of identity (maybe difference) and belonging.

A general discussion is around the role and dynamics found in the dimension of resources, and especially the issues of natural resources in the national economy seem relevant as well. Because there is an important, even crucial importance, in researching the role of resource industries in centre/peripheral dimensions. A recurring argument is identifying the links between a resource-dominated economy and low growth. A questionable approach. The main discussion is focused on the way specific sectors contribute to changes in the dynamic fabric of the economy and the impact in long-term growth. Natural resources – natural systems defined by and linked to land, water, air, etc. – are strategic to "increasingly emphasize the need to identify and valorize rural resources" (Ward and Brown, 2009, p. 1239). The theoretical debate about the general connections between natural resources covers among other things, the relations between resource endowment and economic progress. Surviving quite fruitfully on resources that could drain other sectors from innovative potential is an argument used. The so-called high-tech (defined as high R&D spending relative to turnover) is supposed to create higher growth than low-tech (including resource-based branches).

> there is no unified, coherent and rigorous theoretical argument for an association between long-term low growth and a large proportion of raw materials in the economy.
>
> (Wicken, 2008, p. 26)

A fascinating aspect of a resource economy is that it is, available through technical change, economic change (cost, prices, profit margins, opportunity costs) and social and political change. Resources are defined by availability/accessibility, where the different levels of 'the right to the commons' appear. Resources may be depleted or renewable. Green infrastructure refers to forests, rivers, coastal areas, parks, eco-corridors and other natural or semi-natural qualities that are essential elements for the provision of present and future ecosystem services. They are defined and highlight the benefits that occur naturally, and the losses that may occur if not preserved. Air, water, land, species, soil and lakes are among the natural resources critical for our well-being and to our medium and long-term economic prospects. Resources defined in terms of ownership and control, and different aspects of these, are found in different constellations of interests and conflicts. The basic idea and argument focusing on the common-sense statement that different resources and resource combinations are profiled in different places.

A list comprising resources could appear as essential for the economy and development. Presented in a hierarchical outline, two categories, space and nature, would be on top. Another subdivision is between the built and the constructed and resources and the natural. In development categories, we also have economic, social, human, etc. resources. In this monograph, the approach to different resources defined in space and nature as delimited by peripheral, rural, sparse, etc. This could be complemented by specific and unique examples, like "the castle of Neuschwanstein in Germany, Kleinwalsertal in Austria, the Ice Hotel in Sweden or the Blue Lagoon on Iceland" (ESPON, 2010, p. 45).

One final comment, found within the field of human capital and human endeavour in itself. The presence of an entrepreneurial spirit and entrepreneur offers a case in point:

> It appears to provide a 'low-cost solution' to rural development as it builds upon local people's creativity and their voluntary and economic initiatives.
> (Margarian, 2013, p. 16)

This is manifest in structural patterns referencing 'solutions to circumstances'. At the same time, with population taken as a given, the average frequency of enterprises and entrepreneurship is higher than in urban contexts, although, also on average, smaller in size (Landsbygdspolitiska samarbetsgruppen, 2014, p. 46).

Could resources be described as negative? Not in terms of themselves, but in the process of their realisation, or in the eventual impact outside of intended, or wished for, designations. Terms already indicated in passing, like the 'natural resource curse', describe societies whose economies based on natural resources remained poor, until the whole society was, so to say, redone (Smith, 2008).[2] The 'staple trap'[3] or in historical terms the 'Dutch disease' was the apparent relationship between the increase in the economic development of natural resources and a decline, or lack of development, in the manufacturing sector (or agriculture). High and special incomes strengthen the national economy, making other export products more expensive. Regions stuck in destructive processes (path dependency) or one-sided priorities are primarily beneficial for the state or absent owners but not for the region (Lundgren, 2011). Widening the mega-macro scope of a resource conceptual definition enlarges the picture substantially covering fundamental human challenges (read survival):

> Draws attention to the limits of the economic footprint of major urban centers and advocates greater recognition of the strategic value of small-market towns and villages as catalysts of development and anchors of communities.
> (Marcon, 2011, pp. 1–2)

Production, technologies and activities

The periphery is, as everyplace else, characterised by specific patterns of production and work. Also, as all regions, it is a place of systematic and dynamic change, where structure and process are of central importance. The future exists in the intricacies of existing patterns.

> Future competitive advantages seems [*sic*] premised upon the ability of firms to adopt, integrate and take advantage of the opportunities afforded by a range of evolving technologies.
> (Freathy and Calderwood, 2016, p. 895)

Through reduced distribution and structures of distribution costs, new business models, new ways of working, new knowledge and new infrastructure. Generalisable facts – although a much more detailed and qualitative manner of analysis, with a more thorough approach – try to find specific elements of work and production more suitable for the specific contexts (note plural) of the periphery and patterns not workable, suitable, etc., for the urban, semi-urban contexts. The resource patterns indicated above could be categorised in terms not only of land, earth, climate, but also of clean water, good quality air, etc. These demanding space that is not available, or too costly in urban contexts. Certain production activities demand clean inputs with ecologically approved production, in spite of transport distances. Examples being breweries, cheese production, fruit and wasps and clean-tech (Google and Facebook archives), just to name a few. Agro-processing, the basis of food and drinks, makes a rural location more than desirable. Fresh food and drink demand low transport input in primary production stages and large-scale storage, which are qualitative concerns (Crowley, 2011).

Activities to strengthen the rural economy have often a regional and local scope. Digitalisation has especially changed the creative sector of production, distribution and consumption, and contributed to an expanded concept of culture (Sas, Sunnergren and Jonsson, 2006). Also creating networks and cooperation between rural inhabitants and producers where functions in terms of the social economy and as social capital replace costly investment, are realised. Crowd funding is a fascinating possibility. "This is especially important for rural development, and the new, internet-based communication technology often support the building of such networks" (Bruckmeier and Höj Larsen, 2009, p. 40). The importance is noted especially for those who have the opportunity or are in the position to enjoy its advantages.

> If [rural] firms are unable to capitalize upon its potential, such technologies could be counterproductive and, paradoxically, constitute a real threat to business performance by undermining existing markets and customer segments.
>
> (Freathy and Calderwood, 2016, p. 895)

The problem referred to in examples of the Scottish islands insularity, promoting competition through the ICT competence and network capacity, increased the number of customers. The main problem are the negative consequences of coverage and levels of the ICT having wide implications on social development in general, not only the economy. Investing in broadband capacity in more remote areas is a costly investment and improvement, in some sources, presumed quite substantial (Freathy and Calderwood, 2016, p. 896).

Telecommuting, as a solution, already referred to, first appearing in the 1990s, is still remaining on the same wish lists. Preconditions for adding a flexible working culture have been substantially improving, mobility in work increasing, information technology and information security and capacity as well, as has the complexity and therefore also the capacity of programmes. The vision of the new distance, remote, smart e-worker of the countryside has been a justified optimistic approach. Flexible working solutions complementing rural living are opening up for occupational well-being. Not only in terms of traditional home-based, remote, work. Flexible working solutions offer more alternatives for living *cum* working locations both, as an employee and employer. The basic idea being it's more motivating, less stressing, more productive and time-saving through reductions in commuting. A counter-argument against the notion of de-spatialisation is the realities of face-to-face interaction being important in a substantial number of different interactions. Local collective (cooperative) efforts extending capacity by fibre involves local communities in new capacities. There are, however, aspects of quick-fix technical solutions expected to compensate for cultural and knowledge-related aspects of innovatory processes and entrepreneurship. Technical development has also sides where the pace of introduction is slow. Rural enterprise, when involved, is quite basic in its approach, and necessities of some entrepreneurial skills are not replaceable by ICT.

A qualification is also found in the scope and orientation of technological development in general. Small-scale technology is fundamental and preferable in communities not in the market for large-scale solutions. Technological improvements should be analysed in terms of cost effectiveness – having a larger general impact, due to local backlog in the periphery, while an improvement in the urban environment makes impacts through efficiency and effect on the margin is less impressive although volumes are larger. "Although if density and concentration seems to be a basic need for many human activities, spatial density requirements ought to, in some cases, be replaced by the expanded and improved distance independent networks between centre and periphery" (Westlund, 1998, p. 57, my translation).

Approaches as present in rural-urban, central-peripheral hierarchies should be complemented by considerations of alternative approaches, in technological development, distribution processes. Dominant perspectives do not, to a necessary degree, consider bottom-up and periphery-centre flows of knowledge, innovation and entrepreneurship, be it within the spatial dichotomies or within specific large-scale enterprises (Morgan, 1997).

Structures: complementarity

The idea in this section is to highlight aspects of the structural profiles of the periphery/centre relations, from the viewpoint of complementarity. Today, the description of the centre as a 'benefactor', leading actor, dominates the discussion. Complementarity usually is described in terms of peripheral dependence. How crucial is the latter for overall growth and development? The discussion takes place also within a retroactive resource perspective. Is the relationship symbiotic or parasitic? The dominating dimension is one of peripheral dependency, although rhetorically interdependence is given homage. The issue is one of absolute complementarity, mutual dependence in functional and structural complementarity, the urban not able to do without the countryside, the periphery. Discussing complementarity, remaining on the level of a bipolar analysis, is not very enlightening. Discussing complementarity as a major ingredient of the same functional and social system offers a better analytical viewpoint. Arguing for this approach takes the standpoint from a societal initiative, focusing on policies included as principles – generic, holistic, balanced, development. Identified complementarity in disconnected, unbalanced space, where competition for resources creates imbalances, endangering sought-after long-term stabilities.

The dependency of the region on the urban is there in many aspects and extensively. "The metropolitan area offers high-quality jobs and a diversified labour market, high-order services and cultural activities" (Smetkowski et al., 2011, p. 219). Spontaneous draining of the rural of population/labour, possibly competence at direct costs for the rural and for the urban, the latter in terms of lower environmental quality and looser social fabric. These results are legitimised in terms of urban benefits, exemplified by quality-defined social public goods (especially in terms of health and education). Suggested impacts on the urban contribution to general growth are questioned, but popularly maintained. The framework of the rural is defined in terms of another kind of and another quality of living.

> These trade-offs are generally accepted and it is often evoked that 'people vote with their feet' by choosing different spatial locations.
>
> (OECD, 2011a, p. 32)

The nature of the complementarity also discloses necessities. Starting out with simple things:

> A village household may rely on neighbouring towns or larger urban centres for jobs, shopping, schools, health care and leisure. Urban households may

> use the countryside for travel, sport and recreation and may depend on it for the provision of food, water and energy.
>
> (Gruber and Soci, 2010, p. 62)

It is, however, necessary to remind ourselves of the unequal starting point, founded in the difference of power between the core and periphery. "founded upon territory-based practices . . . especially for those living in less privileged areas" (Lagendijk and Lorentzen, 2007, p. 462).

Complementarity, is highlighted in a whole range of strategic economic sectors/branches where the periphery plays a crucial complementary role for the cities, the urbanites. An example is presented in Euromontana's reaction towards EU policy, elaborating on the degree that the urban structures are supported/dependent upon resources flowing from the periphery. "These essential resources 'hosted' in mountain areas have a value: an economic, social, cultural value" (Marcon, 2011). Mountains are described as the water towers of Europe and its main reservoir also of biomass. The contribution of the Alps to the total discharge of the main European rivers is, for example, 34 percent for the Rhine, 41 percent for the Rhône, 53 percent for the river Po and 25 percent for the Danube. Hydropower is generated by all 7,000 dams on a European level, producing 19 percent of the total European energy production. The relative political and economic importance of water resources increases as times passes. The report from Euromontana also identifies a more general complementarity in long-term perspectives of continuous urban growth, counterbalanced in peripheral development. The complementarity is defined in a broader range of resources found in the periphery, in the rural. Analytical and policy imbalances hinder more holistic approaches where the functional balances between the bipolar positions, not being defined in statistical or monetary values, but in absolute necessities. National and regional value creation processes are ultimately defined by these complementary functionalities (Ølberg, 2012, p. 45).

Structures: size

Another variable of interest is size, which comes in many different appearances and with quite different analytical consequences. Just to name a few: size of turnover, number of workers, areal demand, organisation. The notion of large-scale has been an ideal, a mantra, although with certain caveats, for economic theory for quite a long time. It identifying also, in physical terms, where establishments/entities are located and where, at least, head offices are linked to financial and service centres. Large-scale, manpower-defined outsourcing goes to low-wage, non-unionised, environmentally non-regulated, production sites. Large-scale, high-tech facilities spread all over.

Small-scale has other rules, always more clearly contextually dependent. The size of the activities is the analytical nucleus as statistical definitions identify how small is small is evidently a problem. A councillor in one of the smallest municipalities in Norway pointedly noted: "'you know, we know how to exploit small scale advantages here on the island'" (Kobro, Vareide, and Hartling, 1012, p. 15, my translation).

Small and medium-sized manufacturing show similar locational patterns locating to cheap sites, noting available labour and trying to optimise logistics. Some evidence is found that the establishment of small enterprises seems to be relatively more frequent in the countryside than in the cities.

> He [Keeble] notes that remote rural firms are small and report more problems with the costs of overcoming distance, whilst Smallbone, North and Leigh (1993) comment that rural firms are more likely to serve distant, non-local markets.
>
> (Anderson, 2000, p. 95)

Small-scale farming, moonlighting, seems to be a viable alternative for young couples when considering settling where quality of life and security are important ingredients on the agenda. A newspaper article noted that a Google-search for the Norwegian word of small farms had 3.3 million hits in 2012, for such entities on sale (Pettersen, 2013).

> [T]he families who maintain small-scale agriculture as the base of a diversified enterprise can perhaps be understood as kind of multi-active farmers, not completely different from institutionalised jacks-of-all-trade. It is also within the small farming framework that the new age production of exclusive cuisine has developed.
>
> (Flygare, 2011, p. 85, my translation)

The special case of small-scale food production is discussed as one of the potential development branches within and complementary to the agricultural sector. A special case is noted in the inner parts of Norway, where a special innovation system is identified for this sector. Returning to an argument raised earlier in this book, we do not know how large the production in this sphere is or what the economy is, because it is not measured. Another size-defined aspect noting smallness are dimensions of economic activities largely described as handicraft.

> The projects analysed here are based on natural resources in rural areas such as wood, and the production and processing of resources is organized in small-scale and handicraft forms that can be done by local inhabitants and do not require skills and knowledge that cannot be found or created within the region . . . the revitalization of old practices.
>
> (Bruckmeier and Höj Larsen, 2009, p. 39)

A further variant (home business) exemplifies the theme of size, having to do with complementary and/or supplementary activities which aim to provide the initiator a side income in the rural household. There are a number of types of gainful activities that complement and make part-time farming possible, although scientifically ignored. Linking this together with earlier discussions of the potential setup of mixed objectives, quality of life considerations, measured on a kind of satisfaction-based economy, seems to be an analytical perspective worth penetrating. It is significant as income supplements to other main activities, or aspects of multifunctional rural households in regards to time efficiency. Categories found are service and facility provision, tourism and recreation, crafts and arts, sale of home-grown or refined products. Although the direct economic impact is small, it is complementary enough to make a difference. In some localities, it is also a starting point for local cooperation, conducive to social interaction.

The important point, only exemplified here, is that size matters. The nature of the challenge that faces small SMEs or side activities is pertinent in the peripheral, sparsely populated countryside. The main characterisic of the rural market is its limits, further emphasised by seasonal variations. Geography is a constraint, reinforced by distance to potential extensions, with smallness reinforced by non- or malfunctioning infrastructure. It is also an argument in the potential business network focus, usually discussed in terms of critical mass, however, a dubious measure (Freathy and Calderwood, 2016). Today we can see the strategic impact of e-commerce cutting into the small-market shares that used to be temporary monopolies (Grimes, 2004).

Structural fragments: transport activities

It is a well-known fact that physical infrastructure, in the form of transport networks, is fundamental for human and economic interaction. This simple statement contains many important aspects having to do with accessibilities, etc., covered elsewhere, but also with indirect special advantages.[4] The reason for repeating or referring to the issues in this section again, is to open up for some branch-related arguments, conducive for the identification of rural/peripheral, sparsely populated areas' generalisable uniqueness, a basis for the day-to-day functioning of rural life and defining dimensions of relative vulnerability. Apart from the usual inclusion of roads and transport, energy, water and waste treatment, we also consider tele- and info-communications. All factors together define the status quo and identify necessary policy levels and measures for improvement.

The Weberian optimal location theory, referred to in Chapter 3, worked on minimising total transport work and cost, based on the input of a number of resources located at different alternative locations, distances from alternative production sites. The logic remains repeated in the literature today. Reinforcing the argument that sparsely populated areas tend to be sub-optimal in this respect. The evidence is not self-evident, as transport costs have a relatively smaller impact in general, and, also for peripheral actors. Sparsity could, however hold up the arguments, considering household investments in personal or family car(s) become a necessity, combined with other, more general, infrastructural costs. For example, inhabitants in Copenhagen drive around half as much as the population in the rest of Denmark (Møller, 2009).

Technological change for local communities and their small-market firm survivors increased accessibility but were not always sympathetic to all aspects of rural development: "open them up to competition from other regions (the so called 'pump effect')" (Gløersen et al., 2006, p. 23).

If one, for instance, takes the issue of technological improvement being more costly, either in terms of general and/or per capita, with budgetary constraints, combined with an already diminishing population, the outcome will need to adapt, uphold or even emphasise already-existing sparsity. If, on top of that, services are reorganised (read centralised), especially services needing face-to-face contacts, and their relation to a functioning (time, cost, logistics) transport system, that is successively downsized, the result cannot serve an ambitious periphery.

> In sparsely populated areas, public transport consists mainly of school buses, and the time available for the handling of errands in the municipal centre can be short.
>
> (Landsbygdspolitiska samarbetsgruppen, 2014, p. 23, my translation)

Structural fragments: primary activities

This section pertaining to the development of agriculture, forestry, hunting and fishing, the classical primary economic activities of the countryside. While (post) modern livelihoods emerge in rural contexts, one of the basic roles of the rural areas is and will remain primary production and related, further processing (food, wood, nature, etc.).

> Such a rural economy operates with the natural, social and human capital in the area, but less with economic resources and material from outside the region, as for instance, is the case for industrial production in rural areas.
>
> (Bruckmeier and Höj Larsen, 2009, p. 40)

This naturally depends on the extent of local processing. Still, food on the table, building materials and fuel are traditional products. Forestry and mining are major export sectors, while energy production fluctuates. These primary sectors have stood in the nexus of employment. Rural economics are primarily defined by farm and non-farm agricultural industry. Traditional economic structures and the development of land utilisation in this capacity promote and hinder processes of change. Primary changes are dominated by technological development (progress) in agriculture and forestry. This is followed by changes in land utilisation, production structures, size of activities, decreasing need for labour. Important analytical perspectives, if found, may be the location of production developed in a framework of the value chain, primarily its first stages and varying extensions into the refining process.

Recent patterns of primary production and processing include growing collaboration across intensive and extensive production modes such as organic farming as well as life science research. Product development (primarily on the size of home industry) regard items such as organic vegetables, wild berries, herbs, organic milk and honey. Another strand of development in this field is aquaculture. Refining wood and wood products in an orientation towards composite material (fire resistant and/or hard) with the ambition towards more complete resource utilisation. Renewable energy production embraces numerable options and combinations in terms of organisation, technology, scales and bioenergy processes.

Appearing today are conflicts with the traditional, with space demand, with differentiated ambitions and interests. A number of conflict zones or trajectories are identified. The indigenous people, their rights, their culture being one. In the Sami case the land-demanding conditions for reindeer herding, and its close connections with the Sami culture is a societal issue. Furthermore, multi-utilisation, new special value chains include alternative uses for raw materials. Change of land utilisation or functional areas is also an issue. Forest, nature and natural reserves possess increased positional value. The need for preservation of wildlife, pristine nature, different types of hunting and fishing are important as well. Special variants are golf courses and activities linked to these kinds of leisure pursuits. A major policy issue manifesting the urban-rural is where arable land is used for urban sprawl, instead of allowing for increased urban density. A very pertinent example of the competition in land-use, is locationing, which gives priority to areas not too distant from large settlements. A similar question pertains to other types of activities, like alpine, sailing, etc., resorts. The analytical aspects of leisure activities in general are returned to later in this chapter. A theme touched upon earlier refers to collective, public and private landownership. It is a basic variable in the identification of structural patterns and explanations and the way it affects social and economic processes, and ultimately, the fundamental structure of land-use. Legislation and rules define different levels of exploitation.

Structural fragments: the case of agriculture

Climate zones and change, earth quality, availability and accessibility are among the basic preconditions defining the cultivated landscape at every point in history. From survival to economic margins is also a way to describe an economic-historical process and its impact on present patterns. History has also an important backing for the general role of agriculture in human endeavour – for survival and as a trampoline for industrialisation and as technological development was a key to the early development of the British industrialisation drive. Fundamental technological aspects like exchangeable parts, technological standardisation, the assembly line, aspects of scale of production and distribution were all vital for the dynamism of the technological growth process, all emanating from agricultural development (Smith, 2008, pp. 11–12). Technological development, based on drivers of innovation and diffusion, leading to simultaneous processes of cost and investment increases, reduced shares of manual labour and economies of scale all working together, in changing rural patterns. All development not for the good:

> During the 1980s it became clear that the productivist model of the modernization of agriculture that had prevailed since the 1950s had resulted in a number of negative consequences such as overproduction, environmental degradation, falling incomes at farm level, and a hollowing out of rural development.
>
> (Sæther, 2015, p. 112)

A study of changes in agricultural policy on a national level, is quite complex. Starting out from above, the Common Agricultural Policy of EU has a conservation effect, focusing on well-off regions in the European core. Among member states, the same mechanisms prevail (Schmidt-Thomé and Vihinen, 2006). The combined roles of international competitiveness and preparation for eventual isolation, due to international tension, crisis or of force majeure are also analytical ingredients. Competitiveness linked to changes in the international production profiles, activities on the bourses, etc., are pertinent. National policies defining ideas of equality between the incomes of industrial and rural workers were another example. Custom regimes with impacts on pesticides and fertilisers added to the list. Markets structures loaded with subsidies and quotas and not to say the least, taxes on consumption. Structural changes in the agricultural branches, cooperatives, interest organisations, etc. All this leads to an all-encompassing rationalisation of the sector with an impact on its structure. Among the conditional issues of the history, present and future role of agriculture, we will also find the crucial impact of ownership and control:

> Not only do patterns of landownership provide a context in which land and labour are combined in the production process, but land is also often the primary means through which rural inhabitants of the developing world define their personal, social and political identities . . . the relative and absolute well-being of the population.
>
> (Potter et al., 2008, p. 151)

Linking this to the formation and creation of the agricultural landscape defines its uses, abuses and remaining potentials. Agriculture and agricultural productions systems organised around production chains of components (ending in the farm, starting out in the farm and ending on the shelves of the store). When focusing on this sector within the economy, general growth throughout the country and providing a dynamic countryside is an essential part of the picture. It has created jobs in both industries and with subcontractors. A common estimate is that a dairy farmer provides jobs for five other people. Traditional bulk production has, however, during the last decades, been characterised by far-reaching rationalisation. Encompassing on average 10 percent of the workforce (EU) and 6 percent of value added in rural regions, its strategic implications are so much more than this (OECD, 2006a, p. 2).

The preconditions for present and future development are found in several specialised frameworks with conditions important enough for investment decisions, investment funds, qualified in the form of mortgage and interest terms –an important variable in defining the future. Fragmentary evidence of changes are found in investment and localisation choices in the periphery – this also qualified in alternative terms, such as avoiding traditional large bulk production, and turning to niches or work outside of agriculture or utilising farming facilities for new business activities (Veidal, 2011). The potential and existing list of products, product groups and product categories can be quite extensive, just to name a few: agricultural development with alternative processes in the framework of 'eco', small-scale, alternative, etc. The trends in this field are quite forceful as knowledgeable customers assert themselves on an expanding share of markets. On the other side, the qualities of some of the industrialised food chains, in the light of customer preferences. Societal infrastructure with authoritative controls, promotes dimensions of cultivated security in these kind of branches.

> The promotion of local quality production has thus assumed a high profile in recent rural development strategies as it promises a means of strengthening the position of traditional producers and their products.
>
> (Murdoch, 2000, p. 411)

Complementary off-farm income promotes in general more diversification. The survival of small farms is based on part-time farming and innovative complementary efforts. "It is also within the small-scale farming framework that the new age production of more exclusive food has appeared" (Flygare, 2011, p. 85, my translation). This will naturally develop within a framework of traditions, intergenerational aspects of standard-of-living and in terms of fringe benefits. The individual farmers/farming household's ambitions will contain several motivations, where only one is profit margins. "Diversifying family farms should be conceptualized as households, not as scaled-down capitalist enterprises" (Sæther, 2015, p. 114). Viable agriculture is also a prerequisite for much of the tourism and hospitality industries. Summer visitors are attracted by local delicacies and culinary profiles offered in and by the landscape. A beautiful cultural landscape also attracts tourists and ultimately permanent settlers. New enterprises, not depending on physical proximity to their markets, are stimulated as well. The rural/periphery is an absolute necessary cogwheel in the general functioning of the economy, its profiles serving the core and functions, also as a market for core activities.

A commodity-chain analysis includes a number of important characteristics that encompasses specificities considered in a potential development analysis, unique for the rural and often unique for the locality and farmer. The reason for the argument here is that these various components interlock in a way that the freedom of choice and actions within the food sector – although strongly determined by large-scale actors, especially on issues of costs and price – does provoke temporary strikes, efforts of self-organisation, etc. Large-scale agricultural enterprises and cultivation expand, under the impact of climate change, environmentalism and sustainability, changing consumption patterns towards eco-driven product development and economic space for small-scale, short-travelled production niches, further developed by well-argued branding. Niches are symbolised by words like 'alternative,' 'quality' and 'local' (Watts, Leat and Revoredo-Giha, 2011).

> In rural districts, industrial networks emerge which are integrated, not by the large companies which figures so prominently in commodity-chain analyses, but through the aggregated activities of small, varied and specialized production activities.
>
> (Murdoch, 2000, p. 413)

A systematic approach to the role and function of networks – starting out from the agro-food sector being the most significant user of rural land – also defines a modern version of what rurality is. Murdoch (2000) notes the presence and predominance of 'vertical networks' defined by the included refinement, processing and commodity chains and their rural impact. Horizontal network approaches with a complementary integration between rural and urban spaces include processes of innovation and entrepreneurship, relevant for economic development in a wider sense. There is also a distinct emphasis on the local basis for different products, product lines, where phantasy and the sky is the limit, as to ways and means to promote this dimension. Through the new forms of organisation of the agro-food sector, working against or complementing bulk production, will become more prominent (Watts et al., 2011).

Production profiles, generalised patterns replaced by a kaleidoscopic representation: "multiplicity of technological and organisational productive systems can co-exist. . . . There is thus no longer a model of rural development but many possible trajectories" (Murdoch, 2000, p. 413).

Development is closely linked to the infrastructural networks for research and development, where a presence in the region or in situ is a definite advantage. A scenario played out where a bottom-up potential is in the making. Many spinoffs from traditional farming activity do not rely on research input but on the qualities of social innovations, skills and competence building. Tradition and conventionality are replaced by:

> new knowledge and competence to implement the restructuring strategies poses challenges to both the farmers and the agricultural extension services.
>
> (Sæther, 2010, p. 4)

Structural fragments: the case of forestry and woodworking

Forestry as part of the national economy remains important. In the Nordic countries it remains a prominent part of the economy. In the Swedish economy, forestry has since the mid-19th century played a central role among the export branches. In 2009 its share of exports was 12.4 percent (Lundell, 2011, p. 386). The traditional economic branches of forestry and early stage production remains a prominent feature in quite large territories (Lundgren, 2011). In Norway after intensive logging for timber and firewood, the country consumed through centuries much of this previously vast natural resource. In later days the forest-planted areas have tripled the amount standing and harvesting is below growth, with an ultimate beneficial climate impact. Forests and forestry have also an important impact on trade values and on the economy in general. In 2014, almost 16,000 persons were employed in Norwegian paper mills, sawmills and woodworking industry, and the aggregated turnover in these industries came to NOK 36.5 billion. In 2015, the export value amounted to NOK 10.8 billion (SSB, 2016). Finland is one of the world's largest producers of pulp, paper and cardboard and one of Europe's largest producers of sawn timber. It employs, directly and indirectly 160,000 people. In 2014 the value of production of forest industry in Finland, including the furniture industry, was 20.7 billion euros, accounting for approximately 20 percent of all Finnish exports (Finnish Forest Industries, 2014).

Forestry as part of the rural economy has many interesting dimensions related to the themes covered here. The historical approach, as a background, provides implications into discussions of structural changes in the countryside in general, and its economy in particular. The exploitation of the woodlands has changed patterns through time, and so has the idea of it as a resource, or rather resources. Resources are substantiated when translated in a conceptual background, where trees, woodland and forests are distinguished. Resource use, management and development also reflect ecologies in different kinds of combinations. Based in a dynamic perspective it is possible to identify:

> changing value placed on particular forest product and services, and the many interventions over time which have aimed to secure those resources for human development.
>
> (Potter et al., 2008, p. 467)

The identification of the forest as a working place and a source of income and economic growth, has been complemented by aspects as biological diversity and social values (Klingström, 2016, p. 12). Among these, some are regulated as, for example, reindeer herding, cultural remains, hunting and fishing. Aspects related to tourism, recreational and aesthetic values are also noted, but primarily in passing.

> The concept of multiple use management was introduced in North American and German forest policy during the 1950s and 60s, when resources such as recreation, water, wildlife and fisheries were officially re-introduced as important aspects to consider in addition to timber production.
>
> (Sténs et al., 2016, p. S87)

As an excellent, although still marginal, example of this kind of approach we find *shinrin-yoku*, a Japanese venture. According to the source, this is an therapeutic form of medical treatment, popularly called 'sitting on a stump'. Its concept is, that the forest has an impact on peoples minds, in terms of healing and relaxation. There are five million visits to 50 therapeutic spots per year. The authorities are investing in extention and in research (Ottoson and Ottoson, 2014).

Land-use is an interesting aspect of this, and so are aspects of technological development, with implications in interaction between techniques, productivity and labour. The latter is a continuing process, although the impact on the labour market is not the same in relative terms as it once was. The frame of discussion has to do with aspects of the value production and value chains and systems. Where refinement of wood products takes place and what kind of functional specialisation is what is pertinent. Apart from aspects in regard to the forest stands, alternative uses in direction of hunting, leisure, therapy, bring forward a generalised approach for analysis. Wood products include composites, hard and fireproof wood production and a renaissance for wooden houses, in a substantially wider range of scale and solutions. The role of biomass and the rest of the products in timber working playing a role as well.

Looking into changes of land-use and product development, certain aspects appear of special importance. Multifunctionality of the forest is more in focus today and the competition between classic forestry in terms of timber production, sawing and paper mills is complemented by bioenergy, leisure and habitat. A broader orientation into aspects of preservation and natural reserves is partly accepted. Diversification and further refinement of wood products into aspects of energy production, heat, etc., with biomass as ingredients, has implications on some of the general, 'ordinary' bioprocesses taking place.

Traditional handicraft forms of production – maybe not so large in economic terms, but relevant for the general and specific profiles of the local community and important ingredients in local cultural profiles – maintaining old practices in process and parts of the local labour market (Bruckmeier and Höj Larsen, 2009). Links between biodiversity and economic diversity in product development are a mentionable future for the whole sector.

Structural fragments: energy

The theme of energy production has a prominent place in the present endeavour, based on the fact that the rural/peripheral landscape as a whole provides a major share of energy production, and will continue to be the location of most new energy production and distribution alternatives in the future. Institutional and policy analysis of choices of technology and scale is a pertinent subject. A further perspective, as to the location of production, are issues of environment and security. Rural locations are economically rational and technologically relevant, possibly with a partial exception of solar energy and wind craft on sea and coast. Each energy mode has its geography and rationale, and needs that kind of treatment. Entering the new millennia with priorities linked to climate change and environmental protection emphasises the crucial role of the argument. A realistic, although futuristic approach, is the continuation of the rural/countryside serving the cities and society in general. Although already an existing relation, it includes the idea of a future enlargement with a more profound impact to the socio-economic fabric (Gruber and Soci, 2010, p. 66).

Large-scale plants as well as local or even farm-specific systems, may all be or become energy efficient and profitable depending on technology and organisation. Combinations include e.g. farm-based production, through crops, residuals and manure; forest based production; or wind-based power plants placed in rural areas. Energy, facilities and production processes with an orientation towards local supplies increase in importance. "There is a need for new, simple and economic means to produce heat and electricity communally from renewable resources" (Nieminen-Sundell, 2011, p. 17). Small-scale systems create technological capacities for deliveries during different forms of severe weather conditions, when failures in the general network become more frequent, referring to recent incidents in the Scandinavian context (Landsbygdspolitiska samarbetsgruppen, 2014).

This general outline emphasises an advantage for the periphery, contributing to the solution of energy provision in a number of different chains of energy production futures. The framework sets the agenda for a society, based on biological materials, new energy in terms of biomass, wind, solar and geothermal. All together: "open up for such business opportunities in rural areas that will benefit the whole economy" (Landsbygdspolitiska samarbetsgruppen, 2014, p. 57). This offers "a route by which peripheral economic development policies can be supported" (Allan, McGregor and Swales, 2011, p. 1171).

In the Swedish case the major contribution, hydropower production, takes to a large degree place in sparsely populated areas, without providing any substantial benefits to local communities. Large municipalities in the Swedish countryside, with low populations "delivers a lot of the waterpower billions" (Hörnlund, 2009). The municipality of Jokkmokk produces about 10 percent of the total Swedish hydropower energy. Issues of control, ownership and concessions could have been crucial, when it comes to income profiles for local municipalities. The energy surplus in Vilhelmina (SE), more or less totally exits the locality/region (Åberg, 2013). Where incomes from energy-producing entities should be collected is a political issue. In Iceland, this kind of input/income does not exist, while a number of Norwegian ones do. Water energy, experiences of earlier exploitation and concessions are still leaving positive results to Norwegian local communities and municipalities (Virkkala and Niemi, 2006).

Issues of vested interests, connected with landscape and conflicts around the fact, that to catch the wind the windmills have to be placed, becoming highly visual and with impacts as to noise levels and on the local fauna. Local actors' experience of, and involvement in, rural renewable energy production is central, not always willing to accept changes, the NIMBY[5] effect being activated. Examples multiplied for other energy sources, production and distribution as well. It is notably necessary:

> to ensure that the potential benefits to the local community are accurately identified.
>
> (Allan et al., 2011, p. 1172)

As has been noted continuously in this book, all costs and benefits are not economic. The actual local benefits in economic terms seems, to a high degree, linked with incomes derived from lower energy costs and quotas based on enterprise profits. Tariffs, prices and regulations concerning price control and differentiation are deciding. Backward linkages for construction are not strong. Linkages into the local economy in regard to labour seem negligible. An approach evaluating the impact of wind power projects on the local level makes the potential of alternative income possibilities of marginal interest.

> Sensitivity analysis reveals the relative importance of the level of 'community benefit' payments, 'local sourcing' of intermediate inputs and the level of community ownership of the project to the size of these impacts.
>
> (Allan et al., 2011, p. 1171)

The issue of who benefits will remain, the patterns of differentiation remaining on a national level.

Structural fragments: manufacturing

What about manufacturing – is the era of manufacturing in the periphery over? The question refers to what is happening with what there is. A second, with what is appearing. In regard to existing structures, there is still a substantial presence and a potential, and the specificities in sparsely populated areas have improved. In some aspects, the present structures are sturdy. The reason being that, a certain part of these manufacturing activities are not, primarily, defined by the physical presence of the market or the customer. The main picture, however, is defined by the extent of exogenously determined impact. Issues of ownership and control are here of central importance, their location dominated by activities in the centre. Ownership and outcomes of decision-making shows very clearly differences in regional or local impact, whether the owners are distant or local. Something in between could be discussed by, for example, revenue from stocks, whether the economic results are retained on the local level, partly in the spirit of *usus fructus*. Ownership should and, could be, translated into control, i.e. control over decision-making, control over price, etc. Price agreements for monopolies, be they state or private, are guided, not only by long- and short-term profit margins, but also by traditional values as to centralisation, as to branch and business allocation, as to partnerships, economic and economic-political priorities.

In turn, making large-scale structural changes in the global economy is disturbing, destroying and potentially developing in local presence and networks. At the same time, in the appearance of new, prioritised front-line economic development, emphasis on high and biotech development does not recognise volume effects of low technology, mechanical and technical production. This compares the eventual linkages of the prioritised sectors with manufacturing, by traditional definitions. In an international comparison, however, the latter still stands for a major part of production and labour force activities (Smith, 2008, p. 12).

An important aspect of locational definitions is related to the situational powers of inputs to the production process. Manufacturing contains a large amount of variation, both in its preconditions, processes and treatment of production results, analytically sparsity and peripherality, acting as filters. For instance, the interconnectivity in multi-locational, manufacturing chains, provide restrictions when seeking optimal logistical preconditions, when inputs from other actors are necessary or crucial. Interconnectivity is also a matter of transport solutions, although as noted on the cost side being less and less important (Gløersen et al., 2006).

Another interesting analytical approach of rural and peripheral dimensions, is the distinct emphasis on place rather than sectors for policy and planning purposes, and the role of subsidies, in the investment sphere, although of lesser importance (OECD, 2006b).

Structural fragments: the service sector

The starting point, natural and simple enough, the combined impact of production, provision and consumption of services. Definitions of what kind of services qualify appear in terms of private/public, the nature of the service, face-to-face, online (telephone or net-based) or infrastructural. Also, in terms of frequency in provision and consumption, continuous, on demand or standby. Important for the analysis is whose approach, whose interests are in focus. A high frequency of complex and alternative solutions and possibilities are present. It touches on a range from commercial activities to defined welfare provisions and a lot of in-betweens, but also in complementary directions of the voluntary or social sectors. That the theme has special peripheral/rural connotations is self-evident as sparse population preconditions, most often rules out market solutions. It is furthermore complicated as the provisions could be argued, and promoted, integrated with important labour market considerations. As earlier commented, the service sector is relatively more prominent in peripheral labour markets, replacing the picture of dominant traditional sectors. Analytically integrating the public sector into the total dynamism of the local economy, clarifying the role of public workplace in the total fabric of development. Aspects of local quality-of-life, defined in terms of volume and quality of course include local public service provisions and contributions to place identity/ies, in terms of a good place to live, bring up children, grow old.

An interesting reflection made earlier, however, linked to divisions in economic ideological and policy-related positions, in view of the combination of tax burden and public work, is framed by its implied non-productive outcome. Furthermore, small and peripheral municipalities/communities, negatively influenced by general tendencies of urbanisation and centralisation, remain on expenditure levels not in harmony with negative tendencies on the income side (local taxes) (Johansen, 2009, p. 19). In this controversy, Aasbrenn (1995) suggested an analytical alternative, a focus on the definition of supporting cash flows, financing the activities and by this creating a different and more nuanced picture. The large and economically heavy sectors of service, providing units on local levels, entail considerable and essential state economic transfers. In the proposed outline, other and alternative businesses and activities, like for example tourism, military, energy etc., also become of interest, linked to local tax-based incomes. Transfers and agricultural support another element.

> [D]emonstrates that under various conditions a relatively large public sector can be beneficial for a peripheral region.
>
> (James et al., 2012, p. 447)

National policies of equal service opportunities have provided local opportunities and therefore a considerable impact on the labour market. Measures encompassing labour market impact will therefore have long-term structural and strategic effects on the quality of peripherality in itself, directly related to the volume of the public provision (Westlund, 1998). The substance of policy development has, when changed, important, mainly negative, implications (Aarsæther and Nyseth, 2007).

> Above all, there was a nearly completely new labour market for women outside the cities, namely the care sector. Municipalities increased duties also entailing a series of more advanced services, previously available only to centres appearing in the periphery.
>
> (Westlund, 1998, p. 33, my translation)

An interesting approach is the identification of types of services, of general interest in connection with regional development, in where to find them, and in what way different approaches or identifications have an impact on the general outcome.

> [R]efers to general interest functions and objectives, not to particular activities, sectors/industries, modes of provision or types of provider, etc.
>
> (Littke et al., 2012, p. 3)

Definitions qualifying peripherality, or related or complementary concepts, could and should make a basis for comparisons in two directions. Necessary thresholds or population base, or service levels, standards, etc., per cap, i.e. the nature of the consumption and provision. Strategically, these are aspects of cost-efficiency. What is notable is that size of the locality is not automatically a statement of volume and experienced quality of services provided. It has to be qualified considering, for instance, interaction within a wider spatial framework and budgetary contributions from different sources and consequences of earlier structural development (Arcelus, Arocena, Cabasés and Pascual, 2015). The sparsity most often characterises peripheral locations, meaning that critical economical thresholds of supply are replaced by political considerations for maintaining service at a minimal level and variety. This encounters a position of fundamental rights to fair and/or equal treatment.

When it comes to structural changes pertaining to the peripheral/rural, some basic societal services are provided at longer and longer distances. Amalgamations in both the private and public sectors are resulting in centralising tendencies. Elements of population base and economic viability impose barriers. Road maintenance and travel/transport elements, the cost of operating across the range of services are considered. Even with diminishing transport costs, distance is not always compensated. Regional differentiation has significant consequences for affordance/supply and distribution of welfare. Per capita costs in large, sparsely populated entities, when providing services like school transports etc., have a larger general impact on localities with a small tax base. Structural changes in supply of social and health services are also defined by the quality of accessibility to these very basic services. Dimensions of time and cost are included in the 'longer' accessibility, when public transport is decreasing as well. Personal travel is increasing, but not for all people due to income and other restraints.

> [G]ood health and good income will help to overcome the obstacles that distance impose, while aging, poor health and low income hinder access to services at a distance, if the conditions for use of the service means that you have your own car.
>
> (Landsbygdspolitiska samarbetsgruppen, 2014, p. 23, my translation)

Availability is also a product of time management in the centres, defining the availability of services provided by the centre to the periphery (Fimreite and Selle, 2006), creating a perspective of dependence, but also a structurally defining fundament for development. It is important to note that a disaggregated analysis soon discloses that this does not reflect all service-related activities.

We will also find a large amount of complex and alternative solutions. The frequency of those seem more evident in peripheral locations and sparsely populated areas. Complicating the picture further with category projections, in regions or areas, for instance, an increasing population of older migrants seek settlements for retirement, trying to find quality of life surroundings, which has also to meet "an increment in the number of services available in rural areas" (Cabras, 2014, p. 6).

Some sub-sectors are ultimately determined by urban/centre locations, i.e. urban contexts in relation to demand and supply. In the private sector, transaction costs favour agglomerations, with the lack of innovative milieus, business networks, diseconomies of scale, critical mass, lack of specialised business services like banking, lawyers, tax advisers, translation services, etc. (Gløersen et al., 2006).

Combinations of different types of services and possibilities for temporary, mobile, part-time solutions could have a marginal, positive, impact. "Such are itinerant services, service centres, service kiosks, mobile or outreach, remote services" (Landsbygdspolitiska samarbetsgruppen, 2014, pp. 23, my translation).

A special aspect of the service industry is found under the heading: experiences and leisure. Different kinds of leisure/tourism categories have different impacts. In general, tourism, with its up-front economic impact, counters migratory tendencies and introduces newcomers or potential migrants. This aspect of the private service industry supplies a range of infrastructure, with simultaneous impacts for the tourist and the inhabitant. The latter is a possible argument for settling down in the locality. Seasonal workers (service) are also, in the long run, part of the migrating category. Tourism, in the form of second or holiday homes, creates a special and extra demand on local service provisions.

A special field, crossing the public/private demarcation is the provision of green care, which refers to the utilisation of the rural environment as a base for promoting human mental and physical health, and special quality of life for a variety of client groups. Green care provides new livelihood opportunities for farms and other rural enterprises. It also contributes to rural viability and quality of the rural environment, bringing together rural resources (natural, social and cultural) and ambitions for new alternatives to organise social and health services.

Entering, as above, into a modern field of health care also opens the door for other qualities of the countryside – we could call them natural or nature services. A primary example is silence, and how it is present in and together with rural spaces, places and cultures. While continuous communication, speech and traffic could be described as pacemakers of the contemporary lifestyle, there is a need for counterbalancing. In this sense, the rural landscape is expected to contain a 'healing' potential – a rest home for overworked urbanites. Private-sector activity appears in a small-scale entrepreneurial potential – in the form of hiking routes, exploiting the sense of space, fresh air, wilderness activities, fitness training, contemplation and pilgrimage events, or the more widespread phenomenon of second-home tourism. There is a therapeutic potential in both general and commercial terms. This is a worldwide trend, within affluent societies, of slow culture, etc., where the individuals positioned on the upper reaches of the Maslow pyramid are prominent. The economic impact is prominent in different perspectives. There is an orientation to every step in the planning, development and construction of facilities with this orientation, in these areas. Upon completion, passing over into the economy, defined by the new inhabitants in terms of direct and indirect consumption over the whole range of possible products and services.

The private business service sector is quite another matter. Branch-related private service activities will find the geographical branch profile, a necessary precondition for some logistically optimal locations, indicating that the importance of transport and information infrastructures as crucial. The conventional definition of 'KIBS'[6] as an essentially metropolitan, urban phenomenon is relevant, but there are still interesting issues to raise in regard to its rural dimensions (Crone, 2012). Access in the periphery could be problematic, but fascinatingly enough, the level of provision, when present, has ingredients of higher average R&D level, more local input and more developed interaction with regional networks (Pinto, Fernandz-Esquinas and Uyarra, 2015). KIBS are one of the most innovatively orientated of the service sectors that are present in rural areas and take on a substantial share of the contribution to the economy in more general terms (Johnston and Huggins, 2016).

Structural fragments: new production – new economy

Changes in the economic fabric of society are continuous, and changes makes elements, processes and patterns appear, disappear, reappear, differently in different geographical contexts. Rural, peripheral and sparse are the argumentative definition of the version of new production structures in this short section. Activities are sorted into many different directions, traditional (agriculture and forestry), with sections of their own, has already been covered. What has also been touched upon are parts of new orientations within their extended productions systems. Some others appearing here. A first possible and notable orientation is the relocation of activities from an urban/central to rural/peripheral, often based on special costs for congestion and competition, "decentralisation of this sort is most evident in those segments of the new economy that are relatively routine in nature, but, increasingly, less routine functions are also becoming subjects to the same pressures" (Scott, 2013, pp. 34–35, my translation) found in the framework of changing technological conditions. ICT and improved communication facilities are in the front line.

Bio-economy is a distinction of the economic structure, encompassing activities based on biomass from sea and land. It includes all forms of production, that utilise renewable biomass materials generated by organisms through different processes. The potential sector is much more than the location of alternative and complementary uses of natural resources, raw materials and former waste products. The concept of 'economy' also encompasses ideas of development in different sizes, with extensive room for small-scale production facilities with an orientation towards local demand. Implications include reduction of transport costs and the positive direct implications for the climate, reducing harmful emissions. Small-scale is not rational on its own, but due to material cycles with comparably small-scale volumes, it is potentially highly diversified. Nieminen-Sundell (2011) argues for an impact, by way of denser local clusters, creating new jobs. The same author mentions alternative lines of product development including fungi as base resources for medicine and other innovative materials, like building and packaging material, products. Berries for medical production and cosmetics are also mentioned (2011, p. 18).

Biotechnology is interesting as a development channel in this regard also. Bioplastic products, lignite-based materials, etc., extend the list continuously. Renewable resources and then sustainable practices and their impact – or, should one say, interactivity – with issues in energy climate policy are notable. They are taking their fair share of attention and are identified in strategies for economic development in the EU and USA (Løken, 2015). There is a strategic concern increasing the focus and demand for environmental technologies, eco-friendly products and services and sustainable design ideas. The global market for this kind of orientation is huge.

On the background of an affluent societal development process based on specific rural conditions, a new concept is a specially profiled activity, defined or described as experience – in the cultural, creative, future-oriented entertainment industries. The first, offers personal or group experience to guests, customers, tourists (Lorentzen, 2008). Different directions of the experience sector are found or defined in terms of culture, nature and complementing alternatives. Rurality encompasses a range of 'new commodities' that carries use and commercial values, matching societal trends within the framework of 'environmentalism'. A clear impact found differentiated by consumption patterns appears in generational or sub-cultural categories. For example in

> better availability of organic and local food . . . demand higher among the youngest age-group, 15–24-year-olds. . . . Aesthetic and ecological impacts of food production. . . . Reflected in this idea of becoming a small-scale farmer.
>
> (Nieminen-Sundell, 2011, p. 17)

Pertinent in the present analytical context are the "location-specific advantages that result from the particular aesthetic landscape (shaped or untouched by human activity) or heritage-scape (Mitchell, 2013)" (Korsgaard et al., 2015, p. 13). These, complemented in a number of different directions, satisfy recreational and sport activities, with further examples along the line. Conflicts of purposes are immanent.

> Thus, excessive rural development can result in undermining the character, culture and hence future attractiveness and prosperity of a rural place.
>
> (Korsgaard et al., 2015, p. 17)

Another orientation is where experience is linked and defined by the concept of 'creativity'. It includes a range from specific products to change in behavioural processes, the ways things get done. A term encompassed in descriptions of the innovation process. As a term in the present context, we can talk about artistic expression, inspiration or exceeding some predefined or presupposed limits. It is not only creativity and creation, or performances in themselves, it includes the activities, the realisation. Cultural resources encompass local traditions, language, aspects of everyday (quantity and quality) leisure activities, youth culture, ethnic minorities, voluntary organisations, production and consumption of local products and local craft knowledge (Hultman, 2008). Making these experiences into cultural and competitive products demands alternate types of competences. Different kinds of cultural structures are based on cultural infrastructures, whether institutional/formal or improvised sub-cultural. An interesting aspect, linked to discussions on local and regional identity/ies, is found in the dimension of cultural place dynamics, i.e. cultural identification or formation, defined and found out- and in-doors, natural or created by individuals or groups carrying a fundamental quality of being 'cultural'. Culture is already in place. The definitional exercise encompassing an identification in time and space. Behind this, fundamental structural societal changes are provoked by changes induced by urbanisation, by temporal priorities emphasising leisure and culture, and through this leading to market-induced price or value changes (Sas et al., 2006, p. 15). The future includes measures of participation, of personality/ies, learning and development. A discussion of the type of products found is also of importance. This also appears with an orientation to composite products, where farming and farms are part of the leisure, experience economy. A substantial turn-around for resource production includes product promotion. Eventually this is part of a new priority policy-wise. It is improving the margins through new products and productivity, forced by necessities of maintaining a workable agriculture, through new waves of innovation and entrepreneurship. Not by itself, but in different constellations. Place competition, in this sphere will be rampant, and some of the expressions do not really have a permanent location, but: "need a density of creative and innovative people" (Lorentzen, 2008, p. 8). Actors, attractions and attractivity in this regard are footloose. Experience with implications for destination projects in general summarises – turning from recruiting tourists or spectators on the experience of geology or cultural history – to aspects of experience in terms of happenings, participation and all round services, in terms of guiding, food, transport, beds, etc. I.e. chains of interactive elements in more complete packaged approaches (Mariussen, 2010). This happens when a cultural heritage turns into an economic process. It happens with artefacts linked to happenings – into experiences, even into ways-of-life.

In the same kind of framework, but in other directions we find those activities that have their origin in individual creativity, skill and talent and complementing the exploitation of intellectual property in different directions. Individually linked areas of activities like literature and print media, visual and performing arts, music composition, publishing, new media such as animation, games and internet content design, broadcasting electronic media and film and heritage activities. Creativity and leisure activity industries define the event market (Vasaloppet, Birkebeiner and different types of festivals).

Notes

1 There is a severe complexity related to definitions.
2 His argument is about blocking the potential of innovation outside of these resource areas.
3 One-sidedness – that is, all the eggs are in one basket.
4 Local monopolies, based on inaccessibility from the outside.
5 Not In My Back Yard.
6 Knowledge-Intensive Business Services.

10 Policy frameworks

Introduction

Earlier chapters have outlined the general or popular, but dated picture, of the peripheral/rural. Today this is mainly a legacy of the past, prolongated or promoted partly through fundamental misconceptions into the future. Some or many of its aspects are disputed, some questioned within the framework of theoretical limitations or unsuitability, others on methodological limitations and a combination of misdirection, lack of attention or scrutiny. Through time, processes and therefore structures have changed. Empirical fragments gathered indicate a potentially different logic, a profile or whatever term preferred.

Two more or less overarching legacies ought, at this stage, to be distinguished. The first is linked to tradition, traditional evaluations and, with limited approaches, to development expected or considered where rural areas are concerned. Being dependent on agriculture and other primary activities indicates a low level of economic activity and a remaining source for outmigration (read urbanisation). This is a kind of remaining, historical truth. It is important enough as part of the framework, although "no longer an accurate depiction of the majority of rural regions in the OECD countries" (OECD, 2009b, p. 82). The other remaining illusion of missed opportunities is based on the mentioned unconsidered methods of evaluations and of policies, including misdirected solutions and unfortunate results. Policy measures, entrepreneurship and innovation programmes based on urban contextual criteria end up with mixed and/or disappointing results (Fuduric, 2012, pp. 164–165). The potential of a former and still reigning faulty logic is a tremendous obstacle for proper development.

The field is not only under- or wrongly researched but also carries a burden of a dominant paradigm with methods, ways to measure, choice of problems/cases not capturing the complexity of the combined, new (and old) structures and processes, characterising the periphery in its further and future development. It is hidden behind a centre/core philosophy, defined in terms of the centre, top-down, even in matters concerning the rural/peripheral. It is primarily concerned with the macro, and with the micro only to the benefit of the core, with the desk not the field as a platform and focus of enquiry.

This dominance is so decisive that it seems to reduce most regions to passive by-standers in an urban-driven, centre-dominated, elite-based merry-go-round exploiting the periphery, margins and rurality to a degree that enhances/exploits and transforms even their own future, position and role. This means promoting the urban/ites as the drivers, leaders and funders of the nation, while the 'backwaters' remain dependent on handouts and subsidies. The major concern is that policies outlined and enacted today based on lacking information – or worse, false premises – will at best be ineffectual or at worst counterproductive.

The argument raised has had an ambition to identify the processes, launched without considerations for the periphery/rural dimensions of development, and crucial societal complementarities, through the ways in which policies structurally are defined and power dispersed through definitions and implementation. A discussion of the tug-of-war between different policy-defining levels and the flows of power and control in these processes – some of them with explicit central-peripheral motivations, and therefore concerns – act as undercurrents for more specific policy choices. As a case in point, peripherality is actively and constantly created, and deepened – whether intentionally or not. It occurs in the form of exclusion and marginalisation of different actors or group of actors, of localities, regions and territories.

The discussion in this chapter is taken on in order to reframe a situation where alternative policies and policy measures could and should be contemplated and evaluated. The nature of policymaking in general, where intentions, via interpretations could create a variation and, eventually, an impact on final results. This outline, will in a later stage, act as a precondition for forming or defining the need, distinguishing forms and measures used, evaluated as relevant and worthwhile, up to the point, at least, for serious consideration and debate. "[A] new vision of rural regions as areas with substantive assets; and a focus on investment measures, instead of compensation payments" (Dax, 2014, p. 60).

There is also a more general framework making a re-evaluation of policy and policy systems necessary, being that the rules of the game are already changing and not only piecemeal but by leaps and bounds. Of interest are also the forms that policies take. The field of regional development is popularly categorised in terms of general or large and small/directional. It considering the classical issues between the unique and the general and the degree of necessary differentiation – linked with interacting dimensions of top-down vs. bottom-up. The proposition is valid, when the policy emanates from the national or regional arenas, or channels international agreements and policy structures. The Norwegian example, which, earlier focused on ways and means to maintain a 'living' through a 'liveable' countryside, is a reorientation appearing from what was a special policy for the districts towards a framework of general regional growth-orientated policies. The former also is notable in earlier stages of Swedish rural/peripheral policies – exemplifying, in their general direction, a process including, at least, all European countries. Substantial changes are enacted both in name and substance. The new policies have a clear centre/urban bias (Fimreite and Selle, 2006). The most pertinent today are the change from redistribution schemes to growth schemes appearing on the national level of centre/peripheral relations and in terms of variants of concentration within a general process of centralisation. Based on this growth orientation – innovation and innovation systems theory, cluster approaches, knowledge economy, knowledge spillovers etc. – reorienting the EU towards place-based and smart specialisation may be taking a first, although hesitant, step towards something more strategic. The jury is, however, still out when it comes to actual implementation within the urban/rural, core/periphery dimensions.

The main pillars of economic theory have been considered and will need to be revisited, as economic growth policies, defined with economically orientated definitions of development, are struggling with the issues. The border between the 'traditional' approach and more encompassing policies for sustainability, in their ecological, social and political manifestations, seems to be more permeable, and 'development' more multifaceted (Jonsson, 2013, p. 114). Debates occur around the roles of the market and the state in these processes, when rural locations find themselves poorly served by the market, and state agencies seem unable to overcome market neglect by providing incentives (such as grants or floor space) or infrastructure[1] (here roads, airports, etc.) or by-passing by direct economic transfers. Traditional policy and subsidy structures prevail; a reorientation in policy terms towards the sectors of the countryside in a holistic sense, seems to be wishful thinking, as seems to be the case within the orientation of agricultural policy in Sweden.[2]

> [G]overnments have designed subsidy-based interventions to reduce regional disparities. Such transfers are often not sustainable because they create relations of dependency and, over time, the richest regions become more and more reluctant to finance the lagging ones.
>
> (OECD, 2011a, p. 34)

These are reflections, relevant when it comes to the EU-defined CAP subsidies as well. The already well off are given stronger support than the peripheries, more accessible at the expense of the remote (Schmidt-Thomé and Vihinen, 2006). These are not only problems in the general management of rural policies. The problems approached are seemingly 'mis-specified', focusing on distance to market, rather than competitiveness.

There is a resonance of change also in the way traditional provisions of services are delivered, with an even more profound impact. Changing from societal welfare ambitions to individual solutions defined by central authorities, leaves no room for local variations or adaptation. The earlier defined notion of levelled/equal levels of social service provisions had, as already been noted, an across-the-board impact on local labour markets and increased the share of employment in the public sector substantially and so also the competence level of local administrations (Westlund, 1998). The policy orientation towards larger units on all levels, enforced with economic benefits for those adapting or big enough, seems, however, to be here to stay. Arguments raised about the nature of the development processes, are often focused on reducing costs, increasing efficiency and effectiveness, not only about economic gains, and rarely on user quality. The dominant feature of regional endogenous growth policy is nowadays more and more qualified by the notion of the local uniqueness and everywhere-existing potentials. The impact, however, is very hard to evaluate or promote:

> [M]ost places can contribute to growth. . . . Through a higher utilization of their potential output . . . no . . . organization has adequate ex ante knowledge about which places have a higher potential for growth, whether a given agglomeration is approaching its efficient limits, or how costly it will be to bring a lagging region closer to its potential.
>
> (OECD, 2011a, p. 220)

Arguments are raised, focusing on the need to scrutinise the increasingly important impact of long-term environmental and resource dimensions, in terms of the climate and in terms of future generations widening the scope. Other global issues of concern with implications on development and the economies are terrorism and international migratory flows. Rural and peripheral developments are crucially positioned when considering the green growth agenda and are potentially involved in other aspects as well. This is of special concern when economic functions and traditional growth projections are under the pressure of issues concerning human survival. Referring to a literature review by Massard and Autant-Bernard (2015), there is a need to go beyond general conclusions of the benefits of agglomeration economies and take this as a platform for more specific policies. A place-based policy is a long-term strategy that has as its basic purpose to disclose potentials in the localities "aimed at tackling persistent underutilisation of potential and reducing persistent social exclusion in specific places through external interventions and multilevel governance" (ESPON, 2013, p. 12). In order to be efficient and effective it relies on local knowledge and is described as being "superior to alternative strategies that do not make explicit and accountable their territorial focus, . . . behind a screen of self-proclaimed space-blindness" (ESPON, 2013, p. 12).

Key themes in the framework discussion

The first framework approach is one of defining status quo, how we got there and where we stand. A background to this pertains to the existing knowledge base. A definition by the present author that it is lacking, misdirected, based on questionable theories, and with clear methodological deficiencies, which establish an important, extensive research agenda for the future. There is a need to pool resources (especially knowledge) from a large number of actors (communities or territories), in all societal sectors. This raises implications for how future administration, on all levels, should be organised and function.

The second thematic approach are basic ideas of holism, complementarity and balance. All aspects where the public debate successively has become more frequent and intense. Take as an example the following quotation:

> [H]igher activity levels in the periphery would lead to a better use of the total productive resources of the country, both by preventing bottleneck problems in the central regions and by utilizing resources in the periphery that would otherwise have been wasted.
>
> (Mønnesland, 1994, p. 70)

While also contemplating the opposite:

> [R]egions are often dealt with in an isolated manner, i.e. the interrelationships with other regions and with higher spatial levels (national, international) are left out of consideration.
>
> (Tödtling and Trippl, 2005, p. 1204)

The urban sector, with its focus on the high end of technological and economic growth, is not enough. Past and current rurally based economies remain an absolute and the people necessary to maintain them have to be satisfied at least with a defined minimal threshold of public services and welfare provisions. A more systematic approach in search for complementary assets is relevant not only for providing the urban, but also for maintaining complementary societal functions in general (OECD, 2011a, p. 143). The impact of time should be a considered method for policy analysis. Defined in such terms it will include impacts of substance for the survival of future generations. Which could indicate the necessity of alternative dimensions of lifestyles, etc. (Westholm, 2014).

Holistic, complementary and balanced approaches also mean issues and input of across-the-field, genderised considerations. Issues raised in terms of gender are formally recognised and established in all 'important' positions of society. However, promotion, as such, has not been an automatic pre-stage to implementation. It is notable in the scholarly arena (with a number of well-versed exceptions), where within interests in identity politics, gender issues have generally been ignored, in terms of the rural/urban axis.

> [S]ocial theorists generally fail to acknowledge that a rural woman's experience of gender inequality may be quite different from that of an urban woman.
>
> (Creed and Ching, 1997, p. 3)

In general, whether things happen is when the approach is bottom-up. There is a general support for issues of gender when policies defining women's entrepreneurship are discussed. A reason for that apart from traditional structural obstacles is the structural lack of employment opportunities. Occupations and entrepreneurship defined in male categories make special efforts necessary in order to establish the balance. The ambition in this regard is to assist women to remain in, or migrate back to sparsely populated areas. An issue is the use of words like 'assist', 'support', etc. The balance is naturally taken for granted.

Distance between possible policies and implementation, however, continues to restate the issues:

> The literature also shows that policy measures in rural areas are often devised from the top down, based on a male norm, which should not be the case if women are to benefit.
>
> (Pettersson, 2012, p. 8)

The third framework approach is the institutional preconditions, identifying general policy-defining structural, ideological and pragmatic considerations. This theme, in turn, is developed into a categorisation of sectoral, functional and geographical aspects, trying to find a meaning in a discussion of policies, intentions and implementation. Taxes, laws, regulations, subsidies, channels for exercising dominance, whatever their objectives, should be seriously analysed in consequential and long-term perspectives. Also, seeking for hidden and not so hidden categories i.e. the unwritten policies within policies. Consider the 'obstacles', for example, based on different levels within the European Union: EU procurement rules and their national, regional and local interpretations. EU tender regulations, with implications on local production, and the ways competition are maintained and administered. Consider established principles of the way the organisation of the labour market with national wage agreements holds wages spatially generalised. Where blanket-defined gasoline prices become relatively costlier in a number of ways for the periphery. Where the whole issue of cultural decision-making hides behind an undefined necessity and what constitutes a country's capital is taken for granted. The priorities of impact of national/capital/urban subsidies for Stockholm Opera. City Track and Stockholm Bypass, from the Swedish context, are examples among many.

Rural/peripheral areas have changed substantially, considering functions and structures and the way, they are governed, i.e. in the ways (and if) and means that rural policies are developed, decided and implemented. Traditional steering instruments of the central or nation-state need to be re-evaluated, as they seem insufficient. A tug-of-war between administrative levels is continuously taking place. On a general level, the standing/status/position of the regional entity, of central importance,[3] considers the fundamental forces of society at play. Recognised processes of devolution in general and specific forms put this in the forefront of the present policy agenda in a multitude of countries. Policymakers have "shifted attention towards the consideration of which forms devolution will assume, rather than whether or not it will take place" (Rodriguez-Pose and Gill, 2003, p. 4). Devolution does not only carry decentralised authority, it carries also decentralised responsibilities, primarily of economic concern, where the capacity to adjust varies. The problem being the fact that different regions have different potentials of using, reacting or defending themselves against the consequences of something promoted as or supposed to be, a described advantage. How the burden will fall in each case varies, but the impact on the already relatively poor seems nowadays self-evident. As size matters, as adaptability matters, richer regions have deeper and wider pockets. The problems do not only relate to general power and financial schemes but consider the full play of institutional (read organisational) infrastructure, relative geographical positions, and macro-regional frameworks (Tödtling and Trippl, 2005). In policy, what is ahead is something new, but partly also a revitalisation of values, indicating actions, with philosophical considerations of the nature of future progress. Development should be growth, but in strong consideration of qualitative dimensions.

> [T]ackling local and regional inequalities may be necessary for the achievement of national well-being. In this context, Sen's (1999a) notion that the focus of development should be informed by the formation of 'capabilities' rather than the pursuit of utility would seem to be especially pertinent at the local and regional scale.
>
> (Tomaney et al., 2010, pp. 626–627)

This has to do with the place of the rural/peripheral within societies/nations. Notions of actors and interests are conducive for understanding. Localities, in terms of peripheries or marginal, are perceived as such and the perception is transformed to consequential definitions, descriptions and action. Resources and actors in consequence ignite market processes or empower local actors and forces of community. That is, if the state wants that. Peripheral regions are the ones least favoured by existing government policies. In historical times, this was a dimension of uncontrolled territory. Being in a peripheral location was the territorial equivalent of the unknown, the unexplored, the dangerous. But, also in terms of the unidentified, unplaced. In a more modern version:

> The problem with peripheral areas, seems to be that the government can't find a role for them in their globalisation strategy. Instead of seeing them as an integrated part of Denmark, . . . more and more in the direction of the periphery as a basis for tourism, recreation and traditional activities, or, in other words as an amusement park for the city population.
>
> (Lorentzen, 2012a, p. 107, my translation)

The fourth is the more pragmatic notion of infrastructural, in a broad sense, quality and infrastructural policy measures, i.e. building a physical, institutional and social framework. It is important, to note that infrastructure is an absolute necessary precondition in its widest sense. Transport and communication are complemented by others like economic, competence building, developing settlements also playing prominent roles (Lysgård, 2004, p. 18). Overcoming distance is the basic role of the transport infrastructure. Discussing peripherality through this prism is, of course, self-evident. Different ways to approach it indicate different principles of delimitation and different aspects of consideration. Distance (defined in physical, time or cost measures or in experience) is the starting point. Overcoming distance is a basic parameter when discussing accessibility. Emanating two basic questions: what to reach and how much to spend. This requires redefining some areas, territories and regions, while, at the same time, relocating the designation of periphery, margins to new locations, destinations and regions – where technical changes in all types of communication and transport change the rules of the game and allow for spatial reorganisations. Getting stuck only on physical aspects of infrastructure, losing the holistic objective of general societal infrastructure as fundamental strategic concerns for societies should also be considered in terms of knowledge and social interaction.

The fifth considers the necessity of analytical differentiation, regarding what aspects of the periphery we are considering. Possibly first in generalities like rural, countryside, with the periphery as opposed to the core, in terms of distant and in terms of marginal, harsh, sparsely populated. All of these carry contextual implications with the nature, volume and direction of the flows, in types, categories of actors, defined by roles, positions, locations.

The sixth and here final considers the objective, the strategy/ies. Development and/or growth. Growth and/or equalisation. Sustainability. Long-term effects mean structural changes appearing, while furthermore developing dimensions of sparsity, marginality, etc. Where patterns of settlements, work and leisure are considered, not *post factum*, but as considered and knowledgeable ingredients, combining planned and spontaneous flows into a positive, maybe optimal, geographic future. Avoiding futures consigning:

> the periphery to a subordinate role. However, such general processes are uneven in impact. There is considerable evidence to show that particular local milieu may create conditions that foster endogenous growth, for example the 'industrial district literature'.
>
> (Anderson, 2000, p. 96)

Sectoral distinctions in a general framework

> Although they can be virtually distinct, cities, towns, villages and the open countryside are all part of the same functional economic and social system.
>
> (Gruber and Soci, 2010, p. 62)

Whether growth orientation as a general policy framework and in described variants stands on the agenda or not, the means for identifying the interaction, between the centre/periphery, the urban and rural, appears mostly defined by combinations of profiled sectoral specialisations. The outcome constitutes an identification of special, usually urban-defined advantages/sectors promoting growth. They encompass, front-line, high-tech, research intensive activities, often complemented with aspects of public and especially business services. Much less attention is focused on the sectoral interaction and interdependence, represented and described in terms of holistic complementarity and ideas of a balanced nature. Within the framework of this general standpoint, the groundwork for social policy/contracts – where rural policy is given the right proportions, priorities and the right position – activate a number of more specified policy issues within the context of different general institutional implications of different territorial entities. Income tax systems, fiscal relations between societal levels, education, health care, and so on.

Sectoral policies for agriculture and forestry remain a crucial part of the total rural economy, – its definition in the value creating process, and in its substance of diversification – should be a conscientious process and priority. Also in their role as a platform for further development and an ingredient in a more diversified economy. The interactive properties are also part of the preconditions for the economy based on the tourism sector. The possibility for modern and economic/structurally different conditions in the rural area are underestimated. They already exist or are possible to develop into viable and long-term positive trends. How modern and responsive, alternative and sustainable the structures are relating to investment and skills is still not clear. Aspects of the social economy necessarily integrated as a factor and connected with site-specific/tacit knowledge. Basic issues within the competitive advantage of land-demanding activities in agriculture as well as forest management are important. The periphery is defined by sparse population, complemented by aspects of advantaged environment, referring to pure water, air, etc. Finding the logic that defines the location of production and processing also pertains to the whole spectra of primarily traditional crafts, but also the place-based transfer of innovative practices in these and newer constellations. Impact studies could show long-term consequences with far-reaching societal complexities. An excellent, and already noted, example found in energy production demands space but where the technological possibilities of small production and the digital economy build up for another kind of policy base.

Approaching the periphery in general terms returns necessarily to transport and general facilities found as basic components in any policy consideration. Public service delivery, in its widest sense, is part of such considerations as well. In focus is that "delivery for even basic public services such as education, health care, electricity and transport are complicated by low density, low volume and long distances" (OECD, 2009b, p. 87). What has been identified in this book is the need for considerations in changes in the rules of the game, not only concerning the nature of the issues raised, defined and implemented, but also in the way they are identified.

Geographical distinctions in a general framework

The necessity of analysing geographical distinctions is, on one hand, based on the interrelations of size, form, situation and functional substance and patterns, and problems and policies on the other. It is where geography is defining and being defined. History is full of examples where the discovery and exploitation of a natural resource or locational advantages created/defined/inhabited nodes for mining, oilfields, timber working, agricultural centres, transport hubs, and where the status of mechanisation or transport facilities have and are continuously changing their relative positions in a hierarchy of attraction and provision. Long-term planning or policy activities do have a potential impact on location and status and therefore on their present position. Part of the argument raised here is connected with the fundamental idea of who owns, who exploits and who benefits from the resources or locations, and whether that 'who' is willing to invest in other types of infrastructural (in a wide sense) input, prolonging or establishing any local or regional advantage. For more definite and stable issues related to self-reinforcing investments in financial, medial and political capital is also necessary. A cultural dimension hums in the background. The present is also full of locational disadvantages.

A framework description of changes in regional policy could identify an early focus on redistribution of rural resources, into a policy of industrial location, although modest in volume. An economic growth policy in geographical terms taking place to stimulate relocating mechanisms already on the verge of leaving high-cost urban locations has received substantial inputs of resources in earlier ('60–'70s) times. Headquarters and control remain 'urbanised' and therefore part of a maintained centralisation and localisation. All aspects of general policy issues took part in this, ignoring the specificities of the local communities. For policy-defined regional population growth, ignoring distributive effects below a certain level. Labour market regulations or instruments contained the same kind of setup (space-blind) for city and countryside (OECD, 2011a). The argument for these space-blind policies included the policies for generalised attributes, like agglomerations. Accepting that all agglomerative forces were positive (based, as noted, on liberal dimensions of economic suppositions).

> In this way the migration of people to large cities is an engine of growth for the whole economy. In consequence, policies should not interfere with this optimal allocation of resources and be defined uniformly across all regions (or be blind to space).
>
> (OECD, 2011a, p. 34)

Consider the further consequences in the Norwegian example concerning the distribution of economic resources (*rammetilskuddet*) between communities. This takes place with a clear tendency: away from the smaller peripheral ones to larger, centralising or centrally located (Berg, 2004, p. 75). Without any consideration of the ultimate impact, as the top-down approach cannot encapsulate preconditions and consequences in full. Policy changes within the same process, are the partly forced promotion of mergers between administrative regions and municipalities. In the Nordic countries, instrumental and in focus, are discussions on issues of regional and municipal administrative size. Trying to cut the Gordian knot this way, partly destroying some of the societal fabric in order to create and strengthen other aspects of it. Maybe politically useful, but functionally doubtful. A place-based approach, possibly able to handle these 'mis'-directions will also provide a larger degree of complementarity in the general context of rural-urban. Today with an orientation towards the green growth broad spectrum policy approach:

> migration for the more mobile people to cities can result in disproportionate costs in the supply of public services to the residual population. It therefore

> makes good public policy sense to search for untapped growth potential and look to exploit regionally specific assets in rural areas to the full.
>
> (OECD, 2011a, p. 143)

The EU's maritime, as well as its alpine policies are defined on a macro scale and geographically. The needs identified in an EU-outermost category, with a focus on research and innovation, of information and communication technologies and SME conditions, especially competitiveness, should on this level, be possible to translate into functional inputs (European Union, 2011b, p. 8). This indicates that the specificity of the categorisations are creating priorities of their own. Where, for example, according to §174 of the Treaty of the European Union, the special status of island regions were recognised. Noting

> lack of economies of scale, small markets and limited private investments in a variety of sectors, including transport, energy efficiency (with implications for energy poverty), digital connectivity, etc., all have an impact on businesses and making a living.
>
> (Hatzimarkos, 2016)

Seeking more detail and taking into consideration specific aspects of semi-general nature, pertaining to the periphery in its sparsely populated aspects, sets up challenges, but with the right kind of analytical penetration, possibilities to avoid the pitfalls of traditional land-use planning, based on too dense settlements, with conditions of costs-efficiency, of primary concern, and instead involve:

> issues such as decentralized energy production, development of tourism and an expanding secondary homes market as principal strategies for the development of rural areas.
>
> (Eskelinen and Fritsch, 2006, p. 66)

Based on this example and returning to the basic approach, being that every place could contribute to growth and its own development within the general framework. New sources, better productivity, organisational reforms could realise that. The knowledge beforehand is usually not adequate, at least, there is a lot of room for improvement. The notion of place is increasingly relevant. A mobile society increases reach/availability/accessibility (Formas, 2007). Differences in space and time and involving, interacting participants (multilevel governance) on different levels highlight the important locality and the importance for the locality. Whatever the geographical entity studied it must relate to an extended number of institutional structures to secure property rights, laws, market venues, infrastructure, public communication, risk sharing, capital management, learning and transfer systems, etc. The roles of these functions combine in function/objective perspectives. An orientation from the locality and regional perspective is the new EU orientation of 'smart specialisation', which in essence means to make policy decisions based on the specificities of these entities. This orientation does emphasise 'local' smartness, identifying what is actually there and what is not. Views on lack of capacities, defined as needs for the periphery, are too generalised. Potentials for agreements between administrative entities are a functional and rational compromise. Combining different absolute functionalities on different spatial levels is described as a waste, with functional optimalities, not being considered in correct order and condition. Influence and democratic values are a possible obstacle (Naustdalslid, 2012).

Organisational issues, potentials and deficiencies

Returning to distinctions in relations between interests, interest groups and organisations, where impact, influence, etc. are necessary ingredients in framework policy discussions. On a general level, conscious and spontaneous processes of centralisation and decentralisation are forming and deforming structures. Tug-of-wars brought to the forefront where divisions of decision-making authority are decided. Arguments around institutional structures, positions and influence are frequent.

> No significant or lasting reduction in spatial economic imbalance will be achieved without 'decentering' the key institutional structures
>
> (Martin, Pike, Tyler, and Gardiner, 2015, p. 1)

Part of the policy formation and formulation includes an evaluation of whether the existing system is suitable for handling the type of challenges expected for the future. References could be made to Ostrom (2005), who argues that the main obstacle towards a necessary orientation towards sustainability is within existing institutional interests (Johansson, 2012).

While infighting on the level of federalism vs. statism is both a historical and present example, with turf wars between EU and national actors within the manifest negotiations complementing the *aquis* and taking place within and between the Commission, Parliament and Bureaucracy with a known traditional logic. Within this scope it is fascinating to follow the present EU path, combining *smart specialisation* and *place differentiation*, referred to above, enhancing the special definition of the local, space and place with an organisational issue pertinently orientating towards location as peripheral regions are, by definition, in every dimension least favoured by current government policies. Being in a peripheral location could be described as the territorial equivalent of taking a risk, being automatically, for instance, on the wrong side of the digital divide. Relying on the latter perspectives and practices of the classical dichotomy of top-down and bottom-up approaches. Fighting off or being sceptical to amalgamations in some forms, presently a way of approaching an already reduced influence, impact, control etc., within the general process. However, the potential is there, and proven historically. There is a coincidence between the historically strong influence of the periphery in the Norwegian society and the present problematic issues of changing local and regional structures (Bukve, 2012, p. 253).

In public-choice theories (Shaw, *c.*1998–2008), we will find explanations for centralising and decentralising forces and processes. Actors are identified in their combined positions, roles and ambitions. Politicians and bureaucrats maximise their own, sometimes by way of their masters' interests, whether it is enhancing power or material/economic turnout, in long- or short-term perspectives. Joining large organisations will eventually be the route to higher salaries and fringe benefits. Agendas, then have an ultimate impact of forming policies, where peripheries and rurality do not stand as beneficiaries, and if that is not enough, deforming unwanted consequences. This means that central authorities will take a more or less automatic stand against decentralisation, against the translocation of state institutions. This process is found also in spheres of internal party politics, elections and mandates. Politics, focusing on places with many people, the urbanites by sheer numbers have an impact in the formation. The formal and informal networks among policymakers and others are determinants of this type of governance.

Actors appear in many formats, the main categorisation here are to individuals, as described above, and organisations, which need some further elaboration. The first has to do with aspects of organisational interactions or rather, the lack of these. "Complexity and fragmentation are recurring themes in discussions of multilevel governance" (Green and Orton, 2010, p. 154). Multidimensional analytical considerations are needed where networks are multi-layered, multi-locational and multifaceted in terms of actor abilities, potentials and resources, and not the least ambitions. Leading to diffuse and fragmented patterns where emergent capacities will not be analytically self-evident and results, similarly confusing, misfired or neutralised. "Does the fragmentation of local and regional governance render effective public policy innovation impossible?" (Green and Orton, 2010, p. 155). The special functioning of cooperation and coordination exists between various administrative levels and similar dimensions between units in the same administrative level. The first one makes an issue of responsibilities, budgets and therefore power. The main trend here is a reduction of the importance of the spatial dimension – through the marked importance of actor networks.

> These areas defined through the reach, direction and distribution of linear relationships, rather than through boundaries drawn around contiguous spaces, where everyone belonging to that space is automatically included in the relevant policies.
>
> (Herrschel, 2011, p. 87)

Different functionalities of participation and partnerships, presented as modern methods for increased dynamic development, are in the scope of their (networks') pre-determined delimitation. The processes are, possibly, dead-end streets for democratic considerations and participatory ambitions, when basic definitional aspects of democracy stand in the forefront. Their contents are legitimised by concepts like expediency, efficiency and also a necessary form of activity, where the involvement of the private sectors is given priority, sometimes to a degree that overreaches the sought-for objectives or questions partiality. Major question marks remain as to genderised issues and the possible role and impact within the centre/periphery dichotomy. What is discussed here are some of the drawbacks of 'classical' or 'conventional' ways to organise the peripherality, i.e. coming in from the outside, from the core areas, limiting the potential of the periphery, even adapting it to the preferences of the centre elite. That is not to say that alliances of local brokers with 'outsiders' will not be beneficial. This road is heavily strewn with boulders and blocks.

There are a notable number of tools, orientations, principles, etc., that should be more carefully considered when the periphery/rural is in focus. What kind of forces at play do we find in cross-sectoral approaches, territorial orientation, devolution of political powers to the regional level, involvement of networks at the regional level – including state, private and civic actors, participation from regionally adapted forms of consultancies and regional management. The 'new rural paradigm' introduced by the OECD (2006a), notes the complexity of the issues at stake. Pooling influence and knowledge from a widened group of actors and partly sidestepping traditional hierarchies will by necessity mean adaptations all around, both on local and government levels. Peripheralities will, by the nature of their complexity and profiling, demand pooling efforts. Here, the added necessity of pooling resources and their efficient exploitation is probably much harder to come by, when local 'supplies', leading to entrepreneurial and innovative capacities defined are lacking and also, considering fundamental cultural and attitudinal dimensions (Tödtling and Trippl, 2005).[4]

If we look at aspects of organisational issues, we can identify what makes a community or place an important framework for impact and outcome analysis and locational decision-making significant (Kawachi et al., 1999). A key word reappearing in this context is social capital. Is it possible for this concept to turn from a description of status to an active instrument of policy? How to build trust, how to create norms, how to facilitate cooperation for mutual benefit at the same time as satisfying a direct contribution to the individual, person or enterprise? As earlier quoted:

> Social capital has been claimed to be important for the enhancement of government performance and the functioning of democracy, for the prevention of crime and delinquency, and more recently for the maintenance of population health.
>
> (Kawachi et al., 1999, p. 1187)

Policies, policy measures and criteria – staring into the future

Different actors like decision makers, providers, senders, followed by transferers, transmitters and reaching consumers, receivers, beneficiaries have different interests to defend and promote in society. Distinctions sorted into public, private and voluntary sectors start out with accepting these important distinctions. The supposedly decentralising mechanisms of the market economy will not have the same kind of effects in the countryside, as supposed for the general workings of the theorised economy. Theory and therefore practice will have to be reconsidered. Taking, for example, the issue where strong centralised (inside or outside) ownership in a specific region will push and structure the private economy. These mechanisms will function differently for the public sector (inside or outside) as the hiring and firing do not work in the same way and where even quite simple work – manageable anywhere and supposedly less costly in some places – could and will take place in already designated high-cost locations. No real savings in strict budget allocations but instead a spending spree is to be had, when the budget period ends. Leaving implications of state-private market comparisons and entering into the much more flexible emphasis of network/governance connectivity, makes much of the substance of ways and means of future policy processes, unchartered territory. 'New' patterns and practices within the governance approach, including practical substantiations of concept like 'open', 'flexible', 'non-spatial', 'network-based', 'informal', leading to connectivity and dynamism (Herrschel, 2011).

The question of what is the most efficient and productive way to provide subsidies to needing areas is at stake but not considered in its total complexity. Individuals, households, communities, enterprises, actors in the social economy, etc. are placed in a combination of indicators for defining areas, their thresholds, the nature of their distribution and the nature of the recipients makes room for mixed and complex solutions. They contribute sometimes/most often to a maze of hopefully beneficial outcomes and outputs, interfoliated by inefficient resource utilisation. As earlier indicated, the question could possibly be wrong in itself, as the whole idea of central policy initiatives should be concerned with certain framework aspects not the nuts and bolts of local development elements.

The same caveat refers to the position of the policies directed towards economic entities in question. The general presence of economic actors is not enough, considering the impact on the presence and future of economic development and the possibility of a thriving community. Identifying categories of actors/winners will indicate different types of behaviour in small enterprises with or without owners from the locality. Looking also at smaller entities, their potential as active participants in the local community is much more about overcoming relative isolation and size disadvantages (Dubois and Hedström, 2011). Also considering local entities, defined within conglomerates, with ownership far away and a diffuse stock ownership, reactive to the ups and downs of the stock market. It could be outsourcing, pure production, with no development potential and limitations to functionality. Regulated within a clear company strategy, where, profit margins include or are dependent upon subsidy patterns. Negligence of the local, as in preconditions and ambitions.

The interpretations have to discuss, where the major impact, in a positive way, could be found, i.e. if outside help is expected or granted. Based on the supposition of rather simple administrative practices, there is the cut-off point, in a range from the individual, firm or types of firms, to territories. Of course, all the in-between potentials should be given the attention needed. For example, rural centres and small-town networks, as hubs for service, trade and administration.

This section, contains a humble start, identifying the role of some specific policies within a framework of other, larger, more encompassing ones. These could appear as formalised and agreed documents, in a noted hierarchical approach, in at least two dimensions: geography and function. A general framework example is found in global trade agreements, where terms-of-trade conditions, rules and regulations as to competitive practices appear. The hierarchy becomes prominent in terms of macro-regional agreements, stipulating territorial specificities, ending up with national strategies, with regional and local implications. The place of the periphery, its room for adaptation, is highly regulated – and note that this is only exemplified here in the straight line of market regulations in a direct commercial sense. Complementing this with issues that more or less live a life of their own, but stand as patterns in global frameworks, their implications are complex. Complementary environmental issues must include considerations of the policy implications emanating from global warming. Restoring and preserving ecosystems, related to agriculture and forestry, and the rural territory in general – and especially to promote an efficient utilisation of relevant resources and the shift towards a low carbon and climate-resilient economy in the agricultural, food and forestry sectors – places special demands. The impact on other dimensions of the economy, partly and sometimes come into confrontation with materialistic values and profound hopes for an ultimate survival for humanity.

> However, the current debate about a new development model suggests less social acceptance for these trade-offs, with citizens asking for both greener and more liveable cities, and for rural and intermediate areas providing a minimum of employment opportunities and access to public services.
>
> (OECD, 2011a, p. 32)

It is not only the frameworks, which we can continue to list extensively. Policies also carry presupposed aspects of how to go about doing things. Defining the peripheral within the framework of regional policy and regional development policy is a case in point. What kind of arsenal is available, plausible and acceptable? Analytical ranges include issues of expediency, from support to self-help, based on growth and development potential, choices between growth and equity and combinations in between. Different forms of political and polity solutions range from government to governance, including considerations of sectoral and/or territorial priorities. Furthermore, considerations of bureaucratic expediency. Among the challenges for national and regional governments is the identification of appropriate policy levers for different stages of development processes, and within this catching the specificities of catalytic shortcuts – from knowledge generation and invention to innovation and commercialisation, where we find different spatial dimensions for each.

Finally, there is a consideration of the specificity and/or necessity of special places but also of special cases. The first, concerned with place-specific externalities or 'soft' location factors defines an environment conducive for the development of local firms or making places 'sticky' for mobile capital and skilled workers. This includes improving environmental quality, social stability, cultural resources, educational institutions, the quality of the living environment, and with this local and regional identity and international image. Differentiation is on the agenda providing foundations for a whole range of activities already exemplified; this line of progression has been taken as far as possible. What then, is possible?

After the discussion on general frameworks defining spatial and functional entities on different decision-making levels, and this complemented, exemplifying categorisations of policy areas, we now turn to a discussion on what types, why and how different criteria are used. In studying policy measures in general, there is a clear tendency that recognises the basic proposition that one size does not fit all. All-out efforts with too blunt instruments will be inefficient and even, in worst cases, counterproductive. Combining forces on a number of different platforms will create the potential, the possibility of an orchestra of relevant combinations. What we have, for instance, is the path from single to joint responsibility, from top-down to bottom-up. There is a need for a differentiated approach from integrated and place-related. Structures (both territorial and organisational) of support and the quality of that for rural businesses, provide a broader differentiation in rural areas. This is, by no means, straightforward, as the impacts will not be uniform. Bringing these insights into the field of rural, peripheral studies recognise the potential at the same time as the complexity. Criteria, when analysed, have to answer questions regarding impact. Who should benefit? Who should pay the bills and when shall we start counting? Differentiation includes objectives like growth and/or equality. Gender needs integration as an absolute criterion. Democratic qualities as well. This impacts not only on the object but also, whether the efforts support background prerequisites in regard to centralising or decentralising. This brings the discussion into the reality of peripheries, sparsely populated, lagging. Every category has a potential of different representations.

Principles stand in line to be exemplified: labour to factories or factories to labour? Pupils to schools and teachers or schools and teachers to pupils? Connectivity to urban centres for commuting and service provisions, another case in point. "In practice, spatial mobility of people is often limited and presents a large inertia" (OECD, 2011a, p. 32). Questioning a major instrument of growth and development orientation i.e. the labour market region, in planning terms enlarging, making provisions for a bigger pool of labour and a better flexibility of a larger region. The focus on this side of the issue is quite pertinent. Exemplifying the other with a remark pointing in another, complementary direction, as impacts on the climatological footprint remain a priority. Upgrading and/or widening the skills within the local mini-labour market then makes extensive travelling less necessary:

> [A] wide range of potential research in, e.g. investment into innovative technologies for small and medium-sized companies and public services, green

> energy that would reduce transport costs and promote repopulation as well as the potential for developing a green economy.
>
> (Mendas, 2016, p. 29)

Another distinction lies between front-line direct support and more general provisions for functional infrastructures. What must be created is a framework of technical, transport solutions and advisory, service provisions and connections to rural centres and small-town networks that are clearly defined and equipped as local hubs for service, trade and administration. An argument built on location, where support avoids enforcing flows of centralisation. The focus today is defined in terms of complex info-communication systems development. Per capita cost considerations are questionably up front, in spite of primary importance in regions designated as sparsely populated. When degradation takes place within absolute necessities in service facilities, from waste management to schools, it contributes to spiral effects, as to population levels and gentrification. Another direction, concerning functional infrastructure, has to do with general standards and provisions of local/regional quality-of-life perspectives, related to housing and related functions, cultural events, programmes, traditions and traditional values included. Absolutes in a quest to maintain a potential. Noted should also be the social fabric supporting and strengthening voluntary organisations, local identity and local democratic principles.

However, as a consequence of this multi-directional exemplification, there is a danger in the inclusion of considerations, not for special cases, but for necessary fundamental aspects, based on a malfunctioning society, where deviances and cultural-structural malformations hinder a sound long-term development process. Take, for instance, structural obstacles towards women's entrepreneurship in sparsely populated areas, and in the popular promotion of the labour market regions as a planning instrument, further aggravating imbalances.

Going off in another direction, there is something about words and values. Is the urban, core, centre, helping out? Is it really, or is it payback time? Subsidies or payment for services rendered in earlier decades and centuries. Historically, the agricultural surplus created the market and therefore the system, when the rural provided the impetus for technological development and the funding for its fruition, when technological breakthroughs for agriculture were the basis for the industrialisation drive. Presently, fundamental flows of foodstuffs, raw materials and energy, are at the very foundation of economic development and the guarantor for societal well-being. Discussing subsidies and/or incentives, in perspective of this entrance is a little awkward as the word subsidy carries negative connotations, while incentives focus on dimensions of proactivity.

Lessons to be learned: enlightening frameworks and examples

In order to catch the scientific object (subject) through the art of classification within different types of policy-relevant hierarchies, thematically constructed, the hierarchies that are exemplified have something to do with characteristics like centralisation and concentration, words and concepts that continue as analytical foundations. Further examples, definable in terms of urban, power and control hierarchies. Spatial enters through the back door, and takes care of the process of planning, decision-making and implementation. Methods and techniques are at the same time ways to be studied and investigated. One of the major problems in this process is the necessity of discarding existing biases of spatial models that consider a periphery simultaneously defining unsubstantiated negative properties. An unbiased holistic approach could "provide new opportunities for peripheral regions, and relief from 'overheating' at the core" (Copus, 2001, p. 539). It does, however, necessitate an active peripheral involvement based on local knowledge, and furthermore, a further cultivation of that knowledge.

Arguing for the crucial role of the periphery/margins/rural in this way have implications for a more proactive, general policy. Specification within the realms of regional policy perspectives are steps in the right direction. A basic priority is how to handle the centre/periphery relation in all its connotations. Exploitation, which no one promotes openly or, lifting the periphery to levels of development comparable to the centre. The choice is in what and with what. It is also a perspective related to the kinds of goals/objectives defined in the process. To maintain an acceptable service level for the existing population is maybe more possible than turning the demographic tide, i.e. repopulating the periphery. As described by Westlund (1998, p. 57, my translation) "The question is what is good for the sparsely populated areas: unrealistic objectives that create resignation and contempt for politicians or realistic objectives that make politicians responsible if they are not achieved." Westlund identifies two general directions: to establish industries similar to the centre or trying to complement, in line of comparative advantages. Exploiting the resources that are plentiful, in terms of area-intensive. He concludes, that the picture is benevolent: "optimal affinity is a question of the right combination of similarities and differences" (Westlund, 1998, pp. 45–46, my translation). Policy evolvement from top-down subsidy-based interventions is designed to reduce local and regional disparities, into much broader policies designed to improve regional and local competitiveness, but, maybe of more profound impact, complementarity as a principle.

Approaching the periphery in general terms, transport and general services, as always and everywhere, found to be basic components in such considerations. Public service delivery, in its widest sense, is at the same time, a basic 'infrastructural' prerequisite in rural/peripheral territories. There is a clear, unequivocal argument for financial and infrastructural development. There is a need for a thorough examination of basic budgetary considerations and allocations between different levels of the public sector and the tendencies of key indicators defining the distribution between levels, sizes of municipalities, etc. (Berg, 2004, p. 75). There is a need for extended infrastructural networks both in physical and human terms.

Bottom-up is more than a simple word. It is a substantial part of any financing package, that could, and in all fairness, should be based, on the principle that sparsely populated areas should receive a larger share of the profits/margins, emanating from resource exploitation in their respective territories. Turning the general into the more specific, without losing the general, is the crux of the matter. Devolution of political power to the regional and local levels, involvement of networks and participation of local/regional inhabitants at regional level and local, including state, private and civic actors. Coordinating sectoral policies and general rural objectives in a broad approach do need an authority somewhere. Going more specific, the need is to consider the cultural fabric, defining the unique in combination with the potential. Variants of the scientific community have a strategic role to play in such a society.

> facilitating or constraining the entrepreneurial and innovative capabilities of these places, as well as the means through which the norms and capabilities are reproduced over time, should form a key locus of analysis within the emerging field of evolutionary economic geography.
>
> (Huggins and Thompson, 2015, p. 149)

The need for a holistic and differentiated approach, using the place-based foundation is timely. A proper analysis of the nature of the place – a diagnosis based on in-depth considerations, founded on both top-down and bottom-up information flows and qualitative investigations, focuses on improvements in policies. Instrumentality should constantly be a matter of formation and deformation of and through the local. The kind of analysis needed makes it easier to find ways through the intricacies of structures and processes in rules and regulations, developments schemes, etc. While preparing a list of exemplifying surfaces, fundamental structures remain in hiding: municipal and regional collaboration, government services and programmes, innovation and diversification, education and training, diversity in culture and leisure, safe and easy transportation, structure, stability and resilience of industry, specificities of labour markets, socio-cultural renewal. Threshold signals and points of no return. For example, smaller schools not only provide education for local kids, but are also an important physical facility for volunteer organisations, cultural events etc., and an important symbol for a future, for the survival of the community.

Another approach, by way of the unique, highlights potential problems and problem areas. One of the major variables has to do with distance and accessibility. There is a noticeable second, sometimes turning primary, with improved (distance, time and cost) transport solutions, creating a situation where some locations become less peripheral while others (where the train does not stop) become more. Including a potential demography combined with service and commercial drainage effects. The extension of the broadband network, a good thing in itself, can be a drawback opening up a monopolistic (survival) situation for e-commerce competition. The quality and slow process defining at least parts of the periphery is another case in point.

As noted, an earlier trend within regional policies was the increase in competence in general, but also with a specific purpose, in the public sector. One last item here is a focus on the agenda of knowledge construction, knowledge processing and knowledge dissemination. An ambition to redistribute competence-defined workplaces is described as beneficial also for the social economy through improved exploitation of resources and a higher degree of value creation (Kompetansearbeidsplassutvalget, 2011, p. 13). In order to achieve this, there is a need to focus on a priority for relocating important 'central' authorities to lower-order urban centres. Impact could and should be enhanced promoting active links within the community of peripheral and marginal regions. Social economy, networking and partnerships between these regions would allow learning and more effective dissemination of theories, practices and analysis within the arc of commonality. They are panacea qualifications as to qualities that have to be increased. "Results suggest that volunteer organisations in general positively influence local new firm foundation rates" (Schulz and Baumgartner, 2013, p. 597). The caveat is, however, that enough is enough, too much networking in this direction reduces the rate of establishment, probably because it drains the entrepreneurial body. Knowledge and competence building should be established as a conscious, institutional input into the local fabric.

Based on this changed direction of thought we could argue for necessary consequences in policy, whether it is public or private orientated is not of primary importance. Discussions on exploiting and/or creating local proximal advantages are linked with push factors from congested environments (costs, etc.). This introduces again the discussion on the quality of the infrastructural/communication structure, making integration of sparsely populated areas possible. Copus identifies three general processes being conducive for a change in status: improvements in transport and communications infrastructure, structural changes as, for example, increases in the service sector and light manufacturing and the decline of heavy manufacturing and primary production and, finally, technological change in the field of information society, technology and e-Commerce (Copus, 2001, p. 540).

Notes

1 The concept used in a wide sense includes both physical (like roads and railways) and immaterial (like public advisory capacities).

2 A critique also raised by central control authorities – The National Audit Office – (*Riksrevisionen*).

3 Although down-played by right-wing forces in several European countries.

4 The quotation is followed by a number of specific advices in terms of policy development.

References

Aarsæther, N. (2014). Kommunereform – for morgendagens utfordringer? *Fagbladet samfunn og økonomi*, (1), 18–29.

Aarsæther, N. and Nyseth, T. (2007). Innovasjonsprosesser i den nordiske periferi. *Tidsskrift for samfunnsforskning*, *48*(1), 5–28.

Aasbrenn, K. (1995). Uttynning og regional økonomi – en underbefolkningsspiral. In K. Aasbrenn (Ed.), *Livskraftige uttynningsssamfunn – en nordisk antologi* (pp. 110–127). Stockholm: Nordiska institutet för regionalpolitisk forskning.

Åberg, E. (2013, March 19). Glesbygden kan dö om 60 år. *Dagens Nyheter.*

ACANALYS. (2011). *Hållbar regional utveckling i Västerbotten – en sammanfattning av resulata från ACANALYS.* Retrieved from www.cerum.umu.se/digitalAssets/73/73179_slutrapport1.0.sammanfattning.pdf.

Akgün, A. A., Baycan-Levent, T., Nijkamp, P. and Poot, J. (2011). Roles of local and newcomer entrepreneurs in rural development: A comparative meta-analytic study. *Regional Studies*, *45*(9), 1207–1223.

Allan, G., McGregor, P. and Swales, K. (2011). The importance of revenue sharing for the local economic impacts of a renewable energy project: A social accounting matrix approach. *Regional Studies*, *45*(9), 1171–1186.

Almaas, R. and Elden, K. M. (1997). *Den rurale dimensjon – en teoretisk og geografisk avgrensning.* Trondheim: Senter for Bygdeforskning.

Alonso, W. (1964). *Location and Land Use: Toward a General Theory of Land Rent.* Cambridge, MA: Harvard University Press.

Anderson, A. R. (1998). Cultivating the Garden of Eden: Environmental entrepreneuring. *Journal of Organizational Change Management*, *11*(2), 135–144.

Anderson, A. R. (2000). Paradox in the periphery: An entrepreneurial reconstruction. *Entrepreneurship & Regional Development*, *12*(2), 91–109.

Andersson, K. (2007). *New Rural Goods and Services: The Foundation of the New Countryside.* Helsinki: University of Helsinki.

Andersson, T. (2002). *Politik för tillväxt – internationella trender och den svenska utmaningen.* Östersund: Institutet för tillväxtpolitiska studier.

Arcelus, F. J., Arocena, P., Cabasés, F. and Pascual, P. (2015). On the cost-efficiency of service delivery in small municipalities. *Regional Studies*, *49*(9), 1469–1480.

Arnesen, T., Overvåg, K., Gløersen, E., Schurman, C. and Riise, Ø. (2010). *Fjellområder og fjellkommuner i Sör-Norge – definisjon, avgrensning og karakterisering.* Retrieved from www.ostforsk.no/wp-content/uploads/2014/11/082010.pdf.

Arnesen, T., Overvåg, K., Skjeggedal, T. and Ericsson, B. (2012). Transcending orthodoxy: The multi-house home, leisure and the transformation of core periphery relations. In

M. Danson and P. de Souza (Eds.), *Regional Development in Northern Europe: Peripherality, Marginality and Border Issues* (pp. 182–195). Chippenham: Routledge.

Aronsson, L. and Braunerhielm, L. (2011). Plats för kreativitet. In L. Aronsson and L. Braunerhielm (Eds.), *Kreativitet på plats* (pp. 9–27). Karlstad: Karlstad University Press.

Arzeni, A., Esposti, R. and Sotte, F. (2002). *European Policy Experiences with Rural Development*. Kiel: Wissenshaftsverlag Vauk Kiel KG.

Asheim, B. (2007). Industrial districts as 'learning regions': A condition for prosperity. In R. Rutten and F. Boekema (Eds.), *The Learning Region: Foundations, State of the Art, Future*. Edward Elgar Publishers Ltd.

Ashton, J. K. and Gregoriou, A. (2014). The influence of banking centralization on depositors: Regional heterogeneities in the transmission of monetary policy. *Regional Studies, 48*(9), 1467–1482.

Backman, M. (2013). *Regions, Human Capital and New Firm Formation* (JIBS Dissertation Series No. 086). Retrieved from http://hj.diva-portal.org/smash/get/diva2:605373/FULLTEXT01.pdf.

Baldersheim, H. and Fimreite, A. L. (2005). Norwegian centre – periphery relations in flux: Abolition or reconstruction of regional governance? *West European Politics, 28*(4), 764–780.

Balland, P.-A., Boschma, R. and Frenken, K. (2013). Proximity and innovation networks. In P. Cooke (Ed.), *Re-Framing Regional Development: Evolution, Innovation and Transition* (pp. 188–200). London: Routledge.

Baltzopoulos, A. and Broström, A. (2013). Attractors of entrepreneurial activity: Universities, regions and alumni entrepreneurs. *Regional Studies*, *47*(6), 934–949. doi:10.1080/00343404.2011.602335.

Barca, F. and McCann, P. (2010). The place based approach: A response to Mr. Gill. *Testo disponibile al sito.* Retrieved from *www.voxeu.org/index.php*.

Bathelt, H. and Turib, P. (2011). Local, global and virtual buzz: The importance of face-to-face contact in economic interaction and possibilities to go beyond. *Geoforum, 42*(5), 520–529.

Baumgartner, D. and Schulz, T. (2010). *Volunteer Organisations: Odds or Obstacle for Small Business Formation in Rural Areas? Evidence from Swiss Municipalities*. Paper presented at the Annual Meeting of the Regional Studies Association, Pecs, Hungary.

Beck, E. M., Horan, P. M. and Tolbert II, C. M. (1978). Stratification in a dual economy: A sectoral model of earnings determination. *American Sociological Review, 43*(5), 704–720.

Beck, U. (1992). *Risk Society: Towards a New Modernity*. London: Sage Publications.

Benneworth, P. (2007). Seven samurai opening up the ivory tower? The construction of Newcastle as an entrepreneurial university. *European Planning Studies, 15*(4).

Benneworth, P., Richardson, R., Gillespie, A. and Coombes, M. (2003). *Regional Productivity: A Review of the Rural Perspective: A Research Report to the Rural Economics Unit, the Department for Environment, Food and Rural Affairs*. Newcastle upon Tyne: CURDS.

Berg, N. G. and Forsberg, G. (2003). Rural geography and feminist geography: Discourses on rurality and gender in Britain and Scandinavia. In J. Öhman (Ed.), *Voices from the North: New Trends in Nordic Human Geography* (pp. 173–190). Aldershot: Ashgate.

Berg, N. G. and Lysgård, H. K. (2004). Ruralitet og urbanitet – bygd og by. In N. G. Berg, B. Dale, H. K. Lysgård and A. Löfgren (Eds.), *Mennesker, steder og regionale endringer* (pp. 9–13). Trondheim: Tapir Akademiske Forlag.

Berg, P. O. (2004). Sentralisering og makt – et apropos til Makt- og demokratiutredningen. In J. Amdam and O. Bukve (Eds.), *Det regionalpolitiske regimeskiftet – tilfellet Noreg* (pp. 63–84). Trondheim: Tapir Akademiske Forlag.

Birch, K. (2005). *Colocation and Knowledge: The Relationship between the Science Base and UK Biotech Firms*. Paper presented at the RSA Conference, Regional Growth Agendas, Aalborg.

Bjarnar, O. (2008). Global pipelines and diverging patterns of knowledge sharing in regional cluster. *Working Paper 2008:1*. Retrieved from www.moreforsk.com/publications/reports/industrial-economics/global-pipelines-and-diverging-patterns-of-knowledge-sharing-in-regional-clusters/1196/385/.

Bloch, C. and Bugge, M. M. (2013). Public sector innovation – from theory to measurement. *Structural Change and Economic Dynamics*, *27* (December), 133–145.

Boschma, R. (2005). Proximity and innovation: A critical assessment. *Regional Studies*, *39*(1), 61–74.

Boschma, R. and Frenken, K. (2010). The spatial evolution of innovation networks: A proximity perspective. In R. Boschma and R. Martin (Eds.), *The Handbook of Evolutionary Geography* (pp. 120–135). Cheltenham: Edward Elgar.

Bosworth, G. (2009). *Commercial Counterurbanisation and the Rural Economy*. Paper presented at the European Regional Studies Association Conference, Leuven, Belgium.

Bosworth, G. (2010). Commercial counterurbanisation: An emerging force in rural economic development. *Environment and Planning A*, *42*(4), 966–981. doi:10.1068/a42206.

Bosworth, G. and Willett, J. (2011). Embeddedness or escapism? Rural perceptions and economic development in Cornwall and Northumberland. *Sociologia Ruralis*, *51*(2), 195–214.

Bourdieu, P. (1977). *Outline of a Theory of Practice*. Cambridge: Cambridge University Press.

Brandtzæg, B. A. and Haukeland, P. I. (2011). Naturarven som verdiskaper. Statusrapport 2010. *(TF-notat nr. 21/2012)*. Retrieved from http://evaluering.nb.no/eval-utlevering/innhold/URN:NBN:no-nb_overfortdokument_6619_Eval_0/pdf.

Breska, E. V. (Ed.) (2010). *Investing in Europe's Future: Fifth Report on Economic, Social and Territorial Cohesion*. Luxembourg: Publications of the European Union.

Bristow, G. (2010). *Critical Reflections on Regional Competitiveness: Theory, Policy and Practice*. London: Routledge.

Bruckmeier, K. and Höj Larsen, C. (2009). Sweden: The non-agricultural rural economy as a component of rural sustainable development. In K. Bruckmeier and H. Tovey (Eds.), *Rural Sustainable Development in the Knowledge Society* (pp. 39–59). Aldershut: Ashgate.

Bryceson, D. F. (2002). The scramble in Africa: Reorienting rural livelihoods. *World Development*, *30*(5), 725–739.

Bukve, O. (2012). *Lokal og regional styring: eit institusjonelt perspektiv*. Oslo: Samlaget.

Cabras, I. (2014). Community cohesion and cooperatives in rural Britain: Exploring a sustainable future. *Regions Magazine*, *193*(1), 6–9.

Calignano, G. and Hassink, R. (2016). Increasing innovativeness of SMEs in peripheral areas through international networks? The case of Southern Italy. *Region*, *3*(1), 25–42.

Callaghan, G., Danson, M. and Whittam, G. (2012). Economic and enterprise development in community buy-outs. In M. Danson and P. de Souza (Eds.), *Regional Development in Northern Europe: Peripherality, Marginality and Border Issues* (pp. 196–211). Chippenham: Routledge.

Cardoso, F. H. and Faletto, E. (1979). *Dependency and Development in Latin America*. Berkeley: University of California Press.

Chambers, R. (1983). *Rural Development: Putting the Last First*. London and New York: Routledge.

Champion, A. G. (1989). *Counterurbanization: The Changing Pace and Nature of Population Deconcentration*. London: Arnold.

Cheshire, P. (2006). Resurgent cities, urban myths and policy hubris: What we need to know. *Urban Studies, 43*(8), 1231–1246.

Cheshire, P. and Magrini, S. (2008). *Urban Growth Drivers in a Europe of Sticky People and Implicity Boundaries.* Retrieved from London.

Christaller, W. (1933). *Die zentralen Orte in Süddeutschland: eine ökonomisch-geographische Untersuchung über die Gesetzmässigkeit der Verbreitung und Entwicklung der Siedlungen mit städtischen Funktionen.* Jena: Verlag von Gustav Fischer.

Christensen, L. and Kempinsky, P. (2004). *Att mobilisera för regional tillväxt – regionala utvecklngsprocesser, kluster och innovationssystem.* Lund: Studentlitteratur.

Cloke, P., Goodwin, M. and Milbourne, P. (1998). Inside looking out, outside looking in: Different experience of cutural competence in rural lifestyles. In P. Boyle and K. Halfacree (Eds.), *Migration into Rural Areas: Theories and Issues.* Chichester: John Wiley & Sons.

Cloke, P. J. (1977). An index of rurality for England and Wales. *Regional Studies, 11*(1), 31–46.

Coleman, J. S. (1990). *Foundations of Social Theory.* Cambridge, MA: Belknap Press.

Cooke, P. (2012). *Complex Adaptive Innovation Systems: Relatedness and Transversality in the Evolving Region.* London: Routledge.

Cooke, P., Clifton, N. and Oleaga, M. (2005). Social capital, firm embeddedness and regional development. *Regional Studies, 39*(8), 1065–1077.

Coombes, M. and Champion, T. (2010). Migration and commuting: Local and regional development links. In A. Pike, A. Rodriguez-Pose and J. Tomaney (Eds.), *Handbook of Local and Regional Development* (pp. 182–192). London: Routledge.

Copus, A. K. (2001). From core-periphery to polycentric development: Concepts of spatial and aspatial peripherality. *European Planning Studies, 9*(4), 539–552.

Creed, G. W. and Ching, B. (1997). Recognizing rusticity – identity and the power of place. In G. W. Creed and B. Ching (Eds.), *Knowing Your Place: Rural Identity and Cultural Hierarchy* (pp. 1–38). London: Routledge.

Crone, M. (2012). Re-thinking 'peripherality' in the context of a knowledge-intensive service-dominated economy. In M. Danson and P. de Souza (Eds.), *Regional Development in Northern Europe: Peripherality, Marginality and Border Issues* (pp. 49–64). Chippenham: Routledge.

Crowley, C. (2011). Geography, advice seeking and innovation. *Regional Insights, 2*(1), 18–20.

Cruz, S.C.S. and Teixeira, A.A.C. (2010). The evolution of the cluster literature: Shedding light on the regional studies – regional science debate. *Regiona Studies, 44*(9), 1263–1288.

Curry, N. and Webber, D. J. (2012). Economic performance in rural England. *Regional Studies, 46*(3), 279–291.

Dahl, M. S., Østergaard, C. R. and Dalum, B. (2015). *Entrepreneurial Founder Effects in the Growth of Regional Clusters: How Early Success Is a Key Determinant.* Paper presented at the Regional Studies European Conference, Aalborg. Retrieved from www3.druid.dk/wp/20050018.pdf.

Dahlgren, B. (1989). Some reflections on the periphery – on processes and shifts of perspective. In G. Gustafsson (Ed.), *Development in Marginal Areas* (Vol. 3). Karlstad: University College of Karlstad.

Danson, M. (2009). New regions and regionalisation through clusters – city-regions and new problems for the periphery. *International Journal of Public Sector Management, 22*(3), 260–271.

Danson, M. and de Souza, P. (2012). Periphery and marginality: Definitions, theories, methods and practice. In M. Danson and P. de Souza (Eds.), *Regional Development in Northern Europe: Peripherality, Marginality and Border Issues* (pp. 1–15). Abingdon: Routledge.

Danson, M. and de Souza, P. (2013). Peripheries – the agenda. *Fraser of Allander Economic Commentary* (Special Issue No 4), 5–11.

Davies, S., Michie, R. and Vironen, H. (2012). Can peripheral regions innovate? In M. Danson and P. de Souza (Eds.), *Regional Development in Northern Europe: Peripherality, Marginality and Border Issues* (pp. 118–133). Chippenham: Routledge.

Dax, T. (2014). Shaping rural development research in Europe: Acknowledging the interrelationships between agriculture, regional and ecological development. *Studies in Agricultural Economics, 116*(2), 59–66.

Delfmann, H., Koster, S., McCann, P. and van Dijk, J. (2014). Population change and new firm formation in urban and rural regions. *Regional Studies, 48*(6), 1034–1050.

Delors, J. (2012). Jacques Delors: Reflections on cohesion policy. *Panorama Inforegio*, (47), 4–7. Retrieved from http://ec.europa.eu/regional_policy/sources/docgener/panorama/pdf/mag43/mag43_en.pdf.

de Souza, P. (1989). *Territorial Production Complexes in the Soviet Union: With Special Focus on Siberia.* Göteborg: Göteborgs univ.

Dimitris, S. (2004). The role of business networks and innovation in peripheral regions. In A. Copus (Ed.), *Aspatial Peripherality, Innovation & the Rural Economy (AsPIRE): Finale Report* (pp. 81–104). Aberdeen: AsPIRE.

Döring, T. and Schnellenbach, J. (2006). What do we know about geographical knowledge spillovers and regional growth? A survey of the literature. *Regional Studies, 40*(3), 375–395. doi:10.1080/00343400600632739.

Dubois, A. and Hedström, M. (2011). *Striving for Local Development in the North of Europe.* Paper presented at Regional Studies International Conference 18–20 April, Newcastle upon Tyne, UK.

Eatwell, J., Newman, P. and Milgate, M. (1998). *The New Palgrave Dictionary of Economics.* London: Macmillan.

Echebarria, C. and Barrutia, J. M. (2013). Limits of social capital as a driver of innovation: An empirical analysis in the context of European regions. *Regional Studies, 47*(7), 1001–1017.

Edvardsen, H. M. (Ed.) (2004). *Regional Policy in Sweden and Norway: Same but Different.* Oslo: Norwegian Institute for Urban and Regional Research.

Elander, I. (1978). *Det nödvändiga och det önskvärda: en studie av socialdemokratisk ideologi och regionalpolitik 1940–72.* Stockholm: Arkiv för studier i arbetarrörelsens historia.

Elldér, E. and Larsson, A. (2011). *Improving Regional Transport Accessibility Planning: A GIS-Based Methodology Utilizing Micro-Level Register Data.* Presentation at Regional Studies International Conference 18–20 April, Newcastle upon Tyne, UK.

Eriksson, M. (2008). (Re)producing a 'peripheral' region – Northern Sweden in the news. *Geografiska Annaler, Series B, Human Geography, 90*(4), 369–388.

Eriksson, M. (2010). 'People in Stockholm are smarter than countryside folks' – reproducing urban and rural imaginaries in film and life. *Journal of Rural Studies, 26*(2), 95–104.

Eriksson, R., Lindgren, U. and Malmberg, G. (2008). Agglomeration mobility: Effects of localisation, urbanisation, and scale on job changes. *Environment and Planning A, 40*(10), 2419–2434.

Eskelinen, H. and Fritsch, M. (2006). The reconfiguration of Eastern Finland as an interface periphery. In H. Eskelinen and T. Hirvonen (Eds.), *Positioning Finland in a European Space* (pp. 54–70). Helsinki: Ministry of Environment, Ministry of Interior.

ESPON. (2010). *New Evidence on Smart, Sustainable and Inclusive Territories.* Luxemburg: European Union.

ESPON. (2013). *New Evidence on Smart, Sustainable and Inclusive Territories*. Luxembourg. Retrieved from www.espon.eu/export/sites/default/Documents/Publications/Synthesis Report/FirstOctober10/fullversion.pdf.

European Commission. (2011). The urban and regional dimension of Europe 2020: Seventh progress report on economic, social and territorial cohesion. *Report from the Commission*. Retrieved from http://ec.europa.eu/regional_policy/sources/docoffic/official/reports/interim7/interim7_en.pdf.

European Commission. (2012). Jacques Delors: Reflections on cohesion policy. *Panorama Inforegio*, (43), 4–7.

European Commission. (2014). Cohesion policy, climate change and energy security. *Panorama Inforegio*, (51), 8–11.

European Union. (2011a). Cities of tomorrow: Challenges, visions, ways forward. Retrieved from http://ec.europa.eu/regional_policy/sources/docgener/studies/pdf/citiesoftomorrow/citiesoftomorrow_final.pdf.

European Union. (2011b). Cohesion Policy 2014–2020 investing in growth and jobs. Retrieved from http://ec.europa.eu/regional_policy/sources/docoffic/official/regulation/pdf/2014/proposals/regulation2014_leaflet.pdf.

European Union. (2012). Outermost regions innovation in the outermost regions. *Panorama Inforegio*, *41*(Spring), 12–14.

Fimreite, A. L. and Selle, P. (2006). Den egentlige regiondebatten. *Plan*, *38*(3–4), 10–23.

Finnish Forest Industries. (2014). Statistics. Retrieved from www.forestindustries.fi/statistics/.

Florida, R. (2002). *The Rise of the Creative Class: And How It's Transforming Work, Leisure, Community and Everyday Life*. New York: Basic Books.

Florida, R. (2005). *Cities and the Creative Class*. New York: Routledge.

Fløysand, A. and Jakobsen, S.-E. (2010). Embeddedness and innovation practice in rural areas: A multi-scale approach. In D. E. Lynch (Ed.), *Urban and Rural Schools: Problems, Solutions and Progress* (pp. 103–122). Nova Science Publishers, Inc.

Flygare, I. A. (2011). Svenska småbruk: ett bestående inslag på landsbygden. In H. Antonson and U. Jansson (Eds.), *Jordbruk och skogsbruk i Sverige sedan år 1900* (pp. 70–87). Malmö: Kungl. Skogs- och Lantbruksakademien.

Folke, C., Jansson, A., Larsson, J. and Costanza, R. (1997). Ecosystem appropriation by cities. *Ambio*, *26*(3), 167–172.

Follo, G. and Villa, M. (2010). Å byggje staden stein på stein. In O. J. Borch and A. Förde (Eds.), *Innovative bygdemiljö – ildsjeler og nyskapingsarbeid* (pp. 121–135). Bergen: Fagbokforlaget.

Fontes, M., Sousa, C. and Videira, P. (2009). *Knowledge Access and Location Decisions in Biotechnology: The Spatial Dimension of Social Networks*. Paper presented at the Regional Studies Associations Annual Conference, Leuven, Belgium.

Formas. (2007). *Forskningsstrategi 2006 – Kunskap om landsbygdens utveckling*. Retrieved from www.formas.se/PageFiles/3976/Pdf_Landsbygdens_utv.pdf.

Forsberg, G., Grimsrud, G. M., Jakobsen, L., Jansdotter, M. and Stubberud, K. V. (2006). *Gränsfall: platsens betydelse för omställning och utveckling i en gränsregion*. Stockholm: Nordregio.

Fosso, E. J. (2004). Unges flytting – et spörsmål om identitet og myter om marginale og sentrale steder? In N. G. Berg, B. Dale, H. K. Lysgård and A. Löfgren (Eds.), *Mennesker, steder og regionale endringer* (pp. 119–135). Trondheim: Tapir Akademiske Forlag.

Frank, A. G. (1966). The development of underdevelopment. *Monthly Review*, *1*(4).

Freathy, P. and Calderwood, E. (2016). Coping with change: The implications of e-commerce adoption for island consumers. *Regional Studies*, *50*(5), 894–908.

Fuduric, N. (2012). Entrepreneurship in the periphery: A resource perspective. In M. Danson and P. de Souza (Eds.), *Regional Development in Northern Europe: Peripherality, Marginality and Border Issues* (pp. 164–181). Chippenham: Routledge.

Garcilazo, J. E., Martins, J. O. and Tompson, W. (2010). Why policies may need to be place-based in order to be people-centred. Retrieved from http://voxeu.org/article/why-policies-may-need-be-place-based-order-be-people-centred.

Geurs, K. T. and Wee, B. V. (2004). Accessibility evaluation of land-use and transport strategies: review and research directions. *Journal of Transport Geography*, (12), 127–140.

Gibson-Graham, J. K. (2011). Forging post-development partnerships – possibilities for local and regional development. In A. Pike, A. Rodríguez-Pose and J. Tomaney (Eds.), *Handbook of Local and Regional Development* (pp. 226–236). London: Routledge.

Giles, E. L., Bosworth, G. and Willett, J. (2013). The role of local perceptions in the marketing of rural areas. *Journal of Destination Marketing & Management*, *2*(1), 4–13.

Gløersen, E. (2009). *Strong, Specific and Promising: Towards a Vision for the Northern Sparsely Populated Areas in 2020*. Retrieved from www.diva-portal.org/smash/get/diva2:700388/FULLTEXT01.pdf.

Gløersen, E., Dubois, A., Copus, A. and Schürmann, C. (2006). *Northern Peripheral, Sparsely Populated Regions in the European Union*. Stockholm: Nordregio. In *Nordregio Report 1403-2503*. Retrieved from www.nordregio.se/en/Publications/Publications-2006/Northern-Peripheral-Sparsely-Populated-Regions-in-the-European-Union-and-in-Norway/.

Gløersen, E., Riise, Ø., Schurman, C., Arnesen, T. and Overvåg, K. (2010). *Fjellområder og fjellkommuner i Sør-Norge: definisjon, avgrensning og karakterisering*. Lillehammer: Østlandsforskning.

Gløtvold-Solbu, K. and Ørbeck, M. (2012). Regiondannelser og – forstörring, og konsekvenser av det. In E. Olsson, A. Hauge and B. Ericsson (Eds.), *På gränsen – interaktion, attraktivitet och globalisering i inre Skandinavien* (pp. 45–58). Karlstad: Karlstad University Press.

Goodall, B. (1987). *The Penguin Dictionary of Human Geography*. Harmondsworth: Penguin.

Granovetter, M. S. (1973). The strength of weak ties. *American Journal of Sociology*, *78*(6), 1360–1380. doi:10.1086/225469.

Granovetter, M. S. (1983). The strength of weak ties: A network theory revisited. *Sociological Theory*, *1*, 201–233. doi:10.2307/202051.

Granqvist, M. B. (2012). The political entrepreneur as an unconventional problem solver in a Northern Periphery. In M. Danson and P. de Souza (Eds.), *Regional Development in Northern Europe: Peripherality, Marginality and Border Issues* (pp. 232–246). Oxon: Routledge.

Green, A. and Orton, M. (2010). Policy innovation in a fragmented and complex multilevel governance context: Worklessness and the city strategy in Great Britain. *Regiona Studies*, *46*(2), 153–164.

Gregory, D. (2009). *The Dictionary of Human Geography* (5th ed.). Chichester: Wiley-Blackwell.

Grimes, S. (2003). The digital economy challenge facing peripheral rural areas. *Progress in Human Geography*, *27*(2), 174–193.

Grimes, S. (2004). Information society technology. In A. Copus (Ed.), *Aspatial Peripherality, Innovation & the Rural Economy (AsPIRE): Finale Report* (pp. 61–80). Aberdeen: AsPIRE.

Grönroos, C. (2012). Conceptualising value co-creation: A journey to the 1970s and back to the future. *Journal of Marketing Management*, *28*(13–14), 1520–1534.

Gruber, S. and Soci, A. (2010). Agglomeration, agriculture, and the perspective of the periphery. *Spatial Economic Analysis*, *5*(1), 44–72.

Halfacree, K. (2008). To revitalise counterurbanisation research? Recognising an international and fuller picture. *Population, Space and Place*, *14*(6), 479–495.

Hallén, A. (2013). Innovasjon i offentlig sektor. *Stat og Styring*, *23*(1), 2–3.

Halliday, J. and Coombes, M. (1995). In search of counterurbanisation: Some evidence from Devon on the relationship between patterns of migration and motivation. *Journal of Rural Studies*, *11*(4), 433–446. doi:10.1016/0743–0167(95)00032–1.

Hardt, M. and Negri, A. (2003). *Imperiet*. Göteborg: Glänta.

Harris, C. D. and Ullman, E. L. (1945). The nature of cities. *The Annals of the American Academy of Political and Social Science*, *242*(1), 7–17.

Hatzimarkos, G. (2016). Cohesion policy supporting islands. *Panorama Inforegio*, (57 Summer), 27.

Hauge, A. (2012). Richard Floridas teori om den kreative klassen. In E. Olsson, A. Hauge and B. Ericsson (Eds.), *På Gränsen – interaktion, attraktivitet och globalisering i inre Skandinavien*. Karlstad: Karlstad University Press.

Hauge, A. and Thulemark, M. (2012). Florida i fjällen. In E. Olsson, A. Hauge and B. Ericsson (Eds.), *På gränsen – interaktion, attraktivitet och globalisering i inre Skandinavien*. Karlstad: Karlstad University Press.

Haugen, K. (2012a). *The Accessibility Paradox: Everyday Geographies of Proximity, Distance and Mobility*. Umeå: Umeå University.

Haugen, K. (2012b). *Miljöbilens förutsättningar i glesa bygder. Tillgänglighet samt sociala och ekonomiska aspekter för individer och hushåll*. Retrieved from http://umu.diva-portal.org/smash/get/diva2:525763/FULLTEXT01.pdf.

Haugen, M. S. and Lysgård, H. K. (2006). Discourses of rurality in a Norwegian context. *Norwegian Journal of Geography*, *60*(3), pp. 174–178.

Hedlund, M. (2016). Mapping the socioeconomic landscape of rural Sweden: Towards a typology of rural areas. *Regional Studies*, *50*(3), 460–474.

Hegrenes, A. (2004). Landbrukspolitikk som distriktspolitikk. In R. Amdam and O. Bukve (Eds.), *Det regionalpolitiske regimeskiftet – tilfellet Noreg* (pp. 44–62). Trondheim: Tapir Akademiske Forlag.

Hellevik, O. (2011). Verdier. In S. Naess, T. Moum and J. Eriksen (Eds.), *Livskvalitet: forskning om det gode liv* (pp. 237–244). Bergen: Fagbokforlaget.

Helliwell, J. F. and Putnam, R. D. (2004). The social context of well-being. *Philosophical Transactions of the Royal Society of London B.*, *359*(1449), 1435–1446.

Hermelin, B. and Rusten, G. (2007). The organizational and territorial changes of services in a globalized world. *Geografiska Annaler: Series B, Human Geography*, *89*(Supplementary 1), 5–11.

Herrschel, T. (2011). Regional development, peripheralization and marginalisation – and the role of governance. In T. Herrschel and P. Tallberg (Eds.), *The Role of Regions? Networks, Scale, Territory* (pp. 85–102). Kristianstad: Region Skåne.

Herrschel, T. (2012). Regionalisation and marginalisation – bridging old and new divisions in regional governance. In M. Danson and P. de Souza (Eds.), *Regional Development in Northern Europe: Peripherality, Marginality and Border Issues*. Chippenham: Routledge.

Herrschel, T. and Tallberg, P. (2011). *The Role of Regions? Networks, Scale, Territory*. Kristianstad: Region Skåne, Region Västra Götaland, Regional Growth and Planning Sveriges kommuner och landsting, Kommunesektorens interesse- og arbeidsgiverorganisasjon (KS).

Higdem, U. (2007). *Regional Partnerships and Their Constructions and Implementations: A Case Study of the Counties of Oppland, Hedmark, and Østfold*. Ås: Norwegian University of Life Sciences.

Hincks, S. (2016). Towards inclusive cities: Learning lessons from the UK and Brazil. *Regions Magazine*, *303*(1), 8–9.

Hirschman, A. O. (1958). *The Strategy of Economic Development*. New Haven, CT: Yale University Press.

Hjelm, J. (1991). The chain saw in Swedish forestry. *Technological Forecasting and Social Change*, *39*(1–2), 221–231.

Hofstede, G. and Hofstede, G. J. (2005). *Cultures and Organisations: Software of the Mind* (2nd ed., revised and extended). New York: McGraw-Hill.

Hoggart, K. (1988). Not a definition of rural. *Area*, *20*(1), 35–40.

Horlings, I. and Marsden, T. (2010). *The Interplay between Social Capital, Leadership and Policy Arrangements in European Rural Regions*. Paper presented at the Regional Studies Association Conference, Hungary.

Hörnlund, B. (2009, February 26). Regeringen diskriminerar med rena maffiametoderna. *Dagens Nyheter. Debatt*.

Hospers, G.-J. (2004). Place marketing in Europe: The branding of the Oresund region. *Intereconomics*, *39*(5), 271–279.

Höyer, H. C. (2013). Det regionale innovasjonsbyråkratiet. In T. Ringholm, H. Teigen and N. Aarsaether (Eds.), *Innovativa kommuner*. Cappelen Damm.

Hoyt, H. (1939). *The Structure and Growth of Residential Neighborhoods in American Cities*. Washington, DC: Federal Housing Administration.

Hoyt, H. (1954). Homer Hoyt on development of economic base concept. *Land Economics*, *30*(2), 182–186.

Hudson, R. (2000). *Production, Places and Environment: Changing Perspectives in Economic Geography*. Harlow: Prentice Hall.

Hudson, R. (2007). Regions and regional uneven development forever? Some reflective comments upon theory and practice. *Regional Studies*, *41*(9), 1149–1160.

Huggins, R. and Thompson, P. (2015). Culture and place-based development: A socio-economic analysis. *Regional Studies*, *49*(1), 130–159.

Hultman, J. (2008). GIS, makt och magi – regional utveckling och kultur som strategisk resurs. In F. Andersson, R. Ek and I. Molina (Eds.), *Regionalpolitikens geografi: regional tillväxt i teori och praktik*. Lund: Studentlitteratur.

Isaksen, A. and Onsager, K. (2010). Regions, networks and innovative performance: The case of knowledge-intensive industries in Norway. *European Urban and Regional Studies*, *17*(3), 227–243.

Isard, W. (1956). *Location and Space-Economy: A General Theory Relating to Industrial Location, Market Areas, Land Use, Trade, and Urban Structure*. Cambridge, MA: MIT Press.

Iyer, S., Kitson, M. and Toh, B. (2005). Social capital, economic growth and regional development. *Regional Studies*, *39*(8), 1015–1040.

Jacobs, J. (1961). *The Death and Life of Great American Cities*. New York: Random House.

James, R., Midmore, P. and Thomas, D. (2012). Public sector size and peripherality. *Spatial Economic Analysis*, 7(4), 447–460.

Joas, H. (1996). *The Creativity of Action*. Cambridge: Polity Press.

Joffer, B. (2015, August 28). Det här är ett nytt slag mot oss i Dalarna. *Dalarnas Tidningar*.

Johannisson, B. (2005). *Entreprenörskapets väsen*. Lund: Studentlitteratur.

Johansen, S. (2009). 'Sentraliseringens pris' Er sentralisering et problem? Retrieved from www.hioa.no/extension/hioa/design/hioa/images/nibr/files/filer/2009-5.pdf.

Johansen, S., Bjørnsen, M., Hagen, K.-E. and Juvkam, D. (2006). Distriktpolitisk virkeområde for Norge 2006. *TÖI*. Retrieved from www.toi.no/getfile.php?mmfileid=3025.

Johansson, B. and Karlsson, C. (1991). *Fraan Brukssamhällets exportnät till kunskapssamhällets innovationsnät*. Karlstad: Länsstyrelsen i Värmlands län i Samarbete med Högskolan i Karlstad.

Johansson, S. (2012). Hållbar konsumtion af jordbruksvaror. Hållbar samhällsutveckling – vad innebär det? *(Rapport 2012:40)*. Retrieved from www2.jordbruksverket.se/webdav/files/SJV/trycksaker/Pdf_rapporter/ra12_40.pdf.

Johnston, A. and Huggins, R. (2016). Drivers of university – industry links: The case of knowledge-intensive business service firms in rural locations. *Regional Studies, 50*(8), 1330–1345. doi:10.1080/00343404.2015.1009028.

Johnston, R. J. (2000). *The Dictionary of Human Geography* (4th ed.). Malden, MA: Blackwell Publishers.

Jönsson, C., Tägil, S. and Törnqvist, G. (2007). *Europa, quo vadis?: integration och splittring i tid och rum*. Stockholm: SNS Förlag.

Jonsson, O. (2013). Den dynamiska regionen – hur omvandling, tillväxt och förnyelse kan skapas. In F. Rakar and P. Tallberg (Eds.), *Behövs regioner* (pp. 109–152). Stockholm: Reglab i samarbete med Sveriges Kommuner och Landsting.

Kasabov, E. (2011). Towards a theory of peripheral, early-stage clusters. *Regional Studies, 45*(6), 827–842.

Kawachi, I., Kennedy, B. P. and Glass, R. (1999). Social capital and self-rated health: A contextual analysis. *American Journal of Public Health, 89*(8), 1187–1193.

Keeble, D., Tyler, P., Broom, G. and Lewis, J. (1992). *Business Success in the Countryside: The Performance of Rural Enterprise*. Retrieved from http://agris.fao.org/agris-search/search.do?recordID=GB9130724.

Kitson, M., Martin, R. and Tyler, P. (2004). Regional competitiveness: An elusive yet key concept? *Regional Studies, 38*(9), 991–999.

Kleinknecht, A., Monfort, K. V. and Brouwer, E. (2002). The non-trivial choice between innovation indicators. *Economics of Innovation and New Technology, 11*(2), 109–121.

Klingström, L. (2016). Samma mål – fem skogsbruksmodeller. Sverige har valt mer-av-allt-vägen. *Skog & framtid*, (1), 8.

Knudsen, J. P. (2011). Innovation, culture and politics: An outline for investigating criss-crossing Nordic cleavages. In H.C.G. Johnsen and Ö. Paalshaugen (Eds.), *Hva er innovasjon? Perspektiver i norsk innovasjonsforskning. Bind 1: system og institusjon* (pp. 314–342). Oslo: Cappelen Damm.

Kobro, L. U., Vareide, K. and Hartling, M. (1012). Suksessrike distriktskommuner – en studie av kjennetegn ved 15 norske distriktskommuner. *(TF-Rapport 303)*. Retrieved from www.telemarksforsking.no/publikasjoner/filer/2097.pdf.

Kogler, D. F. (2015). Editorial: Evolutionary economic geography – theoretical and empirical progress. *Regional Studies, 49*(5), 705–711.

Kompetansearbeidsplassutvalget. (2011). Kompetansearbeidsplasser – drivkraft for vekst i hele landet. *(NOU 2011:3)*. Retrieved from www.regjeringen.no/contentassets/a90bf4e1e5f740ea9f810ff4e1519fb4/no/pdfs/nou201120110003000dddpdfs.pdf.

Korsgaard, S., Müller, S. and Tanvig, H. W. (2015). Rural entrepreneurship or entrepreneurship in the rural – between place and space. *International Journal of Entrepreneurial Behavior & Research, 21*(1), 5–26.

Kosonen, K.-J. (2005). *Linking Less-Favoured Regions to the Knowledge Economy: Finnish Experiences*. Paper presented at the Regional Studies Association International Conference 'Regional Growth Agendas', Aalborg.

Kristensson, P. (2013). Glöm innovation. Tänk tjänsteinnovation. Innovationsprocesser i förändring. In C. Nahnfeldt and M. Lindberg (Eds.), *Är det nå'n innovation? Att nyttiggöra hum/sam-forskning* (pp. 178–188). Karlstad: Karlstad University Press.

Krugman, P. R. (1991). *Geography and Trade*. Leuven: Leuven University Press.

Kulu, H. (2013). Why do fertility levels vary between urban and rural areas? *Regional Studies*, *47*(6), 895–912.

Lagendijk, A. and Lorentzen, A. (2007). Proximity, knowledge and innovation in peripheral regions: On the intersection between geographical and organizational proximity. *European Planning Studies*, *15*(4), 457–466.

Landsbygdspolitiska samarbetsgruppen. (2014). *Möjligheternas landsbygd – Landsbygdspolitiska program 2014–2020.* Edita Publishing Oy.

Le Heron, R. (2013). Political projects, changing urban – rural relations and mediating investment: Insights from exploring dairying and Auckland's spatial planning in New Zealand. *Regional Studies*, *47*(8), 1191–1205. doi:10.1080/00343404.2013.783690.

Lind, M. (2002). Det svårgripbara nätverket: en sociologisk studie av företagare i nätverk. (Dissertation), Örebro.

Lindegaard, K. (2012). Dynamics of peripherality. In M. Danson and P. de Souza (Eds.), *Regional Development in Northern Europe* (pp. 78–97). Chippenham: Routledge.

Lipton, M. (1977). *Why Poor People Stay Poor: A Study of Urban Bias in World Development.* London: Temple Smith.

Littke, H., Foss, A. and Rauhut, D. (2012). Services of general interest and regional development in the European Union. *Romanian Journal of Regional Science*, 7(June 15), 88–107.

Løken, J. C. (2015, March 3). Bioøkonomi på topp. *Østlendingen* (p. 26).

Lorentzen, A. (2008). *Territorial Development in the Experience Economy: An Evolutionary Approach.* Paper presented at the Peripherality, Marginality and Border Issues in Northern Europe, Rena, Norway.

Lorentzen, A. (2012a). Yderomraader i Danmark. Hvad er problemet. In J. L. Christensen (Ed.), *Nordjyske Udviklingsperspektiver: afvikling eller udvikling?* (pp. 99–121). Aalborg: Aalborg Universitetsforlag.

Lorentzen, A. (2012b). The development of the periphery in the experience economy. In P. de Souza and M. Danson (Eds.), *Regional Development in Northern Europe: Peripherality, Marginality and Border Issues.* London: Routledge.

Lösch, A. (1940). *Die räumliche Ordnung der Wirtschaft: eine Untersuchung über Standort, Wirtschaftsgebiete und internationalen Handel (The Spatial Organization of the Economy).* Jena: Gustav Fischer.

Lunde, L.-H. (2012). *Alder ingen hindring: vekst og utvikling hele livet.* Oslo: Gyldendal akademisk.

Lundell, S. (2011). Familjeskogsbruket i förändring: tider av frihet, ansvar och ökad kunskap. In H. Antonson and U. Jansson (Eds.), *Jordbruk och skogsbruk i Sverige sedan år 1900* (pp. 386–401). Malmö: Kungl. Skogs- och Lantbruksakademien.

Lundgren, N.-G. (2011). Frontier i Norrbotten: skogsarbete, teknik och inkomster. In A. Antonson and U. Jansson (Eds.), *Jordbruk och skogsbruk i Sverige sedan år 1900* (pp. 337–352). Malmö: Kungl. Skogs- och Lanbruksakademien.

Lundqvist, S. and Johnson, L. (2014). *Grön Entreprenör – skogens sociala värden – forskningen visar vägen.* Uppsala: Sveriges Lantbruksuniversitet.

Lundqvist, T. (2006). Ett kreativt samhälle. *Framtider nr 3.* Retrieved from www.politiken.se/tidskrifter/fram/fram06/fram0603-07.pdf.

Lysgård, H. K. (2001). *Produksjon av rom og identitet i transnasjonale regioner: et eksempel fra det politiske samarbeidet i Midt-Norden.* Trondheim: Geografisk institutt, Fakultet for samfunnsvitenskap og teknologiledelse, Norges teknisk-naturvitenskapelige universitet.

Lysgård, H. K. (2004). Romlighet i studier av mennesker, steder og regioner. In N. G. Berg, B. Dale, H. K. Lysgård and A. Löfgren (Eds.), *Mennesker, steder og regionale endringer* (pp. 17–26). Trondheim: Tapir Akademiske Forlag.

Magrini, S. and Cheshire, P. (2008). Urban growth drivers in a Europe of sticky people and implicity boundaries. *SERC Discussion Paper*. Retrieved from http://eprints.lse.ac.uk/33182/.

Malmberg, B. (2011). Landsbygdens befolkning: jordbruk, barnafödande och demografisk transition. In H. Antonson and U. Jansson (Eds.), *Jordbruk och skogsbruk i Sverige sedan år 1900* (Vol. Skogs- och lantbrukshistoriska meddelanden). Malmö: Kungl. Skogs- och Lantbruksakademien.

Mangset, P. and Røyseng, S. (2009). *Kulturelt entreprenørskap*. Bergen: Fagbokforlaget.

Marcon, A. (2011). Euromontana's contribution to the public consultation on the Vth Cohesion Report 28 January 2011. Retrieved from www.euromontana.org/wp-content/uploads/2014/08/euromontana_vcohesionreport_en.pdf.

Margarian, A. (2013). Public entrepreneurship for rural development: What hinders women's engagement? *Regions, 292*(1), 16–17.

Mariussen, Å. (2010). *Regional mobilisering genom jämförelse och lärande – kommuner, turister, potatis och mjölk*. Retrieved from www.vasa.abo.fi/rurban/pub/6_2010.pdf.

Markantoni, M., Koster, S. and Strijker, D. (2013). The wish to grow – growth expectations for side activities in rural areas. *Journal of Small Business and Enterprise Development, 20*(3), 584–602.

Marsden, T., Banks, J. and Bristow, G. (2002). The social management of rural nature: Understanding agrarian-based rural development. *Environment and Planning A, 34*(5), 809–825.

Marshall, A. (1920). *Principles of Economics* (8th ed.). London and Basingstoke: The Macmillan Press Ltd.

Martin, R. (2012). *Knowledge Bases and the Geography of Innovation*. Lund: Lund University Press.

Martin, R., Pike, A., Tyler, P. and Gardiner, B. (2015). Spatially rebalancing the UK economy: The need for a new policy model. Retrieved from www.regionalstudies.org/uploads/documents/SRTUKE_v16_PRINT.pdf.

Martin, R. and Sunley, P. (2012). Forms of emergence and the evolution of economic landscapes. *Journal of Economic Behavior & Organization, 82*(2–3), 338–351.

Maslow, A. H. (1943). A theory of human motivation. *Psychological Review, 50*(4), 370–396.

Massard, N. and Autant-Bernard, C. (2015). Editorial: Geography of innovation: New trends and implications for public policy renewal. *Regional Studies, 49*(11), 1767–1771.

Massey, D. (1984). *Spatial Divisions of Labour: Social Structures and the Geography of Production*. New York: Routledge.

Massey, D. (1992). Politics and space/time. *New Left Review, 196*(November/December), 65–84.

Mendas, Z. (2016). Promoting sustainable rural island archipelagos. *Regions, 301*(1), 29–30.

Meslier-Crouzille, C., Nys, E. and Sauviat, A. (2012). Contribution of rural banks to regional economic development: Evidence from the Philippines. *Regional Studies, 46*(6), 775–791.

Mezzandra, S. and Neilson, B. (2013). *Border as Method: Or, the Multiplication of Labor*. Durham: Duke University Press.

Millennium Ecosystem Assessment. (2005). Guide to the millennium assessment reports. Retrieved from www.millenniumassessment.org/en/index.html.

Mitchell, B. (2013). *Resource and Environmental Management* (2nd ed.). London and New York: Routledge.

Mitra, J. (2012). *Entrepreneurship, Innovation and Regional Development: An Introduction*. Abingdon, Oxon and New York: Routledge.

Mitze, T. (2011). Mapping clusters: To see or not to see? *Regional Insights, 2*(2).

Moe, S. (2010). *Tid – en sosial konstruksjon?* Oslo: Abstrakt forl.

Möller, C., Ericsson, B. and Overvåg, K. (2012). Säsongsarbetare i svenska och norska skidorter – tillfällig arbetskraft eller potentiella inflyttare. In E. Olsson, A. Hauge and B. Ericsson (Eds.), *På gränsen – interaktion, attraktivitet och globalisering i inre Skandinavien*. Karlstad: Karlstad University Press.

Møller, J. (2009). Mellem udvikling og afvikling – en minianalyse af de danske landdistrikter og landsbyer. *Plan, 41*(3–4), 38–45.

Møller, J., Staunstrup, J. and Winter Johansen, H.H.W. (2010). *Villages and Hamlets in Denmark Revisited: A Spatial Planning Challenge in the Making*. Paper presented at the Conference Nordic Rural Futures, Uppsala.

Möller, P. (2012). Unga vuxna i Sälen. In E. Olsson, E. Hauge and B. Ericsson (Eds.), *På Gränsen – interaktion, attraktivitet och globalisering i inre Skandinavien* (pp. 215–228). Karlstad: Karlstad University Press.

Mondragón Corporation. (2017). In *Wikipedia*. Retrieved September 21, 2017, from https://en.wikipedia.org/wiki/Mondragon_Corporation.

Mønnesland, J. (1994). *Regional Policy in the Nordic Countries*. Stockholm: Nordrefo.

Monsson, C. K. (2013). Understanding the peri-urban economy: The case of Copenhagen. *Regional Insights, 4*(2), 6–8. doi:10.1080/20429843.2013.10795996.

Morgan, K. (1997). The learning region: Institutions, innovation, and regional renewal. *Regional Studies, 31*(5), 491–503.

Morgan, K. (2007). The learning region: Institutions, innovation and regional renewal. In R. Rutten (Ed.), *The Learning Region: Foundations, State of the Art, Future* (pp. 101–124). Cheltenham: Edward Elgar Publishers.

Morrison, P. S. (2011). Local expressions of subjective well-being: The New Zealand experience. *Regional Studies, 45*(8), 1039–1058.

Moulaert, F. and Mehmood, A. (2010). Analysing regional development and policy: A structural-realist approach. *Regional Studies, 44*(1), 103–118.

Müller, A and Segerstedt, E. (2015). *Norrlandsparadoxen. En utvecklingsdröm med problem*. Skellefteå: Ord&Visor.

Murdoch, J. (2000). Networks: A new paradigm of rural development. *Journal of Rural Studies, 16*(4), 407–419.

Myrdal, G. (1957). *Economic Theory and Under-Developed Regions*. London: G. Duckworth.

Myrdal, G. (1982). *Hur styrs landet?: 1* (Vol. 1). Stockholm: Rabén & Sjögren.

Nahnfeldt, C. and Lindberg, M. (2013). *Är det nå'n innovation? Att nyttiggöra hum/sam-forskning*. Karlstad: Karlstads universitet.

Naustdalslid, J. (2012). Framtida for kommunane. *Plan, 44*(2), 20–23.

Nicholls, A. (2006). *Social Entrepreneurship: New Models of Sustainable Change*. New York: Oxford University Press.

Niedomysl, T. (2008). Residential preferences for interregional migration in Sweden: Demographic, socio-economic and geographical determinants. *Environment and Planning A, 40*(5), 1109–1131. doi:10.1068/a39177.

Niedomysl, T. (2010). Towards a conceptual framework of place attractiveness: A migration perspective. *Geografiska Annaler: Series B, Human Geography, 92*(1), 97–109. doi:10.1111/j.1468–0467.2010.00335.x.

Niedomysl, T. and Amcoff, J. (2011a). Is there hidden potential for rural population growth in Sweden? *Rural Sociology, 76*(2), 257–279. doi:10.1111/j.1549–0831.2010.00032.x.

Niedomysl, T. and Amcoff, J. (2011b). Why return migrants return: Survey evidence on motives for internal return migration in Sweden. *Population, Space and Place, 17*(5), 656–673. doi:10.1002/psp.644.

Nieminen-Sundell, R. (2011). Beautiful scenery, but no jobs. Retrieved from https://media.sitra.fi/2017/02/28142229/Beautiful_scenery_but_no_jobs.pdf.

Nordström, A. (2014, June 20). Kulturbristen på landet vigdar klyftan. *Dagens Nyheter* (pp. 4–5).

Nordström, A. (2015, February 24). Storstaden har blivit norm. *Dagens Nyheter. Kultur.*

Norman, J. (2014). Skogen – upplevelsevärden och friluftsliv. In S. Lundqvist and L. Johnson (Eds.), *Grön entreprenör – skogens sociala värden – forskningen visar vägen.* Uppsala: Sveriges Lantbruksuniversitet.

North, D. and Smallbone, D. (2000). Innovative activity in SMEs and rural economic development: Some evidence from England. *European Planning Studies, 8*(1), 87–106. doi:10.1080/096543100110947.

North, D. C. (1990). *Institutions, Institutional Change, and Economic Performance.* Cambridge: Cambridge University Press.

Northern Peripheral, Sparsely Populated Regions in the European Union. (2005). Stockholm: Nordregio.

NUTEK. (2004). Lokal ekonomi for hållbar tillväxt. Retrieved from www.helasverige.se/fileadmin/user_upload/HSSL_Kansli/Vad_vi_goer/ekonomi/Lokal_ekonomi.pdf.

Nyseth, T. (2009). Place reinvention at the Northern rim. In T. Nyseth and A. Viken (Eds.), *Place Reinvention* (pp. 1–14). Farnham: Ashgate.

O'Brien, D. J., Phillips, J. L. and Patsiorkovsky, V. V. (2005). Linking indigenous bonding and bridging social capital. *Regional Studies, 39*(8), 1041–1051.

OECD. (2006a). *The New Rural Paradigm Policies and Governance.* Paris: OECD Publishing.

OECD. (2006b). Reinventing rural policy. *Policy Brief.* Retrieved from www.oecd.org/regional/37556607.pdf.

OECD. (2009a). How regions grow. *Policy Brief.* Retrieved from www.oecd.org/regional/searf2009/42576934.pdf.

OECD. (2009b). *Regions Matter: Economic Recovery, Innovation and Sustainable Growth.* Paris: OECD Publishing.

OECD. (2011a). *OECD Regional Outlook: Building Resilient Regions for Stronger Economies.* Retrieved from http://dx.doi.org/10.1787/9789264120983-en.

OECD. (2011b). *OECD Territorial Reviews: NORA Region 2011: The Faroe Islands, Greenland, Iceland and Coastal Norway.* Retrieved from www.oecd.org/countries/greenland/oecdterritorialreviewsnoraregionthefaroeislandsgreenlandicelandandcoastalnorway.htm.

Öjehag-Pettersson, A. (2015). *Space Craft: Globalization and Governmentality in Regional Development.* (Doctoral thesis), Karlstad University, Karlstad. Retrieved from http://kau.diva-portal.org/smash/get/diva2:801356/FULLTEXT01.pdf.

Ølberg, B. (2012). Verdiskipingsevnen i norske storbyregioner. *Plan, 44*(2), 42–47.

Onsager, K. and Selstad, T. (2004). Regional politikk for regioner i utakt. In K. Onsager and T. Selstad (Eds.), *Regioner i utakt.* Trondheim: Tapir Akademiske Forlag.

Østrem, S. (2015). Akademisk skrivkultur. *Forskerforum,* (9), 36–37.

Ostrom, E. (1990). *Governing the Commons: The Evolution of Institutions for Collective Action.* Cambridge: Cambridge University Press.

Ostrom, E. (2005). *Understanding Institutional Diversity.* Princeton, NJ: Princeton University Press.

Ottoson, M. and Ottoson, Å. (2014). Skogsbad. *Turist,* (4), 46–51.

Overvaag, K. (2012). Fritids- og naturbasert utenlandsk flytting till Indre Skandinavia – illustrert med hundekjörere i Folldal. In E. Olsson, A. Hauge, and B. Ericsson (Eds.), *På gränsen – interaktion, attraktivitet och globalisering i inre Skandinavien* (pp. 253–267). Karlstad: Karlstad University Press.

Overvaag, K., Arnesen, T. and Hagen, S. E. (2009). Reiselivsnæringene i Lillehammer: området og Midt- Gudbrandsdalen. In K. Overvaag, T. Arnesen and S. E. Hagen (Eds.), *Samhandling og innovasjon Vallset* (pp. 301–324). Vallset: Oplandske bokforlag.

Özylildirim, S. and Önder, S. (2008). Banking activities and local output growth: Does distance from centre matter? *Regional Studies, 42*(2), 229–244.

Paasi, A. (2013). Regional planning and the mobilization of 'regional identity': From bounded spaces to relational complexity. *Regional Studies, 47*(8), 1206–1219. doi:10.1080/00343404.2012.661410.

Park, R. E., Burgess, E. W. and McKenzie, R. D. (1925). *The City*. Chicago: The University of Chicago Press.

Parr, J. B., Hewings, G.J.D., Sohn, J. and Nazara, S. (2002). Agglomeration and trade: Some additional perspectives. *Regional Studies, 36*(6), 675–684.

Pasquinelli, C. and Teräs, J. (2011). Branding peripheral knowledge-intensive regions: An insight into international innovation brands. *Regional Insights, 2*(2), 9–11.

Peiró-Palomino, J. and Tortosa-Ausina, E. (2015). Social capital, investment and economic growth: Some evidence for Spanish provinces. *Spatial Economic Analysis, 10*(1), 102–126.

Percoco, M. (2012). Entrepreneurship, social capital and institutions: Evidence from Italy. *Spatial Economic Analysis*, 7(3).

Perroux, F. (1949). Theory of choice and utilization of resources I: Les choix de l'etat producteur et l'application de la theorie des surplus du producteur et du consommateur. *Econometrica, 17*(July Supplementary Issue), 147–156.

Petrov, A. N. (2012). Redrawing the margin: Re-examining regional multichotomies and conditions of marginality in Canada, Russia and their Northern Frontiers. *Regional Studies, 46*(1), 59–81.

Pettersen, B. H. (2013, February 2). Derfor ønsker vi å bo her. *Østlendingen.*

Pettersson, K. (2012). Supporting women's entrepreneurship in Nordic sparsely populated areas. *Nordregio Working Paper 2012:1.* Retrieved from www.nordregio.se/en/Publications/Publications-2012/Supporting-Womens-Entrepreneurship-in-Nordic-Sparsely-Populated-Areas/.

Pinto, H., Fernandz-Esquinas, M. and Uyarra, E. (2015). Universities and knowledge-intensive business services (KIBS) as sources of knowledge for innovative firms in peripheral regions. *Regional Studies, 49*(11), 1873–1891.

Platt, K. (2011). Periphery: A spatial concept ripe for metaphorical extension. *Penn Humanities Forum on Peripheries.*

Poot, J. (2008). Demographic change and regional competitiveness: The effects of immigration and ageing. *International Journal of Foresight and Innovation Policy, 4*(1–2), 129–145.

Porter, M. E. (1990). *The Competitive Advantage of Nations*. Basingstoke: The Macmillan Press Ltd.

Porter, M. E. (1998). Clusters and the new economics of competition. *Harvard Business Review, 76*(6), 77–90.

Potter, R., Binns, T.A.J.E. and Smith, D. (2008). *Geographies of Development: An Introduction to Development Studies* (3rd ed.). Edinburgh: Pearson Education.

Price, L. (2011). *The Relationship between Skills and Productivity in Rural Areas.* Paper presented at the Regional Studies Association Conference, Newcastle upon Tyne, UK.

Putnam, R. D. (1993). *Making Democracy Work: Civic Traditions in Modern Italy*. Princeton, NJ: Princeton University Press.

Putnam, R. D. (2000). *Bowling Alone: The Collapse and Revival of American Community*. New York: Simon & Schuster.

Raunio, M. (2005). *Connectivity and Rewards: Capitalization of Human Interaction and Intelligence: Where to Invest?* Paper presented at the Regional Studies Associations Conference in Aalborg, 28–31 May 3, Aalborg.

Rees, J. (1990). *Natural Resources: Allocation, Economics and Policy*. London: Routledge.

Rehfeld, D. and Terstriep, J. (2013). Socio-cultural dynamics in spatial policy: Explaining the on-going success of cluster politics. In P. Cooke (Ed.), *Re-Framing Regional Development: Evolution, Innovation and Transition* (pp. 274–294). London: Routledge.

Ricardo, D. (2001). *Principles of Political Economy and Taxation*. London: GBR, Electric Book Co.

Rizov, M. and Walsh, P. P. (2011). Is there a rural-urban divide? Location and productivity of UK manufacturing. *Regional Studies*, *45*(5), 641–656.

Rodriguez-Pose, A. and Gill, N. (2003). *Is There a Global Link between Regional Disparities and Devolution?* Retrieved from https://pdfs.semanticscholar.org/f24c/4f0b1b8eda48fcae325aabe49685d71b08c9.pdf.

Rodríguez-Pose, A. and Gill, N. (2005). On the 'economic dividend' of devolution. *Regional Studies*, *39*(4), 402–405.

Röe, P. G. (2009). Forstaden som sted. In N. G. Berg, S. H. Jörgensen, A. Karlsen and A. Aase (Eds.), *Mennesker og steder i samspill: festskrift til Britt Dale* (pp. 43–60). Trondheim: Tapir Akademisk Forlag.

Rokkan, S. (1987). Sentrum og periferi, ökonomi og kultur: modeller og data i kliometrisk sosiologi. In *Stat, nasjon, klasse* (pp. 216–238). Oslo: Universitetsforlaget.

Rokkan, S. (1997). Territories, centres, and peripheries: Toward a geoethnic-geoeconomic-geopolitical model of differentiation within Western Europe. In J. Agnew (Ed.), *Political Geography: A Reader*. London: Arnold.

Rokkan, S. and Urwin, D. W. (1983). *Economy, Territory, Identity: Politics of West European Peripheries*. London: Sage Publications.

Rønning, L. (2008). *Social Capital in Farm-Based Entrepreneurship and Rural Development* (no. 15–2008). Bodø: Handelshøgskolen i Bodø.

Rønningen, M. (2012). Innovativ bygdeturisme? In T. Kvam and M. Rønningen (Eds.), *Turisme i distriktene* (pp. 109–132). Lillehammer: Tapir Akademiske Forlag.

Roper, S., Bryson, J., Hales, C. and Love, J. H. (2008). *Measuring Sectoral Innovation Capability in Nine Areas of the UK Economy*. Retrieved from www.nesta.org.uk/publications/measuring-sectoral-innovation-capability-nine-areas-uk-economy.

Rostow, W. W. (1960). *The Stages of Economic Growth: A Non-Communist Manifesto*. Oxford: Oxford University Press.

Sæther, B. (2010). Agricultural extension services and rural innovation in inner Scandinavia. *Norsk Geografisk Tidskrift – Norwegian Journal of Geography*, *64*(1), 1–8.

Sæther, B. (2015). Microfirms in peripheral areas: How can evolutionary economic geography contribute in studies of diversification? A case study from Norway. *Norsk Geografisk Tidskrift – Norwegian Journal of Geography*, *69*(2), 112–120.

Said, E. W. (1979). *Orientalism*. New York: Vintage Books.

Sas, M., Sunnergren, F. and Jonsson, H. (2006). Den kreativa sektorn – Ett verktyg utvecklat för att beskriva och förstå den kreativa sektorn – tillämpat i Norrköping: Regionförbundet Östsam.

Saxenian, A. (2006). *The New Argonauts: Regional Advantage in a Global Economy*. Cambridge, MA: Harvard University Press.

Schmidt-Thomé, K. and Vihinen, H. (2006). Rural areas – urban-rural interaction and beyond. In H. Eskelinen and T. Hirvonen (Eds.), *Positioning Finland in a European Space* (pp. 41–53). Helsinki: Ministry of the Environment, Ministry of the Interior.

Scholten, C. L. (2013). Att få syn på vardagens innovationspotentialer. In C. Nahnfeldt and M. Lindberg (Eds.), *Är det nå'n innovation? Att nyttiggöra hum/sam-forskning* (pp. 90–110). Karlstad: Karlstads University.

Schön, L. (2012). Går den kapitalistiska tillväxtepoken mot sitt slut? [review]. *Respons.* Retrieved from http://tidskriftenrespons.se/recension/kollaps.

Schulz, T. and Baumgartner, D. (2013). Volunteer organizations: Odds or obstacle for small business formation in rural areas? Evidence from Swiss Municipalities. *Regional Studies, 47*(4), 597–612. doi:10.1080/00343404.2011.587799.

Scott, A. J. (2013). A world of emergence – notes towards a resynthesis of urban-economic geography for the twenty-first century. In P. Cooke (Ed.), *Re-Framing Regional Development: Evolution, Innovation and Transition* (pp. 29–53). Oxon: Routledge.

Scott, W. R. (1995). *Institutions and Organizations.* Thousand Oaks: Sage.

Selstad, T. (2004). Regionbegrepet. In K. Onsager and T. Selstad (Eds.), *Regioner i utakt* (pp. 19–32). Trondheim: Tapir Akademiske Forlag.

Shaw, J. S. (c. 1998–2008). Public choice theory. In D. R. Henderson (Ed.), *The Concise Encyclopedia of Economics.* Liberty Fund.

Shields, R. (1991). *Places on the Margin: Alternative Geographies of Modernity.* London: Routledge.

Simmie, J. (2002). Knowledge spillovers and reasons for the concentration of innovative SMEs. *Urban Studies, 39*(5–6), 885–902.

Singh, J. (2005). Collaborative networks as determinants of knowledge diffusion patterns. *Management Science, 51*(5), 756–770.

Smailes, P. J. (2002). From rural dilution to multifunctional countryside: Some pointers to the future from South Australia. *Australian Geographer, 33*(1), 79–95.

Smallbone, D., North, D. and Leigh, R. (1993). The use of external assistance by mature SMEs in the UK: Some policy implications. *Entrepreneurship & Regional Development, 5*(3), 279–295.

Smetkowski, M., Gorzelak, G., Kozak, M., Olechnicka, A., Ploszaj, A. and Wojnar, K. (2011). *The European Metropolises and Their Regions: From Economic Landscapes to Metropolitan Networks.* Retrieved from www.euroreg.uw.edu.pl/dane/web_euroreg_publications_files/191/smtkowski_et_al._2011_the_european_metropolises_and_their_regions_from_economic_landscapes_to_metropolitan_networks.pdf.

Smith, K. (2008). Innovasjon og vekst i ressursbaserte ökonomier. In J. Hanson and O. Wicken (Eds.), *Rik på natur – innovasjon i en ressursbasert kunnskapsökonomi* (pp. 11–24). Bergen: Fagbokforlaget.

Sørensen, J.F.L. (2012). Testing the hypothesis of higher social capital in rural areas: The case of Denmark. *Regional Studies, 46*(7), 873–891.

Sørensen, J.F.L. (2014). Rural-urban differences in life satisfaction: Evidence from the European Union. *Regional Studies, 48*(9), 1451–1466.

Sørensen, J.F.L. (2016). Rural-urban differences in bonding and bridging social capital. *Regional Studies, 50*(3), 391–410.

Sørensen, T. (2011). Sosial støtte, lokalsamfunn. In S. Næss, J. Eriksen and T. Moum (Eds.), *Livskvalitet: forskning om det gode liv* (pp. 199–206). Bergen: Fagbokforlaget.

SSB. (2016). Agriculture and forestry in Norway 2011: Agriculture, forestry, hunting. Retrieved from www.ssb.no/en/jord-skog-jakt-og-fiskeri/artikler-og-publikasjoner/agriculture-and-forestry-in-norway-2011.

Stenbacka, S. (2011). Othering the rural: About the construction of rural masculinities and the unspoken urban hegemonic ideal in Swedish media. *Journal of Rural Studies, 27*(3), 235–244.

Sténs, A., Bjärstig, T., Nordström, E.-M., Sandström, C., Fries, C. and Johansson, J. (2016). In the eye of the stakeholder: The challenges of governing social forest values. *Ambio, 45*(Supplement 2), S87–S99.

Stimson, R. J., Stough, R. R. and Roberts, B. H. (2006). *Regional Economic Development: Analysis and Planning Strategy* (2nd ed.). Berlin: Springer.

Strøksnes, M. A. (2006). *Hva skjer i Nord-Norge?* Oslo: Kagge.

Svensson, R. (2012). Varenda by behöver inte hållas vid liv. *Dagens Samhälle*, (pp. 12–15).

Sylwan, P. (2011). Jorden och skogen – en essä om de areella näringarnas förändring. In H. Antonson and U. Jansson (Eds.), *Jordbruk och skogsbruk i Sverige sedan är 1900* (Vol. Skogs- och lantbrukshistoriska meddelanden). Malmö: Kungl. Skogs- och Lantbruksakademien.

Syrett, S. (2012). Conceptualising marginalisation in cities and regions. In M. Danson and P. de Souza (Eds.), *Regional Development in Northern Europe: Peripherality, Marginality and Border Issues*. Chippenham: Routledge.

Tarschys, D. (2011). How small are the regional gaps? How small is the impact of cohesion policy? *European Policy Analysis, 1epa*. Retrieved from www.sieps.se/sites/default/files/2011_1epa.pdf.

Teigen, H. (1999). *Regional økonomi og politikk*. Oslo: Universitetsforl.

Ter Wal, A.L.J. and Boschma, R. (2011). Co-evolution of firms, industries and networks in space. *Regional Studies, 45*(7), 919–933.

Tödtling, F. and Trippl, M. (2005). One size fits all? Towards a differentiated regional innovation policy approach. *Research Policy, 34*(8), 1203–1219.

Tomaney, J., Pike, A. and Rodríguez-Pose, A. (2010). Local and regional development – reflections and futures. In A. Pike, A. Rodríguez-Pose and J. Tomaney (Eds.), *Handbook of Local and Regional Development* (pp. 618–630). Oxon: Routledge.

Torre, A. and Rallet, A. (2005). Proximity and localization. *Regional Studies, 39*(1), 47–59.

Tura, T. and Harmaakorpi, V. (2005). Social capital in building regional innovative capability. *Regional Studies, 39*(8), 1111–1125.

Ullman, E. L. (1956). The role of transportation and the bases for interaction. In L. T. William, C. O. Sauer, M. Bates and M. Lewis (Eds.), *Man's Role in Changing the Face of the Earth* (pp. 862–880). Chicago: University of Chicago Press.

Ulver, S. (2012). Den nygrona manniskan – En översikt av landsbygdens status i förändring. Retrieved from www.jordbruksverket.se/download/18.724b0a8b148f52338a326d6/1413535932592/DEN+NYGR%C3%96NA+M%C3%84NNISKAN.pdf.

Uyarra, E. (2011). Regional innovation systems revisited. In T. Herrschel and P. Tallberg (Eds.), *The Role of the Regions? Networks, Scale, Territory*. Kristianstad: Region Skåne.

Valentine, G. (2007). Theorizing and researching intersectionality: A challenge for feminist geography. *The Professional Geographer, 50*(1), 10–21.

van den Bosch, M. (2014). Skog och hälsa – forskningen visar vägen. In S. Lundqvist and L. Johnson (Eds.), *Grön entreprenör – skogens sociala värden – forskningen visar vägen* (pp. 2–15). Uppsala: Sveriges Lantbruksuniversitet.

Veidal, A. (2011). Gårdsbasert entreprenörskap. *(Notat 2011–6)*. Retrieved from http://nilf.no/publikasjoner/Notater/2011/gardsbasert_entreprenorskap_en_kvalitativ_studie_av_muligheter_motiver_og_ressurser_for_entreprenorskap_i_landbruket.

Virkkala, S. (2007). Innovation and networking in peripheral areas: A case study of emergence and change in rural manufacturing. *European Planning Studies, 15*(4), 511–529. doi:10.1080/09654310601133948.

Virkkala, S. and Niemi, K. (Eds.) (2006). *Peripheral Localities and Innovation Policy*. Oslo: Nordic Innovation Centre.

von Thünen, J. H. (1966). *Der isolierte Staat: in Beziehung auf Landwirtschaft und Nationalökonomie* (4th ed.). Stuttgart: Fischer.

Wagner, A.K.H., Strömqvist, S., Uppstad, P. H. and Jakobsson, U. (2010). *Den flerspråkiga människan: en grundbok om skriftspråkslärande*. Lund: Studentlitteratur.

Wahlström, L. (1989). Integrating local development work with municipal planning – some examples. In G. Gustafsson (Ed.), *Development in Marginal Areas* (pp. 77–88). Karlstad: Karlstad University College.

Wallentin, H. (1985). Inledning. In H. Wallentin (Ed.), *Informell ekonomi i glesbygd*. Borås: LT förlag.

Wallerstein, W. (1976). A world-system perspective on the social sciences. *The British Journal of Sociology*, *27*(3), 343–352.

Ward, N. and Brown, D. L. (2009). Placing the rural in regional development. *Regional Studies*, *43*(10), 1237–1244.

Watts, D., Leat, P. and Revoredo-Giha, C. (2011). Local food activity in Scotland: Empirical evidence and research agenda. *Regional Studies*, *45*(9), 1187–1205. doi:10.1080/00343400903380416.

Weber, A. (1971). *Theory of the Location of Industries (Über den Standort der Industrie 1909)* (2nd ed.). New York: Russell & Russell.

Westholm, E. (2014, January 8). Generationsmålet – ett rop på en radikal omställning. *Mora Tidning* (p. 2).

Westlund, H. (1998). Att riva gränser och bygga nätverk – Strategiska vägval för Mittskandinaviens framtid. In H. Westlund (Ed.), *Mellan Atlanten och Bottenhavet* (pp. 11–72). Östersund: Statens institut för regionalforskning (SIR).

Westlund, H. and Bolton, R. S. (2003). Local social capital and entrepreneurship. *Small Business Economics*, *21*(2), 77–113.

Westlund, H. and Nilsson, E. (2005). Measuring enterprises' investments in social capital: A pilot study. *Regional Studies*, *39*(8), 1079–1094.

Whittam, G. and Danson, M. (2001). Power and the spirit of clustering. *European Planning Studies*, *9*(8), 949–963.

Wicken, O. (2008). Manna fra himmelen eller kunnskapsbaserte produkter? In O. Wicken and J. Hanson (Eds.), *Rik på natur – Innovasjon i en ressursbasert kunnskapsøkonomi* (pp. 25–48). Bergen: Fagbokforlaget.

Willis, K. (2011). *Theories and Practices of Development* (2nd ed.). London: Routledge.

Wood, D., Fels, J. and Krygier, J. (2010). *Rethinking the Power of Maps*. New York: Guilford Press.

Woods, M. (2005). *Rural Geography: Processes, Responses and Experiences in Rural Restructuring*. London: Sage Publications.

World Bank. (2009). World development report 2009: Reshaping economic geography. Retrieved from https://openknowledge.worldbank.org/handle/10986/5991.

Young, D., Wood, P. B. and Keil, R. (2011). *In-Between Infrastructure: Urban Connectivity in an Age of Vulnerability*. Retrieved from www.praxis-epress.org/IBT/inbetween.pdf.

Index